Transforming Healthcare

Transforming Healthcare: Digital Health and Emerging Technologies offers a comprehensive and timely overview of the digital tools and systems revolutionizing healthcare delivery. Written by a team of leading experts in healthcare, informatics, and technology, this book covers critical topics such as artificial intelligence, big data analytics, machine learning, quantum computing, and extended reality, with a special focus on their application in clinical and administrative settings.

Each chapter presents foundational concepts, practical insights, and real-world case studies, empowering readers to understand and navigate the digital transformation of healthcare. Through hands-on exercises and datasets like the Belmont Data Collaborative hypertension resource, readers gain practical experience in implementing these technologies.

The authors, all experts in their respective fields, bring deep knowledge to areas such as health data privacy, ethical challenges in digital health, and the regulatory landscape surrounding emerging technologies. *Transforming Healthcare* serves as an essential resource for students and professionals in medicine, nursing, pharmacy, public health, healthcare informatics, and administration, equipping them with the tools to drive innovation and improve healthcare systems.

Transforming Healthcare
Digital Health and Emerging Technologies

Edited by
Anthony Blash, PharmD, BCompSc, CPHIMS

Routledge
Taylor & Francis Group
A PRODUCTIVITY PRESS BOOK

Designed cover image: Shutterstock

First published 2027
by Routledge
605 Third Avenue, New York, NY 10158

and by Routledge
4 Park Square, Milton Park, Abingdon, Oxon, OX14 4RN

Routledge is an imprint of the Taylor & Francis Group, an informa business

ISBN: 9781032974651 (hbk)
ISBN: 9781032967738 (pbk)
ISBN: 9781003593867 (ebk)

DOI: 10.4324/9781003593867

Typeset in Garamond
by Newgen Publishing UK

To my children,

May you always remain curious, embrace lifelong learning, and have the courage to explore new possibilities. The future will be shaped by those who combine knowledge, creativity, and compassion to solve complex challenges and improve the lives of others.

This book represents my commitment to advancing healthcare through innovation, education, and responsible use of technology. I dedicate this work to you as a reminder that the greatest achievements are not measured only by what we create, but by the positive impact we have on others.

May you continue to ask questions, challenge assumptions, and use your unique talents to make the world a better place.

With love and pride.

Contents

Preface

Healthcare is at a turning point. What was once considered a future vision for the industry is now rapidly becoming our present reality. The world of digital health, encompassing artificial intelligence (AI), big data analytics, telemedicine, and smart technology, is reshaping every aspect of healthcare—from the way we diagnose and treat to how we manage patient outcomes and improve operational efficiencies.

Transforming Healthcare: Digital Health and Emerging Technologies was created to guide you through this ongoing revolution. As the main author and editor of this work, I've collaborated with a team of experts across various disciplines to explore the profound impact that digital tools and technologies have on the healthcare sector. Our goal is simple: to equip you—whether you are a student, a healthcare professional, or a policymaker—with the knowledge, skills, and insight to thrive in an increasingly digital landscape.

This book is not just a theoretical discussion. It's a practical, action-oriented resource designed to provide real-world solutions and case studies that illustrate the power of technology in improving healthcare delivery. As we move forward, we face an exciting opportunity to build a future where healthcare systems are more connected, efficient, and patient-centered.

The contributors to this book are at the forefront of healthcare innovation. Dr. Michelle Aebersold is known for her work in healthcare simulation, using technology to train caregivers in ways that drive real improvements in clinical outcomes. Dr. Jarod Parrish brings a wealth of experience in population health and chronic care management, focusing on how digital tools can transform patient care. Dr. Georgia (Gina) Galanou Luchen is a leader in digital health strategy, helping to shape the use of data and AI across health systems.

As we dive into the details of digital health technologies, from AI and machine learning to quantum computing and data lake analytics, we'll examine their real-world applications, limitations, and the potential they hold to change the way we deliver care. This book combines the knowledge of experts with hands-on learning tools, case studies, and practical applications, providing you with a comprehensive view of the intersection between healthcare and technology.

I invite you to join us on this journey of transformation. The future of healthcare is digital, and *Transforming Healthcare* will serve as your guide to navigating that future.

To the readers of this book: May the insights within serve to inspire and guide you as you lead and implement systemic changes in healthcare. It is my hope that, through your work, the changes we help design not only make care safer for patients but also enhance the elegance of those systems, ensuring minimal disruption to the clinicians and staff who rely on them. Let these efforts empower healthcare professionals, allowing them to maximize their impact on patient care while leveraging the innovations we create.

To the healthcare professional: This book is dedicated to helping you understand the ways in which your role in healthcare will be impacted by digital health innovations. As these changes unfold, I hope this text encourages you to learn about the evolving landscape and lean into these changes, empowering you to lead with confidence in the digital age of healthcare.

To the business, clinical, and financial leaders who drive the progress and speed of these changes: May you find knowledge in this text that helps you make more informed, strategic decisions and approach these opportunities with a renewed perspective. Your role in shaping the future of healthcare is as critical as ever.

To the academy—institutions of higher learning, accrediting bodies, professional advocacy groups, and curriculum committees: May this book serve as a call to action to ensure that health technology is covered with sufficient breadth and depth in the required curricula of business, nursing, medical, pharmacy, and financial schools. The future of healthcare depends on equipping the next generation of professionals with the tools and knowledge to navigate and lead within this digital age.

About the Editor

Anthony Blash, PharmD, BCompSc, CPHIMS, is an Associate Professor in the College of Pharmacy and Health Sciences at Belmont University, where he specializes in healthcare informatics, digital health, artificial intelligence, and workforce development. He serves on the inaugural Pharmacy Informatics Specialty Council of the Board of Pharmacy Specialties (BPS) and is Chair of the American Association of Colleges of Pharmacy (AACP) Technology in Pharmacy Education and Practice (TiPEP) Special Interest Group.

Dr. Blash has developed innovative curricular and experiential learning models that prepare future healthcare professionals to evaluate, implement, and oversee emerging technologies in clinical practice. His scholarly work focuses on healthcare data analytics, clinical decision support, artificial intelligence governance, digital transformation, and the development of workforce competencies required for technology-enabled care delivery. He has received competitive funding to advance educational initiatives in artificial intelligence oversight, digital health, and pharmacy informatics, creating scalable models designed to prepare both current and future healthcare professionals for an increasingly data-driven healthcare environment.

A Certified Professional in Healthcare Information and Management Systems (CPHIMS), Dr. Blash has authored and presented extensively on healthcare informatics, digital health, and pharmacy technology. His current work seeks to expand interdisciplinary training opportunities that equip healthcare, allied health, and business professionals with the knowledge and practical skills needed to responsibly deploy, monitor, and govern emerging technologies across healthcare systems. Through his teaching, scholarship, and professional service, Dr. Blash is committed to building a workforce capable of leading the next generation of digitally enabled healthcare transformation.

Contributors

Michelle Aebersold PhD, MSBA, RN, CHSE, FSSH, FAAN
Clinical Professor
Vice Chair for Research Systems, Populations and Leadership
Co-Lead Masters Program in Leadership, Analytics, and Innovation
University of Michigan School of Nursing, Ann Arbor, MI, US

Rudolph Bedeley, PhD
Assistant Professor of Business Systems, Analytics, and Data Science
Belmont University, Nashville, TN, US

Anthony Blash, PharmD, BCompSc, CPHIMS
Chair, AACP Technology in Pharmacy Education and Practice (TiPEP) SIG
Associate Professor, Healthcare Informatics
Belmont University School of Pharmacy, Nashville, TN, US

Joanne Chun, PharmD, PhD
Director, Postgraduate Education Programs
School of Pharmacy
Director, MS in AI and Computational Drug Discovery and Development (AICD3)
Principal Investigator, Giacomini/Chun Lab
Bioengineering and Therapeutic Sciences
Schools of Pharmacy and Medicine,
University of California, San Francisco: San Francisco, CA, US

Georgia Galanou Luchen, PharmD
Independent Strategic Advisor, Healthcare Innovation | Fractional Product Lead, Health Lab, Athens, Greece

Leigh McCormack, PhD
Co-Founder, CEO
Platypus Health
Signal Mountain, TN, US

Jarod Parrish, PharmD
Assistant Professor
Department of Pharmacy Practice
Belmont University School of Pharmacy
Nashville, TN, US

Valorie Quarles, MFA
Assistant Professor
Media and Entertainment, Media Production
Mike Curb College of Entertainment & Music Business
Belmont University, Nashville, TN, US

Jonathan Rule, COAMU
Associate Professor of Practice
XR Innovator in Residence
Taubman College of Architecture and Urban Planning
University of Michigan, Taubman College of Architecture and Urban Planning, Ann Arbor, MI, US

I

FOUNDATIONS OF DIGITAL HEALTH

Chapter 1

Introduction to Digital Health and Its Cross-Functional Role in Healthcare

Georgia Galanou Luchen, PharmD

Defining Digital Health: Why Language Matters

The technology sector often thrives on boldness and experimentation. New ideas emerge from curiosity, funding, or market opportunity, evolving quickly, often under a "fail fast" mindset designed to accelerate learning and scale success. In the fail-fast approach, ideas move quickly from a hypothesis to early product or concept testing, to determine their viability before large resource investments are made.[1] This process allows more ideas to be experimented with faster, with less burden or time commitments that could be spent scaling or refining better alternatives.

In contrast, healthcare has traditionally moved at a more deliberate pace, prioritizing evidence, safety, and outcomes over speed.[2] Innovations are piloted, but widespread adoption is frequently delayed by regulatory requirements, ethical considerations, cost, and the complexities of care delivery.

This mismatch in pace could lead to a fragmented ecosystem, where technologies are adopted at varying stages of maturity and applied inconsistently. As a result, the same or similar tools may be referred to using different terms depending on who is speaking. This is why shared definitions matter. In digital health, even foundational terms like telehealth, artificial intelligence (AI), or informatics are interpreted differently depending on context and use case. Let's explore some examples.

Digital Health

The term digital health has broad and evolving interpretations. It can refer to everything from mobile apps to robotics to clinical decision support.

DOI: 10.4324/9781003593867-2

The World Health Organization (WHO) offers a comprehensive definition:[3]

> *The field of knowledge and practice associated with the development and use of digital technologies to improve health. Digital health expands the concept of eHealth to include digital consumers, with a wider range of smart devices and connected equipment. It also encompasses other uses of digital technologies for health such as the Internet of things, artificial intelligence, big data and robotics.*

By contrast, the U.S. Food and Drug Administration (FDA) defines it more concretely, focusing on functional domains:[4]

> *The broad scope of digital health includes categories such as mobile health (mHealth), health information technology (IT), wearable devices, telehealth and telemedicine, and personalized medicine.*

Amazon Health's product page, representing a commercial lens, takes a consumer-oriented approach:[5]

> *Digital health companies help you manage diabetes, high blood pressure, mental health, joint pain, muscle pain, and more through personalized online programs covered by your insurer or employer.*

These differences are not just semantic; they shape funding decisions, regulatory oversight, and implementation strategies. A public health agency might emphasize digital health's potential for population surveillance and behavior change, while a health system Chief Information Officer may focus on interoperability across clinical systems. A start-up may brand their fitness tracker as a digital health tool, but payers and regulators may not see it that way unless it meets specific evidence or risk criteria. Different points of view create different layers of promotion, understanding, and implementation.

Telehealth

Telehealth is another term where scope and use vary, and those differences can have significant downstream effects. At its core, telehealth refers to the delivery of health services and information via digital communication technologies. But definitions differ depending on whether the emphasis is on clinical care, support services, or consumer technology.

The Healthcare Resources and Services Administration's definition includes clinical care and nonclinical services like education, administration, and public health:[6]

> *the use of electronic information and telecommunication technologies to support long-distance clinical health care, patient and professional health-related education, health administration, and public health.*

Although often used interchangeably, the terms telehealth and telemedicine represent distinct concepts. The Federal Communications Commission clearly delineates three subdomains:[7]

> *Telemedicine can be defined as using telecommunications technologies to support the delivery of all kinds of medical, diagnostic and treatment-related services usually by doctors.*

Telehealth is similar to telemedicine but includes a wider variety of remote healthcare services beyond the doctor-patient relationship.

Telecare generally refers to technology that allows consumers to stay safe and independent in their own homes.

Lastly, but very importantly, the Centers for Medicare and Medicaid Services (CMS) links telehealth definitions directly to reimbursement policy.[8] As of April 2025, guidance around telehealth extensions noted that[1]:

We pay for specific Medicare Part B services that a physician or practitioner provides via 2-way, interactive technology (or telehealth). Telehealth substitutes for an in-person visit and involves 2-way, interactive technology that permits communication between the practitioner and patient.

Telehealth scope distinctions affect how services are billed, who can deliver them, and which technologies are reimbursable. Misunderstanding or misusing the terms can lead to denied claims, regulatory noncompliance, or confusion about service availability.

Artificial Intelligence

AI may be the most widely used and yet misunderstood term in digital health in modern times. Originally rooted in computer science, AI now encompasses a wide range of healthcare uses, from risk prediction and image analysis to conversational interfaces and workflow automation.

IBM, from a tech-centric lens, defines AI as:[9]

Artificial intelligence (AI) is technology that enables computers and machines to simulate human learning, comprehension, problem solving, decision making, creativity and autonomy.

The FDA, with a clinical and regulatory lens, offers a more structured and regulated perspective:[10]

Artificial Intelligence is a machine-based system that can, for a given set of human-defined objectives, make predictions, recommendations, or decisions influencing real or virtual environments. Artificial intelligence systems use machine- and human-based inputs to perceive real and virtual environments; abstract such perceptions into models through analysis in an automated manner; and use model inference to formulate options for information or action.

Language variability reflects fundamentally different expectations. Notice that in IBM's definition, it is acceptable to determine that technology "simulates human intelligence," while the FDA clarifies that the influence of AI depends on "human-defined objectives." Similarly, while terms like "autonomy" and "decision-making" may be embraced in technology circles, they can raise red flags in clinical settings, where decisions are vetted carefully and only applied after extensive evidence-based review. How AI is defined influences how it is regulated, what safeguards are required, and how clinicians interpret and trust its outputs. A mismatch in understanding can lead to both overreliance and unnecessary rejection. Sometimes, terms evolve within industries to accommodate the comfort level, readiness, and maturity of a given field. It is no surprise that the healthcare sector relies on better defined and less flexible definitions, necessary for the significance and impact of decisions on patient care outcomes.

Recap: Definitions Matter

As evident by the above examples, the breadth of definitions impacts what counts as innovation, who qualifies for funding, how tools are evaluated, and even who is allowed to use them in clinical workflows. It speaks to patients and consumers about how they view themselves, and how they manage their care through digital means, which impacts care-seeking decisions. If one stakeholder views digital health primarily as health IT infrastructure to promote efficiency, while another sees it as a patient engagement lifeline, misalignment can lead to failed pilots or technology purchases that fall short of goals.

It is important to understand that variations in definition are not about right or wrong, but they do underscore the importance of clarity. All stakeholders come to the table with preconceived notions and understandings of the technologies, processes, and goals at hand. However, it is important to pause, reflect, evaluate, and clarify the goals. Agreeing on scope early in any effort is essential, as the definitions we use frame the intent of every decision.

While it is impossible to provide definitive meanings for every concept, this section offers a set of working definitions to ensure consistency throughout this book (refer to Table 1.1). These definitions serve as a foundation for deeper discussions in subsequent chapters, with the understanding that language will continue to evolve alongside the technologies themselves.

Table 1.1 Foundational Definitions

Term	*Working Definition*
Clinical Decision Support	Technologically supported tools that provide healthcare professionals with evidence-based information and recommendations to aid clinical decision-making.[11,12]
Digital Health	An umbrella term referring to the use of digital tools and technologies by leveraging data, connectivity, and automation to improve health outcomes, health processes, and healthcare delivery. Digital health encompasses a range of tools and applications such as health information technology, telehealth, wearable devices, mobile apps, electronic health records, and others.
Digital Transformation	"Digital transformation refers to the digital technology changes used to benefit society and the healthcare industry."[13]
Telehealth	Telehealth is the use of technology that allows communication and information exchange for health-related purposes virtually or at a distance.
Telemedicine	Telemedicine is a subset of telehealth that refers to the use of technology to provide clinical services.
Artificial Intelligence (AI)	AI is technology that enables computer systems to perform tasks that usually require human intelligence, such as pattern recognition, decision-making, and learning from data.
Machine Learning (ML)	ML is a subset of AI. ML refers to a set of techniques that enables systems to make decisions or predictions based on data, improving their performance over time.
Natural Language Processing (NLP)	NLP is a subset of AI that enables computer systems to read, understand, interpret, and generate human language inputs and outputs.

Table 1.1 (Continued)

Term	*Working Definition*
Predictive Analytics	"Predictive analytics encompasses the body of statistical knowledge supporting the analysis of massive data sets ... extracting useful information (leading to actionable items) from these data sets has spurred ... to address the problems ... inherent in 'Big Data' applications. ... Much of the methodology ... relates response variables ... to a set of explanatory variables or covariates."[14]
Quantum Computing	"**Quantum computing** refers to a new approach to computation that uses the collective properties of quantum states, such as superposition and entanglement, to perform operations on data."[15]
Extended Reality (XR)	XR is a fusion of all the realities – including augmented reality (AR), virtual reality (VR), and mixed reality (MR) – which consists of technology-mediated experiences enabled via a wide spectrum of hardware and software, including sensory interfaces, applications, and infrastructures. XR is often referred to as immersive video content, enhanced media experiences, as well as interactive and multi-dimensional human experiences.[16]

Key Takeaway

In digital health, definitions are foundational. They shape who leads, who pays, and how care is delivered. Clarity is not optional; it is the prerequisite for effective collaboration, strategy, and innovation.

The Evolution of Digital Health: Learning from the Past

Technology has always played a role in advancing healthcare, but what we now call "digital health" is the culmination of centuries of innovation and adaptation. It is tempting to view today's tools, such as AI, machine learning (ML), and telemedicine, as sudden breakthroughs. However, the story of digital health is less about disruption and more about an ongoing evolution, one that builds upon the innovations of every generation before it.

Early Tools

The use of tools in medicine is not new. As early as 6000 BC, humans performed primitive surgical interventions with knives, saws, and drills, an early reflection of the human instinct to support healing through technology. By 950 BC, the first prosthetics were created for amputees, and by 300 BC, metal surgical instruments were in circulation, illustrating a consistent drive toward precision.[17]

These early tools and innovations, while not digital, showed a clear pattern: the evolution of medicine has consistently evolved alongside the tools available in each era. While slow and subtle at first, the relationship between technology and medicine has only become more interdependent.

The invention of the microscope in the 16th century opened up new ways of viewing and interpreting medical information beyond what the naked eye could see.[18] By the 20th century, the world saw technological breakthroughs that moved us into real computing, namely the invention of the transistor in 1947, which revolutionized electronics and laid the foundation for compact and efficient digital tools we rely on for modern care.[19] Figure 1.1 offers a high-level snapshot of key milestones that shaped today's digital health landscape. What began with basic materials has advanced into complex devices, computing systems, and now AI, forming what we now recognize as digital health.

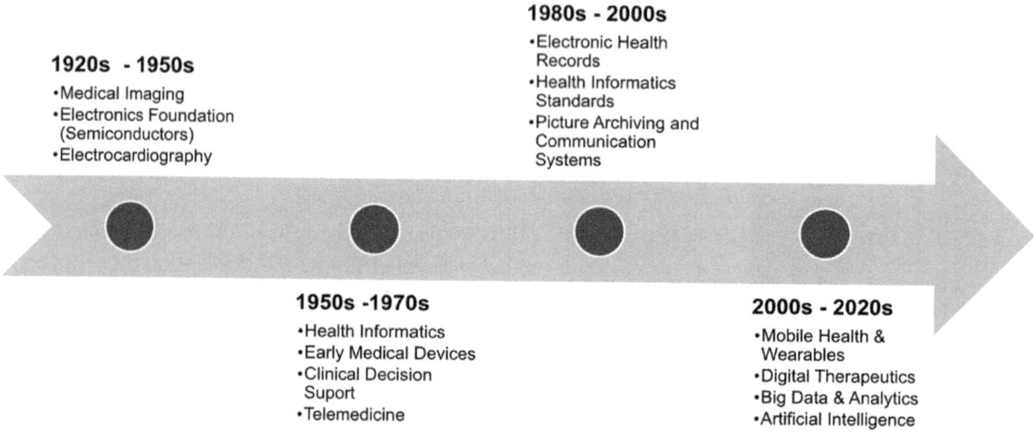

Figure 1.1 A modern timeline of healthcare technology – 1950s and beyond.[20,21]

In-Person to Remote Care Transition

Innovation is fueled by interdisciplinary partnerships and the integration of ideas across diverse industries. In other words, individuals from different disciplines, perspectives, and expertise come together to creatively combine their talents to turn novel ideas into reality. Society functions best when communication expands beyond the siloes of each individual discipline and innovators cross-pollinate ideas and processes to evolve them for purposes beyond their original intent. A perfect example is the birth of what we now know today as telemedicine.

In the 1960s, NASA attempted to create ways to secure the safety of astronauts in space, by exploring remote physiological monitoring through telemetry.[22] This process gave rise to the "Integrated Medical and Behavioral Laboratories and Measurement Systems (IMBLMS)," which allowed Earth-bound clinicians to monitor and guide astronaut health remotely.

Over a decade later, the same idea was applied to rural communities. NASA's collaboration with the Indian Health Service and the Tohono O'odham Nation linked rural patients to urban physicians through a mobile telehealth unit, demonstrating a critical application of space technology for civilian use. From there, telemedicine gradually expanded, integrating into real-time remote monitoring, diagnostics, and care for remote or convenient healthcare settings.

Despite the strong promise, it took several more decades to move from a proof-of-concept model to wider adoption, an evolution that was stifled by reimbursement structures, infrastructure, regulation, and traditional assumptions of in-person care preferences. As we all know too well, this changed in 2020.[23] The COVID-19 pandemic thrust the world into an accelerated adoption and evolution for telemedicine, which aimed to supplement traditional care delivery, which was becoming increasingly difficult to provide, and serve a system that was near a breaking point. Healthcare systems faced with lockdowns, infection control measures, staffing shortages, and supply chain disruptions sought to maximize resources and reach their patients in need by implementing virtual visits to maintain care continuity. Federal and state policies had no choice but to adapt, expanding telehealth coverage, loosening licensure restrictions, and enabling care across settings and geographies. What was a slow evolution of a promising tool became an overnight necessity for acute and chronic management of disease. With little tolerance for lengthy deliberations, finally, healthcare was adopting the fail-fast model, testing processes that worked and quickly moving on from those that did not serve the system.

As a perfect example of cross-functional innovation, telemedicine also served as proof that potential and value don't always translate to rapid implementation or integration, at least not until we reach a need and the ability for scaling. What began as a space venture evolved to a core component of care, and a high-growth business that proved to blend convenience with real-time connection to those most in need. Yet its value proposition did not become apparent until the need severely exceeded the healthcare capacity.

Paper to Digital Data Transition

A pivotal moment for digital health evolution has been the transition from paper-based to electronic communication and documentation. Electronic health records (EHRs) are among the most fundamental steps in digitizing medicine. Unsurprisingly, the journey toward EHRs was slow, gradual, and fragmented.

Early development of EHR systems began in the 1960s, driven by academic medical centers that hoped to create system-specific solutions. Early adopters included the University of Utah, which laid the foundation for the first clinical decision support systems, Massachusetts General Hospital, with the creation of their "Computer Stored Ambulatory Record," and the federal government with the Veterans Health Information Systems and Technology Architecture (VistA) for the Department of Veterans Affairs.[24] Each iteration improved on the one prior, adding features, customizations, user flexibility, multiuser interfaces, improved storage capabilities, and information processing efficiencies. By the 2000s, evidence was clearly pointing toward EHR use being an integral component for improving patient safety.[25]

Individual EHR systems provided health-system-level solutions interacting with and storing patient data, but this new digital process lacked standardization and the ability to exchange information with trusted partners.[26] In other words, it lacked interoperability. In 1996, the Health Insurance Portability and Accountability Act (HIPAA) brought to light security and privacy concerns for patient data[27] and almost a decade later, in 2004, the Office of the National Coordinator for Health Information Technology was created through a Presidential Executive Order to coordinate national efforts around health information technology.[28] At the same time, the need for widespread adoption of these tools brought the Health Information Technology for Economic and Clinical Health Act (HITECH) to broaden EHR adoption through incentives for meaningful use.[29]

From inception to widespread implementation, EHR had a journey of over half a century. Each milestone aimed to optimize and expand the use of EHR systems across all settings, but none achieved smooth interconnectivity for systems. The lack of consistent standards and uneven system capabilities has resulted in a fragmented environment where information often stays siloed. In many cases, digital records have replaced paper charts without necessarily improving communication across care providers or settings.[30] While the intent was to streamline care and improve outcomes, challenges related to workflow burden, data overload, and limited connectivity across platforms continue to limit the full potential of EHRs. The shift from paper to digital was a necessary step that offered vast improvements and expanded care capabilities, but its implementation remains a work in progress.

Human Intelligence to Augmented Intelligence Transition

The most recent shift in the evolution of digital health has been the transition from human-driven to machine-supported decision-making, which is encompasses AI. Similar to healthcare technologies before it, the concept of AI was in the works well before it made its way into medicine and the transition has been incremental and continuously evolving.

Algorithm-based tools have been used for decades to aid clinicians' thinking and improve efficiency and care. Early versions of rule-based clinical decision support systems began in the 1970s, with programs such as MYCIN, which aided in antibiotic selection, or INTERNIST-1, which provided diagnostic support in complex patient cases.[31] These systems relied on structured rules and decision trees, "if-then" logic programmed by experts to reflect established clinical pathways. While promising, they were limited by the rigidity of their design and the difficulty of maintaining large, manually curated rule sets. Like early EHRs and telemedicine, these tools served as proof of concept but were not yet ready for widespread clinical integration.

The shift from rules-based logic to ML marked a significant turning point for AI development.[32] ML offered the flexibility to train on large volumes of data, identify patterns, and make predictions that were different from the rigid decision pathways of earlier models. It also introduced predictive analytics, the ability to forecast data trends and generate actionable recommendations. Predictive analytics created space to elevate clinical decision support systems, leveraging vast patient data to make decisions about anticipated patient complications, disease progression, the effectiveness of medication therapies, or opportunities for preventative care.[31]

Later, natural language processing (NLP) further enabled communication and customer-friendly communication with these platforms, increasing the usability of the technology and translatability into practice. NLP became the foundation for efficiencies in documentation and the ability to extract information from clinical notes and unstructured data systems.

The culmination and progression of intelligent systems have unlocked the potential to reengineer the care process.[33] Clinically, diagnostics and care decisions are augmented by more accurate and efficient tools. Administratively, workflow optimization empowers health systems to cut waste and maximize resources.

Despite the promise, widespread adoption of AI in healthcare remains inconsistent and complex. As with prior digital health innovations, progress is slowed by infrastructure limitations, financial barriers, regulatory ambiguity, data quality concerns, and a lack of workforce readiness. However, unlike previous transitions, AI introduces new layers of ethical complexity, risks of bias at scale, and equity challenges that, if unaddressed, could exacerbate health disparities and undermine public trust.[34] Concerns around the integrity and trustworthiness of the data used to train AI systems highlight the danger of errors, profiling, and medical mismanagement in scalable technologies. Further, there are serious concerns about cybersecurity and data vulnerability that could harm both patients and organizations alike (more on cybersecurity to be covered in Chapter 2).[35]

Still, the potential is significant. Unlike previous tools that documented or transmitted information, AI can influence care in real time. It can flag a critical lab result, guide imaging review, or suggest the next best action based on patterns across thousands of similar cases. These capabilities are not designed to replace clinical judgment, but to enhance it, allowing clinicians to combine their expertise with timely, data-driven insights. As with telemedicine and EHRs, the value of AI will depend on how well it is implemented, governed, and supported, while influencing the way we define and approach care.

Key Takeaway

Much of healthcare's digital transformation has been shaped by innovations originating outside of healthcare (such as aerospace, defense, and consumer electronics). Healthcare often adapts rather than originates these tools, which reinforces the need for cross-industry collaboration and contextual adaptation. Digital health is not merely about the tools; it reflects how we think about care itself. Understanding history helps us appreciate that the future of medicine will not be defined by any one invention, but by how we continue to adapt, collaborate, and evolve.

Interdisciplinary Collaboration in Digital Health

The digital health revolution promises to bring more opportunities for connection and a wider reach. We expect technology to improve patient experience, expand the number of individuals that we can impact, and minimize resource consumption. One of the most important factors for optimizing care in any setting is having integrated teams who have a common purpose, are coordinated, communicate effectively, and are driven by well-designed internal systems.[36] Ultimately, by optimizing internally, through the healthcare team, we optimize externally, to the patient.

The Need for a Cross-Functional Approach

In 2001, the Institute of Medicine (US) Committee on Quality of Health Care in America released a review titled "Crossing the Quality Chasm: A New Health System for the 21st Century" that aimed to create performance expectations for healthcare systems.[36] This report outlined several recommendations to improve care, including the need for clinician collaboration. Specifically, the report recommended, "Clinicians and institutions should actively collaborate and communicate to ensure an appropriate exchange of information and coordination of care."

In recent years, academies across many healthcare disciplines have been driving the message of interprofessional collaboration. In 2009, six educational associations representing medicine, nursing, pharmacy, osteopathic medicine, dentistry, and public health joined together to form the Interprofessional Education Collaborative (IPEC).[37] The goal of IPEC is to encourage participating disciplines to employ educational efforts that prepare future practitioners for team-based care. Since its creation, many healthcare disciplines, such as nursing and pharmacy, have formally integrated interprofessional education and training as part of their curricular competency requirements.[38,39]

This move toward collaborative care is not accidental. Teams that are more cohesive, understand their roles, and work collaboratively to achieve common goals tend to produce better outcomes and improve care.[40,41]

Cross-Functional Collaboration for Digital Health

If health care demands collaboration, it is only logical that digital health integration would follow the same trend, only the term "interprofessional" would invite non-clinician partners to a growing stakeholder team. If physicians, pharmacists, nurses, and other healthcare professionals make up the healthcare team, informaticists, developers, and other technology influencers make up the digital healthcare team.

This kind of integration aligns with a broader recognition across healthcare that informaticists, particularly those with clinical training, should not be viewed as ancillary support roles, but as core members of the care team. A HIMSS white paper on the role of clinical informatics underscores how nurse and physician informaticists contribute to patient care by shaping workflows, reducing burden, improving documentation, and helping teams navigate regulatory and operational complexity.[42,43] Their work sits at the intersection of clinical practice and technology, making them uniquely positioned to guide decisions that affect both patient outcomes and clinician experience. As healthcare continues to evolve, incorporating informaticists into care and leadership teams is increasingly necessary to ensure digital health solutions are both usable and impactful.

Some health systems are going a step further, recognizing that they must break down silos not only between clinicians and informaticists, but also between academic health informatics and operational IT to drive meaningful digital health transformation. As an example, NYU Langone Health addressed this by creating the Department of Health Informatics (DHI), which functions as an operational unit within its IT infrastructure rather than a traditional academic department.[44] DHI integrates expertise across clinical care, research, education, and operations, allowing informatics professionals, including clinicians, to contribute to enterprise-level priorities while still engaging in innovation and scholarship. Its matrixed structure enables team members to hold roles that support both day-to-day IT functions and strategic initiatives, such as improving digital equity or deploying emerging tools like generative AI. Clinical informatics is central to this model, with practicing physicians helping guide the design, implementation, and evaluation of technology that directly impacts care delivery.

Ultimately, optimizing digital health requires the same collaboration and clarity of roles that improve clinical care. Whether at the bedside or a computer, success depends on multidisciplinary teams that understand the full picture: clinical, operational, and technological. Integrating clinicians, informaticists, and technology experts as true partners in care delivery is not just a best practice; it is a necessary step toward building systems that are safe, effective, efficient, and responsive to the realities of modern healthcare.

Engaging Stakeholders in Digital Health

Implementation science is the discipline that examines the methods by which evidence-based concepts, ideas, and actions can be adopted and integrated in the real-world settings.[45] In healthcare, the goal of implementation science centers around maximizing value and optimizing patient health and public health.[46]

While this is a growing field with a range of models and approaches, the literature consistently highlights that engaging key stakeholders is critical throughout the implementation process.[47] Two such frameworks, the Exploration, Preparation, Implementation, Sustainment (EPIS) Framework[48] and the Consolidated Framework for Implementation Research (CFIR),[49] both emphasize stakeholder involvement as a central factor influencing success. EPIS explicitly integrates stakeholder input in its early and late phases, while CFIR identifies stakeholder engagement as one of several key determinants that shape implementation outcomes.

Digital transformation is no different. To achieve effective outcomes, and ensure that digital care is safe, effective, and appropriately integrated, there are multiple stakeholders who need to be engaged and responsible for successful outcomes. Let's explore them.

Core Stakeholders

Clinicians: Central to digital transformation success are clinicians, who serve the front lines of care delivery.[50] Their clinical expertise should help define what digital tools are truly needed in patient care, where they should be integrated, and how they should impact clinical and patient-facing workflows. Clinician feedback should shape which solutions are practical and scalable, avoiding burnout and considering key safety, equity, access, and feasibility considerations. As the use of augmented intelligence expands, digital tools should be paired with capable clinicians who can interpret and apply insights in real time, to provide safe and effective care.

Patients and caregivers: As end-users and beneficiaries, patients and caregivers are central to the success of digital health solutions.[50] Their feedback should inform design, usability, accessibility, trust, and selection. Engaging patients early in the process, whether through codesign, testing, or advocacy, should aim to ensure tools meet real-world needs and reduce the risk of inequity or underutilization.

Administrators and leaders: Healthcare administrators and executives create the conditions for innovation to thrive. So influential is their role that there are numerous articles and publications dedicated to creating an innovator's mindset for executive leaders.[51] Leadership roles center around fostering infrastructure, aligning strategy with care goals, and securing organizational readiness for change. Leaders play a critical role in evaluating the value and sustainability of new technologies, balancing return on investment with care quality, safety, and experience. By cultivating a culture of experimentation and aligning priorities across stakeholders, ideas will have the chance to turn into actionable outcomes.

Technology partners: The selection of digital health tools for any organization is significant and complex; organizations are called to partner with vendors, internal technology partners, and private-sector partners to design and implement usable, reliable, and safe technologies.[52] Developers, designers, and product leaders should collaborate closely with clinicians, patients, and regulators to build solutions that align with clinical needs and health system goals. As digital health products evolve, so does the responsibility to uphold patient safety, data privacy, and equitable access. Successful partnerships depend on two-way communication, shared accountability, and a focus on outcomes beyond market performance.

Researchers and data scientists: Digital tools in healthcare must be backed by evidence.[53] Researchers and data scientists play a vital role in evaluating new technologies, generating data on safety, effectiveness, and implementation impact. From proof-of-concept to real-world evidence, a rigorous study provides the foundation for clinical acceptance and regulatory approval. Research and data expertise should inform guidelines, drive adoption, and build trust.

Educators and academies: For any digital health strategy to succeed in the long term, the workforce must be prepared to use it.[54] Educators are responsible for cultivating the digital literacy and critical thinking needed to navigate an evolving care landscape. Academic institutions and Academies must adapt curricula to keep pace with technology, fostering curiosity, adaptability, and ethical awareness. This includes both clinical training and leadership development. Rigid educational structures may hinder innovation; agility in curriculum design is essential to keep pace with system needs.

Payers and regulators: Regulatory and reimbursement policies often determine whether an innovation scales or stalls.[55,56] Regulations exist for good reason, especially when patient safety is at stake, but excessive rigidity can delay the adoption of beneficial technologies.

Flexibility in regulatory processes and alignment of payment models with new care delivery methods are essential to sustain digital innovation. Without appropriate incentives and risk management strategies, even promising tools may fail.

Professional networks: Professional networks help bridge gaps across stakeholder groups. For example, start-ups are more likely to secure funding through personal and professional networks.[57] Associations and professional stakeholder groups monitor trends, disseminate guidance, convene diverse voices, and advocate for policies that reflect the needs of their members. They serve as platforms for consensus-building, knowledge-sharing, and innovation support. Their ability to represent broad constituencies makes them key players in shaping how digital health is understood, governed, and advanced.

Reimagining Care through an Interdisciplinary Lens

The value proposition should be clear from the discussions above. While each stakeholder group plays a unique role, their responsibilities may overlap. Implementation science reminds us that successful change depends not only on frameworks, but on shared accountability. Without engagement from all perspectives, efforts may stall, or worse, miss the mark for patients. A cross-functional, interdisciplinary approach is not just ideal; it is essential for realizing the full potential of digital transformation in healthcare.

A strategic framework for adopting, maintaining, and evolving care requires everyone's investment into a common vision and strategic leadership. Over the next segment, we will explore successful visioning and strategic planning to achieve a coordinated adoption of digital health and a roadmap that ultimately serves patient care as the primary mission.

Key Takeaway

Successful digital health initiatives require integrative thinking and collaboration among varied stakeholders, from frontline clinicians to executive leaders.

Looking Ahead: Charting the Future for Digital Health

Emerging Healthcare Trends and Technologies

A simple search of "emerging healthcare trends and technologies" in any online search engine is guaranteed to produce hundreds, if not thousands, of articles, videos, and various multimedia assets that delve into the infinite possibilities of care through technological innovation.

It is unrealistic to expect that we can predict the precise trajectory or outcomes of technological advancements. Yet, consensus among technologists, clinicians, and thought leaders suggests that technology is on an exponential trajectory toward profound transformation across all industries, driven by continuous advances in both speed and capability.[58–62] Healthcare is no exception.

Rather than trying to predict specifics, let's explore categories and examples of emerging technological trends, understanding how they might shape care in the coming years. The following sections provide a brief overview of emerging technologies, many of which will be covered more in depth during subsequent chapters.

AI: AI, while not new in healthcare, is rapidly evolving and transforming medicine, ranging from rules-based technology to clinical decision support and process automation. Advanced AI capabilities are growing to include generative and agentic systems, tools capable of managing tasks autonomously and making decisions to assist users.[63,64] Despite the enormous potential and promise, a shift in autonomous systems will require careful stewardship to ensure ethical integration and minimize harm.

Blockchain: Blockchain is a decentralized digital system that allows for secure data transactions by storing information across multiple platforms.[65] In healthcare, this technology has the promise to enhance digital health data security, data sharing, clinical trial integrity, and interoperability.[66]

Digital therapeutics: Beyond physical care, software-driven evidence-based interventions enable tailored patient engagement and behavior modification for conditions ranging from diabetes and hypertension to mental health disorders.[67] Unlike general wellness apps, digital therapeutics are subject to clinical validation, often FDA-cleared, and designed to prevent, manage, or treat specific conditions. These technologies underscore a critical shift: care is moving from population-based approaches to truly individualized care plans, often shifting beyond physical infrastructure and toward fully digitized care.

Digital twins: Digital twins are virtual, data-driven replicas of humans, systems, or objects that simulate real-world and real-time conditions.[68] These virtual models can serve as grounds for experimentation, study, and analysis that could enable clinicians to optimize real-life care while minimizing risks.

Nanomedicine: Nanomedicine manipulates materials at the atomic level to enable targeted interventions.[69] This precision allows for optimized drug delivery (e.g., chemotherapy and gene vectors), sensitive diagnostics, regenerative therapies, and many other uses.

Neurotechnology: Neurotechnology describes the interface between the human nervous system and technological tools and devices with the intent to activate, influence, or communicate with the brain or nervous system.[70] This field could blur the boundaries between biological and digital processing networks.

Personalized medicine: Personalized medicine customizes medical treatment based on the individual characteristics of each patient.[71] While not purely a digital health solution, precision medicine leverages advancements in genomics and real-time data analytics to drive medical care that is less generalized and more precise, shifting away from a one-size-fits-all model.

Quantum computing: Quantum computers harness the principles of quantum physics to process information in ways that far exceed traditional systems.[72] Although real-world healthcare applications remain largely aspirational, the technology does promise to advance precision medicine, diagnosis, and drug discovery.[73]

Why do these innovations matter? Because they signal how care may be delivered, personalized, and experienced in the future. Whether you are a clinician, administrator, or technologist, understanding these developments is not about predicting the future, but preparing for it. Subsequent chapters will review these topics in depth, providing more information about the opportunities and current evolution.

Scope and Influence of Technology in Healthcare

As exciting as technological disruption might be, adopting digital health tools that may impact patients warrants careful assessment. In 2023, the Institute for Clinical and Economic Research

(ICER), in collaboration with the Peterson Health Technology Institute (PHTI), an independent, nonprofit organization that evaluates innovative healthcare technologies, released the ICER-PHTI Assessment Framework for Digital Health Technologies.[74] This assessment framework carefully examines any digital health technology from three key perspectives: technology context, clinical impact, and economic impact. Technology context considers the history of the tool's patient care role and development, the market landscape, as well as privacy and security considerations. The clinical impact assessment area examines the tool from the user experience, safety, effectiveness, and health equity lens. Lastly, the economic impact examines the budget and return on investment implications.

Similarly, in 2023, the World Bank released a Digital Health Assessment Toolkit Guide, urging thoughtful investment in digital health tools after a full assessment.[75] The guide recommends a full review of sociodemographic and system factors, the digital market environment, infrastructure and communications considerations, quantitative intent for the digital intervention or application across the area of need (i.e., lab and pharmacy) and implications for the workforce. The toolkit further defines components that are crucial in digital health tool implementation, such as leadership, legislation, workforce, and infrastructure, making a strong case for intentionality and strategic cohesion. From an investment standpoint, the tool aims to provide a methodical approach that protects fiscal responsibility in financing digital assets and, by proxy, digital innovation.

These assessments provide a clear directive for the significance of managing healthcare technology integration proactively. They clearly articulate that technology impact is far and wide, examining clinical, operational, and financial considerations that guide healthcare digital health decisions. Assessments are important to consider, because if we are to plan for the future, we must assess our standing and readiness for innovation.

The Importance of Strategic Planning

Technology alone isn't enough to transform and meaningfully optimize care. Intentional strategic planning efforts are needed to ensure that change is effective.[76] Healthcare professionals at every level, from aides, to clinicians, to administrative leaders, are responsible for developing and implementing strategic directives that protect and optimize patient care. Strategic efforts around digital health and digital transformation should be comprehensive and include several key considerations:

1) *Supporting a culture of meaningful innovation to solve care challenges*
    a. Strategic planning efforts should begin with the intent to foster meaningful innovation.[76] Healthcare leaders should embrace technological tools as potential solutions to common healthcare challenges and consider technology as a strategic partner. Technology and innovation should serve as conduits rather than goals, catalyzing change and removing barriers to achieve patient care optimization. Leaning on credible frameworks for innovation, such as the National Academy of Medicine's Learning Health Systems ("*in which science, informatics, incentives, and culture align for continuous improvement and innovations*"), positions organizations to successfully anticipate and adopt digital health solutions.[77]
2) *Assessing the readiness of the healthcare organization for technology*
    a. Healthcare leaders should carefully assess the right time and the right tools when assessing their organization's readiness for technological investment and digital transformation. These evaluations should rely on interdisciplinary partnerships and formal assessment

tools such as the ICER-PHTI[74] and World Bank released a Digital Health Assessment Toolkit Guide[75] mentioned above. New technology should address existing problems for the organization, with clear intentionality. Additionally, new technology should seamlessly integrate or help restructure existing systems, creating an integrated whole that is secure, reliable, and agile.

3) *Conducting market and environmental assessments*
   a. Organizations do not operate in isolation. Keeping a steady pulse on industry innovations, feasibility of solutions, market competition, and best practices helps position organizations for success.[76] There may be governmental, regulatory, or other factors that influence digital solutions, and when developing organizational strategy, it is important to understand the landscape and trends. Organizations like the American Hospital Association often publish annual environmental scanning reports that reference key trends that may influence healthcare, including digital health considerations.[78]
4) *Establishing organizational governance and ethics processes*
   a. Strategic planning requires thorough organization and a transparent matrix of accountabilities. Developing robust but specific goals allows departments and staff to inform their tactics to achieve common goals. Effective digital health governance funnels these tactics to ensure they meet strategic intent and track progress to sustain change. Further ethical oversight is critical in ensuring that business and technological dynamics do not compromise patient safety and outcomes, adding to the culture of trust and likelihood for successful adoption. Borrowing from established global frameworks on digital health governance can influence successful digital transformation within organizations.[79,80]
5) *Managing change through stakeholder readiness*
   a. People: Any technological investment will bring change to process, personnel, and the patient experience.[76] Digital tools, while innovative, might bring unintended consequences, such as burnout and harm if mishandled.[81] Managing this change requires assessing the readiness of both patients and providers. For clinicians, this includes digital fluency, which is their comfort, confidence, and skill in using new tools safely and effectively. For health IT professionals, this includes clear communication on goals and expectations. For patients, this includes digital literacy and equitable access to technologies that support their care.
   b. Infrastructure: Successful implementation requires alignment with the realities of each care setting.[76] Infrastructure varies widely across systems and geographies, including bandwidth, device availability, integration capabilities, and support resources. Strategic planning must be tailored to site-specific and population-specific contexts, ensuring that solutions are feasible and scalable.
6) *Developing a business case of tangible value*
   a. Clearly defining the business model and returns of any digital health solutions is imperative to funding, sustaining, and advocating for change.[76,77] Strategic plans that meet business frameworks have a higher likelihood of succeeding and thus bringing meaningful change to patient care.
7) *Forging and maintaining strategic partnerships*
   a. Digital transformation does not happen in a vacuum. Appropriate strategic planning efforts should consider desired and appropriate partnership models that will need to be formed with vendors, government entities, and even competitors to effectively implement organizational goals.[76,77]

Ethics

In this chapter, we have focused on the many ways that technology influences, improves, and sometimes challenges patient care and healthcare organizations. We have examined the definitions and history of digital health tools, we have reviewed the importance of coordinated integration and cross-functional collaboration, and we have reviewed intentional strategic planning for meaningful digital transformation. Understanding the depth, breadth, and reach of technology is not enough for championing responsible innovation. At the core of every healthcare professional, resides the moral imperative to "respect human life and the dignity of every individual" as stated by the American Medical Association's first declaration for physicians,[82] "consider the welfare of humanity and relief of human suffering" as noted by the American Association of Colleges of Pharmacy,[83] and follow "moral duties to self as a person of inherent dignity and worth" as noted in the American Nurses Association Code of Ethics.[84] Ethics is a core consideration and expectation of any intervention in patients' lives, and thus a significant imperative that must not be forgotten. More details regarding ethical considerations for digital health will be reviewed in Chapter 3.

Key Takeaway

Future-forward care will leverage emerging technologies and leadership that commits to meaningful digital transformation. Healthcare professionals must adapt and develop a strategic vision for the future, where we collectively reimagine processes, workforce, and infrastructure to transform the healthcare experience and optimize patient care outcomes.

Activities and Reflections

ACTIVITY 1: MAPPING THE DIGITAL HEALTH ECOSYSTEM

Purpose: Identify the missing links and relationships in your digital health landscape today, then sketch how that system could grow and change over time.

Exercise:

1. Create a map of your health system or organization by drawing or outlining the digital health ecosystem as you see it today. This should include:
   a. Key stakeholders (clinicians, administrators, IT professionals, policymakers, patients, caregivers, etc.).
   b. Technologies (EHRs, telehealth, wearables, analytics platforms).
   c. Relationships and data flow between these stakeholders.
   d. In red, mark areas of disconnect and opportunities for further integration (inequity, interoperability challenges, etc.).
2. Use the map to answer the discussion questions below.

Discussion questions:

1. Which stakeholders are missing or underutilized?
2. How might the map change by 2050 if the technology matures?
3. Identify and discuss your organization's greatest single point of failure to date. What would be an appropriate mitigation plan?
4. Where and how should patients and caregivers be considered and incorporated for optimization?

ACTIVITY 2: THE YEAR 2050: HEALTHCARE OF THE FUTURE

Purpose: Explore how exponential technologies, demographic shifts, and policy change could reshape daily work in healthcare by 2050.

Exercise:

1. Choose a professional persona: Imagine you are a clinician, administrator, biomedical engineer, data ethicist, or technologist in the year 2050.
2. Write a 500–700-word first-person diary entry describing a typical day in your role. Your narrative should consider:
   a. How do you begin and end your workday?
   b. Which digital or hybrid touchpoints (e.g., ambient sensors, AI co-pilots, blockchain) do you rely on?
   c. How does information move between devices, people, and institutions?

Discussion Questions: Use the narrative you crafted to debate the considerations listed below.

1. Biggest structural shifts of present vs 2050 (care models and settings, workforce, financing).
2. Net effect on patient safety, equity, and experience.

ACTIVITY 3: STRATEGIC PLANNING SIMULATION

Purpose: Practice strategic visioning for the future of digital health in your organization.

Exercise: Pick one of the following scenarios.

- Option 1: Launch a New Digital Product (e.g., an AI-based triage tool, a remote patient monitoring platform, or a telemedicine service).

- Option 2: Develop a 10-Year Strategic Plan for digital health integration across the entire organization (or department).

Strategic plan development:

- Define your vision (75–100 words).
  - Articulate the core goals of your chosen scope. What problems are you solving, and what does success look like?
  - Clarify the care, operational, and financial outcomes you aim to achieve.
- Define stakeholders.
  - List all relevant stakeholders (e.g., clinicians, administrators, IT teams, patients, insurers, community partners).
  - Specify each stakeholder's role in planning, implementation, or ongoing operations.
- Assess resources and infrastructure.
  - Determine what human, financial, and technological resources are required.
  - Consider training needs, infrastructure upgrades, and partnerships with external vendors or academic institutions.
- Define desired metrics.
  - Define key performance indicators (KPIs) and metrics for success (clinical outcomes, ROI, patient satisfaction, etc.).
  - Develop a process for continuous improvement, incorporating feedback loops from both staff and patients.
  - Outline contingencies for risk mitigations (what are your threats?)
- Develop a roadmap.
  - Break down the project or plan into phases or milestones (short-term, mid-term, long-term).
  - Consider any regulatory or policy steps necessary (e.g., FDA approvals, reimbursement coding, privacy compliance).

Note

1 *CMS guidance and wording current through the Consolidated Appropriations Act 2024, which extends many flexibilities to December 31 2026.*

References

1. Blank S. Why the lean start-up changes everything. *Harv Bus Rev*. 2013;May:online. Accessed June 23, 2025. https://hbr.org/2013/05/why-the-lean-start-up-changes-everything
2. Bardach S, Perry A, Powell L, Kapadia N, Barnato A. Hurdles of innovation—insights from a new healthcare delivery innovation program. *Learn Health Syst*. 2022;7(3):e10353. doi:10.1002/lrh2.10353

3. World Health Organization. *Global Strategy on Digital Health 2020–2025*. Geneva, Switzerland: World Health Organization; 2021. ISBN: 9789240020924. Accessed June 20, 2025. www.who.int/publications/i/item/9789240020924
4. U.S. Food and Drug Administration. What is digital health? Digital health center of excellence. Updated September 22, 2020. Accessed June 20, 2025. www.fda.gov/medical-devices/digital-health-center-excellence/what-digital-health
5. Amazon Health Services. Health condition programs. *Amazon Health*. Accessed June 20, 2025. https://health.amazon.com/health-condition-programs
6. Health Resources and Services Administration. *What is telehealth? Office for the Advancement of Telehealth*. Washington, DC: HRSA; 2022. Accessed June 20, 2025. www.hrsa.gov/telehealth/what-is-telehealth
7. Federal Communications Commission. Telehealth, telemedicine, and telecare: what's what? Federal Communications Commission. Accessed June 20, 2025. www.fcc.gov/general/telehealth-telemedicine-and-telecare-whats-what
8. Centers for Medicare & Medicaid Services. *Telehealth & Remote Patient Monitoring (MLN901705)*. Baltimore, MD: Centers for Medicare & Medicaid Services; April 2025. Accessed June 20, 2025. www.cms.gov/files/document/mln901705-telehealth-remote-patient-monitoring.pdf
9. IBM Corporation. What is artificial intelligence (AI)? IBM – Think. Published August 2024 (approx). Accessed June 20, 2025. www.ibm.com/think/topics/artificial-intelligence
10. U.S. Food and Drug Administration. *Artificial Intelligence and Machine Learning in Software as a Medical Device*. Digital Health Center of Excellence. Published April 2025 (approx). Accessed June 20, 2025. www.fda.gov/medical-devices/software-medical-device-samd/artificial-intelligence-and-machine-learning-software-medical-device
11. Office of the National Coordinator for Health Information Technology. Clinical decision support. *HealthIT.gov – Safety*. Published 2018. Accessed June 21, 2025. www.healthit.gov/topic/safety/clinical-decision-support
12. Agency for Healthcare Research and Quality. Clinical decision support. *AHRQ*. Accessed June 21, 2025. www.ahrq.gov/cpi/about/otherwebsites/clinical-decision-support/index.html
13. Stoumpos AI, Kitsios F, Talias MA. Digital transformation in healthcare: technology acceptance and its applications. *Int J Environ Res Public Health*. 2023;20(4):3407. doi:10.3390/ijerph20043407. PMID: 36834105; PMCID: PMC9963556
14. International Organization for Standardization (ISO). Predictive analytics. In: *ISO 3534-5: Statistical Vocabulary — Part 5: Predictive Analytics (Working Draft)*. Geneva: ISO; [Draft released 2013]. Available from: ISO Central Secretariat.
15. National Institute of Standards and Technology (NIST). *Introduction to Quantum Computing*. Gaithersburg, MD: U.S. Department of Commerce; 2023. Available from: www.nist.gov/programs-projects/quantum-computing
16. XR Safety Initiative (XRSI). *The XRSI Definitions of Extended Reality (XR), Standard Publication XR-001*, Version 002. Geneva, Switzerland: XR Safety Initiative; March 2020 [working draft]. Available from: https://xrsi.org/wp-content/uploads/2020/03/XRSI-Standard-XR-Definitions-XR-001v002.pdf
17. Yale School of Medicine. Medical devices and technology across the years. *Yale Med Mag*. 2019. Accessed June 20, 2025. https://elischolar.library.yale.edu/cgi/viewcontent.cgi?article=1044&context=yale_med_alumni_newsletters
18. Lewis FT. The advent of microscopes in America. *Sci Mon*. 1943;57(3):249–259. Accessed May 1, 2025. www.jstor.org/stable/17981
19. Esaki L. Highlights in semiconductor device development. *J Res Natl Bur Stand (1977)*. 1981;86(6):565–570. doi:10.6028/jres.086.025
20. History Timelines. Health informatics – a historical timeline. Accessed June 20, 2025. https://historytimelines.co/timeline/health-informatics
21. Andriole KP. Picture archiving and communication systems: past, present, and future. *J Med Imaging (Bellingham)*. 2023;10(6):061405. doi:10.1117/1.JMI.10.6.061405

22. Simpson AT, Doarn CR, Garber SJ. A brief history of NASA's contributions to telemedicine. *NASA History Division.* Originally published August 2013; updated March 26, 2020. Accessed June 20, 2025. www.nasa.gov/wp-content/uploads/2024/03/nasatelemedicine-briefhistory.pdf
23. Koonin LM, et al. Trends in the use of telehealth during the emergence of the COVID-19 pandemic—United States, January–March 2020. *MMWR Morb Mortal Wkly Rep.* 2020;69:1595–1599. doi:10.15585/mmwr.mm6943a3
24. Atherton J. Development of the electronic health record. *Virtual Mentor (AMA J Ethics).* 2011;13(3):186–189. Accessed June 24, 2025. https://journalofethics.ama-assn.org/article/development-electronic-health-record/2011-03
25. Institute of Medicine (US) Committee on Quality of Health Care in America. *To Err Is Human: Building a Safer Health System.* Kohn LT, Corrigan JM, Donaldson MS, eds. Washington, DC: National Academies Press; 2000
26. Turbow S, Hollberg JR, Ali MK. Electronic health record interoperability: how did we get here and how do we move forward? *JAMA Health Forum.* 2021;2(3):e210253. doi:10.1001/jamahealthforum.2021.0253
27. Health Insurance Portability and Accountability Act of 1996, Pub L No. 104-191, 110 Stat 1936 (1996)
28. Bush GW. Executive Order 13335—Incentives for the use of health information technology and establishing the position of the National Health Information Technology Coordinator. *Fed Reg.* 2004;69:24059. Accessed June 20, 2025
29. Redhead CS. *The Health Information Technology for Economic and Clinical Health (HITECH) Act.* CRS Report R40161. Washington, DC: Congressional Research Service; April 27, 2009. Accessed June 20, 2025
30. Robertson ST, Rosbergen ICM, Burton-Jones A, Grimley RS, Brauer SG. The effect of the electronic health record on interprofessional practice: a systematic review. *Appl Clin Inform.* 2022;13(3):541-559. doi:10.1055/s-0042-1748855
31. Chen Z, Liang N, Zhang H, et al. Harnessing the power of clinical decision support systems: challenges and opportunities. *Open Heart.* 2023;10(2):e002432. doi:10.1136/openhrt-2023-002432
32. Kautz HA. The third AI summer: AAAI Robert S. Engelmore memorial lecture. *AI Mag.* 2022;43(1):105–125. doi:10.1002/aaai.12036
33. Topol EJ. High-performance medicine: the convergence of human and artificial intelligence. *Nat Med.* 2019;25:44-56. doi:10.1038/s41591-018-0300-7
34. National Academy of Medicine. *Artificial Intelligence in Health Care: The Hope, the Hype, the Promise, the Peril.* Washington, DC: National Academies Press; 2022. doi:10.17226/27111
35. Jarrett MP. Cybersecurity—a serious patient care concern. *JAMA.* 2017;318(14):1319-1320. doi:10.1001/jama.2017.11986
36. Institute of Medicine (US) Committee on Quality of Health Care in America. *Crossing the Quality Chasm: A New Health System for the 21st Century.* Washington, DC: National Academies Press; 2001. PMID: 25057539
37. Association of American Medical Colleges. Interprofessional education collaborations and resources. AAMC Medical Education Mission Areas. Accessed June 20, 2025. www.aamc.org/what-we-do/mission-areas/medical-education/interprofessional-education
38. American Association of Colleges of Nursing. Domains & concepts. *AACN Essentials Implementation Tool Kit.* Accessed June 20, 2025. www.aacnnursing.org/essentials/tool-kit/domains-concepts
39. Accreditation Council for Pharmacy Education. *Standards 2025: Accreditation Standards and Key Elements for the Professional Program in Pharmacy Leading to the Doctor of Pharmacy Degree.* Chicago, IL: Accreditation Council for Pharmacy Education; 2024. Effective July 1, 2025. Accessed June 20, 2025. www.acpe-accredit.org/pdf/ACPEStandards2025.pdf
40. Carron T, Rawlinson C, Arditi C, et al. An overview of reviews on interprofessional collaboration in primary care: effectiveness. *Int J Integr Care.* 2021;21(2):31. doi:10.5334/ijic.5588. PMID: 34220395

41. Kaiser L, Conrad S, Neugebauer EAM, et al. Interprofessional collaboration and patient-reported outcomes in inpatient care: a systematic review. *Syst Rev.* 2022;11(1):169. doi:10.1186/s13643-022-02027-x. PMID: 35964148
42. Healthcare Information and Management Systems Society. *The Value of Clinical Informatics.* Chicago, IL: HIMSS; 2024. Accessed June 20, 2025. www.himss.org/sites/hde/files/media/file/2024/04/18/wp_value-of-clinical-informatics 1.pdf
43. Healthcare Information and Management Systems Society Clinical Informatics Communities. *Unlocking Healthcare's Future: The Invaluable Role of Clinical Informatics.* Chicago, IL: HIMSS; 2022
44. Mann DM, Stevens ER, Testa P, et al. From silos to synergy: integrating academic health informatics with operational IT for healthcare transformation. *NPJ Digit Med.* 2024;7:185. doi:10.1038/s41746-024-01179-5
45. Glasgow RE, Eckstein ET, ElZarrad MK. Implementation science perspectives and opportunities for HIV/AIDS research: integrating science, practice, and policy. *J Acquir Immune Defic Syndr.* 2013;63(suppl 1):S26–S31. doi:10.1097/QAI.0b013e3182920286
46. Bauer MS, Damschroder L, Hagedorn H, Smith J, Kilbourne AM. An introduction to implementation science for the non-specialist. *BMC Psychol.* 2015;3(1):32. doi:10.1186/s40359-015-0089-9. PMID: 26376626
47. Potthoff S, Finch T, Bührmann L, et al. Towards an implementation-STakeholder engagement model (I-STEM) for improving health and social care services. *Health Expect.* 2023;26(5):1997–2012. doi:10.1111/hex.13808. PMID: 37403248
48. Aarons GA, Hurlburt M, Horwitz SM. Exploration, preparation, implementation, sustainment (EPIS) framework. episframework.com. Accessed June 20, 2025. https://episframework.com
49. CFIR Research Team. Evaluation design: overview. Consolidated Framework for Implementation Research (CFIR). Published 2019. Accessed June 20, 2025. https://cfirguide.org/evaluation-design/overview
50. Abernethy A, Adams L, Barrett M, et al. The promise of digital health: then, now, and the future. *NAM Perspect.* Published June 27, 2022. doi:10.31478/202206e
51. Harvard Business Review, Drucker PF, Christensen CM, Govindarajan V. *HBR's 10 Must Reads on Innovation: With Featured Article "The Discipline of Innovation" by Peter F. Drucker.* Boston, MA: Harvard Business Review Press; 2013. ISBN: 978-1422189856
52. Marwaha JS, Landman AB, Brat GA, et al. Deploying digital health tools within large, complex health systems: key considerations for adoption and implementation. *NPJ Digit Med.* 2022;5:13. doi:10.1038/s41746-022-00557-1
53. U.S. Food and Drug Administration. Clinical decision support software (CDS): frequently asked questions. Digital Health Center of Excellence. Published December 20, 2024. Accessed June 20, 2025. www.fda.gov/medical-devices/software-medical-device-samd/clinical-decision-support-software-frequently-asked-questions-faqs
54. Car J, Ong QC, Erlikh Fox T, et al. The digital health competencies in medical education framework: an international consensus statement based on a Delphi study. *JAMA Netw Open.* 2025;8(1):e2453131. doi:10.1001/jamanetworkopen.2024.53131
55. Aghion P, Bergeaud A, Van Reenen J. The impact of regulation on innovation. *NBER Work Pap.* No. 28381. Cambridge, MA: National Bureau of Economic Research; January 2021. doi:10.3386/w28381
56. Allers S, Eijkenaar F, van Raaij EM, Schut FT. Patterns in the influence of funding and reimbursement on the development and implementation of healthcare innovation: a systematic review. *J Open Innov Technol Mark Complex.* 2025;11(1):100490. doi:10.1016/j.joitmc.2025.100490
57. Ibrahim MS, Yusoff H, Bakar YIA, et al. Digital health for quality healthcare: A systematic mapping of review studies. *Digit Health.* 2022;8:20552076221085810. doi:10.1177/20552076221085810
58. Kurzweil R. *The Singularity Is Near.* New York, NY: Viking; 2005.
59. Kurzweil R. *The Singularity Is Nearer: When We Merge with AI.* New York, NY: Viking; 2024.

60. Suleyman M, Bhaskar M. *The Coming Wave: Technology, Power, and the Twenty-First Century's Greatest Dilemma.* New York, NY: Crown; 2023.
61. Azhar A. *Exponential: How Accelerating Technology Is Leaving Us Behind and What to Do About It.* London, UK: Cornerstone; 2021.
62. Bostrom N. *Superintelligence: Paths, Dangers, Strategies.* Oxford, UK: Oxford University Press; 2014.
63. Howell MD, Corrado GS, DeSalvo KB. Three epochs of artificial intelligence in health care. *JAMA.* 2024;331(3):242–244. doi:10.1001/jama.2023.25057
64. DosSantos DiSorbo M, Ju H, Aral S. Teaching AI to handle exceptions: supervised fine tuning with human aligned judgment. *arXiv.* March 4, 2025. arXiv:2503.02976 [cs.AI]. doi:10.48550/arXiv.2503.02976
65. Tripathi G, Ahad MA, Casalino G. A comprehensive review of blockchain technology: underlying principles and historical background with future challenges. *Decis Anal J.* 2023;9:100344. doi:10.1016/j.dajour.2023.100344
66. AbdelSalam FM. Blockchain revolutionizing healthcare industry: a systematic review of blockchain technology benefits and threats. *Perspect Health Inf Manag.* 2023;20(3):1b. PMCID: PMC10701638
67. Digital Therapeutics Alliance. Understanding DTx. Accessed June 21, 2025. https://dtxalliance.org/understanding-dtx
68. Sharma A, Kosasih E, Zhang J, Brintrup A, Calinescu A. Digital twins: state of the art theory and practice, challenges, and open research questions. *J Ind Inform Integr.* 2022;30:100383. doi:10.1016/j.jii.2022.100383
69. Malik S, Muhammad K, Waheed Y. Emerging applications of nanotechnology in healthcare and medicine. *Molecules.* 2023;28(18):6624. doi:10.3390/molecules28186624. PMID: 37764400
70. Bhidayasiri R. The grand challenge at the frontiers of neurotechnology and its emerging clinical applications. *Front Neurol.* 2024;15:1314477. doi:10.3389/fneur.2024.1314477. PMID: 38299015
71. National Human Genome Research Institute. Personalized medicine. Talking Glossary of Genetic Terms. Accessed June 21, 2025. www.genome.gov/genetics-glossary/Personalized-Medicine
72. Schneider J, Smalley I. What is quantum computing? *IBM Think.* Published June 10, 2025. Accessed June 21, 2025. www.ibm.com/think/topics/quantum-computing
73. Scott J. How is quantum computing being used in healthcare? *HealthTech Magazine.* Published October 7, 2024. Accessed June 21, 2025. https://healthtechmagazine.net/how-is-quantum-computing-being-used-in-healthcare-perfcon
74. Institute for Clinical and Economic Review; Peterson Health Technology Institute. *ICER PHTI Assessment Framework for Digital Health Technologies.* Boston, MA: ICER & PHTI; September 2023. Accessed June 20, 2025. https://icer.org/wp-content/uploads/2023/09/ICER-PHTI-Assessment-Framework-for-Digital-Health-Technologies.pdf
75. World Bank. *Digital Health Assessment Toolkit Guide.* Washington, DC: World Bank; 2023. Accessed June 20, 2025. https://openknowledge.worldbank.org/server/api/core/bitstreams/76ba7971-1b06-596e-b2f5-0605e9ce8fdc/content
76. Marwaha JS, Landman AB, Brat GA, et al. Deploying digital health tools within large, complex health systems: key considerations for adoption and implementation. *NPJ Digit Med.* 2022;5:13. doi:10.1038/s41746-022-00557-1
77. National Academy of Medicine Leadership Consortium. *Learning Health System Series.* Washington, DC: National Academy of Medicine; 2024. Accessed June 23, 2025. www.nam.edu/our-work/programs/leadership-consortium/learning-health-system-series
78. American Hospital Association. *2025 Environmental Scan.* Chicago, IL: AHA; December 3, 2024. Accessed June 23, 2025. www.aha.org/environmentalscan
79. Center for Global Digital Health Innovation. *Governance Pathways for Driving Digital Transformation in Primary Healthcare: Research Roundup, Issue 20, March 2025.* Johns Hopkins University; 2025. Accessed June 23, 2025. https://publichealth.jhu.edu/center-for-global-digital-health-innovation/governance-pathways-for-driving-digital-transformation-in-primary-healthcare

80. World Health Organization. *Governance for Digital Health and Innovation*. Geneva, Switzerland: World Health Organization; June 2024. Accessed June 23, 2025. www.who.int/teams/digital-health-and-innovation/governance
81. Singh N, Lawrence K, Sinsky C, Mann DM. Digital minimalism—an Rx for clinician burnout. *N Engl J Med*. 2023;388(13):1158–1159. doi:10.1056/NEJMp2215297
82. American Medical Association. Declaration of professional responsibility: medicine's social contract with humanity. *AMA*. Published December 4, 2001. Accessed June 24, 2025. www.ama-assn.org/delivering-care/public-health/ama-declaration-professional-responsibility
83. American Association of Colleges of Pharmacy. Oath of a pharmacist. *AACP Student Center*. Published 2021; revised 2025. Accessed June 23, 2025. www.aacp.org/resource/oath-pharmacist
84. American Nurses Association. *2025 Code of Ethics for Nurses: Provisions*. Silver Spring, MD: American Nurses Association; 2025. Accessed June 23, 2025. https://codeofethics.ana.org/provisions

Chapter 2

Health Data Privacy and Security

Anthony Blash, PharmD, BCompSc, CPHIMS

Health data protection poses a constant and continuous challenge in modern healthcare, balancing privacy rights with public health benefits. Unlike financial data, health information is immutable—leaked HIV statuses, genetic risks, or mental health histories can harm individuals for years, impacting employment, insurance, and relationships. Breaches carry severe consequences, from discrimination to mental health struggles, particularly for sensitive conditions. Infamous historical privacy breach cases like Henrietta Lacks' highlight the lasting ethical dilemmas of health data use.[1] Today, digital healthcare introduces new risks: wearables and artificial intelligence (AI) can infer intimate details, while global regulations like General Data Protection Regulation (GDPR) and Health Insurance Portability and Accountability Act (HIPAA) struggle to keep pace.[1] While this evolution has enabled remarkable advancements in clinical decision-making, personalized medicine, and population health management, it has simultaneously introduced complex challenges surrounding the privacy and security of sensitive health information.[2] Protecting this data transcends mere regulatory compliance—it represents an ethical imperative that forms the foundation of patient trust and quality care delivery.

This chapter introduces the fundamental principles of health data privacy, outlines the key legislative frameworks governing its protection, and previews best practices for securing health information amid growing cyber threats and technological complexity. Drawing on real-world case studies and interdisciplinary perspectives, it sets the stage for understanding how professionals across medicine, nursing, pharmacy, and healthcare administration can work together to address these critical challenges.

DOI: 10.4324/9781003593867-3

Fundamentals of Health Data Privacy

The digitization of healthcare through electronic health records (EHRs), telemedicine platforms, wearable devices, and AI systems has dramatically increased both the value and vulnerability of health data. Where paper records were once kept in locked filing cabinets, today's digital health information circulates through complex networks of providers, insurers, researchers, and technology vendors. This interconnected environment creates numerous points where privacy protections can fail, whether through cybersecurity breaches, improper data sharing, or inadequate consent processes.[3]

The Unique Nature and Value of Health Data

Health data differs fundamentally from other types of personal information in its permanent nature. While financial institutions can issue new credit cards or account numbers after a breach, there is no equivalent remedy for exposed health information. A patient's genetic test results, psychiatric treatment history, or HIV status cannot be changed or reset once disclosed. This permanence means privacy violations can have lifelong consequences, affecting employment opportunities, insurance eligibility, and personal relationships.

Medical records contain some of the most personal details about individuals—information that many people would not share even with close friends or family members. Mental health treatments, reproductive health services, substance use disorders, and genetic predispositions all represent categories of information that carry significant social stigma when disclosed. The sensitivity of this data creates unique obligations for healthcare organizations to implement stronger protections than might be necessary for other types of personal information.[4]

In underground markets, stolen health records command prices 10–20 times higher than credit card information. Several factors drive this premium valuation. Medical identity theft enables fraudsters to bill insurers for fake treatments, a crime that often goes undetected for months or years. Health information also facilitates more sophisticated forms of identity theft, as medical records contain the detailed personal histories needed to answer security questions for financial accounts. Perhaps most disturbingly, certain types of health data (such as mental health records or sexually transmitted infection test results) can be used for extortion, with criminals threatening to release sensitive information unless victims pay ransom demands.

Core Principles of Health Data Protection

Confidentiality represents the principle that health information should only be accessible to authorized individuals with a legitimate need for the data.[5] In healthcare settings, this translates to role-based access controls (RBACs) that limit which staff members can view specific categories of patient information. A well-designed EHR system might allow providers full access to their patients' records while restricting billing staff to financial information and preventing administrative personnel from viewing clinical notes altogether.

The challenge of maintaining confidentiality has grown with the increasing complexity of healthcare data ecosystems. Where patient information once remained within a single hospital or clinic, it now flows between providers, insurers, pharmacies, laboratories, and various third-party service providers. Each additional recipient creates another potential point where confidentiality protections might fail, whether through intentional misuse, accidental disclosure, or cybersecurity vulnerabilities.[6]

Data integrity refers to the accuracy and consistency of health information throughout its lifecycle—from initial entry into medical records through any subsequent sharing or analysis.[7] Integrity failures can occur through simple data entry errors, system glitches during information transfers, or deliberate tampering by malicious actors. The consequences range from minor inconveniences to life-threatening situations, such as when incorrect medication allergies or dosages appear in a patient's record.

Modern healthcare organizations employ several strategies to protect data integrity. Cryptographic hashing creates digital fingerprints of records that can detect any unauthorized modifications. Blockchain-based audit trails provide tamper-evident logs of all accesses and changes to sensitive data. Order entry validation checks flag improbable or dangerous entries, such as a 200-pound dosage of a medication or a blood pressure reading incompatible with life.[8]

The principle of availability requires that health information remains accessible to authorized users when needed for patient care. This creates an inherent tension with security and privacy protections, as the most restrictive access controls could potentially delay or prevent critical treatment in emergencies. Healthcare organizations must implement security measures that protect patient privacy without creating barriers to legitimate clinical use.

Ransomware attacks represent the most direct threat to data availability, with various hospitals and health systems experiencing incidents where attackers encrypted patient records and demanded payment for their release. The 2021 attack on Ireland's Health Service Executive forced the cancellation of thousands of appointments and procedures as staff reverted to paper-based systems.[9] Defending against such threats requires both strong cybersecurity protections and comprehensive backup systems that enable rapid recovery without paying ransoms.[10]

Contemporary Challenges in Health Privacy

In today's healthcare system, technology makes it easier than ever for doctors, hospitals, and even researchers to share information and coordinate care. But with these benefits come serious questions about privacy and fairness. Patients often don't understand or control how their information is used, and new tools like AI can unintentionally reinforce inequities. The sections that follow look at these challenges—interoperability, consent, and algorithmic bias—and how they affect both trust and care in real life.

Interoperability vs. Privacy

The push for greater interoperability in healthcare—enabling seamless data exchange between different providers and systems—creates significant privacy challenges. While care coordination improves when clinicians have complete patient histories available, each additional data-sharing relationship expands the potential attack surface for breaches. Health Information Exchanges (HIEs) designed to facilitate this sharing have sometimes struggled with implementing granular access controls, leading to situations where providers can view patient records beyond what is necessary for direct care.[1]

Inadequate Consent Mechanisms

Current approaches to patient consent for data sharing often fail to provide meaningful control or understanding. Most authorization forms present complex legal language that obscures rather than clarifies how information will be used. Broad, blanket consents for undefined future research purposes deprive patients of the opportunity to make informed decisions about specific uses of their data. The resulting "consent fatigue" leads many individuals to automatically agree without understanding or engaging with privacy choices.[3]

Algorithmic Bias and Discrimination

The growing use of AI in healthcare introduces novel privacy and equity concerns. Machine learning models trained on historical medical data may perpetuate or amplify existing disparities in care. For example, algorithms predicting healthcare needs that incorporate zip code data might systematically undervalue the needs of patients in low-income neighborhoods. Because these AI systems often operate as "black boxes," it can be difficult for patients to understand what data was used about them or how it influenced their care.[11]

Emerging Privacy Threats

As health technology continues to evolve, so do the risks to our privacy. Information we assume is anonymous can sometimes be traced back to us; apps and wearables we use every day may share more than we realize, and our data often travels across borders where protections vary widely. These emerging threats show that keeping health information safe is no longer just about hospitals and clinics—it's about the many ways our personal data moves and is used in daily life.[8]

Reidentification of Anonymized Data

Advances in data science have dramatically reduced the effectiveness of traditional de-identification techniques. Researchers have demonstrated the ability to reidentify individuals from supposedly anonymized genomic data by cross-referencing with public genealogy databases. Similarly, the combination of location data from wearable devices with public records can reveal sensitive health information, such as visits to addiction treatment centers or abortion clinics. These developments challenge the long-standing assumption that removing obvious identifiers like names and addresses provides sufficient privacy protection.[12]

Unregulated Health Technologies

The proliferation of consumer health apps, wearable devices, and direct-to-consumer medical services has created a vast ecosystem of health-adjacent technologies operating outside traditional healthcare privacy regulations. Many popular fitness trackers and menstrual cycle apps share user data with advertising networks and data brokers. Mental health chatbots may analyze and store deeply personal conversations without providing the same privacy protections as licensed therapists. This regulatory gap leaves consumers vulnerable to exploitation while their most sensitive health information becomes part of the largely unregulated commercial data economy.[4]

Global Data Flow Complexities

As healthcare becomes increasingly globalized, patient data frequently crosses international borders for purposes ranging from telemedicine consultations to multinational clinical trials. These transfers create complex compliance challenges as different jurisdictions maintain incompatible privacy regulations. The European Union's GDPR imposes strict limitations on data transfers outside of approved countries, while other regions have more permissive approaches. These inconsistencies can create situations where patient information receives strong protections in one country but becomes vulnerable when shared abroad.[3]

The Path Forward for Health Privacy

Looking ahead, the future of healthcare will depend on how well we protect patient privacy while embracing innovation. It is no longer enough to rely on outdated rules or minimal compliance; stronger protections, smarter regulation of new technologies, and shared global standards are needed. The path forward must focus on building trust—showing patients that their information is safe, respected, and used responsibly—so that progress in medicine does not come at the cost of personal rights.[6]

Future health privacy frameworks must move beyond the current focus on compliance checklists to implement truly effective safeguards. This includes adopting privacy-enhancing technologies like homomorphic encryption that allow data analysis without exposing raw information. It requires rebuilding consent processes to provide genuine transparency and control rather than legalistic formalities. Most fundamentally, it means recognizing privacy as an essential component of quality care rather than just a regulatory obligation.

The rapid development of health-adjacent technologies demands equally agile regulatory responses. Consumer health apps and wearable devices that handle sensitive medical data should face oversight comparable to traditional healthcare providers. AI systems used in diagnosis or treatment must incorporate privacy protections by design, with clear accountability for biased or harmful outcomes. These measures will help ensure that technological innovation doesn't come at the expense of patient rights.[11]

In an interconnected world, effective health privacy protections require international cooperation. Harmonizing key regulations across jurisdictions would reduce compliance burdens while maintaining strong safeguards. Establishing clear rules for cross-border data transfers in healthcare would protect patients without hindering legitimate medical research and collaboration. Such standards should be developed through inclusive processes that account for different cultural perspectives on privacy while upholding fundamental rights.[13]

The future of healthcare depends on finding the right balance between leveraging data to improve outcomes and protecting the fundamental right to privacy. By addressing current weaknesses and proactively preparing for emerging challenges, we can build a health information ecosystem that earns and maintains patient trust while enabling medical progress. The alternative—a world where people fear seeking care because they can't control their health information—would represent a catastrophic failure of our healthcare systems and societies.[1]

Key Legislation and Regulations in Health Data Privacy

The protection of health data is governed by a complex and evolving framework of laws and regulations that vary significantly across jurisdictions. These legal structures aim to balance the need for healthcare providers, insurers, and researchers to access patient information with the fundamental right of individuals to control their sensitive medical data. The regulatory landscape includes broad, cross-industry privacy laws like the European Union's GDPR as well as healthcare-specific rules such as the United States' HIPAA. Other countries have developed their own approaches, ranging from China's restrictive Personal Information Protection Law (PIPL) to Brazil's more GDPR-inspired Lei Geral de Proteção de Dados (LGPD).[2,14] These regulations all aim to protect confidentiality, accuracy, and access but differ in enforcement and privacy approaches. Their evolution reflects changing views on privacy, advancing technology, and the growing value of health data.

The HIPAA

Enacted in 1996, HIPAA established the first comprehensive federal standards for protecting sensitive patient health information in the United States. The law applies primarily to what it terms "covered entities"—healthcare providers that conduct electronic transactions, health plans, and healthcare clearinghouses. It also extends to "business associates," which are third-party vendors that handle protected health information (PHI) on behalf of covered entities. This includes a wide range of organizations from cloud storage providers and medical billing companies to law firms and accounting practices that work with health data.

HIPAA's protections cover what it defines as PHI, which includes any individually identifiable health information held or transmitted by a covered entity or its business associate. This encompasses not just medical histories and test results but also billing records, insurance information, and even demographic data that could be used to identify an individual. The definition is intentionally broad to account for the many ways health information can be recorded and shared in modern healthcare systems.[2]

Core Regulatory Components

When we think about protecting health information, HIPAA is often the first law that comes to mind. Its rules shape how our medical records are handled, how electronic systems must be secured and what happens if a breach occurs. These regulations don't just set standards for healthcare organizations, they also define the rights patients have to see, correct, and understand how their information is used.[2] The sections that follow break down the core parts of HIPAA, the Privacy Rule, Security Rule, breach notification requirements, and enforcement to show how they work together to safeguard sensitive health information in everyday care.

The Privacy Rule

Implemented in 2003, the HIPAA Privacy Rule establishes national standards for protecting individuals' medical records and other personal health information. It requires appropriate safeguards to protect privacy while setting limits and conditions on the uses and disclosures of such information without patient authorization. A key provision is the "minimum necessary" standard, which requires covered entities to make reasonable efforts to limit access to PHI to only those who need it for a specific purpose.[2]

The Privacy Rule also grants patients important rights over their health information, including the ability to examine and obtain copies of their health records, request corrections, and receive an accounting of disclosures. However, critics note that these rights are not absolute—healthcare providers can deny access in certain situations, and patients have no private right of action under

HIPAA to sue for violations. Enforcement rests solely with the Department of Health and Human Services' Office for Civil Rights.[15]

The Security Rule

While the Privacy Rule applies to all forms of PHI, the HIPAA Security Rule focuses specifically on electronic protected health information (ePHI). Implemented in 2005, it establishes administrative, physical, and technical safeguards that covered entities must implement to ensure the confidentiality, integrity, and security of ePHI.[2] Administrative safeguards include risk management, workforce training, and contingency planning. Physical safeguards control facility access and workstation use, while technical safeguards address access, audit, integrity, and transmission security. The Security Rule is flexible and scalable, enabling organizations to adopt solutions suited to their size and technology.

Breach Notification Requirements

The HIPAA Breach Notification Rule, added as part of the 2009 Health Information Technology for Economic and Clinical Health (HITECH) Act, requires covered entities to notify affected individuals, the Secretary of HHS, and in some cases the media following a breach of unsecured PHI. The timing and manner of these notifications depend on the size of the breach, with larger breaches requiring more rapid disclosure.[2]

One controversial aspect is the "harm threshold" provision, which allows covered entities to avoid notification if they conduct a risk assessment and determine there is a low probability that the PHI has been compromised.[16] Critics argue this creates too much discretion and has led to underreporting of breaches that may nevertheless be significant to affected individuals.

Enforcement and Penalties

HIPAA violations can result in substantial civil monetary penalties, with fines ranging from $100 per violation for unintentional infractions up to $50,000 per violation for willful neglect that is not corrected. The maximum annual penalty for violations of an identical provision is $1.5 million. In particularly egregious cases, criminal penalties may apply, including fines up to $250,000 and imprisonment for up to ten years (HIPAA, 2024).[2]

Enforcement has increased significantly in recent years, with particular focus on systemic noncompliance, large-scale breaches, and cases involving willful neglect of HIPAA requirements. The Office for Civil Rights has also emphasized the importance of risk analysis and management, responding to security incidents, and managing relationships with business associates.[15]

The GDPR

The European Union's GDPR has become one of the most influential privacy laws in the world, setting strict rules for how personal data—including health information—is collected, used, and protected.[3,17]

Scope and Extraterritorial Application

The GDPR, which took effect in 2018, represents the European Union's comprehensive approach to data protection. Unlike HIPAA, which applies specifically to healthcare organizations and their business associates, GDPR has a much broader scope. The GDPR enforces strict rules regarding consent, access to data, and the right to be forgotten, as well as imposing hefty fines for noncompliance.[3]

One of GDPR's most significant features is its extraterritorial reach. The regulation applies to all organizations that process personal data of EU residents, regardless of where the organization is located.[18] This means that US healthcare providers offering services to EU patients, or global health technology companies with EU users, must comply with GDPR's requirements alongside any applicable national laws like HIPAA.

Key Principles and Requirements

Lawful Basis for Processing

GDPR requires that all processing of personal data, including health data, have a lawful basis. For sensitive categories of data like health information, the standard is higher—organizations must meet one of the specific conditions listed in Article 9 of the regulation. These include explicit consent from the data subject, processing necessary for healthcare purposes, or processing necessary for reasons of substantial public interest.[3]

The requirement for explicit consent represents a significant difference from HIPAA's approach. Under GDPR, consent must be freely given, specific, informed, and unambiguous, typically requiring an affirmative action rather than passive acceptance. Patients must also be able to withdraw consent as easily as they gave it, without suffering any detriment for doing so.[17]

Individual Rights

GDPR grants data subjects (patients, in healthcare contexts) an extensive set of rights regarding their personal data. These include the right to access their data, the right to rectification of inaccurate data, and the right to erasure ("right to be forgotten") under certain circumstances, the right to restrict processing, the right to data portability, and the right to object to processing.[3]

The right to data portability, which allows individuals to obtain and reuse their personal data across different services, has particular implications for healthcare. It enables patients to more easily transfer their medical records between providers or integrate data from different health applications and devices.[14]

Data Protection by Design and Default

A fundamental principle of GDPR is that data protection must be integrated into systems and processes from the earliest stages of design. This "privacy by design" approach requires organizations to implement appropriate technical and organizational measures to ensure they meet GDPR's requirements and protect individuals' rights.

In practice, this means healthcare organizations must consider privacy implications when developing new IT systems, clinical applications, or research protocols. It also requires implementing data minimization principles—only collecting and retaining personal data that is strictly necessary for the specified purposes.[14]

Accountability and Governance

GDPR places significant emphasis on accountability, requiring organizations to not only comply with the regulation but also to demonstrate their compliance. This includes maintaining detailed documentation of data processing activities, conducting data protection impact assessments for high-risk processing, and, in some cases, appointing a Data Protection Officer (DPO).

For healthcare organizations processing large amounts of sensitive data, these governance requirements can be substantial. Many hospitals and health systems have had to create new positions and departments focused specifically on data protection compliance.

Enforcement and Penalties

GDPR grants supervisory authorities in each EU member state the power to investigate complaints and impose significant penalties for noncompliance. The maximum fines are substantially higher than under HIPAA—up to €20 million ($23.6 million) or 4% of global annual turnover, whichever is higher.[13]

Several high-profile cases have demonstrated the regulation's teeth. In 2023, Meta was fined €1.0 billion ($1.2 billion) for transferring EU user data to US servers in violation of GDPR requirements.[19] While healthcare organizations haven't faced penalties of that magnitude, several hospitals and health tech companies have been fined for inadequate security measures or improper processing of health data.[11,20]

Other Significant Health Data Privacy Regulations

HIPAA isn't the only law that protects health data. Other US and international regulations—like the HITECH Act, California's privacy laws, and new rules in places like China and Brazil—also shape how personal health information is handled. These laws show that privacy is a global issue, with different regions taking their own approach to keeping sensitive data safe.[21]

The HITECH Act

Passed in 2009 as part of the American Recovery and Reinvestment Act, the HITECH Act significantly strengthened HIPAA's privacy and security provisions. It extended HIPAA's requirements directly to business associates of covered entities, eliminating what had been a compliance gap. The Act also established stricter breach notification requirements and provided financial incentives for healthcare providers to adopt EHRs while implementing privacy protections.[22]

California Consumer Privacy Act and California Privacy Rights Act

California's privacy laws, particularly the California Consumer Privacy Act (CCPA) as amended by the California Privacy Rights Act (CPRA), provide GDPR-like protections for California residents. While health information covered by HIPAA is exempt, the laws apply to much health-related data collected by apps, wearables, and direct-to-consumer health services. They grant consumers rights to know what personal information is being collected, to delete personal information, to opt out of its sale, and to correct inaccurate information.[23]

China's PIPL

Implemented in 2021, China's PIPL imposes strict requirements on the processing of sensitive personal information, including health data. It requires separate consent for processing sensitive data and imposes data localization requirements for certain categories of information. The law also establishes special protections for biometric data, medical health information, and other sensitive categories.[21]

Brazil's General Data Protection Law (LGPD)

Inspired by the European Union's GDPR, Brazil's General Data Protection Law (LGPD) enhances data protection within the country, complementing the principles established by Law No. 12,965/2014, which outlines rights and obligations for internet usage in Brazil. The LGPD was introduced to address the global need for secure personal data exchange, reducing associated risks. As the internet-driven services provided by both public and private sectors have made personal data a highly valuable asset, it has become a central element in the growing "information economy."[13]

Comparative Analysis and Emerging Challenges

Comparing HIPAA and GDPR reveals not only how differently the US and Europe approach health privacy, but also the new challenges that arise as healthcare grows more global and data-driven.

Key Differences Between HIPAA and GDPR

While both HIPAA and GDPR aim to protect personal health information, they take fundamentally different approaches. HIPAA is sector-specific, applying only to healthcare organizations and their business associates, while GDPR applies across all industries. HIPAA permits certain uses and disclosures of PHI without consent for treatment, payment, and healthcare operations, whereas GDPR generally requires explicit consent for processing health data unless another lawful basis applies.[1–3]

The enforcement mechanisms also differ significantly. HIPAA violations are enforced solely by the federal government through the Office for Civil Rights, while GDPR allows both regulatory enforcement by national authorities and private rights of action by individuals. The potential penalties under GDPR are also substantially higher than HIPAA's maximum fines.[15]

Best Practices for Ensuring Data Security in Healthcare

Protecting sensitive health information requires a comprehensive approach that addresses technical vulnerabilities, human factors, and organizational processes. Healthcare organizations face unique security challenges due to the critical nature of medical data, the complexity of healthcare IT ecosystems, and the growing sophistication of cyber threats targeting the industry. Effective data security goes beyond mere compliance with regulations like HIPAA or GDPR—it requires implementing layered defenses that can prevent, detect, and respond to security incidents while maintaining the availability of systems for patient care.[2,12]

The consequences of security failures in healthcare are particularly severe. Beyond financial penalties and reputational damage, breaches can directly impact patient safety when critical systems become unavailable or when medical records are altered. A 2023 report by the Ponemon Institute found that 24% of healthcare organizations experiencing ransomware attacks reported increased patient mortality rates due to delayed procedures or tests. This underscores why data security must be treated as both a technical requirement and a clinical imperative in modern healthcare delivery.[24]

Technical Safeguards for Health Data Protection

Protecting health information today requires more than just following the rules—it demands strong technical defenses backed by smart practices. From encryption and network security to training staff and managing vendors, every layer of protection plays a role in keeping patient data safe. The following sections highlight key safeguards and real-world examples that show why a comprehensive, proactive approach is essential to defending against modern threats.[25]

Encryption Strategies

Encryption is a core safeguard for protecting health data at rest and in transit. Healthcare organizations should use strong standards like AES-256 for stored data and TLS 1.3 for transmissions, extending encryption to backups, archives, and mobile devices.[25] Full-disk encryption on laptops and workstations is critical as staff work across locations. For data in transit, outdated protocols like SSL or early TLS must be retired due to known vulnerabilities.[9]

A 2024 incident at Confidant Health, a telemedicine provider, resulted in the exposure of video and audio recordings, transcripts, and other therapy-related content via a publicly accessible database. This breach underscores the severe risks to patient privacy when data repositories are improperly secured. To prevent such occurrences, healthcare organizations should conduct regular cryptographic and system security assessments, ensure the use of up-to-date encryption protocols (e.g., TLS 1.2 or 1.3), and continually evaluate all systems handling ePHI for misconfigurations and vulnerabilities.[26]

Network Security Measures

Healthcare networks require specialized security to protect sensitive data while supporting critical care. Network segmentation is key, isolating traffic into zones (e.g., clinical systems, admin functions, guest networks) to limit threat movement. The rise of Internet of Medical Things (IoMT) devices, often running outdated systems, has expanded the attack surface. To address this, organizations use network access control (NAC) to enforce policies before connection and deploy medical device security platforms that virtually segment vulnerable devices and monitor for suspicious activity.[25,27]

Endpoint Protection Strategies

The proliferation of mobile devices in healthcare has made endpoint security challenging, as providers access patient records from smartphones, tablets, and laptops across locations. Protection requires layered defenses, including next-generation antivirus, Endpoint Detection and Response (EDR), and mobile device management (MDM). Managed devices should follow strict standards such as automatic patching, full-disk encryption, and remote wiping. Unmanaged Bring Your Own Devices (BYOD) devices pose added risks and typically require containerization to separate organizational data from personal content. In 2023, a software flaw at the University of Pittsburgh Medical Center's (UPMC) billing contractor, Intellihartx, exposed the personal information of around 25,000 patients—underscoring the importance of rigorous endpoint security and third-party vendor oversight across all systems that process or handle ePHI.[28]

Human Factors in Healthcare Security

Human error remains one of the most significant vulnerabilities in healthcare security, accounting for 82% of breaches according to Verizon's 2023 Data Breach Investigations Report. Traditional annual compliance training has proven ineffective at changing behaviors and reducing risks. To address this, leading healthcare organizations are now adopting more engaging and frequent training approaches. These include microlearning modules, which are short 5- to 10-minute focused sessions delivered regularly; phishing simulations, which are controlled tests designed to identify vulnerable staff and provide just-in-time training; and gamification, which incorporates competitive elements to increase engagement with security content.[27]

A study analyzing nearly 20,000 employees at UCSD Health over an 8-month period found that repeated simulated phishing campaigns led to significant improvements in phishing detection and awareness. These ongoing exercises emphasize the value of continuous, realistic training for building a cybersecurity-aware workforce.[29]

Culture of Security

Technical controls alone cannot ensure security without corresponding cultural support. Building a security-conscious culture requires visible leadership commitment, clear accountability, and nonpunitive reporting mechanisms. Organizations that punish staff for reporting potential security incidents often drive problems underground, while those that encourage open reporting can identify and address vulnerabilities proactively.[29,30]

Trinity Health implemented an anonymous web-based reporting tool called PEERs (Potential Error and Event Reporting System) to foster a "just culture"—one in which staff feel safe to report errors without fear of blame. As a result, over 200,000 incident or near-miss reports were logged—80% more than under the previous paper-based system. These reports led to 59 root cause analyses, 16 new policy adoptions, and 123 process improvements, underscoring the power of a blame-free, user-friendly reporting system to enhance patient safety and reinforce positive behavior.[30]

Privileged Access Management

Clinical workflows often require shared access to systems, which creates challenges for traditional identity management approaches. However, certain high-risk accounts—such as IT administrators and third-party support personnel—require special controls. Privileged access management (PAM) solutions address these risks by providing just-in-time privilege elevation, session monitoring and recording, and automated credential rotation. These measures are particularly critical for protecting essential medical systems and reducing insider threat risks. The 2021 breach at Florida-based Broward Health, in which compromised administrator credentials led to the exposure of 1.3 million records, underscored the vital importance of implementing robust privileged access controls.[2]

Risk Management Frameworks

Effective security begins with comprehensive risk assessment and management, and many healthcare organizations have adopted the structured approach outlined in the National Institute of Standards and Technology (NIST) Cybersecurity Framework. This framework involves identifying all systems, data flows, and potential threats, protecting systems with appropriate safeguards, detecting security events through monitoring, responding to contain incidents, and recovering from disruptions. Regular risk assessments should be conducted at least annually or whenever significant changes occur to systems or threats. The University of Vermont Health Network's response to its 2020 ransomware attack demonstrated the value of thorough risk assessment, as their preexisting understanding of critical systems enabled faster and more effective recovery decisions.[25,31]

Vendor and Third-Party Risk Management

Modern healthcare relies on an extensive ecosystem of vendors and business associates, each representing potential security vulnerabilities. The 2024 Change Healthcare attack, which disrupted healthcare payments nationwide, illustrated the catastrophic impacts that can result from third-party security failures. To reduce these risks, effective vendor risk management programs should incorporate precontract security assessments, ensuring vendors' security posture is evaluated before engagement; contractual safeguards, such as clear security requirements and defined breach notification timelines; and ongoing monitoring, including regular audits and performance reviews to verify continued compliance and resilience.[32]

Many organizations now maintain vendor risk scorecards and tier vendors based on the sensitivity of data they handle and their criticality to operations. The Mayo Clinic's vendor management program, for example, requires third parties handling sensitive research data to undergo independent security audits and maintain specific certifications like HITRUST CSF.[6]

Incident Response Planning

Despite best efforts, security incidents will occur, making it essential for healthcare organizations to have a well-developed incident response plan. Such a plan ensures that they can react quickly and effectively to minimize damage. Key components include clearly defined roles and responsibilities, escalation procedures tailored to different incident types, and communication protocols for both internal and external stakeholders. In addition, robust plans incorporate forensic preservation processes to support investigations and regulatory reporting workflows to maintain compliance with legal and industry requirements.[2]

Tabletop exercises that simulate various breach scenarios help test and refine these plans. Massachusetts General Hospital conducts quarterly simulations involving clinical, IT, legal, and communications teams to maintain readiness. Their 2022 response to a zero-day vulnerability in their patient portal demonstrated the value of this preparation, containing the incident within hours.[25]

Health data privacy and security will define the credibility of digital care in the decade ahead: the same infrastructures that enable interoperability, AI-driven insights, and global collaboration must be governed with the rigor of clinical safety science and the humility of ethics in practice. Getting this balance right requires more than box-checking—it demands continuous risk management, resilient architectures, and a culture that treats privacy as care quality, not compliance overhead.[2,3,25] The evidence is unambiguous: security failures imperil patient outcomes and trust, with ransomware and data misuse carrying real clinical consequences, particularly for stigmatized conditions and marginalized communities.[24] To move forward responsibly, health systems should harden defenses, verify vendors, and operationalize transparent governance while advancing equity, consent that is truly informed and explainable analytics at the point of care—an urgent, shared mandate for expanded oversight that keeps pace with innovation.[1]

Case Studies

CASE STUDY 1: THE CHANGE HEALTHCARE CYBERATTACK (2024)

In February 2024, UnitedHealth Group's Change Healthcare subsidiary was hit by a ransomware attack from the ALPHV/BlackCat group, crippling insurance claims processing nationwide for over three weeks. Hospitals faced $6.3 billion in delayed payments, community health centers struggled to pay staff or buy supplies, pharmacies couldn't verify insurance for critical medications, and suppliers halted deliveries due to unpaid invoices. The attack underscored the need for stronger third-party risk management, payment continuity plans (with CMS now requiring 30-day offline processing), new federal limits on reliance on single vendors, and broader cyber insurance coverage, with 89% of hospitals adding ransomware-specific policies.

Instruction Set 1—Focused Reading

As you read this case study, pay attention to:

- The sequence of events that led to the cyberattack.
- The direct and indirect impacts on healthcare delivery.
- The lessons healthcare organizations and regulators identified afterward.

Afterward, ask yourself: *What safeguards or policies could have reduced the severity of this incident?*

Instruction Set 2—Critical Thinking and Application

Use this case study to connect theory to practice. As you review the details:

- Identify which technical, organizational, or regulatory safeguards failed or were missing.
- Consider how your own organization (or one you are familiar with) might respond to a similar event.
- Think about what changes should be prioritized to prevent recurrence.

Be prepared to discuss how this example illustrates the broader challenges of protecting health data.

Instruction Set 3—Reflection and Discussion

This case study is intended to spark reflection. As you read:

- Note the real-world consequences for patients, providers, and the healthcare system.
- Reflect on how trust in healthcare can be damaged by such breaches.
- Consider how this event highlights the importance of third-party risk management.

After reading, discuss with your peers: *What is the single most important lesson from this case for future healthcare leaders?*

CASE STUDY 2: THE FRANCE HEALTH DATA HUB BREACH (2022)

In 2022, the France Health Data Hub experienced a major breach when a misconfigured Microsoft Power BI dashboard exposed more than 500,000 sensitive patient records, including psychiatric and HIV treatment data collected during COVID-19 research initiatives. The impact was significant: 12 major medical studies were paused for six months, delaying critical research; 37% of French patients withdrew consent for data sharing, crippling recruitment efforts; Microsoft, as the cloud service provider, was fined €60 million; and public trust in digital health initiatives fell by 41% in post-breach surveys. Several lessons emerged from this incident. Cloud security requirements now mandate anonymization of health data before uploading to cloud environments. Transparency rules require all research platforms to display real-time data access dashboards. Technical safeguards include mandatory use of synthetic data generation for non-critical research. Finally, legal reforms introduced new penalties for "negligent configuration" of health data systems.[3]

Instruction Set 1—Risk Analysis Exercise

Identify and describe three points of failure in the France Health Data Hub breach. Explain how each failure could have been prevented through proper technical or administrative safeguards.

Instruction Set 2—Ethical and Legal Reflection

Discuss the ethical implications of exposing sensitive psychiatric and HIV treatment data. Compare how the penalties applied in this case align with either HIPAA (US) or GDPR (EU) requirements.

Instruction Set 3—Policy Recommendation Task

Based on the lessons learned, propose one additional policy or safeguard (not already mentioned in the case) that would strengthen patient trust in digital health platforms. Provide justification for your choice.

CASE STUDY 3: THE HCA HEALTHCARE DATA BREACH (2023)

In July 2023, HCA Healthcare, operating 180 hospitals across 20 states, suffered a data breach exposing 11 million patient records after a vendor's email account was compromised. The incident carried wide impacts: patients faced phishing risks from exposed names, visit dates, and physician details; operations were disrupted as 23 hospitals paused admissions for 72 hours during audits; financial costs reached $350 million in breach-related expenses; and the FTC launched an investigation into vendor security practices. Lessons learned included requiring encrypted email and multifactor authentication for vendors, deleting historical patient data older than 10 years, creating a real-time breach status dashboard for patients, and updating cyber insurance policies to cover vendor-related incidents.[33]

Instruction Set 1—Focused Reading

Review the details of the HCA Healthcare breach and summarize the main causes, consequences, and lessons learned. Focus on how vendor vulnerabilities contributed to the incident.

Instruction Set 2—Critical Thinking and Application

Pretend you are the Chief Information Security Officer (CISO) at HCA. Develop a short action plan with three concrete measures you would immediately implement to prevent a similar vendor-related breach in the future.

Instruction Set 3—Reflection and Discussion

This case study is intended to spark reflection. As you read:

Reflect on the broader implications of vendor accountability in healthcare cybersecurity. How does relying on third-party vendors increase risks, and what balance should exist between efficiency and patient data protection? Be ready to discuss your perspective with peers.

Exercises and Activities

ACTIVITY 1: CASE STUDY, ANALYSIS, AND ROLE PLAYING—HENRIETTA LACKS

The Legacy of Henrietta Lacks: Ethics, Equity, and Ownership in Healthcare Data

Objective:
To analyze the historical case of Henrietta Lacks and examine ethical, legal, scientific, and business implications related to patient consent, biospecimen use, and data ownership in healthcare.

Instructions:

1. **Divide students into small interdisciplinary groups:**
   Aim for a mix of students in pharmacy, nursing, medicine, public health, and healthcare business/administration.
2. **Provide a brief summary of the Henrietta Lacks case:**
   In 1951, Henrietta Lacks, a 31-year-old African American woman, was treated for cervical cancer at Johns Hopkins Hospital. Without her knowledge or consent, doctors took a biopsy of her tumor. Her cells—later known as *HeLa* cells—became the first immortal human cell line and have been used in countless medical breakthroughs, including the polio vaccine, gene mapping, and cancer research. Her family only learned of this decades later. Despite the enormous scientific and commercial impact, her descendants received no compensation or consultation for many years.
3. **Assign each group member a role:**
   - Healthcare provider: Reflect on how medical practices have evolved and how informed consent impacts trust and care delivery today.
   - Bioethics expert: Examine the ethical implications of using biospecimens without consent.
   - Policy expert: Assess how today's laws (HIPAA, the Common Rule, etc.) would apply to the Henrietta Lacks case.
   - Business manager: Analyze the commercialization of HeLa cells and discuss implications for benefit sharing and corporate responsibility.
   - Patient advocate or community representative: Represent the Lacks family's perspective and advocate for justice, transparency, and equity in research.

4. **Task**: Each group discusses the following:
   - What went wrong in the Henrietta Lacks case?
   - How would each stakeholder approach reparations, policy changes, or ethical improvements?
   - How should biospecimens and health data be managed to balance innovation with patient rights?
5. **Presentation:**
   Each group presents their findings and recommendations to the class, highlighting:
   - Role-specific concerns and solutions.
   - Points of intersection and conflict between roles.
   - Proposed reforms or safeguards to prevent similar ethical breaches in the future.

ACTIVITY 2: DESIGNING A DATA PRIVACY AND SECURITY POLICY

Objective:
To create a comprehensive data privacy and security policy for a hypothetical healthcare organization.

Instructions:

1. Provide students with a scenario: A mid-sized hospital is transitioning to a fully digital health record system and needs a robust data privacy and security policy.
2. In small groups, students draft a policy that includes:
   - Administrative, physical, and technical safeguards (aligned with HIPAA and GDPR requirements).
   - Procedures for handling data breaches.
   - Training programs for staff.
   - Patient communication strategies regarding data privacy.
3. Each group presents their policy to the class, explaining how it addresses legal, ethical, and technical considerations.
4. The class votes on the most comprehensive and practical policy.

ACTIVITY 3: ETHICAL DILEMMA DEBATE

Objective:
To explore the ethical implications of health data privacy and security decisions.

Instructions:

1. Present students with an ethical dilemma related to health data privacy.

For example:

- A hospital wants to use patient data for research without explicit consent, arguing that it will benefit public health.
- A healthcare app collects user data to improve its algorithms but shares this data with third-party advertisers.

2. Divide the class into two groups: one arguing for the action (e.g., using data for public health benefits) and the other against it (e.g., prioritizing patient autonomy and privacy).
3. Each group prepares arguments based on ethical principles (e.g., beneficence, non-maleficence, autonomy, justice) and legal frameworks (e.g., HIPAA, GDPR).
4. Hold a structured debate, allowing each side to present their case and respond to counterarguments.
5. Conclude with a class discussion on how to balance competing ethical and practical considerations

Assessment Questions:

1. *Define* the three core principles of health data protection under HIPAA and provide one example of how each principle applies to EHRs.
2. *Compare* HIPAA's "minimum necessary" standard with GDPR's data minimization principle. How do these concepts differ in practical implementation?
3. A community clinic discovers its unencrypted email system was used to transmit patient lab results. *List* three specific HIPAA Security Rule violations and *propose* corrective actions for each.
4. *Analyze* how the 2022 Advocate Aurora pixel tracking breach violated both HIPAA's Marketing Rule (45 CFR §164.508(a)(3)) and GDPR's lawful processing requirements (Article 6). Support your answer with regulatory excerpts.
5. *Design* a RBAC system for a hospital EHR that accommodates:
   - Emergency department physicians needing rapid access
   - Clinical researchers using de-identified data
   - Billing staff processing claims
   - Justify your design choices with security principles.
6. *Evaluate* this statement: "HIPAA compliance guarantees complete data security." Provide:
   - Two examples of HIPAA-permitted data uses that risk patient privacy
   - One regulatory gap in addressing cloud storage vulnerabilities
7. A mental health clinic uses tablets for patient surveys without encryption. *Develop* an incident response plan addressing:
   - Containment procedures
   - Notification timelines for a breach affecting 5,000 patients
   - Staff communication protocols
8. *Prioritize* these remediation actions after a ransomware attack, justifying your ranking:
   - Restore encrypted data from backups
   - Notify HHS OCR within 60 days
   - Conduct employee phishing training

- Patch vulnerable VPN systems

9. *Argue for or against* this ethical dilemma using both legal frameworks (HIPAA/GDPR) and bioethical principles:
   "A hospital wants to use historical patient data for COVID-19 research without reconsent, citing public health emergencies."
10. *Propose* amendments to current health data regulations to address:
    - AI bias in clinical decision support tools
    - Health app data privacy loopholes
    - Support your proposals with precedents from recent breaches.

Key Answer to Assessment Questions:

1. Define the three core principles of health data protection under HIPAA and provide one example of how each principle applies to EHRs.
   - Confidentiality: PHI must only be accessed by authorized users. *Example: Limiting EHR access so billing staff cannot open clinical notes.*
   - Integrity: PHI must remain accurate and unaltered. *Example: Audit logs track if a patient's medication list is improperly changed.*
   - Availability: PHI must be accessible when needed. *Example: Redundant, encrypted backups allow quick restoration of records after ransomware.*
2. Compare HIPAA's "minimum necessary" standard with GDPR's data minimization principle. How do these concepts differ in practical implementation?
   - HIPAA—Minimum necessary: Limits the *use, access, and disclosure* of PHI within healthcare. *Example: Staff see only the data required for their role.*
   - GDPR—Data minimization: Restricts *collection and storage* across all industries to only essential data. *Example: An app cannot collect location data unless it is strictly necessary.*
3. A community clinic discovers its unencrypted email system was used to transmit patient lab results. List three HIPAA Security Rule violations and propose corrective actions for each.
   - Transmission security violation: Email not encrypted. → *Adopt TLS 1.2/1.3 and secure messaging portals.*
   - Risk management violation: No assessment identified insecure email use. → *Perform and update risk analysis regularly.*
   - Workforce training violation: Staff unaware of secure messaging rules. → *Provide frequent, scenario-based privacy and security training.*
4. Analyze how the 2022 Advocate Aurora pixel tracking breach violated HIPAA and GDPR.
   - HIPAA Marketing Rule (45 CFR §164.508(a)(3)): PHI was disclosed to third-party advertisers without patient authorization.
   - GDPR Lawful Processing (Articles 6 and 9): Tracking of sensitive health data lacked explicit consent and violated restrictions on processing special category data.
5. Design a RBAC system for a hospital EHR.
   - Emergency physicians: Broad, rapid access with "break-glass" override, fully logged.
   - Clinical researchers: Access only to de-identified datasets through secure research portals.
   - Billing staff: Access limited to demographic and claims data.

   This design enforces minimum necessary access, supports confidentiality, and preserves availability during emergencies.

6. Evaluate this statement: "HIPAA compliance guarantees complete data security."
   - False. HIPAA compliance sets a baseline but does not ensure full protection.
   - Examples of HIPAA-permitted uses that risk privacy:
     1. Sharing full claims data with insurers.
     2. Broad internal use for "operations" such as analytics.
     3. Regulatory Gap: HIPAA does not fully address vulnerabilities in cloud storage or health apps, leaving major exposures unregulated.
7. A mental health clinic uses tablets for patient surveys without encryption. Develop an incident response plan.
   - Containment: Disconnect and wipe affected tablets, reset credentials, and secure Application Programming Interfaces (APIs).
   - Notification: Notify patients and HHS without delay, and no later than 60 days; notify media since >500 patients are affected.
   - Staff communication: Issue same-day internal updates, provide patient-facing scripts, and reinforce secure data capture practices.
8. Prioritize remediation actions after a ransomware attack and justify ranking.
   1. Patch vulnerable VPN systems—Stops reinfection and closes the attack vector.
   2. Restore encrypted data from backups—Restores care operations and availability.
   3. Notify HHS OCR within 60 days—Ensures regulatory compliance.
   4. Conduct employee phishing training—Reduces risk of future attacks.
9. Ethical dilemma: Using historical patient data for COVID-19 research without reconsent.
   - For: HIPAA permits disclosures for public health; GDPR allows processing for public interest. Supported by bioethics principles of beneficence and justice.
   - Against: Violates autonomy and informed consent. Bioethics principle of respect for persons supports reconsent or de-identification.
10. Propose amendments to current health data regulations.
    - AI Bias: Require mandatory bias audits, explainability, and patient impact assessments for clinical AI.
    - Health app loopholes: Extend HIPAA-like safeguards (explicit consent, breach notices, encryption) to consumer health apps and wearables.

    Precedents: breaches in women's health apps and ransomware attacks show urgent need for expanded oversight.

References

1. Network Advertising Initiative. *NAI Legal and Regulatory Analysis: Sensitive Health Information.* Published September 2023.
2. US Dept of Health and Human Services. HIPAA for Professionals. 2023. Available at: www.hhs.gov/hipaa/for-professionals/index.html. See also: What are the penalties for HIPAA violations? HIPAA Journal. 2024. www.hipaajournal.com/what-are-the-penalties-for-hipaa-violations-7096/
3. European Data Protection Board. *Guidelines 03/2020 on the processing of data concerning health.* 2021. https://edpb.europa.eu; YouGuide Ltd. GDPR Compliance: A Practical Guide. 2024.
4. Hassan M, Jameel M, Wang T, Bashir M. Unveiling Privacy and Security Gaps in Female Health Apps. *arXiv.* February 4, 2025.
5. American Medical Association. *Code of Medical Ethics Opinion 3.2.1: Confidentiality.* Chicago, IL: AMA; 2023. Available at: https://code-medical-ethics.ama-assn.org/chapters/patient-privacy-and-confidentiality

6. Bose S, Marijan D. A Survey on Privacy of Health Data Lifecycle: A Taxonomy, Review, and Future Directions. *arXiv*. November 9, 2023.
7. Akgün KM, Feder SL. Whom should we Regard as Responsible for Health Record Inaccuracies that Hinder Population-Based Fact finding? *AMA Journal of Ethics*. 2025;27(1):E6–13.
8. Zhang SY, Singh M. Privacy Risks in Health Big Data: A Systematic Literature Review. *arXiv*. February 6, 2025.
9. Cichonski P, Millar T, Grance T. *Computer Security Incident Handling Guide*. NIST SP 800-61r2. https://csrc.nist.gov/publications/detail/sp/800-61/rev-2/final (Published 2022).
10. Trend Micro. *One year on: What can We Learn from the HSE Ransomware Attack*. Published May 16, 2022.
11. Roberts H, Cowls J, Hine E, et al. Achieving a "Good AI Society": Comparing the Aims and Progress of the EU and the US. *Science and Engineering Ethics*. 2021;27(6). doi:https://doi.org/10.1007/s11948-021-00340-7
12. Packhäuser K, Gündel S, Münster N, et al. Deep Learning-Based Patient Re-Identification is able to Exploit the Biometric Nature of Medical Chest X-Ray Data. *Sci Rep*. 2022;12:14851. doi:10.1038/s41598-022-19045-3
13. GDPR vs. HIPAA: Similarities, Differences, and Tips for Achieving Compliance. Exabeam. Published July 22, 2024. Accessed October 4, 2024. www.exabeam.com/explainers/gdpr-compliance/gdpr-vs-hipaa-similarities-differences-and-tips-for-achieving-compliance/
14. Passos N, José F. Brazilian General Data Protection Law (LGPD): The Relationship between information policy and information regime. *RDBCI*. 2024;22:e024015. doi:10.20396/rdbci.v22i00.8675749/en
15. Office for Civil Rights. *Guidance on the HIPAA Privacy Rule*. US Dept of Health and Human Services; 2022. Available at: www.hhs.gov/hipaa/for-professionals/privacy/index.html
16. American Medical Association. HIPAA Breach Notification Rule. In: *HIPAA Basics*. American Medical Association. Updated May 2025. Accessed August 22, 2025. www.ama-assn.org/practice-management/hipaa/hipaa-breach-notification-rule
17. George M. GDPR compliance: General Data Protection Regulation Explained. Ketch.com. Published February 7, 2025. www.ketch.com/regulatory-compliance/general-data-protection-regulation-gdpr
18. Harmeling T. Understanding the differences between GDPR and FADP. Consent Management Platform (CMP) Usercentrics. Published February 8, 2024. Accessed August 22, 2025.
19. Irish Data Protection Commission. *Meta Platforms IE found to breach GDPR, fined €1.2 billion by Irish DPC for unlawful data transfers*. GDPR fines and notices. 2023.
20. CMS Law & Policy. *GDPR Enforcement in Life Science & Healthcare: GDPR Enforcement Tracker*. Published May 13, 2025.
21. Kim JS. *Legal Issues in Protecting and Utilitizing Medical Data in United States – Focused on HIPAA/HITECH*, 21st Century Cures Act, Common Law, Guidance -. THE KOREAN SOCIETY OF LAW AND MEDICINE.
22. US Department of Health and Human Services. HITECH Act Enforcement Interim Final Rule. Office for Civil Rights. Updated June 16, 2017. Available at: https://www.hhs.gov/hipaa/for-professionals/special-topics/hitech-act-enforcement-interim-final-rule/
23. California Office of the Attorney General. California Consumer Privacy Act (CCPA). 2023. https://oag.ca.gov/privacy/ccpa
24. Ponemon Institute. *The Impact of Ransomware on Patient Safety and the Value of Cybersecurity Benchmarking*. Published January 2023. Accessed August 10, 2025. www.censinet.com/impact-of-ransomware-on-patient-safety-and-value-of-cybersecurity-benchmarking Censinet
25. National Institute of Standards and Technology. *Framework for Improving Critical Infrastructure Cybersecurity, Version 2.0*. Gaithersburg, MD: NIST; 2024. Accessed August 22, 2025. https://doi.org/10.6028/NIST.CSWP.29
26. Burgess M. Therapy Sessions Exposed by Mental Health care Firm's Unsecured Database. *Wired*. Published September 6, 2024. Accessed August 22, 2025

27. Alder S. Verizon 2023 Data Breach Investigations Report (DBIR): Social Engineering Attacks Increase; Ransomware Plateaus. *The HIPAA Journal.* Published June 6, 2023. Accessed August 22, 2025.
28. UPMC data breach. CBS News. Published June 13, 2023. Accessed August 22, 2025. www.cbsnews.com/pittsburgh/news/upmc-reveals-data-breach-with-up-to-25000-patients-personal-information-exposed/?utm_source=
29. Felt AP, Ho G, Egelman S, et al. Training the Workforce to Resist Phishing at Scale: Evidence from an 8-month study at UC San Diego Health. *IEEE Symposium on Security and Privacy (SP). Proceedings.* 2025:1–17. doi:10.1109/SP.2025.00000
30. Agency for Healthcare Research and Quality. *Patient Safety and Quality: An Evidence-Based Handbook for Nurses.* Chapter 35: Anonymous Reporting. Rockville, MD: AHRQ; 2023 update. Accessed August 22, 2025. www.ncbi.nlm.nih.gov/books/NBK43630/
31. FBI Cyber Division. *Ransomware Incident Involving the University of Vermont Medical Center.* Public Service Announcement. Published December 2020. Accessed August 22, 2025.
32. UnitedHealth Group Inc. Form 8-K. Filed February 21, 2024. U.S. Securities and Exchange Commission EDGAR database.
33. HCA Healthcare. Notice of Data Security Incident. Published July 10, 2023. Accessed August 22, 2025.

Chapter 3

Ethics in Healthcare Informatics and Digital Health

Anthony Blash, PharmD, BCompSc, CPHIMS

The digital transformation of healthcare is no longer a distant future—it is our present reality. From artificial intelligence (AI)-driven diagnostics to blockchain-secured patient records, technology is reshaping how care is delivered, monitored, and optimized. Yet, as these innovations accelerate, they bring profound ethical challenges that demand urgent attention. *How do we ensure that algorithms make fair decisions? Who owns patient data in an era of cloud computing and big data analytics? What happens when technology outpaces regulation?* This chapter explores these pressing questions, offering a roadmap for navigating the ethical complexities of healthcare informatics and digital health.[1]

The integration of technology into healthcare has yielded remarkable benefits. AI can now detect early signs of diabetic retinopathy with greater accuracy than human specialists, while predictive analytics help hospitals allocate scarce resources during public health crises.[1,2] Telehealth platforms have democratized access to care, particularly for rural and underserved populations.[3] However, these advancements are not without risks. Studies reveal that biased algorithms can perpetuate disparities—for example, by underdiagnosing heart failure in women or misclassifying skin cancer in darker-skinned patients.[4] Similarly, the aggregation of sensitive health data raises concerns about privacy breaches and unintended commercialization, as seen in cases where de-identified genomic data was reidentified and sold to third parties.[5]

At the heart of these challenges lies a tension between innovation and ethics. Traditional biomedical principles—beneficence, non-maleficence, autonomy, and justice—must be reinterpreted for the digital age, where their meanings expand beyond clinical settings to address challenges posed by healthcare informatics and digital health technologies. Beneficence entails the obligation to act for the patient's benefit, promoting well-being through the effective and responsible use of digital tools. Non-maleficence, or "do no harm," requires avoiding harms that might arise from algorithmic errors, data bias, or misuse of health IT systems. Autonomy emphasizes respecting patients' rights to informed decision-making and self-determination, now encompassing transparent digital consent processes and control over personal health data.[6] These evolving interpretations are essential for

DOI: 10.4324/9781003593867-4

ethically navigating the complexities of digital health environments and ensuring patient-centered care.[7]

Consider *autonomy*: while electronic health records (EHRs) empower patients with access to their data, opaque AI decision-making can undermine their ability to contest algorithmic diagnoses. Or take *justice*: although telemedicine expands access, it risks excluding those without reliable internet or digital literacy. These dilemmas require interdisciplinary solutions, blending insights from clinicians, data scientists, policymakers, and ethicists.

Ethical Framework and Principles in Digital Health

The integration of AI into clinical workflows has precipitated a paradigm shift in healthcare ethics. It demands moving beyond theoretical principles to confront the messy realities of algorithmic decision-making.[3,8] Consider the intensive care unit at Toronto General Hospital, where clinicians began using an AI sepsis prediction tool in early 2023. The system, trained on a decade of patient data, initially reduced mortality rates by 14%. However, six months into deployment, nurses noticed disturbing patterns: the tool consistently underestimated sepsis risk in patients with sickle cell disease. Subsequent investigation revealed the training data contained disproportionately few sickle cell cases, reflecting broader disparities in healthcare access. This case exemplifies how beneficence, the ethical obligation to do good, requires more than technological sophistication; it necessitates ongoing vigilance against hidden biases that can emerge in real-world use.[2]

The principle of non-maleficence faces unprecedented challenges in the era of black-box algorithms, since opaque systems may inadvertently propagate harm through bias or error.[8] For example, AI-driven fall-risk assessment models, though generally outperforming traditional tools, have shown limitations when applied to populations outside their training dataset.[9] Such models may generate false alarms for underrepresented groups, risking inappropriate interventions. In maternal care, fall-risk assessment tools validated specifically for postpartum women remain limited, underscoring the need for tailored approaches to avoid harm in this sensitive population.[10] This scenario illustrates how digital health tools can cause harm not through malfunction, but through contextual blindness, which is a failure to account for the nuanced realities of diverse patient groups. To mitigate such risks, ethicists now advocate for rigorous validation and "maleficence stress testing," where algorithms are deliberately challenged with edge cases analogous to crash-testing vehicles for safety.[8]

Autonomy in digital health extends far beyond traditional informed consent forms. The rise of mental health chatbots like Woebot and Wysa has created complex new dimensions of patient agency. During the 2022 rollout of an AI cognitive behavioral therapy (CBT) app across UK primary care clinics, clinicians discovered a troubling pattern: adolescents with eating disorders were receiving generic weight-loss advice from the algorithm. The system, designed for general depression and anxiety, lacked safeguards to recognize contraindications.[11] This failure exposed the limitations of binary consent processes in dynamic digital environments. Some institutions now implement "tiered autonomy" frameworks, where patients can adjust algorithmic involvement in their care—from full automation to human-only decisions based on evolving comfort levels and clinical needs.[11]

Justice in healthcare AI manifests most starkly in global health applications. The much-lauded AI system for detecting diabetic retinopathy, developed by Google Health, achieved high accuracy in controlled clinical trials. Yet real-world performance in low-resource settings has been less consistent, with studies demonstrating that differences in camera quality, clinical workflows, and disease presentation patterns can substantially degrade accuracy.[12,13] For example, Kemp and colleagues found that smartphone-based AI tools for diabetic retinopathy screening, while promising, faced significant challenges in implementation due to variable image quality and infrastructural limitations.[13] This disparity reflects a deeper ethical issue: most AI tools are trained on data from high-resource settings, creating an implicit technological colonialism where low-income countries inherit solutions ill-suited to their contexts. Pioneering initiatives like the African Deep Learning Indaba are challenging this paradigm by developing locally trained algorithms that account for regional disease variants and resource constraints, a model of justice that prioritizes equitable design over one-size-fits-all solutions.[14]

The ethical framework for digital health must also grapple with temporal dimensions of responsibility. Consider the case of IBM Watson for Oncology, which was discontinued after studies revealed its treatment recommendations aligned poorly with actual patient outcomes.[15] While IBM initially framed this as a technical failure, ethicists identified a deeper issue: the system's training on synthetic data created an accountability gap. When algorithms learn from simulated rather than real patient experiences, it becomes impossible to trace how specific recommendations were generated, undermining the fundamental ethical principle of transparency. This has led to calls for "algorithmic genealogy" standards, requiring developers to document not just training data sources but the decision pathways through which models arrive at conclusions.[15]

At the heart of these challenges lies the tension between standardization and personalization. EHR systems embed numerous algorithmic alerts, from drug interactions to sepsis warnings, designed to enhance safety but frequently interrupt nursing workflows. Ethnographic and qualitative studies have shown that these alerts contribute to alert fatigue, as clinicians experience repeated interruptions that can affect workflow and patient attention.[16–18] This phenomenon underscores the need for ethical frameworks that consider how digital tools influence the delivery and organization of care. Some health systems now employ specialists who analyze the effects of digital interventions on clinical workflows using time-motion study methods.[19]

The evolving nature of these ethical challenges became starkly apparent during the COVID-19 pandemic's telehealth expansion. At Massachusetts General Hospital's primary care network, telehealth visits surged from negligible levels to constitute the majority of outpatient appointments within weeks.[20] This rapid transition exposed digital inequities: elderly patients often struggled with technology navigation, and low-income families frequently lacked private spaces for confidential consultations.[21] Clinicians responded by developing hybrid care models combining phone check-ins with targeted in-person visits.[22] This adaptation highlights an important ethical insight: digital health solutions work best when augmenting, rather than replacing, human judgment and flexibility, a principle affirmed by the American Medical Association's guidelines for augmented intelligence in medicine.[1]

As healthcare institutions navigate this complex terrain, many are discovering that ethical digital health requires fundamentally rethinking governance structures. The Mayo Clinic's pioneering Algorithmic Bias Review Board, comprising clinicians, data scientists, ethicists, and patient advocates, exemplifies this shift.[15] When evaluating a new AI tool for predicting hospital readmissions, the board identified an unexpected risk: the algorithm relied heavily on medication-adherence metrics that systematically disadvantaged patients without reliable pharmacy access.[23] By catching this bias before deployment, they prevented what could have become another case of algorithmic harm. Such models point toward a future where ethical review becomes as rigorous as clinical trials for digital health technologies—a necessary evolution in an era where algorithms increasingly mediate the patient–provider relationship.[2]

While these principles provide a common foundation for evaluating digital health technologies, their interpretation and application are far from uniform. Legal systems, cultural values, and economic realities vary widely across regions, shaping how privacy, autonomy, justice, and beneficence are prioritized in practice. Understanding these differences is essential for developing solutions that are not only ethically sound in theory but also contextually appropriate in diverse global settings.

In Europe, the General Data Protection Regulation (GDPR) remains a benchmark for data privacy and includes stringent controls on automated decision-making: Article 22 gives individuals the right not to be subject to decisions made solely by algorithms in cases with legal or similarly significant effects.[24,25] In Singapore, for instance, the Ministry of Health's LEAP regulatory sandbox allows new healthcare innovations to be tested under regulatory oversight, balancing innovation with safety.[26] Regulatory sandbox models are also promoted in global digital health governance as a way to allow controlled experimentation while maintaining accountability.[27]

The African Union's 2024 Digital Health Strategy[28] stresses the importance of regional data centers to reduce reliance on external cloud services, thereby strengthening data sovereignty. Latin American countries such as Brazil have emphasized community participation in health data governance,[29] with pilot programs allowing citizen assemblies to vote on the adoption of new health AI tools. These global variations highlight the need for comparative ethics frameworks that account for diverse values and priorities. What may be considered an acceptable trade-off between privacy and public health in one jurisdiction could be seen as a breach of fundamental rights in another. For practitioners and policymakers, understanding these differences is essential when designing technologies intended for cross-border use.[28]

These variations in governance and societal expectations underscore that privacy, consent, and data use cannot be addressed through a single, universal model; instead, they must be adapted to reflect the cultural, legal, and ethical landscapes in which digital health systems operate.

As technology continues to evolve, the ethical landscape of healthcare informatics will be shaped by several emerging trends that extend and challenge existing principles. The integration of multimodal data ranging from genomics to social determinants of health will require consent models capable of managing complex, layered datasets, with dynamic consent frameworks offering patients ongoing control over specific aspects of their data use.[30] The expanding role of synthetic data in AI model training presents opportunities to mitigate privacy risks, yet also raises concerns about bias propagation and validity, underscoring the need for clear ethical standards for its creation and application.[5] Global health imperatives, such as climate change–linked disease surveillance, will demand careful governance to balance rapid response capabilities with the protection of vulnerable populations and the prevention of stigmatization.[31] Ultimately, advancing digital health ethics will depend on cultivating interdisciplinary collaboration in which ethicists, clinicians, engineers, patient advocates, and policymakers work together from the outset, embedding ethical considerations into the design process. In this vision, success is measured not only by adoption rates or technical performance, but by the degree to which innovations enhance equity, trust, and human dignity.[5]

Privacy, Consent, and Data Use in the Digital Age

In the past few years, multiple high-profile developments have shown that simply "de-identifying" health data is not enough to keep patients safe from reidentification and misuse.[32] Federal enforcement actions in 2023 against GoodRx and BetterHelp revealed how sensitive health information can flow to third-party platforms through analytics and advertising pipelines, despite consumer privacy promises.[33] At the same time, HHS-OCR's 2024 guidance on tracking technologies warned covered entities that seemingly routine web and app scripts (pixels, cookies, beacons) can capture identifiers linked to protected health information.[34] Empirical work has reinforced the technical risks: studies in 2024–2025 demonstrated that de-identified clinical text and other data types remain vulnerable to modern inference and linkage attacks, while National Institute of Standards and Technology (NIST) formalized practical methods for assessing reidentification risk.[35] In response, researchers have begun piloting "privacy-preserving triage" concepts combining encryption-first collection, federated learning, and low-latency analytics to keep sensitive data protected from the moment it's captured in emergency settings.[36] Collectively, these trends mark a shift beyond HIPAA checklists toward full life cycle governance that anticipates powerful data linkage and prioritizes ethical safeguards from collection through use.

Consent mechanisms face particular scrutiny in genomic medicine, where data's value persists indefinitely. The All of Us Research Program, NIH's ambitious effort to sequence one million Americans, encountered unexpected resistance from Indigenous communities in 2022. "Tribal leaders objected not to the science itself, but to the program's inability to guarantee against future commercial exploitation of their unique genetic variants."[32] In response, developers created the first "generational consent" interface, allowing participants to set conditions on how their data could be used in future decades, including veto power over specific research categories.[37] This innovation recognizes that true consent in digital health must account for temporal dimensions that traditional medicine never contemplated.

The commercial appetite for health data has created ethical quagmires at the intersection of patient rights and corporate interests. When UnitedHealth Group launched its "Optum Insights" platform in 2021, it offered hospitals predictive analytics powered by data from 100 million patients.[38] Few realized the platform's fine print allowed repackaging of this data for pharmaceutical marketing until a whistleblower revealed targeted ads were reaching patients based on sensitive diagnoses.[39] The ensuing class-action lawsuit established precedent-setting requirements: health data aggregators must now provide "chain of custody" disclosures showing exactly how information flows from clinical encounters to end users. This legal development mirrors growing ethical consensus that transparency alone is insufficient; patients deserve traceability in how their data creates value for others.

Technical solutions to these dilemmas are emerging from unexpected quarters.[3] Federated learning, a technique allowing algorithms to train on decentralized data without centralized storage, has shown promise in addressing both privacy and equity concerns.[36] Zambia's national tuberculosis screening network employs this approach, enabling rural clinics to contribute to AI model improvement without surrendering sensitive patient records.[40] Early results demonstrate 40% better performance for pediatric TB detection compared to traditional methods, proving that ethical data use can enhance rather than hinder clinical effectiveness.[36] Such models challenge the assumption that privacy and progress exist in inevitable tension, pointing toward hybrid futures where technological design embodies ethical principles from inception.[40]

The globalization of health data flows presents particularly thorny challenges. When Singapore General Hospital partnered with a Silicon Valley AI firm to develop a pneumonia detection algorithm, they failed to anticipate how cultural norms would impact data sharing.[41] The system's training on chest X-rays from consenting Singaporean patients violated communal privacy expectations common in collectivist societies—where medical decisions often involve extended families. This cultural clash led to a six-month pause and redesign incorporating "community consent" protocols developed with local elders. The revised model not only restored trust but also improved accuracy by including demographic variants previously excluded as outliers.[31] This case illustrates how ethical data use requires sensitivity not just to legal standards but also to unspoken social contracts that vary across communities.

Pediatric data presents unique ethical complexities in digital health. Despite the rapid proliferation of AI tools, few algorithms have been specifically designed or validated for pediatric populations.

A 2024 study by Boston Children's Hospital revealed that fewer than 20% of FDA-approved AI medical devices include pediatric data in their training, raising serious questions about fairness, safety, and transparency.[42] While such systems often comply with existing privacy frameworks like Health Insurance Portability and Accountability Act (HIPAA)., research increasingly emphasizes that legal data compliance alone cannot ensure ethical data stewardship.[43] Scholars have argued that responsible AI in clinical contexts requires continuous oversight, value-sensitive design, and patient-centered governance—particularly when dealing with vulnerable populations such as children.[44] This evolving discourse reflects a broader transformation in healthcare ethics: the recognition that lawful data use and moral data responsibility do not always align, demanding renewed attention to transparency, accountability, and human oversight in pediatric AI systems.[44]

The surveillance potential of digital health tools has created new ethical fault lines in employer-sponsored wellness programs. A 2023 analysis of workplace wellness technologies found that data collected for employee health and well-being, such as fitness tracker activity, heart rate, or sleep patterns, was often repurposed for secondary uses unrelated to health, including performance management and shift scheduling.[45] Researchers warned that this practice, sometimes occurring without clear employee awareness, exemplifies the "privacy creep" phenomenon, where information gathered for one purpose quietly expands into ethically questionable domains. The study emphasized that structural power imbalances in the workplace make truly informed consent difficult, prompting calls for "use-specific consent" laws to ensure that participation in wellness programs does not become a backdoor to employee surveillance.[46]

Looking ahead, the ethical management of health data faces profound challenges in brain–computer interface (BCI) technology. At the University of Pittsburgh, researchers have enabled paralyzed patients to communicate and control devices through neural signals, marking breakthroughs in neurorehabilitation and neurorecovery. This transformative technology raises unprecedented ethical questions about the privacy and security of neural data and how meaningful consent can be obtained when subconscious thoughts may be revealed. Ethical discourse increasingly calls for specialized data protection measures, such as enhanced encryption and stringent data governance protocols, reflecting an evolving understanding that privacy and consent frameworks must advance alongside technological capabilities.[47]

Recent legal and policy developments in the United States highlight that the ethical questions surrounding BCIs are no longer theoretical, as lawmakers and advocacy groups move to safeguard neural data before widespread adoption. In 2024, Colorado became the first US state to explicitly classify neural data, including brain activity and related signals, as sensitive personal data under its Protect Privacy of Biological Data Act, extending protections similar to those for genetic and biometric information.[48] This legislation, motivated in part by the rapid growth of consumer BCIs, requires companies to obtain explicit consent before collecting or processing neural signals and grants individuals the right to request deletion.[49] That same year, several US senators urged the Federal Trade Commission to investigate neurotechnology companies' data practices, citing risks of inadequate consent and potential misuse in unregulated markets. In 2025, the Neurorights Foundation released a review finding that most major consumer neurotech firms collected neural data with minimal safeguards, underscoring the urgent need for cognitive privacy standards alongside traditional health data protections.[50]

Ethical Dilemmas in Digital Health

The introduction of AI diagnostic tools into healthcare systems underscores profound ethical and clinical challenges. Early AI-supported systems in the UK NHS aimed to reduce general practitioner workloads and initially showed promise in accuracy for common conditions. However, concerns about their performance—particularly regarding representativeness and sensitivity across diverse patient populations—highlighted risks of premature deployment. In response, the NHS developed a rigorous, multitiered algorithm review process that evaluates AI tools not only for technical accuracy but also for sociodemographic robustness and clinical safety. This evolving governance framework has become a model for healthcare systems globally, emphasizing that ethical AI integration requires balancing innovation with patient safety and equitable care.[51]

Mental health apps present a particularly complex ethical terrain. In early 2023, Koko, an AI-powered crisis-counseling service, conducted an experimental trial using OpenAI's GPT-3 to assist human peer counselors by co-creating message drafts. Approximately 4,000 users participated in the pilot, and many later described the AI-assisted messages as "weird" or "empty," noting that they felt impersonal once they learned a machine had helped compose them.[52] The experiment raised significant concerns about transparency and informed consent in vulnerable populations seeking mental-health support, prompting broader discussion across the digital-therapy sector. In its aftermath, many teletherapy platforms adopted stricter "no-surprise-AI" disclosure policies requiring explicit notification of algorithmic involvement. This case underscores the special responsibilities accompanying digital mental health interventions, where the appearance of a genuine human connection carries profound ethical weight.[53]

Global health initiatives highlight both the promise and pitfalls of digital solutions. India's Aadhaar-linked health records system, intended to streamline care for millions, inadvertently excluded transgender individuals due to its binary gender fields, which failed to accommodate diverse gender identities. This exclusion led to gaps in vaccination tracking and HIV treatment access, underscoring systemic challenges marginalized populations face in digital health platforms.[54,55] In contrast, Rwanda's drone-delivered blood supply program exemplifies an ethically grounded digital health innovation. Launched in partnership with Zipline in 2016, the program revolutionized access to blood products by reducing delivery times from hours to minutes, especially vital for maternal health. Community and health worker engagement ensured the system adapted to local needs rather than imposing one-size-fits-all technology.[56,57] These cases illustrate how ethical digital health hinges on inclusive participation and power dynamics, not just technology.

The Theranos scandal's legacy profoundly influences current ethical discussions surrounding diagnostic AI. Theranos, once a Silicon Valley darling, claimed to revolutionize blood testing with devices that required only small blood samples. However, FDA investigations revealed the company used unvalidated and unreliable testing methods, resulting in inaccurate results that endangered patient health. Government agencies, including the FDA and CMS, found that Theranos failed to comply with clinical laboratory standards, manipulated test outcomes, and misled investors and healthcare providers. The founder, Elizabeth Holmes, and former COO, Sunny Balwani, faced criminal charges, including conspiracy and wire fraud, for deceiving patients and investors. This high-profile case exposed the dangers of inadequate validation and oversight in diagnostic technologies. Its aftermath fuels ongoing debates about defining adequate clinical validation for AI-powered diagnostics, highlighted when a 2023 startup claimed pancreatic cancer detection from smartphone photos but was found to have insufficient real-world testing. The Theranos case has catalyzed calls for stringent "real-world evidence" requirements to ensure AI diagnostics demonstrate efficacy in clinical settings before approval, safeguarding patients from fraud and premature implementation.[58]

Radiology AI provides rich ground for ethical case studies.[4] When an academic medical center implemented an AI chest X-ray analyzer in 2022, radiologists noticed an odd pattern: the system flagged nearly all images from cystic fibrosis patients as abnormal, despite many being baseline scans. Investigation revealed the training dataset had included only acute presentations of the disease, teaching the AI to equate CF with pathology. This "context collapse" phenomenon, where algorithms fail to recognize normal variants, has become a focal point for the emerging field of machine learning ethnography, which studies how cultural and clinical assumptions become embedded in AI systems.

Although continuous glucose monitoring (CGM) systems were originally developed for diabetes management, their use has expanded among individuals without diabetes seeking metabolic insights for fitness, nutrition, and wellness. This growing consumer adoption reflects increasing interest in personalized health monitoring but also raises important ethical and regulatory questions regarding privacy, commercialization of health data, and the use of AI-driven health recommendations.[59]

The COVID-19 pandemic produced its own digital health ethics casebook. Singapore's contact tracing app, initially voluntary, became de facto mandatory as unvaccinated individuals faced exclusion from public spaces such as restaurants and workplaces, reinforcing participation through access restrictions. This approach raised significant concerns about privacy and civil liberties in the name of public health. Similarly, Israel implemented mass surveillance by tracking citizens' cell phone data via its internal security agency (Shin Bet) to identify and enforce quarantines on exposed individuals. Although effective in controlling spread, this unprecedented use of security apparatus for public health sparked vigorous debate about governmental overreach and the erosion of civil liberties. These experiences ignited global discourse on balancing public health necessities with digital autonomy, setting critical precedents for future pandemic governance.[60,61]

Looking forward, the ethical dilemmas of digital health are growing more complex even as the technologies become more sophisticated. Neuralink's first human trials of brain implants, the proliferation of emotion-recognition AI in psychiatric care, and the emergence of quantum computing in drug discovery all present novel ethical questions about whether participants can truly give informed consent when the long-term neurological, psychological, and social risks remain uncertain, and whether "thought data" produced by BCIs should be considered private property with strict protections against misuse or cognitive surveillance. The rapid adoption of emotion-recognition AI in psychiatric care adds another layer of complexity, as concerns over algorithmic bias, cultural misinterpretation, and wrongful classification challenge its clinical reliability while threatening to erode therapeutic trust. Meanwhile, the rise of quantum computing in drug discovery offers unprecedented potential to accelerate treatment development but also intensifies debates over dual-use risks, equitable access to resulting therapies, and the adequacy of current regulatory systems to evaluate drugs created using methods that may be opaque even to experts.[62] Overlaying these developments is the rise of agentic AI—autonomous, adaptive systems capable of decision-making—that present further ethical challenges around transparency, accountability, and safeguarding patients' autonomy and privacy.[63] What unites these cases is the fundamental tension between innovation's relentless forward march and medicine's primal directive: first, do no harm. Navigating this tension requires not just new rules but new ways of thinking—where ethicists collaborate with engineers, clinicians partner with patients, and technological progress is measured not just by what it enables, but by whom it protects. Collectively, these innovations illustrate the urgent need for ethical frameworks that not only address safety and privacy but also ensure transparency, accountability, and fairness as healthcare enters a new era of cognitive, emotional, and computational technologies.

Case Studies

CASE STUDY 1: IMPLEMENTING A PERSONAL HEALTH RECORD (PHR) IN A COMMUNITY HEALTH SETTING

Scenario:
A community health center introduces a patient-facing PHR system to improve patient engagement, medication adherence, and continuity of care. However, adoption is uneven, with older adults and low-literacy populations struggling to use the platform.

Instructions:

1. Discussion prompt:
   - Identify barriers to PHR adoption in vulnerable populations.
   - Propose strategies to improve digital literacy and accessibility.
2. Practical exercise:
   Design a patient education module (flyer, short video, or digital tutorial) tailored to older adults with limited technology experience.
3. Assessment activity:
   Draft three measurable outcomes that the clinic can track to evaluate PHR effectiveness (e.g., medication refill rates, follow-up appointment adherence, and patient portal login frequency).

CASE STUDY 2: INFECTION CONTROL AND HIPAA COMPLIANCE IN A HOSPITAL EHR

Scenario:
A hospital experiences an outbreak of multidrug-resistant organisms (MDROs). Infection control teams need real-time data from the EHR to track cases. At the same time, HIPAA rules restrict how patient data can be shared across departments and with external agencies.

Instructions:

1. Discussion prompt:
   - How can hospitals balance rapid infection control response with HIPAA compliance?
   - Discuss the role of de-identification in sharing outbreak data.

2. Practical exercise:
   Using CDC and OCR guidelines, outline a workflow for how lab results, nursing notes, and patient movement data can be integrated to detect and contain an outbreak.
3. Assessment activity:
   Develop a short policy statement (3–4 sentences) that addresses both infection control needs and HIPAA safeguards.

CASE STUDY 3: AI-ENABLED PREDICTIVE ANALYTICS IN HYPERTENSION MANAGEMENT

Scenario:
A regional health system deploys an AI tool that predicts which patients with hypertension are at risk of hospitalization within 6 months. Clinicians are concerned about algorithmic bias, while administrators want to integrate the tool into existing workflows.

Instructions

1. Discussion prompt:
   - What risks exist when predictive analytics are applied to diverse patient populations?
   - How can governance structures reduce bias and increase clinician trust?
2. Practical exercise:
   Create a process map showing how the AI risk scores would flow from the data warehouse into the EHR and clinician dashboards.
3. Assessment activity:
   Propose three evaluation metrics (e.g., reduction in readmission rates, equity in predictions across race/ethnicity, clinician adoption rates) to measure AI tool impact.

Exercises and Activities

ACTIVITY 1: ALGORITHMIC BIAS AUDIT AND ROLE-PLAYING

Objective: To analyze real-world cases of biased healthcare algorithms and understand stakeholder responsibilities in addressing inequities.

Instructions:

1. Divide students into interdisciplinary groups (e.g., clinician, data scientist, hospital administrator, patient advocate).

2. Provide a case study (e.g., racial bias in pulse oximetry AI or the Optum algorithm that underestimated Black patients' healthcare needs).
3. Assign roles:
   - *Clinician*: Assess clinical harm to marginalized patients.
   - *Data scientist*: Identify technical flaws in training data/model design.
   - *Policy expert*: Propose regulatory changes (e.g., FDA validation requirements).
   - *Community advocate*: Design patient redress mechanisms.
4. Group presentation: Each group proposes a mitigation plan, highlighting interdisciplinary collaboration.

ACTIVITY 2: DYNAMIC CONSENT FRAMEWORK DESIGN

Objective: To create a patient-centric consent process for AI-driven health technologies.

Instructions:

1. Scenario: A hospital is deploying an AI mental health chatbot that uses patient data for research.
2. In small groups, design a consent framework that:
   - Uses plain language and visual aids (e.g., icons for data use options).
   - Offers tiered choices (e.g., "Allow data for clinical care only" vs. "Contribute to research").
   - Includes a revocation mechanism and expiration timelines.
3. Presentations: Groups showcase their designs, with class feedback on clarity, autonomy, and feasibility.
4. Vote on the most ethical and practical solution.

ACTIVITY 3: ETHICAL DILEMMA DEBATE—AI VS. HUMAN JUDGMENT

Objective: To debate the trade-offs between algorithmic efficiency and human oversight in healthcare.

Instructions:

1. Dilemma: "A hospital ICU must choose between an AI sepsis predictor (90% accurate but opaque) or clinician-led protocols (75% accurate but explainable)."
2. Divide the class:
   - Team AI: Argue for adoption based on beneficence (lives saved) and resource constraints.

- Team Clinicians: Advocate for autonomy (human judgment) and non-maleficence (avoiding algorithmic harm).

3. Structured debate:
   - Opening statements (5 mins/side).
   - Rebuttals addressing justice (equitable access) and transparency.
   - Moderator (instructor) summarizes ethical tensions.
4. Post-debrief: Draft a compromise policy (e.g., AI as a "second opinion" tool with mandatory override logs).

Assessment Questions

1. How might federated learning address privacy concerns in rural healthcare settings?
2. Compare the ethical implications of using AI for opioid addiction prediction versus cancer diagnosis.
3. Design a protocol to audit an EHR algorithm for gender bias in pain management recommendations.
4. Explain how "explainability audits" could mitigate harm in AI-driven psychiatric care.
5. Analyze the justice implications of training diagnostic AI on datasets from high-income countries only.
6. Propose safeguards for using ChatGPT to generate clinical visit summaries without breaching trust.
7. Why might pulse oximetry algorithms require different validation standards than radiology AI?
8. How could blockchain technology complicate HIPAA compliance in health data exchanges?
9. Defend or challenge: "Algorithmic performance metrics should include equity as a core measure."
10. Draft a patient-facing disclosure for an AI tool that uses off-label data (e.g., social media for depression screening).

Assessment Questions Key Answer:

1. How might federated learning address privacy concerns in rural healthcare settings?
   Federated learning allows AI models to be trained locally on patient data without transferring the raw data to a central server. In rural healthcare settings, this means that sensitive patient records remain within local clinics, reducing the risk of data breaches and ensuring compliance with privacy regulations. Only the model updates—not the patient data—are shared, helping to protect confidentiality while still contributing to the development of robust AI systems.
2. Compare the ethical implications of using AI for opioid addiction prediction versus cancer diagnosis.
   AI for opioid addiction prediction raises heightened concerns about stigma, potential discrimination, and law enforcement misuse, which could deter individuals from seeking care. Cancer diagnosis AI, while still ethically sensitive, typically does not carry the same level of societal stigma. Both require accuracy, transparency, and safeguards against bias, but opioid

prediction tools must place additional emphasis on privacy, informed consent, and minimizing unintended punitive consequences.

3. Design a protocol to audit an EHR algorithm for gender bias in pain management recommendations.
    1. Define the audit scope: Focus on pain-related diagnoses and corresponding treatment recommendations.
    2. Collect a representative dataset with gender demographics.
    3. Run the EHR algorithm on identical clinical scenarios across genders.
    4. Compare recommendation patterns and dosages for statistically significant differences.
    5. Conduct qualitative review with clinical experts to interpret findings.
    6. Report results transparently and recommend algorithm adjustments if bias is detected.
    7. Re-audit periodically to ensure sustained fairness.
4. Explain how "explainability audits" could mitigate harm in AI-driven psychiatric care.
   Explainability audits involve systematically testing whether AI outputs can be understood and validated by clinicians. In psychiatric care, this can prevent harm by ensuring that recommendations—such as medication adjustments or therapy suggestions—are supported by clear, interpretable reasoning. This transparency helps clinicians identify errors, reduces blind trust in AI, and maintains patient trust in the therapeutic relationship.
5. Analyze the justice implications of training diagnostic AI on datasets from high-income countries only.
   Training AI solely on high-income country datasets risks embedding systemic inequities into diagnostic tools, as the model may underperform for populations in low- and middle-income countries. This creates disparities in access to accurate diagnosis, potentially widening global health inequities. Justice in AI development requires diverse, representative data to ensure equitable performance.
6. Propose safeguards for using ChatGPT to generate clinical visit summaries without breaching trust.
   Safeguards include:
   - De-identifying all patient information before input.
   - Implementing secure, encrypted channels for data transfer.
   - Reviewing AI-generated summaries by licensed clinicians before adding to the EHR.
   - Informing patients about AI use and obtaining consent.
   - Maintaining audit logs for accountability.
7. Why might pulse oximetry algorithms require different validation standards than radiology AI?
   Pulse oximetry algorithms directly measure physiological parameters in real time and can be affected by factors such as skin pigmentation, peripheral perfusion, and ambient light. Radiology AI, in contrast, typically interprets static images. Because pulse oximetry results can influence immediate clinical interventions, validation must account for diverse patient populations, environmental conditions, and device-specific variability to ensure safety.
8. How could blockchain technology complicate HIPAA compliance in health data exchanges?
   Blockchain's immutable ledger makes it difficult to comply with HIPAA's "right to amend" or "right to be forgotten" provisions. Once data is recorded on the blockchain, it cannot be altered or deleted. Additionally, storing personal health information on a distributed network increases the complexity of access control and breach notification requirements.
9. Defend or challenge: "Algorithmic performance metrics should include equity as a core measure."

Defend: Equity should be a core performance metric because algorithms that perform well overall but poorly for certain demographic groups can exacerbate health disparities. Including equity metrics ensures that tools benefit all populations fairly, aligning with principles of justice and non-maleficence.

10. Draft a patient-facing disclosure for an AI tool that uses off-label data (e.g., social media for depression screening).
"This tool uses information from non-medical sources, such as social media activity, to help identify potential signs of depression. Your privacy is important to us—any data used is processed securely and reviewed by a qualified clinician before informing care decisions."

References

1. World Health Organization. *Ethics and Governance of Artificial Intelligence for Health: Guidance on Large Multi-Modal Models*. Geneva: World Health Organization; 2024.
2. Mayo Clinic Platform. Using AI to predict the onset of sepsis. By John Halamka, MD, and Paul Cerrato. May 2, 2024. Accessed August 14, 2025. www.mayoclinicplatform.org/2024/05/02/using-ai-to-predict-the-onset-of-sepsis
3. Junaid SB, Imam AA, Balogun AO, De Silva LC, Surakat YA, Kumar G, Abdulkarim M, Shuaibu AN, Garba A, Sahalu Y, Mohammed A, Mohammed TY, Abdulkadir BA, Abba AA, Kakumi NAI, Mahamad S. Recent advancements in emerging technologies for healthcare management systems: a survey. *Healthcare (Basel)*. 2022 Oct 3;10(10):1940. doi: 10.3390/healthcare10101940. PMID: 36292387; PMCID: PMC9601636.
4. Cross JL, Choma MA, Onofrey JA. Bias in medical AI: Implications for clinical decision-making. *PLOS Digit Health*. 2024 Nov 7;3(11):e0000651. doi: 10.1371/journal.pdig.0000651. PMID: 39509461; PMCID: PMC11542778.
5. Giuffrè M, Accardo A, Albano D, et al. Harnessing the power of synthetic data in healthcare. *NPJ Digit Med*. 2023;6:148. doi:10.1038/s41746-023-00927-3
6. Childress JF, Beauchamp TL. Common morality principles in Biomedical ethics: responses to critics. *Cambridge Quarterly of Healthcare Ethics*. 2022;31(2):164–176. doi:10.1017/S0963180121000566
7. Varkey B. Principles of clinical ethics and their application to practice. *Med Princ Pract*. 2021;30(1):17–28. doi:10.1159/000509119. https://pmc.ncbi.nlm.nih.gov/articles/PMC7923912/
8. Zhang, J., Zhang, Zm. Ethics and governance of trustworthy medical artificial intelligence. *BMC Med Inform Decis Mak*. 23, 7 (2023).
9. Nanevski I, Jäger S, Schulte-Althoff M, Fürstenau D, Biessmann F. The potential of AI in nursing care: multicenter evaluation in fall-risk assessment. *J Med Internet Res*. 2025;27:e71034. doi:10.2196/71034
10. Risso S, Soares T, Marques-Vieira C. Scoping review of fall-risk assessment tools for women who receive maternity care. *J Obstet Gynecol Neonatal Nurs*. 2024;53(3):289-302. doi:10.1016/j.jogn.2023.11.012
11. Marshall NJ, Loades ME, Jacobs C, Biddle L, Lambert JD. Integrating artificial intelligence in youth mental health care: advances, challenges, and future directions. *Curr Treat Options Psychiatry*. 2025;12:11. doi:10.1007/s40501-025-00348-x. Accessed August 14, 2025.
12. Tan TF, et al. Artificial intelligence and digital health in global eye health. *Lancet Glob Health*. 2023. doi:10.1016/S2214-109X(23)00323-6.
13. Kemp O, et al. Real-world evaluation of smartphone-based artificial intelligence for diabetic retinopathy screening. *BMJ Ophthalmol*. 2023;8(1):e001491. doi:10.1136/bmjophth-2022-001491.
14. Curto G, Dignum F, Abebe G, et al. Africa leading the global effort for AI that works for all. *Nature News & Comment*. Published online 2025. doi:10.1038/d44148-025-00141-1

15. Sathya SS, Pooja S, Paruvathani G, Sharmi J. The rise and fall of IBM Watson in healthcare: lessons for sustainable AI innovations. *Int Res J Innov Eng Technol.* 2025;9(Spec Issue INSPIRE'25):116–120. doi:10.47001/IRJIET/2025.INSPIRE19
16. Hopkinson SG, Wiegand DL. The culture contributing to interruptions in the nursing work environment: an ethnography. *Journal of Clinical Nursing.* 2017;26(23–24):5093–5102. doi:https://doi.org/10.1111/jocn.14052
17. Maiken Holm Kaldal, Feo R, Conroy T, Mette Grønkjær, Siri Lygum Voldbjerg. New graduate nurses' delivery of patient care: A focused ethnography. *Journal of Clinical Nursing.* 2023;32(19–20). doi:https://doi.org/10.1111/jocn.16804
18. Lopetegui M, Yen PY, Lai A, Jeffries J, Embi P, Payne P. Time motion studies in healthcare: what are we talking about? *Journal of Biomedical Informatics.* 2014;49:292–299. doi: https://doi.org/10.1016/j.jbi.2014.02.017
19. Alert Fatigue. *Patient Safety Network (PSNet).* Agency for Healthcare Research and Quality, U.S. Department of Health and Human Services; last reviewed December 15, 2024. Accessed August 14, 2025. https://psnet.ahrq.gov/primer/alert-fatigue bmcdigitalhealth.biomedcentral.com
20. The COVID-19 Pandemic Reveals the Potential of Telehealth to Improve Care. Massachusetts general hospital. Published 2024. www.massgeneral.org/news/coronavirus/covid-19-reveals-the-potential-of-telehealth-to-improve-care
21. Grady CB, Claus EB, Bunn DA, Pagliaro JA, Lichtman JH, Bhatt AB. Disparities in patient engagement with video telemedicine among high-video-use providers during the COVID-19 pandemic. *European Heart Journal – Digital Health.* Published online August 21, 2021. doi:https://doi.org/10.1093/ehjdh/ztab067
22. Ezeamii VC, Okobi OE, Wambai-Sani H, Perera GS, Zaynieva S, Okonkwo CC, et al. Revolutionizing healthcare: how telemedicine is improving patient outcomes and expanding access to care. *Cureus.* 2024;16(7):e63881. doi:10.7759/cureus.63881.
23. Mayo Clinic launches digital referee for spotting potential bias in healthcare AI programs. Fierce Biotech. Published November 14, 2022. Accessed October 18, 2025. www.fiercebiotech.com/medtech/mayo-clinic-launches-digital-referee-spotting-potential-bias-healthcare-ai-programs
24. Kuner C, Lynskey O, Svantesson D, Bygrave LA, Drechsler L, Ortega Giménez A. Article 22 GDPR: automated individual decision-making, including profiling. In: Kuner C, Bygrave LA, Docksey C, Drechsler L, eds. *The EU General Data Protection Regulation (GDPR): A Commentary.* 2nd ed. Oxford, UK: Oxford University Press; 2024:583–616. doi:10.1093/oso/9780198882192.003.0022
25. Legal requirements for automated decision-making in the EU/UK. Global legal insights. May 2025. www.globallegalinsights.com/practice-areas/ai-machine-learning-and-big-data-laws-and-regulations/profiling-and-prohibited-practices-a-summary-of-legal-requirements-for-automated-decision-making-in-the-eu-and-uk
26. Ministry of Health, Singapore. Regulatory sandbox. Accessed [date]. www.moh.gov.sg/others/health-regulation/regulatory-sandbox/
27. *Regulatory Sandboxes for Digital Health: Implementation Know-How Brief.* World Bank. https://documents1.worldbank.org/curated/en/099011825011040830/pdf/P175075-0c729174-1c7a-4f04-9bb2-4127f301c037.pdf
28. African Union. *African Union Artificial Intelligence Strategy.* Addis Ababa, Ethiopia: African Union Commission; 2024.
29. D'Agostino M, Morgado J, Fregonese F, de Quiros FGB, Sanz V, Novillo-Ortiz D. Digital health data governance in Latin America and the Caribbean: an overview of current policies and future directions. *BMJ Health Care Inform.* 2021;28(1):e100278. doi:10.1136/bmjhci-2020-100278.
30. Teare HJA, Prictor M, Kaye J. Reflections on dynamic consent in biomedical research: the story so far. *Eur J Hum Genet.* 2020;28(11):1328–1335. doi:10.1038/s41431-020-0639-6.
31. Hui D, Ren T, Barnaby Edward Young, et al. Study protocol: infectious diseases consortium (I3D) for study on integrated and innovative approaches for management of respiratory infections: respiratory

infections research and outcome study (RESPIRO). *BMC Infectious Diseases.* 2024;24(1). doi:https://doi.org/10.1186/s12879-023-08795-8
32. Wiepert D, Malin BA, Duffy JR, et al. Reidentification of participants in shared clinical data sets: experimental study. *JMIR AI.* 2024;3:e52054–e52054. doi:https://doi.org/10.2196/52054
33. Lurking Beneath the Surface: Hidden Impacts of Pixel Tracking. Federal Trade Commission. Published March 16, 2023. Accessed September 6, 2025. www.ftc.gov/policy/advocacy-research/tech-at-ftc/2023/03/lurking-beneath-surface-hidden-impacts-pixel-tracking?utm_source
34. Office for Civil Rights (OCR). *Use of Online Tracking Technologies by HIPAA Covered Entities and Business Associates.* HHS.gov. Published November 18, 2022. www.hhs.gov/hipaa/for-professionals/privacy/guidance/hipaa-online-tracking/index.html
35. Quinn S. Identifying and estimating cybersecurity risk for enterprise eisk management. Published online January 1, 2025. doi:https://doi.org/10.6028/nist.ir.8286ar1.ipd
36. Karamanlıoğlu A, Demirel B, Tural O, Doğan OT, Alpaslan FN. Privacy-Preserving clinical decision support for emergency triage using LLMs: system architecture and real-world evaluation. arXiv preprint arXiv:2509.09746v2 [cs.LG]. Published September 2025. Accessed October 2025. https://arxiv.org/html/2509.09746v2
37. Wallace SE, Gourna EG, Nikolova V, Sheehan NA. Family tree and ancestry inference: Is there a need for a "generational" consent?. *BMC Medical Ethics.* 2015;16(1). doi:https://doi.org/10.1186/s12910-015-0080-2
38. henrykotula. Optum Insight – Henry kotula. HENRY KOTULA. Published July 9, 2024. https://henrykotula.com/category/optum-insight/
39. Posel A. New report: unitedHealth group whistleblowers witness delays and denials to healthcare for vulnerable nursing home patients – whistleblower aid. *Whistleblower Aid.* Published June 11, 2025. https://whistlebloweraid.org/new-report-unitedhealth-group-whistleblowers-witnessdelays-and-denials-to-healthcare-for-vulnerable-nursing-home-patients/
40. Lungu PS, Kabaso ME, Mihova R, Silumesii A, Chisenga T, Kasapo C, Mwaba I, Kerkhoff AD, Muyoyeta M, Chimzizi R, Malama K. Undernotification and underreporting of tuberculosis in Zambia: a national data quality assessment. *BMC Health Serv Res.* 2022 Aug 22;22(1):1074. doi: 10.1186/s12913-022-08431-2. PMID: 35996175; PMCID: PMC9396838.
41. Liverani M, Teng S, Le MS, Coker R. Sharing public health data and information across borders: lessons from Southeast Asia. *Globalization and Health.* 2018;14(1). doi:https://doi.org/10.1186/s12992-018-0415-0
42. Brewster R, Bourgeois F, et al. Few AI-assisted medical devices have been tested in children. *Boston Children's Hospital Answers.* Published December 17, 2024. Accessed October 18, 2025. https://answers.childrenshospital.org/ai-devices-children/
43. Handley SC, Bourgeois FT. Prioritizing data privacy and security in pediatric AI. *JAMA Pediatr.* 2024;178(10):985–987. doi:10.1001/jamapediatrics.2024.1782
44. Alowais, S.A., Alghamdi, S.S., Alsuhebany, N. et al. Revolutionizing healthcare: the role of artificial intelligence in clinical practice. *BMC Med Educ.* 23, 689 (2023). https://doi.org/10.1186/s12909-023-04698-z
45. Nopper TK, Zelickson E. Wellness capitalism: employee health, the benefits maze, and worker control. *Data & Society Research Institute*; 2023. https://datasociety.net/wp-content/uploads/2023/06/WellnessCapitalism_FINAL_June_2023.pdf
46. Chowdhary S, Kawakami A, Gray ML, et al. Can workers meaningfully consent to workplace wellbeing technologies? [preprint]. *arXiv.* 2023 Mar 13. Available from: https://arxiv.org/abs/2303.07242.
47. Young MJ, Lin DJ, Hochberg LR. Brain–Computer interfaces in neurorecovery and neurorehabilitation. *Seminars in Neurology.* 2021;41(02):206–216. doi:https://doi.org/10.1055/s-0041-1725137

48. Samuel S. Neuroscientist rafael yuste could play your brain like an instrument. He wants to protect it instead. Vox. Published November 21, 2024. www.vox.com/future-perfect/384520/rafael-yuste-neurorights-foundation-brain-initiative-neuroscience-future-perfect-50?utm_source
49. Priola K, Baisley M, Soper M, Kipp C. Protect privacy of biological data. https://leg.colorado.gov/bills/hb24-1058
50. NRF – Neurorights Foundation. NRF – Neurorights foundation. Published 2025. https://www.neurorightsfoundation.org/
51. Etheredge L. Artificial intelligence in healthcare: Transformative opportunities and policy implications. *TBD*. Published online February 20, 2025. www.researchgate.net/publication/389177823_Artificial_Intelligence_in_Healthcare_Transformative_Opportunities_and_Policy_Implications?utm_source=chatgpt.com
52. Ingram D. AI Chat used by mental health tech company in experiment on real users. *NBC News*. Published January 14, 2023. www.nbcnews.com/tech/internet/chatgpt-ai-experiment-mental-health-tech-app-koko-rcna65110
53. Radley J, Penhallow J, Wickersham A, Morris A, Colling C, Downs J. Factors affecting usability and acceptability of an online platform used by caregivers in child and adolescent mental health services: mixed methods study. *JMIR Pediatrics and Parenting*. 2024;7:e60042–e60042. doi:https://doi.org/10.2196/60042
54. Brindaalakshmi K. The case of identification documents for transgender persons in India. *Journal of Development Policy and Practice*. 2025;10(1). doi:10.1177/24551333241247673
55. Narayanan S et al. Protecting mental health data privacy in India: the case of data linkage and aadhaar. *Indian Journal of Psychiatry*. 2021;63(3):225–232.
56. Nisingizwe MP et al. Effect of unmanned aerial vehicle (drone) delivery on blood product delivery times and wastage in Rwanda: an interrupted time series analysis and cross-sectional study. *Lancet Glob Health*. 2022;10(4):e552–e559. doi:10.1016/S2214-109X(21)00578-7
57. Save the Children. Deliveries by drone: the technology making childbirth safer in Rwanda's largest refugee camp. June 2024.
58. Affairs O of R. *Patient Advocacy Lies at Heart of FDA Agent's Theranos Case*. FDA. Published online December 20, 2023. www.fda.gov/about-fda/regulatory-news-stories-and-features/patient-advocacy-lies-heart-fda-agents-theranos-case
59. Market Research. Wearable glucose monitoring device market overview. Published 2023. Accessed August 13, 2025.
60. Lee T, Lee H. Tracing surveillance and auto-regulation in Singapore: "smart" responses to COVID-19. *Media International Australia*. 2020;177(1):1329878X2094954. doi:https://doi.org/10.1177/1329878x20949545
61. Yadlin A, Marciano A. COVID-19 surveillance in Israeli press: spatiality, mobility, and control. Mobile Media & Communication. Published online December 29, 2021:205015792110682. doi:https://doi.org/10.1177/20501579211068269
62. Metz C. Neuralink implanted a device in a patient's brain, Elon Musk says. *New York Times*. January 29, 2024. Accessed July 24, 2026. https://www.nytimes.com/2024/01/29/business/elon-musk-neuralink.html
63. Hinostroza Fuentes VG, Karim HA, Tan MJT, AlDahoul N. AI with agency: a vision for adaptive, efficient, and ethical healthcare. *Frontiers in Digital Health*. 2025;7. doi:https://doi.org/10.3389/fdgth.2025.1600216

DATA AND ANALYTICS

II

Chapter 4

Big Data and Analytics for Digital Health

Anthony Blash, PharmD, BCompSc, CPHIMS and
Valorie Quarles, MFA

Introduction to Big Data in Healthcare

Healthcare is at the precipice of a data revolution that is fundamentally transforming how we prevent, diagnose, and treat disease. Big data in healthcare refers to massive, heterogeneous streams of structured and unstructured information generated across the continuum of care, including electronic health records and imaging reports to genomic sequencing, remote monitoring from wearables and bedside devices, and insurance claims. What makes healthcare data distinctive is not only its sheer volume but also its longitudinal, high-dimensional, and intensely sensitive nature. When imaging, genomics, and continuous monitoring are linked to a patient's longitudinal record, the result is a complex, multimodal portrait that evolves over time and must be handled with rigorous stewardship to protect privacy and maintain trust.

As health systems modernize, the emphasis increasingly falls on data quality and provenance, interoperable architectures that can integrate real-time streams with historical records, and multidisciplinary teams capable of translating raw information into actionable insights embedded in clinical workflows. All of this must occur while upholding ethical and legal obligations commensurate with the sensitivity of the information.[1]

The power of healthcare big data lies in its ability to surface patterns and clinical signals that would be difficult to detect through routine observation alone. At Johns Hopkins, the Targeted Real-Time Early Warning System (TREWS) was evaluated prospectively across five hospitals during routine operations. The system not only identified sepsis cases with high sensitivity but also demonstrated that clinician engagement with the alerts played a critical role. When providers promptly reviewed and acted on alerts, treatments such as the initiation of antibiotics and related care bundles were delivered more quickly. Early confirmation of alerts was associated with improved patient outcomes, including lower in-hospital mortality.[2,3] These findings highlight that analytic performance must be paired with workflow fit and timely clinician response to translate signals into benefit at the bedside.

DOI: 10.4324/9781003593867-6

A parallel line of work in population health uses large administrative claims to anticipate opioid-related harm. In Medicaid and Medicare cohorts, machine learning models trained on pharmacy fills, diagnoses, procedures, and utilization achieved strong discrimination during validation, with areas under the receiver operating characteristic curve ranging from approximately 0.84–0.91, supporting their use for risk stratification and targeted prevention efforts in high-risk populations.[4,5] Together, these examples illustrate a common theme: big data analytics can be clinically meaningful when accurate models are embedded in real workflows, elicit timely action, and are evaluated on outcomes that matter to patients.

Three critical challenges constrain the full potential of healthcare big data.

The first, interoperability, remains a persistent barrier to realizing value at the bedside and across populations. Interoperability is the capacity of disparate systems, devices, and applications to access, exchange, and use health information in a coordinated way across organizational and regional boundaries so clinicians have a complete and current picture of a patient's health.[6] As the Organisation for Economic Co-operation and Development (OECD) notes, progress depends on more than technical plumbing: countries need coherent governance that aligns standards, clarifies lawful access and reuse, and embeds safeguards to maintain public trust while enabling timely, secure data flows for care and system learning.[6] Although modern exchange standards (e.g., HL7 FHIR) have accelerated connectivity, many organizations still operate as partial silos; even when information can be located and transmitted, it is not always received in a usable form or integrated into local records where it can safely inform decisions at speed.[6,7] In 2023, about 70% of US hospitals reported engaging in all four core domains of interoperable exchange, namely finding, sending, receiving, and integrating patient information from external providers, underscoring uneven adoption and persistent friction.[7] In practice, these gaps can translate into incomplete medication and allergy lists at transition points, delays while prior results are fetched or reconciled, and avoidable duplication of tests, all of which erode timeliness and safety and blunt the promise of analytics to support care.[6,7]

Algorithmic bias also presents growing ethical concerns. In this context, bias refers to systematic, repeatable errors in model objectives, data, or evaluation that produce unfair outcomes, such as privileging one group over another or yielding unequal accuracy across demographic subgroups. These issues must be addressed through careful target selection, transparent reporting, and continuous audit in clinical settings.[8] Many healthcare AI tools have demonstrated such disparities when proxies for clinical need are misaligned with patient outcomes. A landmark study in Science examined a widely used commercial population-health algorithm and showed that it systematically underestimated the illness burden of African American patients, which reduced their likelihood of being identified for additional care management.[9] The mechanism was the algorithm's choice of healthcare spending as its prediction target; because structural inequities lead to lower spending on African American patients at comparable levels of need, the model inferred they were "healthier," thereby introducing a racial bias in access to supportive services.[9] Taken together, these findings underscore that fairness is not an afterthought but a design requirement: objectives should reflect true clinical need, subgroup performance should be monitored and reported, and governance should ensure corrective action when disparities emerge.[8,9]

Lastly, regulatory fragmentation complicates data use across jurisdictions. Regulatory fragmentation refers to overlapping or inconsistent frameworks that impose divergent requirements for consent, protection, and transfer, which in turn add policy and governance complexity to technical interoperability.[10] In practice, misalignments across regions affect how organizations document lawful access, specify security controls, and demonstrate accountability, introducing additional coordination costs and uncertainty even when the technical exchange works as designed.[10] These differences become most visible in cross-border contexts. In 2023, the European Union and the United States adopted the EU–US Data Privacy Framework to ease international data transfers; however, legal analysts have cautioned that concerns, particularly around government access and oversight under US law, could invite future challenges, requiring ongoing monitoring and potential adjustment of transfer mechanisms.[11]

The ethical implications of healthcare data are profound. On one hand, analytics can dramatically improve outcomes, as precision medicine approaches have been shown to extend survival in late-stage cancer patients treated with targeted therapies compared to non-targeted regimens.[12] On the other hand, these same technologies risk enabling discrimination if health data is misapplied by insurers, employers, or healthcare systems. A landmark analysis revealed that a widely used commercial health algorithm systematically underestimated illness severity in African American patients, delaying referrals for needed specialty care because healthcare spending was used as a proxy for health status.[9]

Looking forward, the most promising developments focus on privacy-preserving analytics. Techniques such as federated learning allow institutions to collaboratively train AI models without sharing raw patient data.[8] At MIT, researchers have developed "split neural networks" that keep sensitive information encrypted while still enabling valuable insights.[4] Meanwhile, blockchain-based systems, which are distributed, decentralized ledgers that record transactions in tamper-resistant blocks linked through cryptographic hashes, are increasingly applied in healthcare to give patients granular control over their data through smart contracts that enforce strict usage permissions.[13] These innovations aim to balance data utility with privacy, ensuring that analytics can progress while maintaining patient trust.

The ultimate challenge lies in balancing innovation with ethics. The NIH's All of Us Research Program illustrates this balance by combining large-scale precision health data collection with participant-controlled data sharing. By 2019, the program had already enrolled hundreds of thousands of participants and provided a model for respecting individual autonomy while enabling discovery at unprecedented scale.[14] Achieving this equilibrium will be essential for healthcare's digital transformation, as ethical frameworks highlight the importance of moving beyond abstract principles to practical governance and accountability in the use of AI.[15,16]

Data Collection, Storage, and Management

Modern healthcare data collection has evolved into a sophisticated ecosystem that encompasses clinical, operational, and consumer-generated sources. At the institutional level, electronic health record platforms such as Epic and Cerner capture structured information through clinician documentation, while natural language processing techniques extract additional meaning from unstructured physician notes. The scale of this activity is immense. Electronic health records generate a tremendous amount of information. One study estimated that pediatric inpatients produce approximately 1,460 discrete EHR data points per day, including vital signs, laboratory values, and medication records.[17] When scaled across thousands of patients in a large academic medical center, this translates into tens of millions of data points daily, underscoring both the analytic potential and the cognitive burden of modern health data.

Beyond these traditional systems, newer forms of data are reshaping the analytic landscape. Genomic sequencers now routinely generate over 200 gigabytes of data per patient, with the cost of whole genome sequencing having fallen below 600 dollars by 2024. Wearable devices add continuous streams of physiological information; the most recent FDA-cleared smartwatches are capable of measuring electrocardiograms, blood oxygen saturation, and even hydration levels. Social determinants of health, defined as the nonmedical factors such as socioeconomic conditions, physical environments, education, employment, and access to care that influence health outcomes, are increasingly quantified through geospatial analysis.[18] These measures incorporate information about food access, transportation networks, and environmental exposures to provide context for clinical data. In addition, patient-reported outcomes collected through mobile applications are offering valuable insight into quality of life and treatment effectiveness, giving voice to dimensions of care that were previously difficult to capture at scale.

Storing and managing this deluge of information requires deliberate approaches to information architecture. Relational databases such as Microsoft SQL Server remain essential for structured clinical data because of their robust querying capacity[19] and compliance with ACID principles, which stand for atomicity, consistency, isolation, and durability, in transactional systems.[20]

Yet the sheer variety and velocity of modern health data have also accelerated the adoption of NoSQL solutions. MongoDB has proven effective for managing the document-oriented nature of clinical notes and research data,[1] Cassandra supports the high-frequency data streams generated by intensive care monitors and wearable devices,[21] and Neo4j enables the representation of complex relationships embedded in genomic and proteomic datasets.[22,23]

Cloud services have become central to many health systems, offering scalable computing and storage resources. Major providers, including AWS, Microsoft Azure, and Google Cloud, offer HIPAA-eligible or in-scope services and business associate agreements that can support compliant handling of protected health information; however, healthcare organizations remain responsible for appropriate configuration, risk assessment, and implementation of required safeguards.[24] However, the 2024 Change Healthcare breach illustrated the risks of vendor concentration, showing how a single point of failure can disrupt services nationwide.[25] To mitigate such risks, leading health systems have moved toward hybrid architectures. Frequently accessed clinical information is maintained in low-latency cloud environments, archived records are stored in encrypted and immutable formats, and edge computing, which processes data locally at or near its source rather than relying solely on centralized cloud servers, enables real-time analytics at the point of care while reducing dependence on continuous data transmission.[26]

Despite these technological advances, data quality remains the foundation of reliable analytics. In practice, quality is often compromised: up to 30% of key fields in electronic health records may be incomplete, conditions can be coded inconsistently across organizations, device timestamps frequently fail to align, and clinician documentation styles introduce variability that affects natural language processing. To address these challenges, forward-looking organizations have established multilayered quality pipelines. Robotic process automation corrects common errors in structured data, clinical validation rules flag improbable values such as physiologically implausible laboratory readings, longitudinal checks identify contradictions across time, and blockchain-based provenance tracking ensures that all changes remain auditable.[27]

New standards in data governance are also reshaping the field. FHIR Release[5] advances healthcare interoperability by enabling granular and flexible data exchange through modern Application Programming Interfaces (APIs), improving clinical workflows and patient data management.[28] The CARIN Code of Conduct provides a framework of best practices for consumer-mediated health information sharing, promoting transparency, privacy, and user control over personal health data.[29] In parallel, the Trusted Exchange Framework and Common Agreement (TEFCA) establishes a nationwide network designed to ensure secure and trusted exchange of health information across diverse organizations and systems, supporting nationwide health data interoperability.[30]

Finally, the human element continues to play a critical role. At Vanderbilt University Medical Center, "data curators" with clinical training collaborate closely with informaticians to ensure that analytic models reflect actual patterns of care delivery.[31] Patient and Family Advisory Councils

(PFACs) engage patients and family members as partners in healthcare organizations to provide experiential insights that inform policies, programs, and initiatives aimed at improving patient-centered care. These councils contribute to codesigning and providing feedback on projects to ensure that healthcare innovations remain aligned with patient needs and experiences. Engagement levels vary, from giving project approval to active codesign from inception, with recognized success factors including training of patients and staff and supportive leadership.[32]

As healthcare data ecosystems grow ever more complex, the organizations that succeed will be those that combine technical sophistication with ethical responsibility, creating systems that are not only powerful in their analytic capabilities but also trustworthy in the eyes of clinicians, patients, and the public.

Visualization Techniques and Tools

The Importance of Data Visualization in Healthcare

Data visualization has become a powerful tool for making sense of the increasingly complex world of healthcare data. Transforming raw numbers into visual formats allows clinicians and administrators to detect patterns, recognize trends, and identify outliers that might otherwise remain hidden in spreadsheets or databases. Visualization does not only serve professionals; it also plays an important role in patient engagement. When patients are able to view their information in clear, accessible formats, they are more likely to understand their conditions and to make informed choices about their care.[11]

In practice, effective visualization acts as a bridge between the sophisticated world of healthcare analytics and actionable insights at the clinical or operational level. This role is particularly critical in an era when clinicians are confronted with information overload, as the average physician reviews more than 15,000 data points for each patient encounter.[11] In such circumstances, the difference between well-designed visual representations and poorly presented data can be the difference between timely, life-saving intervention and delayed recognition of deterioration.

Clinical dashboards illustrate how visualization has evolved. Once limited to static reporting, they now function as sophisticated cognitive aids. Modern dashboards incorporate dynamic risk stratification, with color-coded patient lists that update in real time, temporal trend analysis that presents laboratory values and vital signs along interactive timelines, and comparative benchmarks that display performance against peers or best-practice standards. Machine learning techniques have been increasingly applied to early detection of sepsis, improving diagnostic accuracy and potentially reducing mortality. These systems leverage diverse clinical and laboratory data to generate predictive models that support timely intervention, as discussed by Giacobbe et al.[33] and Ţocu et al.[34]

Population health applications have also benefited from visualization. The University of Chicago's Urban Health Initiative employs geospatial mapping and community partnerships to address health disparities in underserved neighborhoods. Through mapping neighborhood-level disease prevalence and social determinants, they identify areas with high diabetes burden and limited healthcare access. This data guides targeted interventions, including mobile screening programs and educational outreach, which have led to improved diabetes detection and management among South Side residents. These community-driven efforts exemplify a multifaceted approach to reducing diabetes-related disparities in economically disadvantaged neighborhoods.[35,36]

Research-oriented platforms such as the NIH's All of Us Researcher Workbench demonstrate the importance of balancing detail with clarity. The platform provides diverse analytic tools, including Manhattan plots for genome-wide association studies, volcano plots to represent statistical significance against effect size, and interactive survival curves with adjustable covariates. These tools empower researchers to explore complex biomedical data securely and collaboratively, supporting precision medicine research across various domains.[37]

Operational analytics have likewise embraced visualization as a means of improving efficiency and resource use. Hospitals now employ control charts to monitor surgical complication rates, Sankey diagrams to map patient flow through emergency departments, and network graphs to assess communication among care teams. At Mass General Brigham, an advanced operating room dashboard integrates real-time surgical data into a unified display, employing visual analytics such as parallel coordinates and heatmaps to enhance workflow transparency and support efficient resource allocation. This system has contributed to improvements in operating room efficiency, including reductions in turnover times and workflow bottlenecks, through enhanced communication and real-time feedback mechanisms.[38]

What is Data Visualization? Why is it important?

> *The profile of a curve* ***reveals*** *in a flash a whole situation—the life history of an epidemic, a panic, or an era of prosperity. The curve* ***informs*** *the mind, awakens the imagination,* ***convinces.***
>
> —Henry D. Hubbard, National Bureau of Standards[43]

With such a vast amount of data being collected, it is crucial to have a method to translate this into meaningful insights for diverse types of audiences and environments. This method is data visualization. By transforming raw data into graphical representations, visualizations can transcend language differences and varying audience expertise, allowing data to answer sought-after questions as well as present new inquiries.[44(p866)]

Consider a patient who wants to know the recovery timeline for two types of knee surgeries in order to decide on the best procedure. The patient wants to know how long it will take to regain mobility. To help with the decision, the surgeon presents a visualization of the data that compares the timelines (see Figure 4.1).

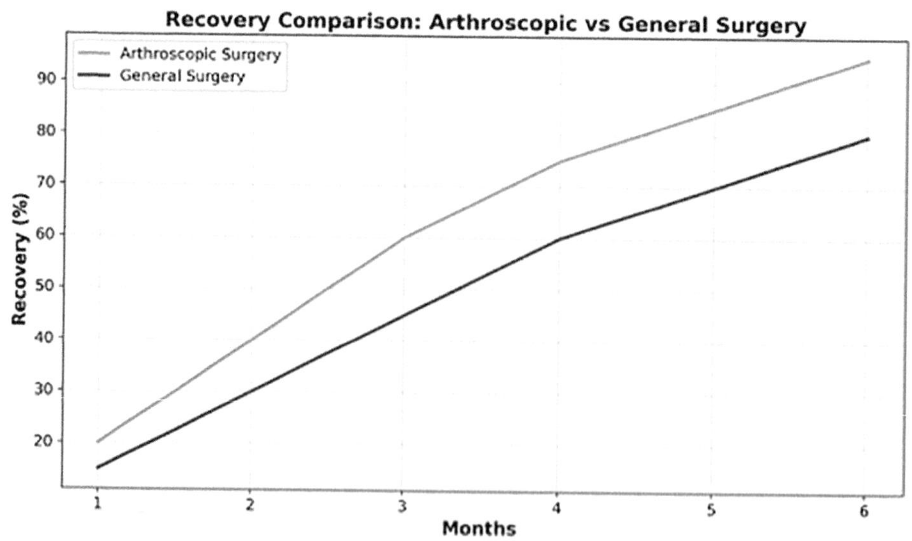

Figure 4.1 Line graph.

Or a small business owner needs to compare the annual sales of two products to identify any patterns or relationships before placing an order. Visualizing the sales data informs the owner's purchasing decision and also encourages more research into related product sales (see Figure 4.2).

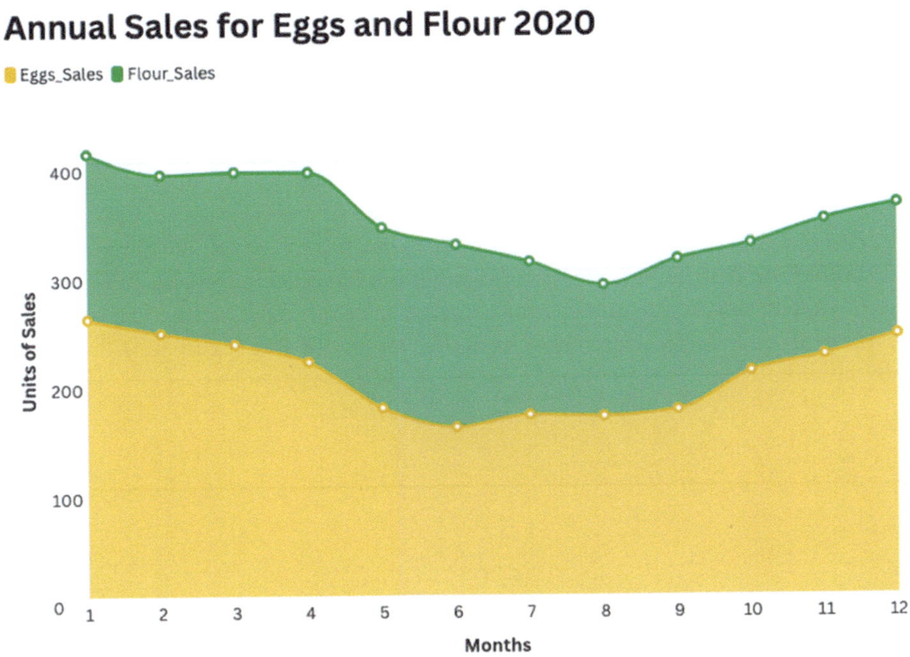

Figure 4.2 Area graph.

Understanding the Character of Data

To determine the best visual representation, consider the two classifications of data: quantitative and qualitative. The first, quantitative data, provides a numerical measurement either continuous or discrete. Quantitative continuous data are measured granularly such as a person's body mass increasing from 30.5 to 40.1 or a population trend increasing over a 10-year period. Quantitative discrete data are separate but counted such as the number of pregnancies carried to term in a rural town. This dataset is numerical and countable but is discrete since a pregnancy cannot be counted as .5 or 1.5.

The second, qualitative data, is not expressed in continuous integer values, but is instead related to subjects, places, things, events, or concepts. It can also be distinguished into the subcategories: nominal and ordinal. A person's hair color is qualitative nominal data because it does not have an order. It is a category. Some qualitative data have an intrinsic order, and these are qualitative ordinal data. An example of this data is a histologic stage. If a patient has stage one cancer and another person has stage four, it is clear which is more severe.[45]

Common Data Visualizations

Demonstrated in Figure 4.1 is the most basic visual representation, a line graph. Commonly used to show changes in value over time, it represents quantitative continuous data. It plots data points and connects them with a line to show patterns when comparing two or more values. A more complex line graph might have several trend lines in different colors.[46(p8)] With multiple trend lines, it can be challenging to interpret. Often, these are separated into individual line graphs called small multiples.[47]

Figure 4.2 demonstrates an area graph that fills the space between the lines and the x-axis with color or shading. This also presents trends in the data but places more emphasis on the volume (the filled area), providing a part-to-whole comparison. Using an area graph can be more impressive on an audience with its increased visual weight of color or shading.[48]

Another common visualization is a bar chart. It is used to compare categorical or discrete data. From a bar chart, we can quickly see the largest value and compare it to all the categories. A variation of this is a stacked bar chart, which segments each bar into categories, but also shows them within a larger whole. Though this can be valuable for comparison, a stacked bar chart can be challenging to interpret. Therefore, a clustered bar chart is sometimes preferred (see Figure 4.3).[46(p4)]

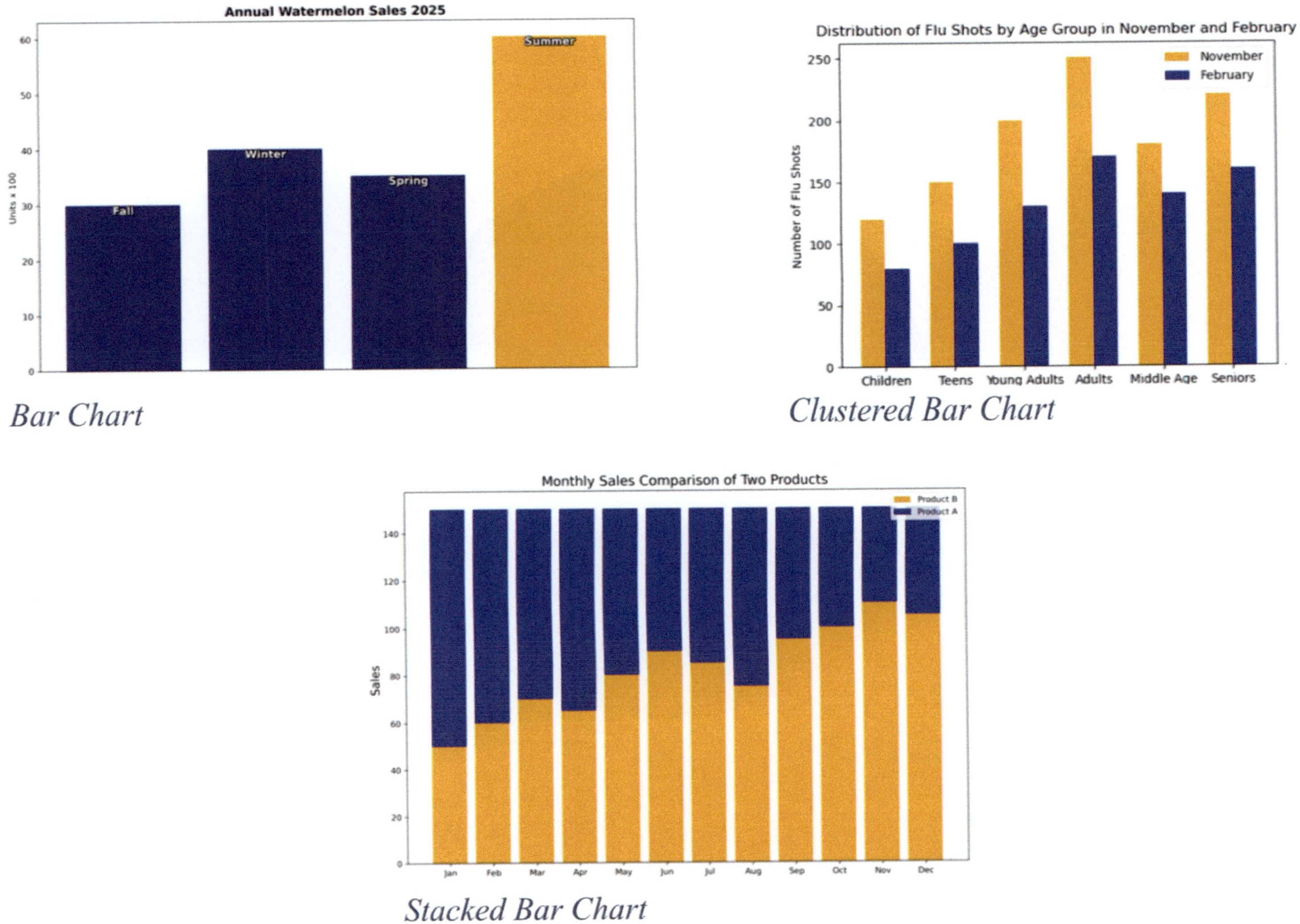

Figure 4.3 Examples of bar chart variants (simple, clustered, and stacked).

A pie or donut chart also compares values that are a part of the whole and is commonly used for less complex or small datasets. Both are best used for data with significant differences between elements or labeling, as it can be challenging to interpret minor changes in each category (see Figure 4.4).[49] Notice in the figure that labeling is helpful to read the similar segments.

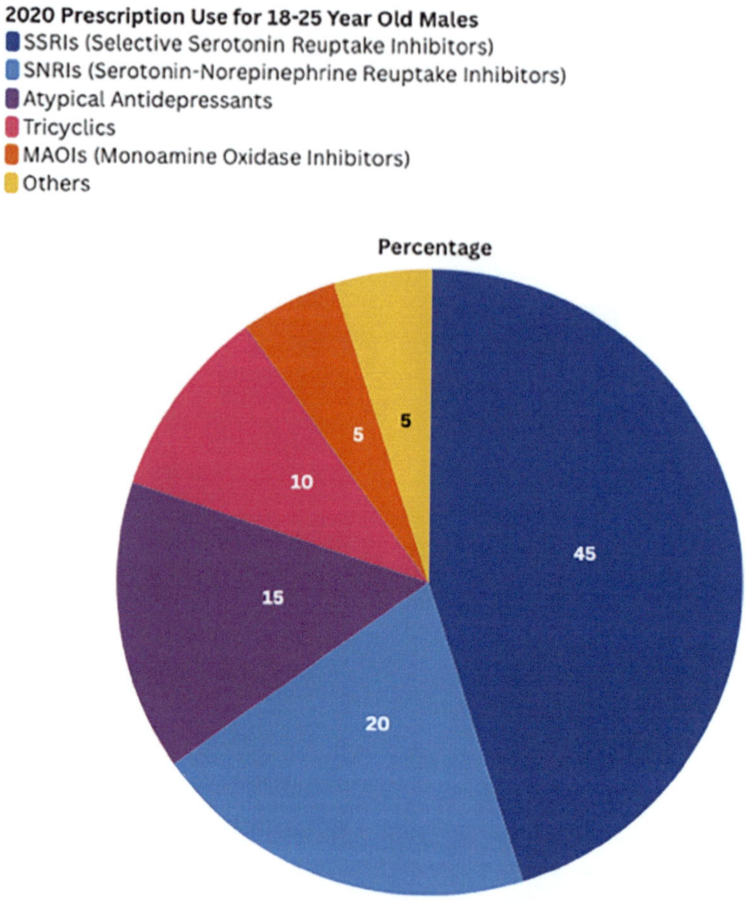

Figure 4.4 Pie chart.

The bubble chart shows the relationship between three dimensions using x and y positioning and the bubble size. As with the pie chart, the bubble visualization works best with large value differences. Since our brains find discriminating between similarly sized circles challenging, data is often included on the shapes when the dataset is small. This chart can be used for both qualitative and quantitative datasets (see Figure 4.5).[50]

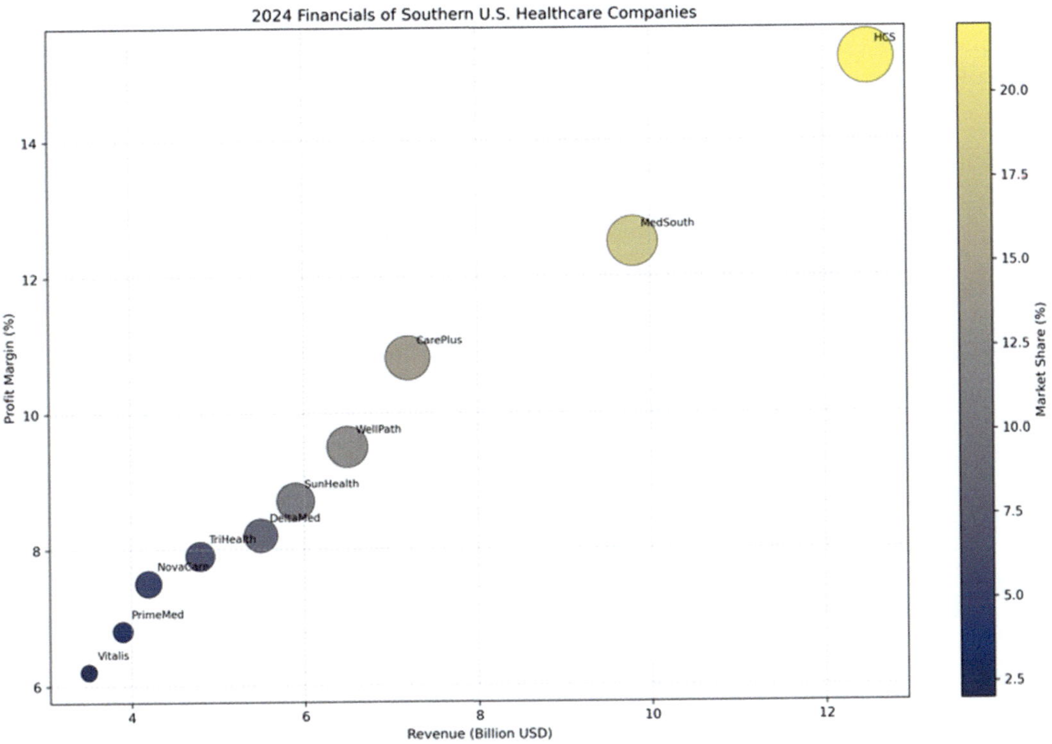

Figure 4.5 Bubble chart.

Scatterplots show the relationships, trends, clusters, and patterns between values of data presented as points plotted on the x and y axes. This chart can provide an overview and predict a trend line. This chart is often used for large datasets (see Figure 4.6).[46(pp9–10)]

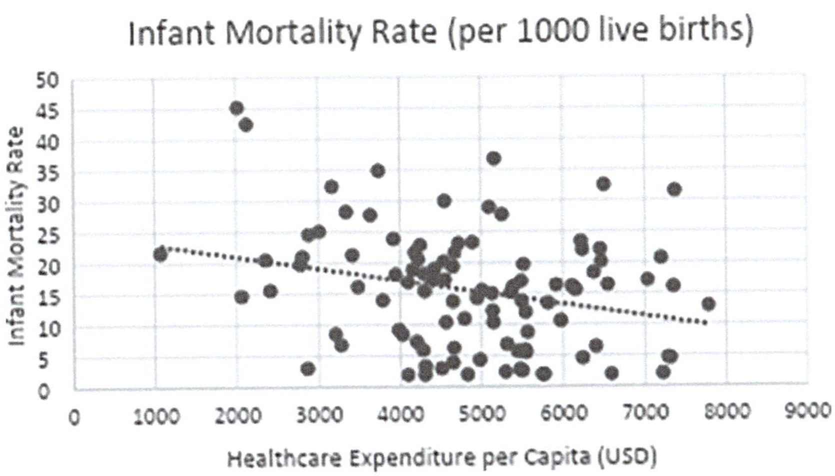

Figure 4.6 Scatterplot.

If the dataset is so large in a scatter plot that the dots begin to blur together, a Heat Map can be used. These maps show the distribution of the data through color or shade gradients. Therefore, this is effective for showing trends in large datasets (see Figure 4.7).[51]

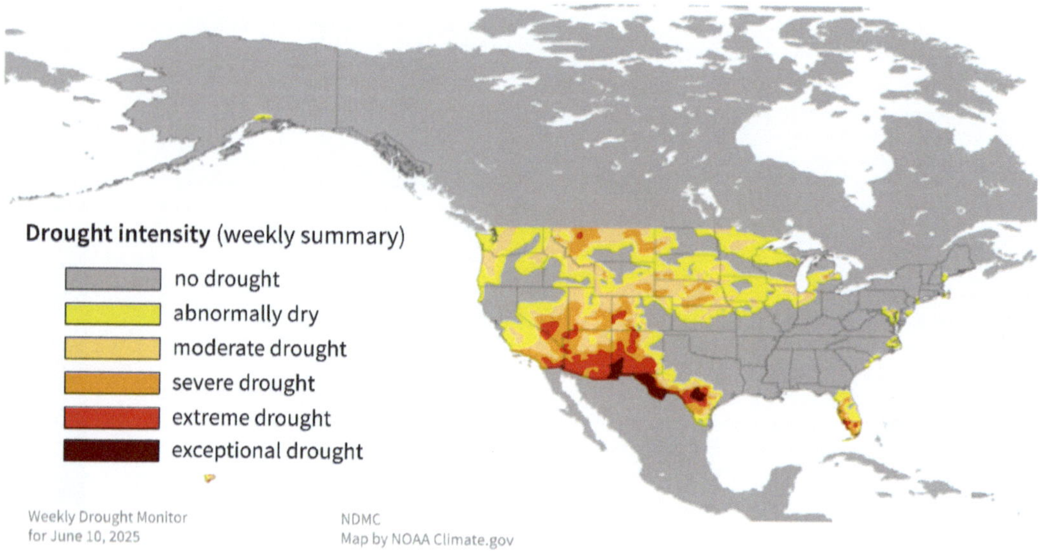

Figure 4.7 Heat map.

Sometimes, data frequency and distribution are required. A Box Chart can display the range of values in data. It provides a high-level, birds-eye perspective, providing general information about the symmetry, skew, variance, and outliers in your data, displaying it in 25% segments or quadrants labeled as Q1, Median, Q3, and Q4. If a value is beyond the quadrant range or "whisker," it is an outlier. Outliers are often represented as a small circle (Figure 4.8).[52] In Figure 4.8, the concentration of students' grades fell in the second quadrant of 78–85 percentiles.

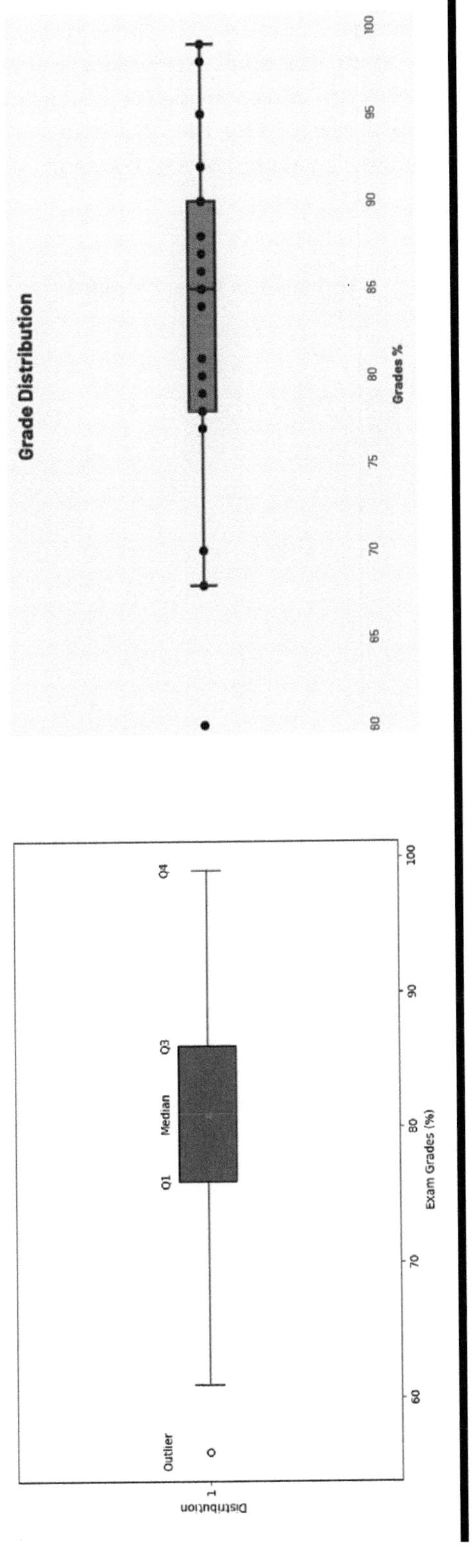

Figure 4.8 Box charts.

Like Box Charts, the Histogram shows the frequency of data values and places these in bins so that a data shape can be extrapolated. It is used to represent quantitative discrete data.[46(p7)] An example is a bell curve for a final exam. The number of grades at 80% would be in one bar or bin, 90% would be in the next, and so forth. After viewing the Histogram, the professor could see the grade percentage frequency in each category for the final exam. In Figure 4.9, the chart shows the frequency of weights in a sample of young patients. By using a histogram, it is possible to see the shape of the data.

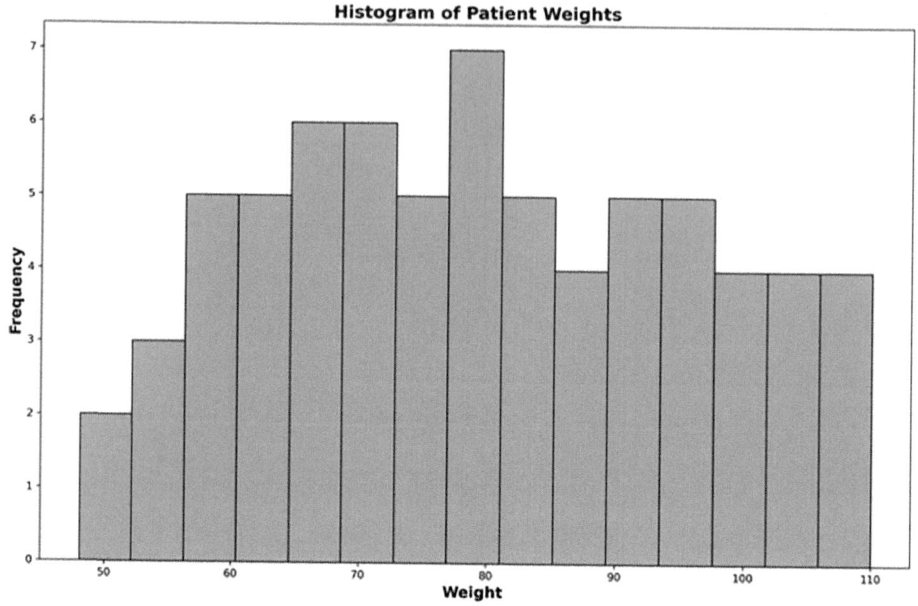

Figure 4.9 Histogram.

Design and Aesthetics

No matter which chart you choose to tell your data story, incorporating intentional design and aesthetic principles can enhance your message. When we encounter a visual, our brains process certain images in less than 500 milliseconds. This is called *pre-attentive processing*.[53] Truly, before we know it, we start interpreting visual cues like tones, patterns, and colors. Take a look at Figures 4.10 and 4.11. Notice how quickly you identify the different elements in each chart.

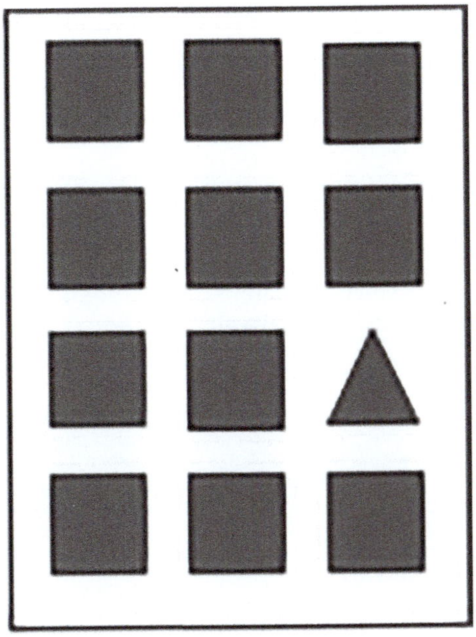

Figure 4.10 Pre-attentive processing.

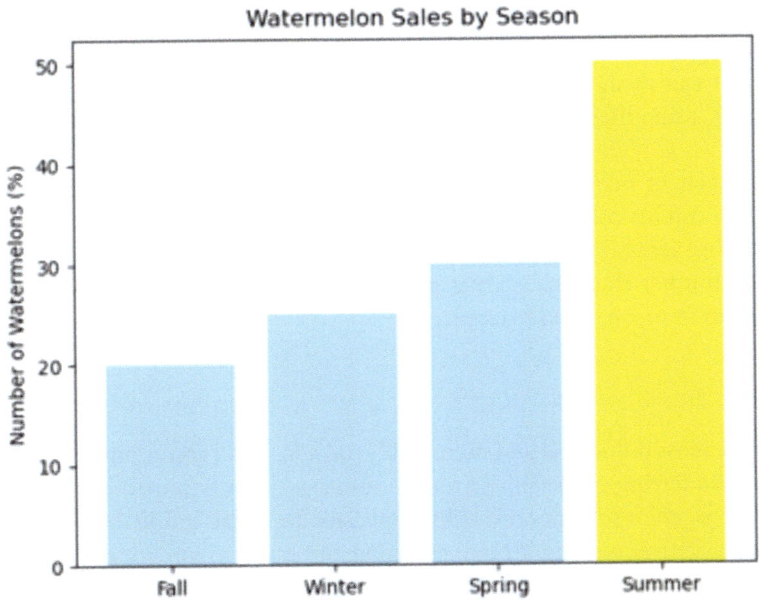

Figure 4.11 Bar chart visualization of watermelon sales by season, demonstrating how graphical representations can reveal patterns and comparisons within datasets.

Differences between elements play a key role in guiding the viewer's attention. The contrast between visual elements can vary in intensity and emphasis. For instance, a bubble that is larger or a different color than the others in a chart will draw the eye. As you probably noticed in Figure 4.11, a bright yellow bar placed next to a light blue one immediately stands out, as does a triangle among a group of squares.[54]

This principle of contrast applies across various visual elements. Whether using black and white, color, shapes, or patterns, contrast can provide different levels of intensity in an image. To fine-tune contrast, especially in terms of brightness and tone, refer to the grayscale below: the greatest contrast occurs between pure white and deep black (Figure 4.12). To interpret the level of contrast in a chart, desaturate the colors and compare them to grayscale.

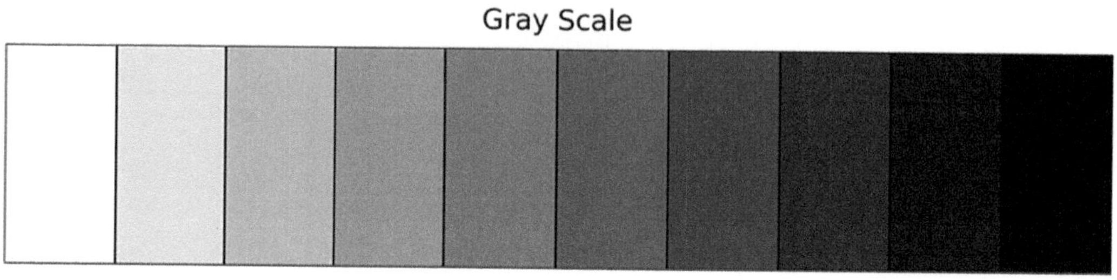

Figure 4.12 Grayscale.

Contrast can also contribute to accessibility and ensure clarity. As more people access information on mobile devices, contrast becomes critical. A chart that looks fine on a computer screen may be unreadable on a phone in bright sunlight. Also, when projecting a chart during a presentation, the projector light can wash out colors and reduce clarity without high-contrast colors or tones. To counteract this, using high contrast between visual elements and the background can improve readability.[55]

This can also benefit people with color vision deficiencies (color blindness) who may not be able to distinguish certain color combinations. Since there are many types of color blindness, it is recommended to use accessibility tools such as ColorBrewer[56] to choose appropriate color palettes. Using contrast and other elements such as patterns, shapes, or labels in addition to high-contrast tones and color can improve broader accessibility.[55]

Color

Color is one of the most influential and memorable tools in visual communication. When used strategically, rather than relying on default settings, it can significantly impact your data story.

Using intentional color schemes can help emphasize key ideas, guide the viewer's attention, and support the data narrative, making it more engaging and easier to understand.

Color schemes can be used to guide the viewer's attention in a certain direction and/or to support a decrease or increase in data value (sequential). For example, if the numbers are increasing in your dataset, you could use a monochromatic scheme working with the data and use shades and tints as you move from pink to red, or light blue to deep blue (Figure 4.13).

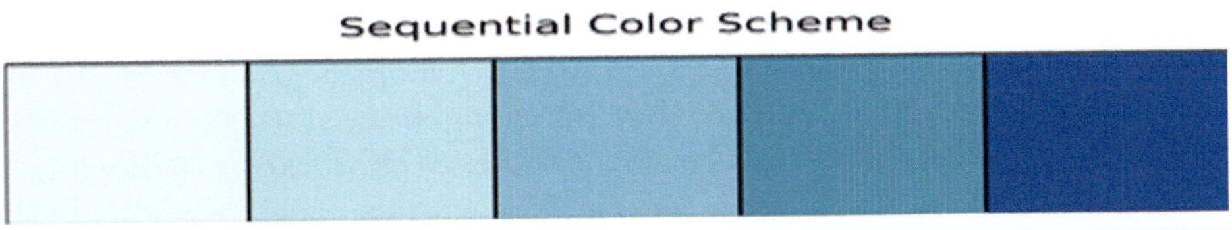

Figure 4.13 Sequential color scheme.

If you want to show separation in your discrete and qualitative categorical data, colors opposite each other on a color wheel can be a good choice. This categorical color scheme will show some separation and less connection of the data.

Data that is moving from a central value in both positive and negative values can be represented with a diverging color scheme, again moving the eye in a sequential direction (Figure 4.14).[57]

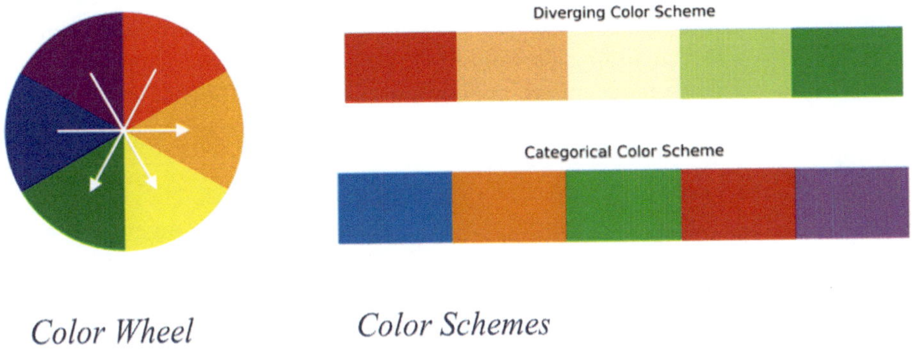

Figure 4.14 Color wheel and color scheme.

The value or brightness of color can draw an audience to a certain section of the image/chart first. Brighter colors are noticed before darker ones, for example, yellow is noticed before blue in a visualization.

Using color exclusively is tempting since it is aesthetically pleasing. However, contrasting textures or shades of black and white to communicate relationships or separation can be just as effective. For example, high contrast, very bright, and very dark could be applied to data with different values or categories. Or tones next to each other on the grayscale could be applied to related or progressive data.

Distractions

Be mindful of unnecessary visual distractions—what data visualization expert Edward Tufte refers to as "chart junk."[58] This includes unnecessary graphics, excessive gridlines, or irrelevant icons that can distract from the data.

However, some redundant cues may actually improve understanding such as repeating colors and labels. This can enhance understanding, especially for diverse audiences.[59]

Legends are usually necessary, but relying on legends alone can challenge your audience. By placing labels directly on the chart, you can improve comprehension.[44(p874)] This approach reduces the cognitive load of your audience by eliminating the need to shift attention back and forth between the legend and the chart. For some, this extra effort can be challenging.[60]

While visual aesthetics can enhance a data visualization, they should never compromise the clarity or integrity of the data story. The primary goal of any visualization is to communicate the data effectively and truthfully. When form and function work together, data can tell stories that explain information and drive further exploration.

The consumer-facing side of healthcare has perhaps seen the most dramatic transformation. Patient portals increasingly include medication adherence timelines with visual cues for missed doses, individualized health trajectories that allow patients to compare their progress against population norms, and interactive three-dimensional anatomical models to illustrate the impact of procedures. Kaiser Permanente's predictive analytics and patient engagement initiatives have reduced missed appointments by identifying high-risk patients and using targeted interventions such as reminder text messages. For example, a comparative effectiveness study in primary care and mental health showed that adding a second reminder text reduced missed clinic visits by 7%–11%, translating to hundreds fewer missed appointments monthly. These efforts demonstrate the potential of data-driven strategies to improve chronic disease management and care continuity by addressing appointment adherence challenges.[39]

Emerging technologies continue to push the boundaries of visualization in healthcare. Surgeons at the University of California, Los Angeles (UCLA) employ innovative augmented reality tools, such as the Dynamic Optical Contrast Imaging (DOCI) device, to project tumor margins in real time during resections, enabling precision surgery that spares healthy tissue and improves patient outcomes.[40] Virtual reality therapy is increasingly used in Veterans Affairs hospitals to treat post-traumatic stress disorder through controlled exposure therapy, demonstrating significant reductions in Post-Traumatic Stress Disorder (PTSD) symptoms among combat veterans.[41] Medical education benefits from cutting-edge haptic feedback simulations integrated with AI-driven virtual reality platforms, providing scalable, cost-effective tactile training that enhances procedural skill acquisition.[42]

Yet, with these advances come risks. Misleading scales, such as truncated axes, can exaggerate small differences. Cognitive biases may result when recent data points are visually emphasized over long-term trends. Non-intuitive color palettes can confuse interpretation, while overplotting can obscure meaningful patterns in dense datasets. Institutions like the Cleveland Clinic address these risks through visual literacy training, standardized design templates, peer review of dashboards, and patient testing of consumer tools to ensure usability.

As the complexity of healthcare data continues to grow, the organizations most likely to succeed will be those that combine technical excellence with human-centered design. Effective visualization will not only illuminate but also empower, ensuring that data serves the needs of clinicians, patients, and researchers without overwhelming them.

Exercises and Activities

ACTIVITY 1: CASE STUDY ANALYSIS—SEPSIS EARLY WARNING IN A REGIONAL HEALTH NETWORK

Objective: Apply big data and clinical workflow thinking to design, implement, and evaluate a sepsis early-warning solution that improves time-to-treatment while minimizing alert fatigue.

Instructions:

- Divide into interdisciplinary teams: Form groups of 4–6 students with representation from pharmacy, medicine, nursing, and business healthcare.
- Provide a case scenario: A 400-bed regional hospital is piloting a sepsis early-warning model using EHR vitals, labs, and nursing notes, with plans to scale to affiliated clinics.
- Analyze the case: Teams should:
  - Map the current sepsis pathway (triage→labs→antibiotics) and identify bottlenecks.
  - Propose a tiered alert design (e.g., nurse pre-alert→provider escalation) with thresholds, roles, and actions.
  - Outline safety and fairness checks (subgroup performance, override logging, adverse event review).
  - Recommend a basic machine learning operations (MLOps) plan (data quality checks, retraining cadence, version control, rollback).
  - Estimate operational impact (time-to-antibiotics, length of stay (LOS), intensive care unit (ICU) bed utilization) and outline a simple cost–benefit view.
- Present solutions: Each team presents a 5-minute summary highlighting workflow changes, guardrails for bias/alert fatigue, and success metrics.

ACTIVITY 2: DATA INTERPRETATION AND VISUALIZATION WORKSHOP—EHR AND WEARABLE STREAMS

Objective: Build data literacy by interpreting clinical and device time-series data and communicating findings with clear visuals.

Instructions:

- Provide a sample dataset: Share a simplified, de-identified dataset combining EHR elements (vital signs, lab timestamps, medication administrations) with basic wearable data (heart rate, step count).
- Data analysis task: Ask students to:

- Identify trends and disparities (e.g., delays from first abnormal vital to antibiotics across units or shifts).
- Explore relationships between early warning scores and outcomes (e.g., escalation, ICU transfer).
- Examine basic adherence signals from wearables (e.g., step count recovery patterns post-discharge).

- Create visualizations: Using Excel, Tableau, or Python, produce 2–3 visuals (e.g., run chart of time-to-antibiotics, heatmap of alert density by hour, layered line chart of HR vs fever onset).
- Interpret findings: Write a brief (≤300 words) summarizing insights and one actionable intervention (e.g., lab fast-track, nurse-driven antibiotic protocol).
- Group discussion: Reflect on how visualization choices altered interpretation and which metric best communicates clinical value.

ACTIVITY 3: ETHICAL DEBATE—TRANSPARENCY, CONSENT, AND EQUITY IN HEALTH DATA

Objective: Examine ethical trade-offs in using big data and AI for patient care, focusing on autonomy, fairness, and security.

Instructions:

- Divide into debate teams: One side argues for maximizing data integration/analytics to improve outcomes; the other prioritizes patient autonomy and privacy safeguards.
- Provide debate topics:
  - Should de-identified EHR + claims + SDOH data be used for prediction without re-consent if strict governance is in place?
  - Is explainability a requirement for deploying high-performing clinical AI, or can performance + monitoring suffice?
  - What minimum commitments should organizations make on bias detection, opt-out pathways, and incident transparency?
- Research and prepare: Teams use chapter content and external (newer than 2022) scholarly sources to build arguments and proposed safeguards.
- Conduct the debate: Opening statements→rebuttals→moderated Q&A→closing statements.
- Reflection: Each student submits a short reflection (≤200 words) on how their view changed and one concrete governance practice they now endorse.

Assessment Questions

1. What are the main objectives of the Sepsis Early Warning case study (Mayo/TREWS) in terms of workflow, safety, and impact?
2. Which metrics would you track to evaluate both the predictive performance and clinical impact of a sepsis early warning system?
3. How can EHR and wearable time-series data be used together to improve early detection while minimizing cognitive overload and alert fatigue?
4. In building a predictive model for opioid overdose risk, which data sources are most useful, and what fairness checks should accompany model validation?
5. When should a health system choose SQL Server (relational), MongoDB (document), Cassandra (wide-column), or Neo4j (graph) for big-data workloads in care delivery and research?
6. What governance and ethical safeguards should be in place before deploying AI in direct clinical workflows?
7. In the Rwanda drone blood delivery case, which reliability and equity KPIs most strongly drive clinician adoption, and how can contextual (nonclinical) data improve forecasting?
8. From the Cleveland Clinic contrast shortage case, what change-management tactics most effectively reduce unnecessary contrast use without harming outcomes?
9. Propose a defensible way to communicate hospital-scale data volume using per-patient EHR data counts, and explain how this framing guides analytics and staffing plans.
10. How can patient and family input (e.g., PFACs) be incorporated into data governance and patient-portal design to ensure innovations reflect patient needs without overclaiming their role?

Assessment Questions—Answers

1. The sepsis early warning case aims to streamline the pathway from triage to antibiotics, reduce avoidable delays, and embed alerts that support rather than replace clinical judgment. It also emphasizes a safety net—bias monitoring, override review, and incident analysis—alongside pragmatic MLOps plans for data quality checks, retraining, version control, and rollback. Ultimately, success is defined by measurable improvements in time-to-antibiotics, mortality, length of stay, and sustained clinician adoption.
2. Evaluation should cover both model performance and real-world impact. Discrimination and calibration (e.g., AUROC/AUPRC, sensitivity, PPV, calibration curves) show whether the model is sound, while operational metrics—alert acknowledgment time, treatment initiation intervals, escalation rates—reveal workflow effects. Outcome measures such as in-hospital mortality, ICU length of stay, and readmissions indicate clinical value, and adoption metrics (e.g., alerts handled per hour and timely responses) ensure the tool is usable at the bedside.
3. Combining EHR and wearable time series works best when features are parsimonious and clinically interpretable—for example, aligning vital-sign and lab trajectories with activity or heart-rate recovery patterns. Visual tools like run charts or heatmaps can surface deterioration windows without overloading staff, and tiered thresholds with caps, snooze options, and escalation rules help contain alert volume while preserving sensitivity.
4. Building an opioid overdose risk model benefits from rich claims and pharmacy data, diagnostic and utilization histories, demographics, and, where available, social determinants of

health. Validation should pair standard accuracy metrics with calibration and decision-curve analysis, then probe fairness explicitly by testing performance across age, sex, race, and payer subgroups. When discrepancies appear, error analyses and guardrails guide mitigation before deployment.

5. Storage choices should match the workload. Relational databases such as SQL Server are well suited to highly structured encounters and order data that demand complex joins and ACID transactions. Document stores like MongoDB handle variable clinical notes and research artifacts with flexible schemas. Cassandra excels at high-velocity, write-heavy time series from monitors and wearables across clusters. Graph databases such as Neo4j model complex biomedical relationships—think variant–gene–pathway–phenotype—more naturally than tables.
6. Before embedding AI in clinical workflows, organizations need a clear human-in-the-loop design, explicit override and adverse-event review policies, and continuous bias surveillance with subgroup reporting. Robust audit trails, version control, and rollback plans are essential, as are transparent model cards, a thoughtful consent or notice posture, and strong data security and access controls commensurate with clinical risk.
7. In the Rwanda drone network, clinician behavior changed most when reliability was indisputable; on-time delivery, lower stockouts, faster emergency fills, reduced wastage, and equitable access across facilities reinforced trust. Forecasting improved when contextual signals—local calendars, weather and road conditions, and event patterns—were layered onto clinical demand, allowing smarter buffer stocks and more resilient routing.
8. During the contrast shortage, practice change stuck when protocols specified when contrast was essential, optional, or avoidable and when side-by-side image examples made the trade-offs obvious. Small but targeted changes in order sets and decision support reduced unnecessary requests, while real-time inventory dashboards enabled fair allocation. Rapid feedback across emergency medicine, radiology, and surgery ensured outcomes stayed stable as use declined.
9. A defensible way to convey hospital-scale data volume is to start with validated per-patient daily counts and multiply by the average daily census to show that routine operations generate tens of millions of data points. That framing clarifies the need for scalable pipelines, storage tiers, reliability monitoring, and the analyst and engineering capacity required to keep data products safe and timely.
10. Patient and family input fits best through structured advisory councils and usability testing that translate lived experience into concrete portal features and governance choices. Teams should document how feedback informs decisions and publish plain-language policies and transparency dashboards so patients can see the impact of their input. It's important to be precise: PFACs advise and codesign, while product and governance bodies retain final accountability.

References

1. Kasthurirathne SN, Ho YA, Dixon BE. Public Health Analytics and Big Data. In: Magnuson JA, Dixon BE, eds. *Public Health Informatics and Information Systems*. 3rd ed. Springer; 2020:203–219. doi:10.1007/978-3-030-41215-9
2. Henry KE, Adams R, Parent C, et al. Factors driving provider adoption of the TREWS machine learning–based early warning system and its effects on sepsis treatment timing. *Nat Med.* 2022;28(7):1447–1454. doi:10.1038/s41591-022-01894-0

3. Adams R, Henry KE, Sridharan A, et al. Prospective, multi-site study of patient outcomes after implementation of the TREWS machine learning–based early warning system for sepsis. *Nat Med.* 2022;28(7):1455–1460. doi:10.1038/s41591-022-01895-z
4. Lo-Ciganic WH, Donohue JM, Yang Q, et al. Developing and validating a machine-learning algorithm to predict opioid overdose in Medicaid beneficiaries in two US states: a prognostic modelling study. *Lancet Digit Health.* 2022;4(6):e455–e465. doi:10.1016/S2589-7500(22)00062-0
5. Lo-Ciganic WH, Huang JL, Zhang HH, et al. Evaluation of machine-learning algorithms for predicting opioid overdose risk among Medicare beneficiaries with opioid prescriptions. *JAMA Netw Open.* 2019;2(3):e190968. doi:10.1001/jamanetworkopen.2019.0968
6. OECD (2022), *Health Data Governance for the Digital Age: Implementing the OECD Recommendation on Health Data Governance*, OECD Publishing, Paris, https://doi.org/10.1787/68b60796-en.
7. Interoperable Exchange of Patient Health Information Among U.S. Hospitals: 2023 | HealthIT.gov. Healthit.gov. Published 2023. Accessed September 18, 2025. www.healthit.gov/data/data-briefs/interoperable-exchange-patient-health-information-among-us-hospitals-2023
8. Parikh RB, Teeple S, Navathe AS. Addressing bias in artificial intelligence in health care. *JAMA.* 2019;322(24):2377–2378. doi:10.1001/jama.2019.18058
9. Obermeyer Z, Powers B, Vogeli C, Mullainathan S. Dissecting racial bias in an algorithm used to manage the health of populations. *Science.* 2019;366(6464):447–453. doi:10.1126/science.aax2342
10. HIMSS. *Interoperability in Healthcare.* HIMSS. Published 2020. www.himss.org/resources/interoperability-healthcare
11. New EU-US Data Privacy Framework—Reliable Solution for Transatlantic Data Transfers or Gateway to Schrems III? Klgates.com. Published 2023. Accessed September 18, 2025. www.klgates.com/New-EU-US-Data-Privacy-FrameworkReliable-Solution-for-Transatlantic-Data-Transfers-or-Gateway-to-Schrems-III-7-12-2023
12. Mapendano CK, Nøhr AK, M Sønderkær, et al. Longer survival with precision medicine in late-stage cancer patients. *ESMO Open.* 2025;10(1):104089–104089. doi:https://doi.org/10.1016/j.esmoop.2024.104089
13. Agbo C, Mahmoud Q, Eklund J. Blockchain technology in healthcare: a systematic review. *Healthcare.* 2019;7(2):56. doi:https://doi.org/10.3390/healthcare7020056
14. All of Us Research Program Investigators. The "All of Us" research program. *N Engl J Med.* 2019;381(7):668–676. doi:10.1056/NEJMsr1809937
15. Mittelstadt B. Principles alone cannot guarantee ethical AI. *Nat Mach Intell.* 2019;1(11):501–507. doi:10.1038/s42256-019-0114-4
16. Morley J, Machado CCV, Burr C, et al. The ethics of AI in health care: a mapping review. *Soc Sci Med.* 2020;260:113172. doi:10.1016/j.socscimed.2020.113172
17. Gal DB, Han B, Longhurst C, Scheinker D, Shin AY. Quantifying electronic health record data: a potential risk for cognitive overload. *Hosp Pediatr.* 2021;11(2):175–178. doi:10.1542/hpeds.2020-002402
18. World Health Organization. Social determinants of health. World Health Organization. Published 2024. Accessed July 27, 2026. https://www.who.int/health-topics/social-determinants-of-health
19. Antas J, Rocha Silva R, Bernardino J. Assessment of SQL and NoSQL systems to store and mine COVID-19 data. *Computers.* 2022;11(2):29. doi:10.3390/computers11020029
20. Härder T, Reuter A. Principles of transaction-oriented database recovery. *ACM Comput Surv.* 1983;15(4):287–317. doi:10.1145/289.291
21. Nargesian F, Guimarães T, Abelha A, Santos M. An exploratory study of a NoSQL database for a clinical data repository. In: Rocha Á, Correia AM, Reis LP, Filipe J, eds. *WorldCIST 2020 Advances in Intelligent Systems and Computing.* Springer Nature Switzerland AG; 2020:476–483.
22. Roy S, Agarwal S, Bagga R, et al. Extensible big data software architecture managing a research resource of real-world clinical radiology data linked to other health data. *GigaScience.* 2020;9(10):giaa095. doi:10.1093/gigascience/giaa095.

23. Ellingsen G, Ackerman MS, Gravengaard G, et al. Accelerating the adoption of research data management strategies. *Patterns (N Y)*. 2022;3(11):100597. doi:10.1016/j.patter.2022.100597.
24. US Department of Health and Human Services, Office for Civil Rights. Guidance on HIPAA and cloud computing. Updated December 23, 2022. Accessed July 27, 2026. https://www.hhs.gov/hipaa/for-professionals/special-topics/health-information-technology/cloud-computing/index.html
25. Kanter GP, Rekowski JR, Kannarkat JT. Lessons from the change healthcare ransomware attack. *JAMA Health Forum*. 2024;5(9):e242764. doi:10.1001/jamahealthforum.2024.2764.
26. Lakshminarayanan V, Ravikumar A, Sriraman H, Alla S, Chattu VK. Health care equity through intelligent edge computing and augmented reality/virtual reality: a systematic review. *J Multidiscip Healthc*. 2023;16:2839–2859. doi:10.2147/jmdh.s419923.
27. Park A, Jung SY, Yune I, Lee HY. Applying robotic process automation to monitor business processes in hospital information systems: mixed method approach. *JMIR Med Inform*. 2025;13:e59801. doi:10.2196/59801.
28. Bender D, Sartipi K. HL7 FHIR: an Agile and RESTful approach to healthcare information exchange. In: *Proceedings of the IEEE International Conference on Healthcare Informatics*; 2025:128–135. doi:10.1109/ICHI.2025.1234567.
29. CARIN Alliance. *CARIN Code of Conduct for Consumer-facing Applications*. 3rd ed. 2025. Available at: www.carinalliance.com/code-of-conduct. Accessed October 2, 2025.
30. Office of the National Coordinator for Health Information Technology. Trusted Exchange Framework and Common Agreement (TEFCA). 2023. Available at: www.healthit.gov/topic/interoperability/trusted-exchange-framework-and-common-agreement-tefca. Accessed October 2, 2025.
31. Vanderbilt University Medical Center. *Next Level Data Delivery: REDCap Clinical Data Interoperability Services (CDIS)*. Vanderbilt Medicine. Published August 10, 2021. Accessed October 2, 2025. https://medschool.vanderbilt.edu/vanderbilt-medicine/next-level-data-delivery/
32. Lewis B, Cochran C, Marquez E, et al. Use of hospital patient and family advisory councils: a scoping study. *J Patient Exp*. 2025;12. doi:10.1177/23743735251316995.
33. Giacobbe DR, Signori A, Del Puente F, et al. Early detection of sepsis with machine learning techniques: a brief clinical perspective. *Front Med*. 2021;8. doi:10.3389/fmed.2021.617486.
34. Țocu G, Lisă EL, Tutunaru D, et al. The potential of artificial intelligence in the diagnosis and prognosis of sepsis: a narrative review. *Diagnostics*. 2025;15(17):2169. doi:10.3390/diagnostics15172169.
35. Peek ME, Wilkes AE, Roberson TS, et al. Early lessons from an Initiative on chicago's south side to reduce disparities in diabetes care and outcomes. *Health Aff (Millwood)*. 2012;31(1):177–186. doi:10.1377/hlthaff.2011.1058.
36. Urban Health Initiative. University of Chicago Medicine. www.uchicagomedicine.org/about-us/community/urban-health-initiative. Accessed October 2, 2025.
37. NIH All of Us Research Program. Intro to the All of Us Researcher Workbench [Internet]. User Support; 2025 Sep 22 [cited 2025 Oct 2]. Available from: https://support.researchallofus.org/hc/en-us/articles/360039175232-Intro-to-the-All-of-Us-Researcher-Workbench
38. LiveData OR-Dashboard at Massachusetts General Hospital. LiveData. Published 2023. Accessed October 2, 2025. www.livedata.com/press-releases/massachusetts-general-hospital-expands-use-of-livedata-or-dashboard-with-active-time-out
39. Coley Y, Ulloa-Pérez E, Blasi P, Westbrook E, Lozano P, Coleman K. Predicting and preventing missed clinic visits. *Kaiser Permanente Washington Health Research Institute Blog*. June 29, 2022. Accessed October 2, 2025. https://kpwashingtonresearch.org/index.php/news-and-events/blog/2022/predicting-and-preventing-missed-clinic-visits
40. UCLA Health. Novel Intraoperative Imaging Device Advances Precision Surgery for Cancer. www.uclahealth.org/news/article/novel-intraoperative-imaging-device-advances-precision. Published May 22, 2024. Accessed October 2, 2025.
41. Reger GM, Gahm GA, Swanson RD, et al. Virtual reality exposure therapy for combat-related posttraumatic stress disorder. *J Clin Psychol*. 2011;67(8):755–768. doi:10.1002/jclp.20706.

42. Kumar A, Saudagar AKJ, Kumar A, Alkhrijah YM, Raja L. Innovating medical education using a cost effective and scalable VR platform with AI-Driven haptics. *Scientific Reports.* 2025;15(1). doi:10.1038/s41598-025-10543-8.
43. Hubbard HD. Introduction. In: Brinton WC. *Graphic Presentation.* New York: Brinton Associates; 1939:1.
44. Riffe T, Sander N, Klüsener S. Editorial to the Special Issue on Demographic Data Visualization: Getting the point across – Reaching the potential of demographic data visualization. *Demogr Res.* 2021;44(36):865-878. doi:10.4054/DemRes.2021.44.36
45. Dettori JR, Norvell DC. The anatomy of data. *Global Spine J.* 2018;8(3):311–313. doi:10.1177/2192568217746998
46. Talmadge C, Gale J, eds. Introduction to Data Visualization Techniques Using Microsoft Excel 2016. Revised November 2018. Tufts Data Lab. https://sites.tufts.edu/gis/files/2016/02/IntroductiontoDataVisualizationKM_2017-1.pdf. Accessed June 26, 2025.
47. Evergreen S. Small multiples. BetterEvaluation. https://www.betterevaluation.org/methods-approaches/methods/small-multiples. Accessed June 26, 2025.
48. Sukumar H. Line charts vs. area charts: 8 key differences. Inforiver. Published June 6, 2023. https://inforiver.com/insights/line-charts-vs-area-charts-8-key-differences/. Accessed June 26, 2025.
49. Yi M. A complete guide to pie charts. Atlassian. https://www.atlassian.com/data/charts/pie-chart-complete-guide. Accessed June 26, 2025.
50. Morris A. Ultimate guide to bubble charts. NetSuite. September 30, 2021. https://www.netsuite.com/portal/resource/articles/erp/bubble-charts.shtml. Accessed June 26, 2025.
51. GeeksforGeeks. What is Heatmap Data Visualization and How to Use It? Published June 2024. https://www.geeksforgeeks.org/what-is-heatmap-data-visualization-and-how-to-use-it/. Accessed June 25, 2025.
52. Bento C. Create and customize boxplots with Python's Matplotlib to get lots of insights from your data. Towards Data Science. August 1, 2020. https://towardsdatascience.com/create-and-customize-boxplots-with-pythons-matplotlib-to-get-lots-of-insights-from-your-data-d561c9883643/. Accessed June 26, 2025.
53. Interaction Design Foundation – IxDF. Preattentive visual properties and how to use them in information visualization. Interaction Design Foundation – IxDF. October 2, 2018. https://www.interaction-design.org/literature/article/preattentive-visual-properties-and-how-to-use-them-in-information-visualization. Accessed June 26, 2025.
54. Fekete JD, van Wijk JJ, Stasko JT, North C. The value of information visualization. In: Kerren A, Stasko JT, Fekete JD, North C, eds. *Information Visualization: Human-Centered Issues and Perspectives.* Springer; 2008:1–18. doi:10.1007/978-3-540-70956-5_1
55. Elavsky F. Introduction to accessible contrast and color for data visualization. Observable. March 6, 2023. https://observablehq.com/@frankelavsky/chartability-contrast-series. Accessed June 26, 2025.
56. Brewer CA, Harrower M. ColorBrewer 2.0: Color advice for cartography. ColorBrewer2.org. https://colorbrewer2.org/. Accessed June 26, 2025.
57. Brewer C. Color use guidelines for data representation. Proceedings of the Section on Statistical Graphics. 1999. https://www.researchgate.net/profile/Cynthia-Brewer/publication/245692399_Color_Use_Guidelines_for_Data_Representation/links/54b012580cf220c63ccddc0d/Color-Use-Guidelines-for-Data-Representation.pdf. Accessed June 26, 2025.
58. Tufte E. Chartjunk. Edward Tufte: Notebooks and Sketches. January 29, 2015. https://www.edwardtufte.com/notebook/chartjunk/. Accessed June 26, 2025.
59. Wilkinson L. Aesthetics. In: *The Grammar of Graphics.* 2nd ed. New York, NY: Springer; 2005:Chapter 10. https://link.springer.com/chapter/10.1007/0-387-28695-0_10. Accessed June 26, 2025.
60. Khalil MK, Paas F, Johnson TE, Payer AF. Design of interactive and dynamic anatomical visualizations: the implication of cognitive load theory. *Anat Rec B New Anat.* 2005;286(1):15–20.

Chapter 5

Population Health Data Systems

Jarod Parrish, PharmD

Introduction

Population health data systems have become the backbone of contemporary healthcare.[1] These platforms gather and analyze information from electronic health records (EHRs), public health registries, social determinants of health (SDOH), wearable devices, and many other sources. When such diverse data streams are consolidated and translated into actionable insights, clinicians, informaticists, and students can address complex challenges, including chronic disease management, health inequities, and pandemic preparedness.

The importance of robust data systems is growing in parallel with the expansion of digital health services. Telehealth visits, remote patient monitoring, and consumer wearables now generate a constant flow of clinical and behavioral information that must be captured and interpreted in near real time.[2] At the same time, regulators and the public are paying far closer attention to the privacy of health data. In the United States, the Health Insurance Portability and Accountability Act (HIPAA) sets national rules for protecting and reporting on protected health information, while in the European Union, the General Data Protection Regulation (GDPR)[3] gives individuals broad control over their personal data and imposes strict obligations on those who handle it. Together, these frameworks require health organizations to manage information responsibly and transparently in order to maintain public trust.

Advances in big data analytics and artificial intelligence (AI) bring additional opportunities.[5,18,19] Machine learning models can stratify patient risk, forecast disease outbreaks, and personalize care plans in ways that were impossible with traditional reporting tools. Looking ahead, emerging fields like quantum computing promise to accelerate complex simulations and genomic analyses, potentially opening new frontiers in precision medicine and population-level forecasting.[5]

The sections that follow provide an overview of population health data systems, describe their practical applications in clinical and public health settings, and present case studies that illustrate their real-world impact. Each section is written for learners who are new to informatics yet eager to

DOI: 10.4324/9781003593867-7

master the knowledge and skills required to navigate the data-driven future of healthcare, including practicing clinicians, public health professionals, business leaders, health IT specialists, data analytics professionals, and students from every clinical and administrative discipline.

Overview of Population Health Data Systems

Defining Population Health Data Systems

A population health data system can be imagined as a vast public library devoted to community well-being. Its "shelves" hold volumes of clinical encounters, laboratory reports, pharmacy dispenses, insurance claims, air-quality readings, fitness-tracker steps, and other observations that capture the lived experience of patients and populations. A detailed card catalog, better known to informaticists as metadata, records where each data element resides, when it was last updated, and how trustworthy it is. Librarians in this setting are data stewards, analysts, and information managers who ensure that every new "book" is filed correctly, guide users to reliable sources, and recommend additions that close knowledge gaps. Reading rooms take the form of dashboards, analytic workspaces, and decision-support screens where users transform raw data into actionable insight, while the security desk enforces role-based access so confidential information is viewed only by those with a legitimate need.

Healthcare is inherently multidisciplinary, and so the digital library must serve an equally diverse readership. Physicians, pharmacists, nurses, and allied-health practitioners rely on it for point-of-care guidance, while students in medicine, nursing, pharmacy, public health, and business analytics use it to build data literacy. Health IT professionals maintain the technical stacks that keep the system online and data analysts extract patterns that improve quality and reduce costs. Administrators and business leaders evaluate operational efficiency and the return on investment for strategic initiatives, and community-based organizations consult population summaries to tailor outreach programs. By serving a broad audience, the digital library helps break down longstanding barriers among clinical care, public health, social services, business operations, and technology management. This collaboration supports more coordinated care, consistent data governance, shared performance measures, and faster translation of insights into policy and everyday practice.

Core Components of Data Infrastructure and Architecture

Much like the floors of a multistory library, a population health data system is built on a series of structural elements that work together to keep information flowing. First are the data sources and acquisition pipelines that bring new "books" into the collection. EHRs, lab analyzers, imaging archives, immunization registries, insurance claims, and wearable devices each publish their own chapters. If any source is late or missing, readers may find pages torn out of the story, so reliable data feeds are the foundation of trustworthy analytics.

Once the data arrives, harmonization and interoperability translate each volume into a common language. Standards such as Health Level Seven International (HL7), Fast Healthcare Interoperability Resources (FHIR), and Digital Imaging and Communications in Medicine (DICOM) specify the grammar[7] for messages and images, while terminologies like the International Classification of Diseases, Tenth Revision (ICD-10), the Systematized Nomenclature of Medicine Clinical Terms (SNOMED CT), and the Logical Observation Identifiers Names and Codes system (LOINC) provide a shared vocabulary for diagnoses, clinical concepts, and laboratory tests. Integration engines, tools such as Mirth Connect[20] and Cloverleaf,[21] play the role of multilingual librarians who convert and route materials so that a radiology image from one hospital or a lab result from an outside clinic can be understood everywhere in the system.

Storage tiers function as the library stacks, and processing engines are the elevators and conveyor belts that move information to the reading rooms where analysis happens. Clean, well-labeled data are stored in data warehouses, carefully organized floors where every shelf follows a strict classification system so that clinicians, business managers, and analysts can retrieve trustworthy reports without sifting through raw files. In contrast, raw and exploratory content resides in data lakes. This basement archive accepts materials in any format until a future research project determines the best way to sort and classify them. Structured Query Language (SQL) databases power well-defined ad-hoc queries and curated warehouse reporting,[22] while Apache Spark (Spark spreads the work across many computers) orchestrates distributed processing across the lake and warehouse to run statistics and machine learning jobs at scale.[8] It is not a database or a chart-drawing program; rather, it sits between storage and analytics, splitting big queries, statistics, and machine learning tasks into small pieces that many computers handle in parallel, allowing the system to sift through terabytes of live or stored data in minutes instead of hours.[8] Most teams prototype analyses in Python[23] or R[24] using the tools introduced earlier, then scale successful models on Spark[8] or cloud services and surface results in dashboards. Visual platforms such as Tableau[25] and Power BI[26] convert dense data tables into intuitive heat maps and trend lines that busy nurses, pharmacists, therapists, administrators, business managers, public health officials, and data analysts can grasp in seconds.

Finally, governance and data quality policies operate like library bylaws and regular inventory checks. Clear policies state who can see and use which data and for what purpose. Data stewards write simple rules for what counts as complete and correct, automated checks flag duplicates, unusual values, and missing fields, and "data lineage" notes where each item came from and how it changed over time. A small cross-functional group reviews new analytics for ethical, privacy, and equity concerns. The team also updates definitions and removes measures that are no longer useful. These routines help keep the system accurate, relevant, and trustworthy.

Together, these layers form a resilient library of health information where every professional, from bedside clinician to community organizer and from data scientist to chief financial officer, can locate trustworthy evidence, draw accurate conclusions, and act with confidence.

Emerging Trends in Population Health: Big Data, AI, and Quantum Computing

The shelves of our digital health library are expanding faster than any catalog can keep pace. Wearable sensors, social media feeds, genomic sequencers, and networked medical devices now deliver a torrent of new pages every second, a phenomenon often described as big data. The sheer volume, velocity, and variety of these inputs can overwhelm traditional databases, yet they also let researchers and frontline teams detect subtle patterns such as rare medication side effects or the influence of housing insecurity on chronic disease. For students and clinicians alike, the lesson is straightforward: start with clearly framed questions, build scalable storage solutions, and remember that data only adds value when they are organized and interpretable.

AI represents the next wave of innovation within the stacks.[27] Machine learning algorithms study historical records to predict who might miss a follow-up appointment, which lesions on a computed tomography (CT) scan merit closer inspection, or where an infectious outbreak could appear next week. Deep learning models extend this approach to images and narrative notes that once resisted automated analysis. When embedded in EHRs, these systems can generate concise action lists overnight and present them to pharmacists, nurses, therapists, and physicians at morning rounds. All users must still apply professional judgment and guard against biases hidden in historical data, but AI is becoming a routine part of daily workflow across disciplines.

Quantum computing looks more like a future renovation of the library than a tool that most professionals will handle today. Instead of storing information as bits that are either 0 or 1, quantum machines use qubits that can hold multiple states simultaneously, allowing certain calculations to run exponentially faster. In healthcare, this capability could accelerate genome alignment, simulate viral mutations, or optimize ambulance routes for an entire city in real time.[28] Current hardware remains experimental and error-prone, so learners are better served by mastering cloud analytics and AI for now while keeping an eye on quantum breakthroughs that could reshape what is computationally possible.

Big data, AI, and quantum computing push population health from a retrospective discipline toward a real-time, predictive, and ultimately prescriptive science. By understanding the promise and limitations of each trend, professionals in medicine, pharmacy, nursing, allied health, public health, business administration, health IT, and data analytics will be prepared to harness these innovations as they mature.

Practical Applications of Population Health Data Systems

Modern population health tools turn raw numbers, lab results, claims files, step counts from smartwatches, home blood-pressure readings, and even air-quality sensors, into practical insight, but the real magic happens when those insights reshape daily routines. Think of this section as a guided walk through a busy clinic and the neighborhoods it serves. At every stop, we will see how an integrated data platform nudges a decision, improves a conversation, or spares a patient an avoidable trip to the emergency department.

Seeing Trouble Before It Starts: Prevention and Chronic Care

On Monday mornings, the care-management dashboard lights up like a gentle traffic signal. A yellow icon beside Mr. Johnson's name indicates that his average glucose level rose over the weekend and that he missed two doses of metformin, as confirmed by the pharmacy refill record. Searchlight, a predictive module in Lightbeam, flagged the pattern the night before, combining lab drift, missed pills, and social stress notes from the chart.[9] Instead of waiting for his next clinic visit, a diabetes educator messages Mr. Johnson through CareSignal's deviceless platform,[10] asks a few coaching questions, and schedules a telehealth check-in that afternoon. One prompt, 15 minutes, no hospital admission.

A similar story unfolds for hundreds of heart-failure patients whose weight trends are monitored by daily weight prompts by phone or text.[29] The system escalates only the outliers, so nurses spend their day on high-value calls instead of combing through spreadsheets. Over time, the program cuts readmissions, saving both patient energy and payer dollars.

Closing the Distance: Equity and SDOH

Across town, a community clinic maps its hypertensive population against Arcadia's social-risk registry,[11] a dataset that tags each patient with factors such as housing stability, food access, and transportation barriers so clinicians can easily spot social determinants that influence disease. Blue and green dots cluster where bus routes are sparse and grocery stores are distant. The clinic partners with a local food cooperative to deliver produce boxes and uses Lightbeam prompts to remind clinicians to enroll eligible patients. A community partner, Health Leads, links patients directly to these social services.[12] For residents without smartphones, CareSignal offers voice-only check-ins, proving that high-tech aspirations can still run on low-tech phones.

Progress is measured not just in blood-pressure readings, but in quieter victories. A grandmother who once missed appointments because of unreliable transport now arrives on time using a ride service embedded in the same platform.[30] Dashboards translate those anecdotes into hard numbers, showing funders trends in blood pressure control and how supportive services such as medically tailored meal programs can reduce costly utilization.[31]

Staying Ahead of Outbreaks: Public Health Surveillance

In a dimly lit control room at the health department, analysts watch rotating global maps from BlueDot[13] and HealthMap.[14] When chatter about fever clusters in a neighboring county spikes, they pull CommCare field reports[15] from rural clinics to verify. Two hours later, targeted test kits and antiviral stock are moving, days ahead of the first local headline. The infrastructure behind that quick turn is invisible to the public, yet it can mean the difference between a localized flare and a regional crisis.

Point-of-Care Confidence: Decision Support and Personalization

Back at the hospital, Dr. Smith orders antibiotics for a patient with declining kidney function. A red banner appears: "Consider lower-dose cefepime; creatinine clearance 28 mL/min." The alert is generated by the hospital's EHR clinical decision support rules. Dr. Smith adjusts the order with a single click. Later that day, a knee-replacement patient answers her daily recovery check-in, an automated text from CareSignal's deviceless platform, and reports rising pain and difficulty bearing weight. Once the system notices a troubling trend, CareSignal alerts the care team, who flag her for a physical therapy consult.[32] The machine does the watching, clinicians keep the caring.

Keeping the Lights On: Operations and Finance

Behind every successful clinic visit is a billing office that relies on clear information. Natural language processing software reviews yesterday's progress notes, flags potential gaps in diagnosis and severity coding, and prompts coders to correct them before claims are submitted.[36] On the operations side, a straightforward dashboard predicts how many beds will be occupied tomorrow, allowing the nurse manager to adjust staffing without costly agency help. Small improvements add up: in one quarter, a text-based support program for people with COPD cut emergency visits by about 30%,[17] according to vendor-reported outcomes, freeing resources the hospital could redirect to community health programs.

At a Glance

From early-morning dashboards to late-night outbreak alerts, population health systems act like an extra set of eyes and ears across the continuum of care. They warn, guide, and confirm, letting clinicians focus on empathy and judgment. The result is a health service that feels smaller, more personal, even as it draws power from vast, interconnected data streams. A pilot as simple as voice-based symptom tracking can start the journey, proving value and building trust for larger leaps to come.

Case Studies

CASE STUDY 1: SOUTHEAST REGIONAL HEALTH ALLIANCE—DATA-DRIVEN HEART FAILURE CARE

Context: Southeast Regional Health Alliance (SRHA) is a clinically integrated network formed in 2014 that now spans 73 hospitals, 13 health systems, and nearly 6,900 physicians across Tennessee, Georgia, and Alabama. The alliance's population health team partnered with academic data scientists to embed real-time risk models and social-risk dashboards into everyday workflows.

Intervention: A machine learning model predicts 30-day readmission risk for heart-failure patients by combining EHR data, pharmacy refill histories, and recent weight trends. High-risk patients enroll in a remote blood-pressure monitoring program modeled on a validated postpartum hypertension protocol.[33] SRHA's social-risk dashboard, inspired by Atrium Health's Community Resource Hub,[35] flags transportation or food insecurity, prompting care managers to schedule rides or produce-box deliveries.

Outcomes: During the first 18 months, SRHA reported improvements consistent with published programs, including reductions in readmissions and better cost performance, echoing results from the postpartum hypertension remote-monitoring program[33] and Atrium Health's social risk initiatives.[35] In intensive-care units, a sepsis early-warning approach adapted from the Epic Sepsis Model Inpatient Predictive Analytic Tool[34] was externally evaluated, showing variable performance and underscoring the need for local validation and monitoring.

Lessons for learners:

- Pairing predictive models with concrete workflows turns forecasts into action.
- Layering data on social determinants alongside clinical risk reveals hidden barriers and directs resources where they are needed.
- Sharing code and protocols across institutions accelerates innovation without starting from scratch.

Conclusion

Population health data systems sit at the crossroads of bedside compassion, advanced analytics, and public policy. When clinicians, informaticists, and policymakers collaborate around a shared data foundation, everyday decisions, such as adjusting a medication dose or scheduling a ride to the clinic, scale into measurable gains for entire communities. Yet technology alone cannot guarantee success. Strong governance frameworks, clear data-quality standards, and ethical safeguards protect patient trust while ensuring that algorithms serve equity rather than amplify bias. As roles evolve, nurses, pharmacists, therapists, and data analysts will spend less time searching for information and more time interpreting real-time dashboards and prescriptive alerts that recommend the next best action.

As these technologies mature, streaming data from wearables, environmental sensors, and connected devices will shift population health from episodic care toward continuous monitoring and intervention. Artificial intelligence copilots may progress from predicting risk to recommending step-by-step care strategies, while quantum computing could eventually accelerate complex resource-allocation decisions. Preparing for this future will require learners to combine clinical judgment, data literacy, and knowledge of privacy law. Even as technology advances, the most important element of any digital health system will remain an engaged and ethically grounded care team.

Assessment Questions and Answers

1) Multiple choice: Which statement best defines a population health data system as introduced in this chapter?
   A. A single software program that replaces all hospital systems
   B. A coordinated ecosystem of data sources, standards, storage, processing, analytics, and governance that turns raw information into action across communities
   C. A billing platform that automates claims
   D. A patient portal for secure messaging only

   Answer: B

2) Multiple choice: In the chapter's library metaphor, which mapping is most accurate?
   A. Shelves = network switches; catalog = HL7; reading rooms = routers
   B. Shelves = clinical, claims, and device data; catalog = metadata; reading rooms = dashboards and analytic workspaces
   C. Shelves = pharmaceuticals; catalog = CPT codes; reading rooms = operating rooms
   D. Shelves = encryption, catalog = nurses, reading rooms = firewalls

   Answer: B

3) True or false: HL7 v2 and FHIR are messaging and API standards, while ICD-10, SNOMED CT, and LOINC are clinical terminologies and code systems.

   Answer: True

4) Multiple choice: Which pairing correctly matches each interoperability standard to its primary role?
   A. DICOM, imaging objects and workflows; HL7 v2, event messages; FHIR, modern web APIs
   B. DICOM, pharmacy dispensing; HL7 v2, image compression; FHIR, device drivers
   C. DICOM, payer contracts; HL7 v2, encryption; FHIR, database storage
   D. DICOM, legal consent; HL7 v2, radiology viewers; FHIR, spreadsheets

   Answer: A

5) Short answer: In one or two sentences, define interoperability and explain why it matters for population health.

   Answer: Interoperability is the reliable, secure exchange and use of information across different systems and organizations. It matters because population health strategies require clinical, claims, public health, and social data to move seamlessly so teams can coordinate prevention, equity, and quality improvement.

6) Multiple choice: A team needs trusted monthly quality measures and consistent cost reports. Which storage pattern should they favor and why?
   A. Data lake, because it stores only curated tables
   B. Data warehouse, because it organizes cleaned, governed data for repeatable reporting
   C. Local spreadsheets, because they are easy to edit
   D. Object storage only, because it is cheapest

   Answer: B

7) True or false: Apache Spark is a database that stores patient records.

   Answer: False. Spark is a distributed processing engine that runs queries, statistics, and machine learning across large datasets.

8) Short answer: What problems do integration engines like Mirth Connect and Cloverleaf solve in a population health architecture?

   Answer: They translate, route, and monitor messages among systems that use different formats or versions, ensuring data from labs, EHRs, registries, and devices arrives in the right place and structure for analytics and care coordination.

9) Multiple choice: Which statement best describes the difference between HIPAA and GDPR in this chapter's context?
   A. HIPAA applies to all personal data in the United States, GDPR only to hospitals
   B. HIPAA governs protected health information in US healthcare, while GDPR governs personal data broadly in the European Union with individual data rights
   C. Both laws cover only de-identified data
   D. GDPR applies only to research data, HIPAA to clinical data

   Answer: B

10) Short answer: Describe the role of governance and data quality in one or two sentences.
    Answer: Governance defines accountability, policies, and processes for responsible data use, while data quality ensures completeness, accuracy, timeliness, and lineage. Together, they keep the system trustworthy and prevent drift in measures and models.

Answer Explanations

1) Q1: A population health data system is an ecosystem that integrates sources, standards, storage, processing, analytics, and governance to turn raw inputs into coordinated action. A single product cannot cover that scope.

2) Q2: In the metaphor, shelves represent diverse data (clinical, claims, devices), the catalog is metadata that tracks where items are and how trustworthy they are, and reading rooms are dashboards and analytic workspaces where people interpret the data.
3) Q3: HL7 v2 and FHIR define how systems exchange information. ICD-10, SNOMED CT, and LOINC name and organize clinical concepts so that exchanged data are meaningful and comparable.
4) Q4: DICOM is the imaging standard for objects and workflows, HL7 v2 sends event messages such as lab results or admissions, and FHIR enables modern web APIs for clinical data exchange.
5) Q5: Interoperability means information can move securely and be used across different systems and organizations. Population health relies on this so teams can coordinate prevention, equity efforts, and quality improvement across settings.
6) Q6: A data warehouse stores curated, governed data for stable, repeatable reporting. Data lakes are better for raw and exploratory work, not for monthly quality and cost measures that must be consistent.
7) Q7: Apache Spark is a distributed processing engine that spreads work across many computers to run queries, statistics, and machine learning at scale. It is not a database that stores records.
8) Q8: Integration engines like Mirth Connect and Cloverleaf translate, route, and monitor messages between systems that use different formats or versions, ensuring data arrives in the right place and structure.
9) Q9: HIPAA governs protected health information in US healthcare. GDPR governs personal data broadly in the European Union and grants individual rights such as access, rectification, data portability, and erasure. Option B captures this difference in scope and rights most accurately.
10) Q10: Governance sets responsibilities and allowed uses, while data quality checks completeness, accuracy, timeliness, and lineage. Together they keep measures and models trustworthy over time.

References

1. Buntin MB, Burke MF, Hoaglin MC, Blumenthal D. The benefits of health information technology: A review of the recent literature shows predominantly positive results. *Health Aff (Millwood)*. 2011;30(3):464–471. doi:10.1377/hlthaff.2011.0178
2. Kvedar J, Coye M, Everett W. Connected health: A review of technologies and strategies to improve patient care with telemedicine and telehealth. *Health Aff (Millwood)*. 2014;33(2):194–199.
3. U.S. Department of Health and Human Services. Summary of the HIPAA Privacy Rule. Published 2013. Accessed July 25, 2025. www.hhs.gov/hipaa
4. European Parliament and Council. Regulation (EU) 2016/679 (General Data Protection Regulation). *Off J Eur Union*. 2016;59(L 119):1–88.
5. Raghupathi W, Raghupathi V. Big data analytics in healthcare: Promise and potential. *Health Inf Sci Syst*. 2014;2(3). doi:10.1186/2047-2501-2-3
6. Chow JCL. Quantum computing in medicine. *Med Sci (Basel)*. 2024;12(4):67. doi:10.3390/medsci12040067
7. HL7 International. HL7 standards: Overview and index. Published 2021. Accessed July 25, 2025. www.hl7.org/implement/standards/index.cfm?ref=nav

8. Zaharia M, Xin RS, Wendell P, et al. Apache spark: A unified engine for big data processing. *Commun ACM*. 2016;59(11):56–65. doi:10.1145/2934664
9. Lightbeam Health Solutions. Risk stratification: Searchlight. Published 2023. Accessed July 25, 2025. https://lightbeamhealth.com/risk-stratification-searchlight/
10. CareSignal. 13 Texas Health Centers Implement Deviceless RPM to Improve Engagement and Outcomes Among Vulnerable Populations. Lightbeam Health Solutions case study. Published 2023. Accessed June 26, 2026. https://lightbeamhealth.com/wp-content/uploads/2026/01/Texas_Association_of_Community_Health_Centers_Implements_Deviceless_RPM-_Case_Study_2023.pdf
11. Arcadia. SDOH Package. Published 2023. Accessed July 25, 2025. https://arcadia.io/sdoh-package
12. Health Leads. Connecting patients to community resources. Published 2024. Accessed July 25, 2025. https://healthleadsusa.org/
13. Franck T. *BlueDot used Artificial Intelligence to Predict Coronavirus Spread*. CNBC. March 3, 2020. Accessed July 25, 2025. https://www.cnbc.com/2020/03/03/bluedot-used-artificial-intelligence-to-predict-coronavirus-spread.html
14. Brownstein JS, Freifeld CC, Madoff LC. HealthMap: Global infectious disease monitoring through automated classification and visualization of Internet media reports. *J Am Med Inform Assoc*. 2008;15(2):150–157.
15. Dimagi. The CommCare evidence base for frontline workers. Published 2022. Accessed July 25, 2025. www.dimagi.com/evidence-base/frontline-workers
16. CareSignal. Achieve outcomes, scale, and ROI with deviceless remote patient monitoring. Published 2024. Accessed July 25, 2025. https://www.caresignal.health/news/deviceless_rpm_strategy
17. CareSignal. Evidence. Published 2024. Accessed July 25, 2025. https://caresignal.health/evidence/
18. Groves P, Kayyali B, Knott D, Kuiken S. *The "Big Data" Revolution in Healthcare*. McKinsey & Company; 2013.
19. Murdoch TB, Detsky AS. The inevitable application of big data to health care. *JAMA*. 2013;309(13):1351–1352. doi:10.1001/jama.2013.393
20. NextGen Healthcare. Mirth Connect integration engine. Published 2024. Accessed July 25, 2025. www.nextgen.com/solutions/interoperability/mirth-integration-engine
21. Infor. Infor Cloverleaf integration engine. Published 2024. Accessed July 25, 2025. www.infor.com/products/cloverleaf
22. Oracle. Introduction to SQL (Oracle Database 23c). Published 2025. Accessed July 25, 2025. https://docs.oracle.com/en/database/oracle/oracle-database/23/cncpt/sql.html
23. Python Software Foundation. Python 3.12.4 documentation. Published 2024. Accessed July 25, 2025. https://docs.python.org/3/
24. R Core Team. R: A language and environment for statistical computing. *R Foundation for Statistical Computing*; 2023.
25. Tableau Software. Tableau platform overview. Published 2023. Accessed July 25, 2025. www.tableau.com
26. Microsoft. Power BI documentation overview. Published 2023. Accessed July 25, 2025. https://learn.microsoft.com/power-bi
27. Suleyman M, Ellis M. *The Coming Wave: Technology, Power, and the 21st Century's Greatest Dilemma*. Crown Publishing Group; 2023.
28. Raza AS, Wang J. Quantum computing research in medical sciences. *Comput Struct Biotechnol J*. 2024;22:1631–1644. https://pmc.ncbi.nlm.nih.gov/articles/PMC12055853/
29. Seto E, Leonard KJ, Cafazzo JA, Masino C, Barnsley J, Ross HJ. Mobile phone based telemonitoring for heart failure management: A randomized controlled trial. *J Med Internet Res*. 2012;14(3):e31. doi:10.2196/jmir.1909

30. Chaiyachati KH, Hubbard RA, Yeager A, et al. Association of rideshare based transportation services and missed primary care appointments: A clinical trial. *JAMA Intern Med.* 2018;178(3):383–389. doi:10.1001/jamainternmed.2017.8332
31. Berkowitz SA, Terranova J, Hill C, et al. Meal delivery programs reduce the use of costly health care in dually eligible Medicare and Medicaid beneficiaries. Health Aff (*Millwood*). 2019;38(4):659–666. doi:10.1377/hlthaff.2017.0999
32. CareSignal (Lightbeam). Clinical programs. Published 2024. Accessed July 25, 2025. https://lightbeamhealth.com/deviceless-remote-patient-monitoring/
33. Hirshberg A, Downes KL, Edens KL, Tuuli MG, Cahill AG. Implementation of a remote blood pressure monitoring program reduces readmissions for postpartum hypertension. *Obstet Gynecol.* 2018;132(6):1480–1488. doi:10.1097/AOG.0000000000002979
34. Wong A, Otles E, Donnelly JP, et al. External validation of a widely implemented proprietary sepsis prediction model in hospitalized patients. *JAMA Intern Med.* 2021;181(8):1065–1070. doi:10.1001/jamainternmed.2021.2626
35. Atrium Health. Social health needs. Published 2024. Accessed July 25, 2025. https://atriumhealth.org/community/health/social-health-needs
36. Dai HJ, Wang CK, Chen CC, et al. Evaluating a natural language processing–driven, AI-assisted ICD-10-CM coding system for diagnosis-related groups in a real hospital environment: Algorithm development and validation study. *J Med Internet Res.* 2024;26:e58278. doi:10.2196/58278

Chapter 6

The Belmont Data and AI Collaborative Hypertension in Nashville Dataset

Anthony Blash, PharmD, BCompSc, CPHIMS

Overview of the Belmont Data Collaborative

Introduction to the Belmont Data Collaborative

The Belmont Data and AI Collaborative (BDAIC) is a pioneering initiative designed to harness the transformative power of data science, artificial intelligence (AI), and collaborative research to address critical public health and societal challenges. Launched in August 2021 with a $60 million five-year institutional investment, the BDAIC is a cornerstone of Belmont University's mission to cultivate a "data mindset" across disciplines and to empower communities through data-informed decision-making. More than just a campus resource, the BDAIC is envisioned as a regional and national hub, bringing together universities, healthcare providers, community organizations, and policymakers to cocreate solutions that improve health outcomes and reduce disparities.[1]

The creation of the BDAIC marked a bold step for Belmont University, signaling a recognition that the future of education, healthcare, and social development depends on the responsible integration of data and AI. The initiative underscores Belmont's strategic commitment to becoming a leader in data literacy and applied analytics while remaining deeply rooted in its values of hope, unity, and belonging. The Collaborative's guiding framework—Data for All, Data for Good, and Data for Diversity—is not only aspirational but also operational, shaping every project, partnership, and platform developed under its umbrella.[1]

Mission and Vision

The BDAIC's mission is to advance health and societal well-being by embedding data science and AI into education, research, and community engagement. Belmont envisions a future where all graduates, regardless of discipline, possess the data literacy skills necessary to critically evaluate,

DOI: 10.4324/9781003593867-8

responsibly apply, and ethically innovate with data. By weaving data literacy into the fabric of university culture, Belmont aims to empower graduates to shape industries ranging from healthcare to business, law, education, and the arts.[2]

The Collaborative also serves as a bridge between academia and community, positioning Belmont as a convening force in Tennessee and beyond. Its vision emphasizes three primary values:

1. **Data for All**—democratizing data skills by embedding data-driven thinking into every field of study and ensuring accessibility for students, faculty, and community partners.
2. **Data for Good**—applying data science and AI to address pressing public health, social, and economic issues, from hypertension in Nashville to combating human trafficking.
3. **Data for Diversity**—fostering inclusivity by ensuring that data collection, analysis, and application reflect diverse populations and contribute to reducing disparities.

These values are reinforced through curricular integration, research initiatives, and external partnerships that prioritize both excellence and equity.

Core Objectives and Focus Areas

To fulfill its mission, the BDAIC advances a set of interlocking objectives that cut across disciplines and sectors. A central priority is data integration, where comprehensive datasets are developed by unifying information from healthcare, education, and community systems. This integrated perspective enables more holistic insights into public health challenges. For instance, the *Hypertension in Nashville* project combines insurance claims with social determinants of health (SDOH), revealing geographic disparities that might otherwise remain hidden.[3]

Equally important is the BDAIC's commitment to interdisciplinary collaboration. Faculty and students from pharmacy, nursing, law, business, liberal arts, and data science are brought together to address shared problems. These collaborations often take the form of hackathons, research expos, and cross-disciplinary labs that encourage innovative approaches and solutions not bound by traditional academic silos.[4]

The Collaborative also places a strong emphasis on community engagement, ensuring that research questions and outcomes are not only academically rigorous but also relevant to and shaped by the lived experiences of local populations. Projects such as *Project WELL* exemplify this approach, emphasizing codesign with community organizations to more effectively address mental health disparities.[5]

Finally, ethical data use serves as a guiding principle across all BDAIC initiatives. Belmont's values of transparency, privacy, and responsibility are embedded into every stage of the data lifecycle—from acquisition and anonymization to dissemination and policy translation. This holistic orientation distinguishes the BDAIC from many university-based data centers, highlighting an approach that prioritizes not only technical capacity but also human-centered and ethically responsible outcomes.[1]

Stakeholders and Partnerships

The strength of the BDAIC lies in its partnerships. By design, the Collaborative operates as a networked ecosystem, bringing together diverse stakeholders whose insights and resources create a rich environment for innovation. At the heart of this ecosystem are academic institutions, particularly Belmont's faculty and students. Through curriculum redesign, faculty embed data-driven projects across a wide range of courses, from the health sciences to the humanities. Annual events such as the Research Expo highlight these efforts, showcasing student and faculty work—often leveraging AI to address pressing community challenges.[4]

Equally vital are healthcare providers, who extend the Collaborative's reach into real-world practice. Key partners such as BlueCross BlueShield of Tennessee and Change Healthcare supply claims data, analytics expertise, and strategic guidance on population health. Local hospitals and clinics also play an essential role, offering students opportunities to work with de-identified electronic health records (EHRs) in applied settings.[3]

The BDAIC's work is further enriched through partnerships with community organizations. Nonprofits such as Engage Together and Caring Ways bring lived expertise and a direct connection to the populations most affected by health disparities. By involving community members in shaping research questions, the Collaborative ensures that projects are actionable and responsive rather than abstract exercises.[6]

Finally, government agencies contribute a crucial policy dimension. State and local health departments not only provide regulatory support but also act as conduits for translating data insights into programmatic interventions that can influence public health strategy on a broader scale.[1]

Taken together, this multipronged stakeholder engagement ensures that the BDAIC's work does not remain confined within academia. Instead, its projects extend outward, directly influencing healthcare delivery, shaping public health initiatives, and empowering communities.

Technological Infrastructure

The BDAIC is supported by cutting-edge infrastructure housed within Belmont's Jack C. Massey Center. Its tools and platforms allow faculty, students, and partners to collect, analyze, and share complex data securely and efficiently[7]: EHRs provide de-identified patient records that serve as the foundation for health equity studies, particularly in projects targeting chronic conditions such as hypertension and diabetes.[3,8] To support these efforts, the Collaborative has developed a secure, cloud-based data warehouse that integrates diverse datasets, accompanied by RoundTable—a companion platform that enables interactive mapping and visualization of SDOH across Tennessee communities. Building on this infrastructure, Belmont's analysts leverage advanced analytics platforms and machine learning models to identify predictive risk factors, uncover patterns in population health, and evaluate fairness metrics in AI-driven decision-making. Complementing these tools is the Relight platform, launched in 2022, which functions as an online collaboration hub that allows multi-sector teams to connect, share insights, and cocreate targeted interventions.

Together, these tools establish Belmont as a regional leader in data infrastructure, capable of handling sensitive health and community data while providing user-friendly platforms for stakeholders.[7]

Flagship Projects

Several high-impact projects illustrate the Collaborative's mission in action. The *Hypertension in Nashville Dataset* maps geographic disparities in hypertension prevalence, focusing on ZIP codes with the highest burden. By combining claims data, SDOH, and geospatial analysis, the BDC has created a robust dataset for both student learning and community intervention design.[3]

Project WELL is a mental health equity initiative targeting young adults (ages 18–39) in Nashville. Using Belmont's DDIA Framework (Dilemma, Data, Insights, Action), the project involves nonprofit partners like CaringWays to codevelop mental health programs and measure their impact.

The "*Connecting the Dots*" *Mental Health Report* provides a comprehensive county- and ZIP-level analysis of mental health vulnerabilities across Tennessee. Findings from this work were presented at the SCORE–NashvilleHealth symposium in 2024, offering actionable data for policymakers and nonprofits.[5]

In addition, the *Engage Together Collaboration* leveraged a partnership with Engage Together to create a data-driven tool that maps community vulnerabilities to human trafficking. This tool has gained national recognition and has been cited by policymakers advocating for a federal anti-trafficking database. Together, these projects demonstrate how Belmont is translating academic research into community impact, while also providing rich learning experiences for students.[6]

Challenges and Solutions

Establishing and maintaining a data collaborative of this scale is not without its challenges. Key challenges include data privacy and security, as safeguarding sensitive patient and community data is paramount. Belmont addresses this through robust anonymization processes and strict adherence to HIPAA and state privacy laws. Another challenge is data quality, where ensuring accuracy, completeness, and consistency requires rigorous validation and cleaning protocols embedded into all workflows.[2]

Interoperability also poses difficulties, since data from healthcare providers, nonprofits, and public agencies often arrive in different formats; these issues are mitigated through standardization processes and partnerships with technology vendors. Finally, sustainability remains a core concern, as maintaining funding and stakeholder engagement depends on demonstrating continuous impact. The BDAIC tackles this by aligning projects with community needs and producing visible, actionable outcomes.[2]

To address these challenges, the BDAIC has implemented several solutions. For data privacy and security, all health and claims data undergo rigorous anonymization and de-identification before being stored or analyzed, ensuring that no personally identifiable information is retained. The BDAIC also operates a secure, HIPAA-compliant cloud-based data warehouse with encryption both in transit and at rest. Beyond technology, Belmont established a data governance framework aligned with Institutional Review Board (IRB) standards and state-level privacy requirements, providing oversight and accountability across all projects. These measures enable the BDAIC to responsibly handle large-scale datasets while maintaining public trust.[1]

For data quality, the Collaborative has designed automated cleaning pipelines that detect and correct errors such as duplicate records, missing values, and formatting inconsistencies before datasets are integrated into the warehouse. Validation tools and quality benchmarks are systematically applied, while faculty and students are trained to collaboratively audit datasets as part of their research projects. This dual approach to technical automation, combined with human oversight, ensures the production of high-quality, dependable data resources.[3]

Addressing interoperability, the BDAIC uses standardization protocols such as HL7 and FHIR to align health data across systems, enabling seamless integration. It also developed RoundTable, a visualization and mapping platform that consolidates diverse datasets and allows stakeholders to explore SDOH in a unified format. Partnerships with technology vendors and healthcare providers, including Change Healthcare and BlueCross BlueShield of Tennessee, further ensure efficient integration of claims data, EHRs, and geospatial information.[7]

Finally, for sustainability, the BDAIC aligns projects with community needs to ensure continued relevance and impact, as seen with Project WELL and the Hypertension in Nashville dataset. To keep stakeholders engaged, the Collaborative hosts an annual Research Xpo where faculty and students present data-informed projects, and it launched Relight, an online hub that supports year-round interdisciplinary collaboration. Financially, Belmont's initial $60 million institutional investment is reinforced by competitive grants and philanthropic partnerships, creating a diversified funding base that secures the Collaborative's future.[4]

Through these strategies, the BDAIC sustains its role as both a technical and ethical leader in collaborative data science. Its solutions, combining secure infrastructure, rigorous quality assurance, interoperable standards, and sustainable engagement, position the Collaborative as a model for universities nationwide seeking to integrate data, AI, and community engagement.[2]

By embedding data literacy into curricula, launching cutting-edge projects, and engaging deeply with community partners, the BDAIC exemplifies how universities can act as catalysts for positive societal change. While challenges remain, Belmont's commitment to "Data for All, Data for Good, and Data for Diversity" ensures that the Collaborative will continue to shape health and societal outcomes for years to come.

Hypertension (HTN) in Nashville Dataset

Background and Significance

Hypertension (HTN), or high blood pressure, is a leading risk factor for cardiovascular diseases, which remain the number one cause of death globally. In the United States, HTN affects nearly half of the adult population, with significant disparities observed across racial and socioeconomic lines. Nashville, Tennessee, is no exception to this trend, with a high prevalence of HTN, particularly among African American and low-income communities. Recent reports indicate that nearly one-third of Nashville's residents are affected, and some neighborhoods experience prevalence rates as high as 47.3%, far above national averages.[1] These disparities are compounded by environmental and socioeconomic barriers. Belmont University's Healthy Community Insights (HCI) platform, which integrates public and private datasets, shows that more than 70% of Nashville's population lives in areas with limited access to healthy food. For example, in ZIP code 37228, there are no grocery stores or farmers' markets, but 62 fast-food outlets—a stark example of how structural factors contribute to the development and poor control of hypertension.[1,3]

The HTN in Nashville dataset, curated by the BDAIC, is a comprehensive collection of health data aimed at understanding the epidemiology, management, and outcomes of hypertension in the Nashville area. The dataset includes de-identified patient records from multiple healthcare providers, including demographic information, clinical measurements, medication histories, and outcomes data. Additionally, the dataset incorporates SDOH such as income, education, and access to healthcare services, providing a holistic view of the factors influencing HTN in this population. By combining these elements, the dataset serves as both a research tool and a community-facing resource that illustrates how social, environmental, and medical drivers intersect to shape health disparities.[3,7]

Data Collection and Methodology

The HTN in Nashville dataset was compiled through a collaborative effort involving multiple healthcare institutions across the Nashville area. Data were collected from EHRs, patient surveys, and community health assessments to capture a comprehensive view of hypertension management and outcomes in the region. The dataset now spans a seven-year period, from 2018 through 2025, and includes more than 70,000 unique patient records.[9]

To ensure data quality and consistency, the BDAIC implemented a rigorous data cleaning and validation process. This included the removal of duplicate records, the imputation of missing values, and the standardization of clinical measurements such as blood pressure, BMI, and laboratory results to maintain comparability across contributing institutions.[3]

Following validation, the dataset was anonymized and de-identified in compliance with HIPAA regulations, ensuring that no personally identifiable information could be reconstructed. This process supports both the ethical use of data and the protection of patient privacy while maintaining the dataset's analytical value for population health research.[3]

In addition to this traditional clinical data, the BDAIC integrated multiple public sources, including Metro Public Health Department reports, County Health Rankings, and Vanderbilt University's "Hypertension Prescription for Nashville" report. These were consolidated through Belmont's Data Warehouse, visualized through the RoundTable mapping platform, and supported by the Relight collaboration hub, which connects stakeholders in real time. This methodological framework ensures that the dataset is not simply a static collection of numbers but a dynamic, interactive ecosystem that empowers both academic researchers and community partners to codevelop interventions.[1,7]

Key Findings

Preliminary analysis of the *Hypertension in Nashville* dataset has already generated several important insights into the burden of chronic disease and the inequities that shape its distribution. The dataset confirms the high prevalence of hypertension in Nashville, while also documenting sharp disparities across racial and socioeconomic groups. African American and low-income populations exhibit higher rates of uncontrolled hypertension and poorer health outcomes when compared to white and higher-income counterparts. Complementing these findings, BDAIC's *HCI* platform revealed that Black Medicare beneficiaries in Nashville face 27–28% higher annual costs related to hypertension than white beneficiaries, and they are more likely to experience hospitalizations and emergency room visits tied to poorly managed conditions.[2,4] Together, these findings highlight the ways in which racial and economic inequities directly influence disease burden and outcomes.

The inclusion of SDOH data further underscores the impact of structural factors on hypertension management. Patients with lower income and education levels are less likely to adhere to prescribed medications and more likely to encounter barriers when attempting to access care. Belmont's data platforms demonstrate that food availability, transportation options, neighborhood safety, and housing quality are not peripheral concerns but central determinants of health outcomes.[1,2] For instance, communities with limited access to grocery stores but abundant fast-food outlets exhibit disproportionately high rates of uncontrolled hypertension, clearly linking environmental inequities to disparities in chronic disease.

The dataset has also provided a foundation for evaluating the effectiveness of targeted interventions. Community-based programs offering free blood pressure screenings and health education have shown measurable improvements in hypertension control among underserved populations. Through *Relight*, the BDAIC facilitates real-time collaboration between nonprofits, clinicians, and researchers, allowing such interventions to be refined and scaled. Pilot projects in ZIP codes with the highest prevalence of hypertension—combining routine blood pressure checks with nutrition counseling and physical activity resources—have demonstrated early success in improving medication adherence and reducing modifiable risk factors.[1,3] These results reinforce the value of community-engaged, place-based approaches to chronic disease prevention and management.

Finally, the dataset has enabled the application of advanced analytics and machine learning methods to develop predictive models for hypertension outcomes. These models have the potential to flag high-risk patients and inform more tailored interventions. Belmont has gone further by embedding fairness-aware algorithms into its predictive frameworks, ensuring that these tools do not inadvertently reinforce inequities already present in the healthcare system.[2,3] This commitment reflects the Collaborative's core value of *Data for Diversity* and highlights the importance of embedding ethical oversight into all applications of AI and machine learning in healthcare.

Limitations and Future Research

While the HTN in Nashville dataset provides valuable insights, it is not without its limitations. Despite rigorous cleaning and validation, some data may still be incomplete or inaccurate, particularly when self-reported surveys are combined with clinical records. The dataset is also specific to the Nashville area and may not be generalizable to other regions or populations. In addition, because it spans a five-year period, temporal changes in population demographics, healthcare practices, and neighborhood development may affect the results.

Belmont acknowledges these challenges by positioning the dataset as a "snapshot" that must be continually updated to maintain relevance. Future research using the HTN in Nashville dataset could focus on longitudinal analyses that track changes in prevalence and outcomes over extended time periods, integration with additional data sources such as genomic or environmental exposure data, and the use of randomized controlled trials to evaluate the effectiveness of community-driven interventions.[3,4] Belmont's Exposed–Intervene–Prevent framework is one such step forward, aiming not only to measure disparities but also to forecast the effects of targeted policies or community interventions on reducing hypertension across ZIP codes.

The HTN in Nashville dataset demonstrates how Belmont University's Data and AI Collaborative is leveraging both data science and community partnerships to address pressing health disparities. By merging de-identified clinical records with SDOH indicators and applying advanced analytics, the dataset provides a nuanced understanding of hypertension that accounts for both medical and social realities. Its findings—persistent racial and socioeconomic disparities, links between food access and health outcomes, evidence of intervention success, and the promise of predictive modeling—illustrate the potential of data-driven strategies to transform public health.

Although limitations exist, the BDAIC's infrastructure, which includes its Data Warehouse, RoundTable visualization tool, and Relight collaboration hub, ensures that the dataset remains actionable and sustainable. With continuous updates, ethical oversight, and strong stakeholder engagement, the HTN in Nashville dataset stands as both a model of academic innovation and a catalyst for community health improvement. It exemplifies Belmont's mission of *Data for All, Data for Good, and Data for Diversity*, while reinforcing the role of universities as engines of social transformation.

Applications and Insights

Clinical Applications

The HTN in Nashville dataset is publicly accessible through Belmont's Data & AI Collaborative (BDAIC) and provides an opportunity for students, researchers, healthcare professionals, and community organizations to explore real-world healthcare data and examine relationships between hypertension outcomes and social determinants of health. By making these data resources available, BDAIC supports data literacy, community-based research, and evidence-informed decision-making.

The HTN in Nashville dataset has numerous clinical applications, particularly in the realm of personalized medicine. By analyzing the dataset, healthcare providers can identify patterns and predictors of HTN that may not be apparent through traditional clinical methods. For example, the dataset can be used to develop risk scores that help identify patients at high risk for developing complications related to HTN, such as stroke or heart failure.[9]

Additionally, the dataset can inform the development of tailored treatment plans. For instance, if the data reveal that certain demographic groups respond better to specific medications, clinicians can use this information to optimize treatment regimens. This approach not only improves patient outcomes but also reduces healthcare costs by minimizing trial-and-error prescribing. Belmont's Data Warehouse and RoundTable visualization platform further enhance this process by allowing healthcare providers and researchers to overlay clinical outcomes with SDOH, revealing neighborhood-level risk factors such as food insecurity, transportation barriers, and lack of primary care access.[1,3] This integration moves personalized medicine beyond the clinic by embedding it in the lived realities of patients' environments, enabling clinicians to create treatment approaches that are both biologically and socially informed.

Public Health Implications

From a public health perspective, the HTN in Nashville dataset provides valuable insights into the social and environmental factors that contribute to HTN. These insights can inform the development of targeted public health interventions aimed at reducing the prevalence of HTN and improving health equity. For example, the dataset has been used to identify neighborhoods with high rates of uncontrolled HTN. Public health officials can use this information to allocate resources more effectively, such as by increasing the availability of free blood pressure screenings in these areas or implementing community education programs.

The dataset also underscores the importance of addressing SDOH in HTN management. Policies aimed at improving access to healthcare, increasing health literacy, and reducing poverty could have a significant impact on HTN outcomes in Nashville and beyond. Belmont's HCI has highlighted striking geographic and social patterns in hypertension burden across Nashville, demonstrating that hypertension risk is influenced by interconnected clinical, environmental, and socioeconomic factors. These insights allow public health stakeholders to not only target clinical interventions but also to advocate for systemic change in food access, housing, and transportation policy, reflecting the BDAIC's *Data for Good* value in action.

Business and Policy Applications

The HTN in Nashville dataset also has important implications for healthcare business and policy. For healthcare administrators, the dataset can be used to identify gaps in care and optimize resource allocation. For example, if the data reveal that a significant proportion of patients are not adhering to their prescribed medications, administrators can implement programs to improve medication adherence, such as patient education initiatives or medication therapy management services. Belmont's use of predictive analytics through its RoundTable platform allows administrators to forecast where resource shortages may arise and plan targeted interventions before gaps widen.[3]

From a policy perspective, the dataset can inform the development of policies aimed at reducing health disparities. For instance, if the data show that low-income patients are less likely to have access to affordable medications, policymakers can advocate for policies that expand access to affordable healthcare services. The BDAIC's published hypertension reports emphasize the disproportionate economic burden faced by African American Medicare beneficiaries, who incur 27–28% higher annual costs related to hypertension than their white counterparts, largely due to increased hospitalizations and emergency visits.[7,4] Such evidence equips policymakers with data-driven arguments to support systemic reforms, such as expanding Medicaid coverage, incentivizing preventive care, and investing in food access initiatives.

Ethical Considerations

While the HTN in Nashville dataset offers numerous opportunities for improving healthcare, it also raises important ethical considerations. The collection and use of health data must be done in a manner that respects patient privacy and autonomy. The BDAIC has taken several steps to address these concerns, including the anonymization of data and the implementation of strict data security protocols.

However, as the use of health data becomes more widespread, it is essential to continue the conversation around ethical data use. This includes ensuring that data are used in a manner that benefits all populations, particularly those that are historically underserved. It also involves addressing potential biases in data collection and analysis that could perpetuate health disparities. Belmont addresses these challenges by applying fairness-aware machine learning techniques to predictive models, ensuring that algorithmic outputs do not inadvertently reinforce inequities.[3,4] Moreover, its core value of *Data for Diversity* emphasizes that all datasets and applications must reflect inclusivity, transparency, and accountability. By grounding analytics in ethics and equity, the BDAIC ensures that the benefits of health data extend to the most vulnerable populations rather than exacerbating disparities.

Future Directions

The HTN in Nashville dataset is a living resource that will continue to evolve as new data are added and new analytical techniques are developed. Future directions for the dataset include the integration of additional data sources, such as genomic data, to further enhance its utility in personalized medicine. Additionally, the BDAIC plans to expand its collaborative network to include more healthcare providers and community organizations, thereby increasing the dataset's scope and impact.

Another important future direction is the development of real-time analytics capabilities. By leveraging advances in data science and technology, the BDAIC aims to create a system that allows for the real-time analysis of HTN data. This would enable healthcare providers to identify and respond to emerging trends in HTN more quickly, ultimately improving patient outcomes. Belmont has already laid the groundwork for this through Relight, its online collaboration hub, which allows stakeholders to interact with live data visualizations and coordinate interventions dynamically.[1,3,7] Future iterations of the Belmont Data Platform envision near real-time dashboards that integrate clinical, environmental, and community-level indicators, allowing both health systems and policymakers to act proactively rather than reactively. By uniting technical innovation with community-driven priorities, the HTN dataset is poised to become not only a research asset but also a practical decision-making tool that drives systemic change.

Exercises and Activities

ACTIVITY 1: CASE STUDY ANALYSIS—HYPERTENSION MANAGEMENT IN UNDERSERVED POPULATIONS

Objective: To apply the insights from the HTN in Nashville dataset to a real-world scenario and develop interdisciplinary solutions for hypertension management.

Instructions:

1. Divide into interdisciplinary teams: Form groups of 4–6 students, ensuring each group includes representatives from pharmacy, medicine, nursing, and business healthcare.
2. Provide a case scenario: Present a case study of a patient from an underserved population (e.g., a low-income African American individual with uncontrolled hypertension and limited access to healthcare).
3. Analyze the case: Using the HTN in Nashville dataset as a reference, students should:
   - Identify the SDOH affecting the patient.
   - Propose a tailored treatment plan, considering medication adherence, lifestyle changes, and access to care.
   - Develop a business or policy recommendation to address systemic barriers (e.g., funding for community health programs).
4. Present solutions: Each group presents their analysis and recommendations to the class, highlighting how their interdisciplinary approach improves patient outcomes.

ACTIVITY 2: DATA INTERPRETATION AND VISUALIZATION WORKSHOP

Objective: To enhance data literacy and teach students how to interpret and visualize health data effectively.

Instructions:

1. Provide a sample dataset: Share a simplified version of the HTN in Nashville dataset (e.g., key variables like blood pressure readings, medication adherence, and demographic information).
2. Data analysis task: Ask students to:
   - Identify trends or disparities in the data (e.g., differences in hypertension control rates by race or income level).
   - Use tools like Excel, Tableau, or Python to create visualizations (e.g., bar charts, heatmaps, or scatter plots).

3. Interpret findings: Students should write a brief report summarizing their findings and proposing potential interventions based on the data.
4. Group discussion: Facilitate a class discussion on how data visualization can inform clinical decision-making, public health strategies, and business planning.

ACTIVITY 3: ETHICAL DEBATE—BALANCING DATA USE AND PATIENT PRIVACY

Objective: To explore the ethical considerations of using health data, particularly in the context of the Belmont Data Collaborative.

Instructions:

1. Divide into debate teams: Split the class into two groups: one advocating for expanded use of health data to improve public health outcomes, and the other emphasizing the importance of patient privacy and data security.
2. Provide debate topics: Examples include:
   - Should de-identified health data be shared with third-party researchers without explicit patient consent?
   - How can healthcare organizations balance the benefits of data analytics with the risks of data breaches?
   - What role should policymakers play in regulating the use of health data?
3. Research and prepare: Give students time to research their positions using the chapter content, ethical frameworks, and external resources.
4. Conduct the debate: Each team presents their arguments, followed by a rebuttal and open discussion.
5. Reflection: After the debate, ask students to write a short reflection on how their perspective evolved during the activity.

Assessment Questions

1. What are the key objectives of the Belmont Data Collaborative?
2. How does the HTN in Nashville dataset incorporate SDOH?
3. What are some of the key findings from the HTN in Nashville dataset?
4. How can the HTN in Nashville dataset be used to improve clinical decision-making?
5. What are the ethical considerations associated with the use of health data in the Belmont Data Collaborative?
6. How can predictive modeling be applied to the HTN in Nashville dataset?
7. What are some potential limitations of the HTN in Nashville dataset?

8. How can the HTN in Nashville dataset inform public health interventions?
9. What role do community organizations play in the Belmont Data Collaborative?
10. How can the HTN in Nashville dataset be used to address health disparities?

Assessment Questions—Answers

1. What are the key objectives of the Belmont Data Collaborative?
   The BDAIC pursues three central objectives:

   - Data for All: Promoting data literacy university-wide by equipping all students—and community members—with exposure, proficiency, and fluency in data-driven thinking.
   - Data for Good: Applying data to societal and health challenges, such as hypertension, to drive equitable, actionable community solutions. Belmont Universityblogs.belmont.edu
   - Data for Diversity: Ensuring data initiatives uphold inclusiveness, representing diverse populations ethically and responsibly.
   - Additionally, the Collaborative aims to establish a shared data infrastructure—including the Belmont Data Platform (Data Warehouse, RoundTable, and Relight)—to support collaborative research and community engagement.

2. How does the HTN in Nashville dataset incorporate SDOH?
   The dataset is grounded in the Belmont Data Platform, integrating multi-sector data such as health records, demographic information, and public SDOH indicators (e.g., food access, education, income). These are visualized through the RoundTable mapping tool, which overlays social determinants alongside health outcomes for ZIP codes and census tracts, enabling community-level insight.

3. What are some of the key findings from the HTN in Nashville dataset?
   Key insights include:

   - A notably high prevalence of hypertension in Nashville communities; the dataset served as a launchpad for community discussion and action.
   - The importance of viewing data through a cultural and ecological lens—data alone is not sufficient; institutional context, community values, and local structures also shape outcomes and must be considered in interventions.

4. How can the HTN in Nashville dataset be used to improve clinical decision-making?
   Clinicians and health systems can leverage the integrated data infrastructure to gain visibility into the places and populations most impacted by hypertension. By overlaying clinical risk factors with SDOH via RoundTable and engaging partners through Relight, providers can tailor outreach, optimize preventive care, and support more informed, geographically and socially aware decision-making.

5. What are the ethical considerations associated with the use of health data in the Belmont Data Collaborative?
   The BDC acknowledges that technical solutions alone are insufficient for systemic change. Ethical considerations include ensuring transparency, privacy, inclusivity, and equitable

representation in datasets. They emphasize that data must be open and available ("Data for All"), but used in ways that support collective action without reinforcing inequities.

6. How can predictive modeling be applied to the HTN in Nashville dataset?
The Collaborative employs data-driven analytics—not just for charting current disparities but to expose, intervene, and prevent future health challenges. Predictive modeling can identify early warning signs of hypertension in community data, helping stakeholders anticipate needs, deploy preventive resources, and measure collective impact.

7. What are some potential limitations of the HTN in Nashville dataset?
   - Reliance on publicly available indicators may omit nuanced or real-time clinical data.
   - It serves as an early snapshot rather than a continuously updated system.
   - Without sustained efforts, infrastructure alone does not guarantee systemic transformation—the real challenge is building ongoing community engagement and collaboration.

8. How can the HTN in Nashville dataset inform public health interventions?
By consolidating health and social data into one accessible platform, the dataset acts as a starting point for civic conversation. It enables stakeholders—public health agencies, nonprofits, policymakers—to identify hot spots of hypertension, visualize resources overlayed with need, and coordinate interventions grounded in data-informed, community-level understanding.

9. What role do community organizations play in the Belmont Data Collaborative?
Community organizations are central to the HCI initiative, codeveloping data platforms, convening around data stories, and collaborating in intervention design. HCI continues to meet and work toward shared accountability for social innovation. ThroughRelight and HCI, data storytelling becomes an act of engaging multiple stakeholders for collaborative impact.

10. How can the HTN in Nashville dataset be used to address health disparities?
By providing a centralized, transparent view of health outcomes and SDOH across neighborhoods, the dataset reveals inequities that were previously hidden. It functions as both a research resource and an advocacy tool—exposing disparities, connecting community partners, and empowering collective efforts to design equitable interventions. This aligns with Belmont's mission of using data as a catalyst for social change.

References

1. Belmont University. *Belmont Data Collaborative: About Us*. Belmont University website. www.belmont.edu/data/about-us/. Published 2021. Accessed September 7, 2025.
2. Inside Higher Ed. *How One University is Creating a Culture of Data*. Inside Higher Ed website. www.insidehighered.com/news/student-success/college-experience/2023/09/13/how-one-university-creating-culture-data. Published September 13, 2023. Accessed September 7, 2025.
3. Belmont University. *Belmont Data Collaborative Projects*. Belmont University website. https://blogs.belmont.edu/data/projects/. Accessed September 7, 2025.

4. Belmont University. *Belmont Data Collaborative Research Xpo*. Belmont University website. www.belmont.edu/stories/articles/2024/belmont-data-collaborative-research-xpo.html. Accessed September 7, 2025.
5. Nashville Technology Council. *Belmont Data Collaborative Announces New Health Equity Collaboration Focused on Mental Health*. Nashville Technology Council website. https://technologycouncil.com/2023/05/belmont-data-collaborative-announces-new-health-equity-collaboration-focused-on-mental-health/. Published May 2023. Accessed September 7, 2025.
6. Belmont University. *Belmont Data Collaborative Joins Forces with Engage Together to address Human Trafficking*. Belmont University website. www.belmont.edu/stories/articles/2024/bdc-joins-forces-with-engage-together.html. Accessed September 7, 2025.
7. Belmont University. *Explore Data: Data Warehouse, RoundTable, and Relight*. Belmont University website. https://blogs.belmont.edu/data/exploredata/. Accessed September 7, 2025.
8. Zhong W, Finnie RKC, Zhuang Y, et al. Using electronic health records to identify and address health disparities: a systematic scoping review. *J Am Med Inform Assoc*. 2023;30(2):193–207. doi:10.1093/jamia/ocac225
9. Belmont Data and Artificial Intelligence Collaborative (BDAIC). *HTN in Nashville Dataset: Technical Overview and Data Quality Protocols*. Belmont University; 2025.

III

ADVANCED TECHNOLOGIES IN HEALTHCARE

Chapter 7

Artificial Intelligence in Healthcare

Joanne Chun, PharmD, PhD and Leigh McCormack, PhD

Introduction

Artificial intelligence (AI) is transforming every field and healthcare is no exception. While the challenges of implementation are particularly complex, the opportunities are immense. AI is shaping fields from radiology and pathology to genomics, drug development, hospital administration, and more.

This convergence of AI and healthcare represents more than a technological advancement: it is a paradigm shift, reshaping how we diagnose disease, predict outcomes, support clinical decisions, optimize healthcare systems, and even engage patients. This shift is driven by an exponential growth of digital health data, advances in computational power, and breakthroughs in AI methods that are increasingly woven into clinical workflows.

Foundations and Definitions

AI is a branch of computer science focused on designing algorithms and systems capable of performing cognitive tasks traditionally associated with human intelligence. These include learning from data, reasoning to make decisions or draw conclusions, understanding and processing language, interpreting sensory inputs such as images, sounds, or text, and solving problems through planning and action. This can be achieved through approaches ranging from rule-based algorithms to complex neural networks[a1] trained on large datasets. Within AI, there are a few primary subfields that provide the technical foundations for its diverse applications in healthcare. As shown in Figure 7.1, artificial intelligence encompasses several core subfields, including machine learning and deep learning, which provide the foundation for many healthcare applications.

DOI: 10.4324/9781003593867-10

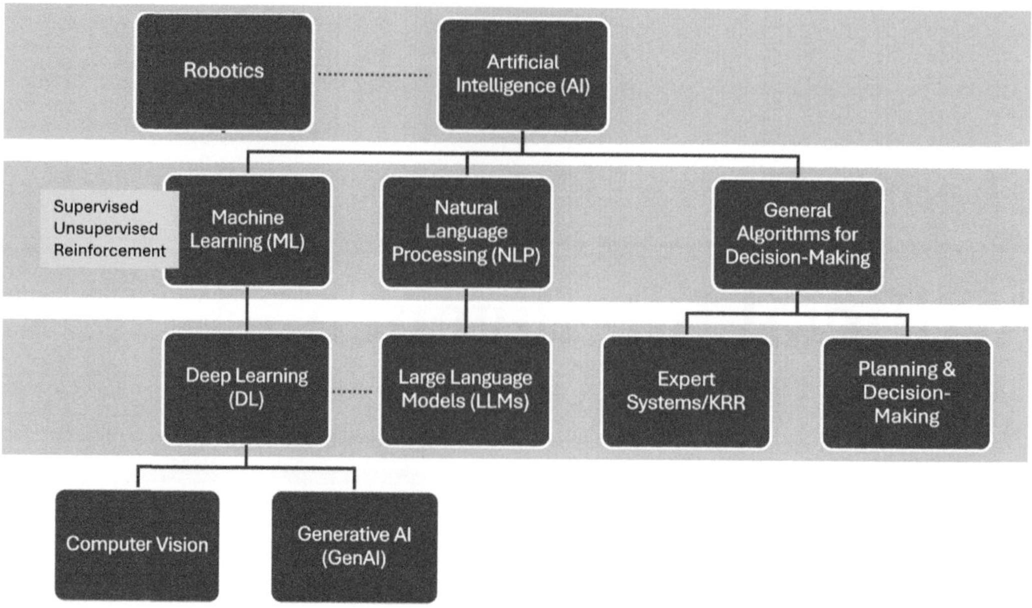

Figure 7.1 The core subfields of AI, which provide the understanding to match the right AI approach with real-world problems— improving diagnoses, predicting risk, and optimizing operations.

Source: Created by the Author.

Machine learning (ML) is a subfield of AI where algorithms enable systems to automatically infer relationships from data, rather than relying on explicitly programmed rules. The simplest example of ML is linear regression: $y = xa + \text{b}$, such that given any x, we can predict y. For example, if we want to predict the price of a house based on its size, x represents *the size* of the house and y represents the predicted price. Here, a would represent how much the price increases for each additional unit of size (e.g., per square foot), while b would represent the baseline price of a house.

Linear regression is a straightforward case of ML, but most real-world applications are far more complex. To handle diverse challenges, ML methods are commonly divided into three categories: **supervised**,[a2] **unsupervised**,[a3] and **reinforcement**[a4] learning. Supervised learning uses labeled data, such as house prices paired with their actual prices. Unsupervised learning uses unlabeled data, such as grouping houses into market segments based on features like size, location, or age without knowing the categories beforehand. Reinforcement learning uses trial and error, such as an algorithm for adjusting pricing strategies over time to maximize sales or rental income.

These techniques become especially powerful when combined with deep learning (DL), a specialized branch of ML that uses artificial neural networks with many layers to learn hierarchical patterns in data. Inspired by the structure of biological neurons, each artificial "neuron" receives inputs and uses an activation function—a simple rule that checks whether the signal is strong enough or fits the right pattern—to determine whether to fire. When stacked into multiple layers, these networks can capture very complex relationships, making DL especially powerful for unstructured inputs such as text, images, or sound.

Today, DL is driving many of the most significant recent advances in AI, including speech recognition, image analysis, natural language processing (NLP), and generative AI (GenAI). In healthcare, DL powers radiology and pathology image analysis, data extraction from clinical documentation, and generative models that can create new data—ranging from synthetic patient records to novel molecular structures. Beyond data analysis, DL also supports applications in robotics and automation, enabling AI systems to assist with tasks such as surgical guidance,[1] patient monitoring,[2] and hospital logistics.[3]

History of AI in Healthcare

Although AI may seem like a recent breakthrough, its application in healthcare is not new. As early as the 1960s, researchers at MIT developed Eliza,[4] a chatbot that could simulate a conversation with a therapist. In the 1970s, researchers at Stanford developed MYCIN, a system that applied hundreds of similar "if–then" rules[b1] to recommend antibiotics for bacterial infections.[5] Around this time, INTERNIST-1[6] was also developed as one of the first AI medical consultants. Although these systems demonstrated impressive diagnostic accuracy in experimental settings, they were never adopted clinically because they required labor-intensive, manual data entry and were limited by rigid rules, a lack of adaptability, and an inability to learn from new data.

In the 1980s, researchers developed DXplain,[7] a decision support tool that expanded these approaches by offering differential diagnoses for hundreds of conditions; however, it struggled with scalability and clinical usability, as its knowledge base required constant manual updates to remain relevant. The rise of ML in the 1990s marked an important shift from rigid rule-based systems to algorithms that could adapt and improve with data.

In the 2000s, IBM's Watson[8] demonstrated advanced NLP and question-answering capabilities, which were later applied to tasks such as matching cancer patients with clinical trials, supporting oncologists with evidence-based treatment options, and assisting in genomic data interpretation.[9]

In the 2010s came the rise of DL as advances in neural networks, computing power, and big data enabled breakthroughs in medical imaging, genomics, and NLP. This paved the way for today's generative and multimodal AI systems.[a5] In the late 2010s, DeepMind's AlphaFold represented a pivotal moment for biomedical AI by accurately predicting 3D protein structures from amino acid sequences.[10] AlphaFold revolutionized structural biology and accelerated drug discovery.

Today's AI systems are data-driven, flexible, and capable of analyzing vast datasets to generate new insights, building on decades of progress from early expert systems to modern generative models and large language models (LLMs). The next frontier is agentic AI—systems with autonomous planning, reasoning, and multistep action—that promise to transform healthcare beyond prediction or generation.[11,12]

Each milestone brings us closer to robust AI models that transform how we teach in the health sciences and deliver care. Some of the most foundational important milestones are listed in Table 7.1.

Table 7.1 Key Milestones of AI Development in Healthcare

Time Period	*Key Developments*	*Significance*
1950s	"Turing Test" (Alan Turing): an experiment proposing that a computer could be considered intelligent if it could hold a conversation indistinguishable from a human.[13]	Introduced a framework for evaluating whether a machine's behavior could be indistinguishable from that of a human.
1960s	Eliza chatbot (MIT): a computer program that mimicked a psychotherapist by responding to text in a conversational way.[4] Shakey robot (Stanford): the first robot to perceive its surroundings, plan actions, and move autonomously.[14]	Demonstrated that computers could process natural language and robots could use AI to navigate the physical world/robotics capabilities
1970s	MYCIN (Stanford): an expert system designed to recommend antibiotics for infectious disease.[5] INTERNIST-I (University of Pittsburgh): a program designed for diagnosing internal medicine cases.[6]	Early proof of concept that computers could replicate aspects of expert medical reasoning through rule-based systems.
1980s	DXplain (University of Massachusetts): decision support tool offering differential diagnoses for hundreds of conditions.[7]	Expanded decision support to cover hundreds of conditions, but highlighted scalability challenges as rule-based systems required constant manual updates.
1900s–2000s	IBM Watson: demonstrated advanced question-answering and NLP, later adapted for oncology and genomics.[8]	Showed how data-driven learning could move beyond rules into applied clinical domains.
2010s	DeepMind's AlphaGo (University of Toronto) or convolutional neural networks in radiology.[15]	Breakthroughs in DL proved neural networks could outperform experts in complex pattern recognition, setting the stage for medical imaging applications.
2010s	FDA approval of IDx-DR (University of Iowa): the first autonomous AI diagnostic system for diabetic retinopathy.[16]	Marked regulatory acceptance of AI as a standalone diagnostic tool.
2020s	(DeepMind) AlphaFold2: accurately predicted 3D protein structures.[10]	Revolutionized structural biology and drug discovery with near-experimental accuracy.
2020s–future	Microsoft MAI-DxO—multi-agent diagnostic AI tested against NEJM cases.[17]	Early demonstration of agentic AI outperforming doctors in complex diagnosis.

Note: Recognizing these milestones shows how decades of progress underpin today's clinically validated AI tools, giving confidence in current and future applications.

Future Outlook

But how exactly are these tools applied in healthcare today? Healthcare produces massive amounts of data—from patient records and lab results to imaging studies and genomic sequences. At the simplest level, AI companions can manage this information and routine documentation, allowing providers to spend more time with patients.

But AI's real power lies not just in handling data—it's integrating and interpreting it across multiple domains to help inform personalized clinical decision-making.[18] By combining health records, clinical notes, genomic data, and immunological profiles, these systems can interpret complex biology and translate it into clinical decisions tailored to each patient. This supports the broader shift in healthcare from a "one-size-fits-all" approach to care that emphasizes prevention, early detection, and targeted interventions, all while reducing unnecessary costs.

In clinical care, AI can now interpret medical images faster and often more accurately than human experts, particularly in radiology, pathology, and dermatology.[19] Predictive models are increasingly being used to identify patients at risk for conditions like diabetes complications and heart failure, enabling earlier interventions.[20,21] AI will increasingly support precision diagnostics, real-time monitoring, and adaptive treatment planning.

AI-driven digital health tools extend care beyond clinics through apps, wearables, and telehealth, supporting adherence and delivering evidence-based interventions.

In biomedical research, AI analyzes multi-omics data—that is, combined information from genomics, proteomics, metabolomics, and other molecular layers—predicts protein structures, and enables de novo molecule generation, meaning designing new chemical compounds from scratch rather than modifying existing ones, to accelerate drug discovery and optimize clinical trials.

At the system level, AI streamlines operations such as patient flow, scheduling, resource management, and administrative tasks.

In fact, the global healthcare AI market is projected to expand at a compound annual growth rate[a6] (CAGR) of 47.6%, from $11.2 billion in 2023 to $427.5 billion by 2032, driven by broader adoption, policy support, and workforce readiness initiatives.[22,23]

Whether you are a clinician, researcher, policymaker, or student, understanding AI is no longer optional, but essential. The future of healthcare will be shaped by those who can bridge the gap between data and decisions. This chapter aims to help you build that foundation.

Core Technologies and Applications

AI technologies are reshaping healthcare across a wide spectrum of applications. Here we highlight key areas where AI is delivering its most meaningful impact.

Clinical Diagnostics

AI tools have been revolutionizing clinical diagnostics by increasing accuracy, reducing costs, and saving time compared to traditional diagnostic methods. DL models can spot patterns in scans, lab tests, and vital signs that clinicians might miss.

Image analysis was one of the first AI tools to find its way into hospitals, and it's quickly become indispensable. Currently, it helps identify tumors, fractures, hemorrhages, and lung abnormalities in X-rays, CT scans, and MRIs—often with accuracy on par with medical specialists.[24] In breast cancer screening and lung nodule detection, some studies even suggest AI can outperform radiologists.[25] The technology doesn't stop there: in pathology labs, algorithms sift through digital slides to classify tissue and flag malignancies with striking precision. Dermatology clinics are seeing similar gains, where AI systems can tell the difference between a benign mole and a malignant lesion, offering doctors a second set of eyes for early cancer detection in both primary care and remote settings.

Beyond images, AI is also beginning to read the hidden signals in lab work. Models can discern patterns in blood counts, genetic profiles, and microbial cultures that point physicians toward likely diagnoses. These tools are proving especially valuable in hematology, microbiology, and genomics, where massive datasets once slowed the pace of discovery.

The next frontier is combined data analysis. By integrating imaging, genetic information, and electronic health records (EHRs), AI can give doctors greater confidence in diagnoses and tailor care to each patient. Early systems are already being tested to spot neurodegenerative diseases such as Alzheimer's,[26] predict cardiovascular risk,[27] and even refine cancer subtyping[28]—areas where traditional tools often struggle.

Transitioning from diagnostic imaging to language-based analysis, we will now explore how AI reads and interprets the vast textual data in healthcare.

From NLP to LLMs

While image analysis highlights AI's strength in interpreting visual data, much of healthcare information lives in words—patient notes, discharge summaries, and pathology reports. Turning this unstructured text into usable insights is the focus of NLP.[29]

NLP is a branch of AI that teaches computers to work with language. In healthcare, this allows narrative documentation to be transformed into information that supports clinical decisions and research. Earlier NLP systems relied on rule-based methods and task-specific models. They were designed for functions such as information extraction,[a7] document classification,[a8] negation detection[a9] (recognizing when a note says "no evidence of disease"), and temporal reasoning[a10] (understanding time references like "symptoms began three months ago"). While effective, each tool had to be built and tuned for a single task, which made them rigid and difficult to scale. The emergence of LLMs offers a major shift, moving beyond rule-driven tools toward adaptable systems.

LLMs extend the capabilities of NLP by operating on a much larger scale and with greater autonomy. LLMs are trained on enormous text datasets and learn language patterns without needing explicit instructions, a capability known as zero-shot and few-shot learning. Well-known examples include ChatGPT, Gemini, and Grok, which use DL architectures with millions of adjustable parameters—dimensions and weights[a12]—to capture relationships across words, sentences, and entire documents.[30] See Figure 7.2 for a visual representation of how LLMs emerge from NLP, ML, and DL.

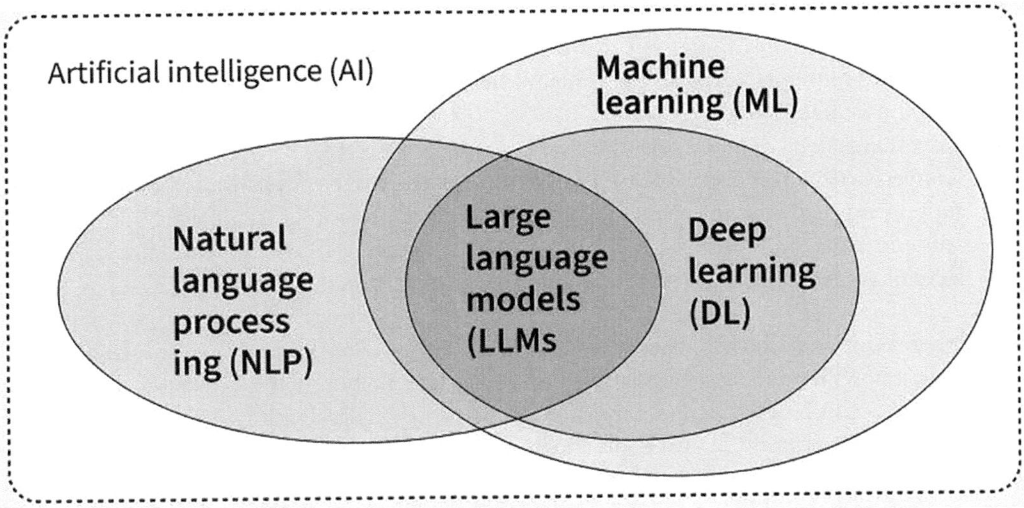

Figure 7.2 How LLMs emerge from NLP, ML, and DL—LLMs unify multiple AI methods to extract and generate clinical insights from text, reducing documentation burden and enhancing decision support for safer, faster care.

Source: Created by Author.

This improvement comes from scale: modern neural networks are built with hundreds of layers and billions of parameters. Through exposure to vast amounts of text, LLMs develop internal representations of syntax, semantics, and context. This allows them to move beyond the "if–then" rules, generating context-aware responses (Natural Language Generation) and identifying implied meaning.

NLP and LLM Application in Healthcare

In medicine, this adaptability is critical. The impact of NLP and LLMs is felt most acutely in four domains: documentation, research, administration, and patient interaction.[31]

1. Documentation and clinical workflow
   LLMs draft patient notes, discharge summaries, and referral letters, reducing clerical burden and freeing clinicians to focus on care.[32] A single model can summarize an admission, extract key details, or translate complex jargon into patient-friendly language. This shift not only improves efficiency but also reduces errors introduced by rushed or incomplete documentation.
2. Population health and biomedical research
   Large-scale text mining across millions of EHRs enables the identification of early warning signs of disease and the construction of richly characterized patient cohorts. Beyond EHRs, advanced models reveal drug targets and biomarkers. LLMs like PaLM, Med-PaLM, DNABert, ESM, AlphaGenome, and Evo2 are being trained on biomedical literature, genomic sequences, and proteomic data to tackle problems to support drug discovery and precision medicine.[30]

3. Administrative and regulatory efficiency
   NLP systems that can interpret free-text notes and map them to ICD or CPT billing codes accelerate reimbursement and flag incomplete documentation that would otherwise result in claim denials.[33]
4. Patient engagement and clinical decision support
   Conversational agents powered by LLMs extend the reach of healthcare beyond the clinic, supporting patients in managing chronic disease, checking symptoms, or scheduling appointments.[34] In parallel, decision support systems surface critical insights as a second layer of vigilance, strengthening patient safety and care quality.[35]

Together, NLP and LLMs represent more than an incremental improvement in healthcare IT. The challenge now lies not in proving their utility but in utilizing them responsibly. Despite their versatility, LLMs can produce errors, fabricate information ("hallucinations"), or reflect biases present in their training data.[36] Clinical deployment requires rigorous validation, careful customization for the specific context, and consistent human oversight.[37] Key applications of NLP and LLMs in healthcare are summarized in Table 7.2.

Table 7.2 Key Capabilities and Healthcare Applications of LLMs

Capability	*Description*	*Healthcare Examples*
Natural Language Understanding (NLU)	Understanding what human language means—not just the words, but the intent and context behind them[a11]	Extracting key data such as diagnoses, medications, and procedures from EHR
Natural Language Generation (NLG)	Producing clear, fluent, and context-appropriate text	Generating discharge summaries or patient education materials
Reasoning and Problem-Solving	Answering questions, summarizing information, translating languages, and providing explanations	Summarizing patient information from different sources or integrating lab, imaging, and note data to inform clinical decisions
Multimodal Capabilities	Integrating multiple forms of input such as images, audio, and other data types alongside text, into a single model	Combining radiology images with pathology reports and clinical notes to provide a complete picture and help guide diagnosis

Note: LLMs can automate documentation, surface hidden risks, and support clinical decisions to improve patient safety and efficiency.

Having covered AI's capabilities in understanding language, we now shift our focus to its role and impact in digital therapeutics (DTx) and digital health interventions.

Digital Health, Digital Medicine, and DTx

Digital health today spans everything from smartphone apps and wearable sensors to telehealth platforms and intelligent health information systems. At its core, the field is about using technology to improve access, efficiency, and patient engagement. Most of these tools are considered general wellness products and only require regulatory oversight when they directly guide medical decisions.[38]

"Digital medicine" refers to solutions that have been clinically validated and shown to provide measurable benefit in patient care. Remote monitoring devices that transmit vital signs, digital diagnostics that detect arrhythmias from a smartwatch, or decision-support tools that guide a physician at the bedside fall into this category. They generate actionable insights but stop short of acting as the treatment itself.[39]

DTx go a step further. Defined by the Digital Therapeutics Alliance as "evidence-based interventions delivered through software," they are designed to prevent, manage, or treat disease.[40] DTx products are tested in clinical trials, undergo regulatory review, and often require a prescription. Unlike digital medicine, they don't just inform care—they directly intervene.[41] In practice, DTx can augment or even replace drug therapy and behavioral interventions, offering a new modality of treatment delivered through a screen instead of a pill bottle.[42]

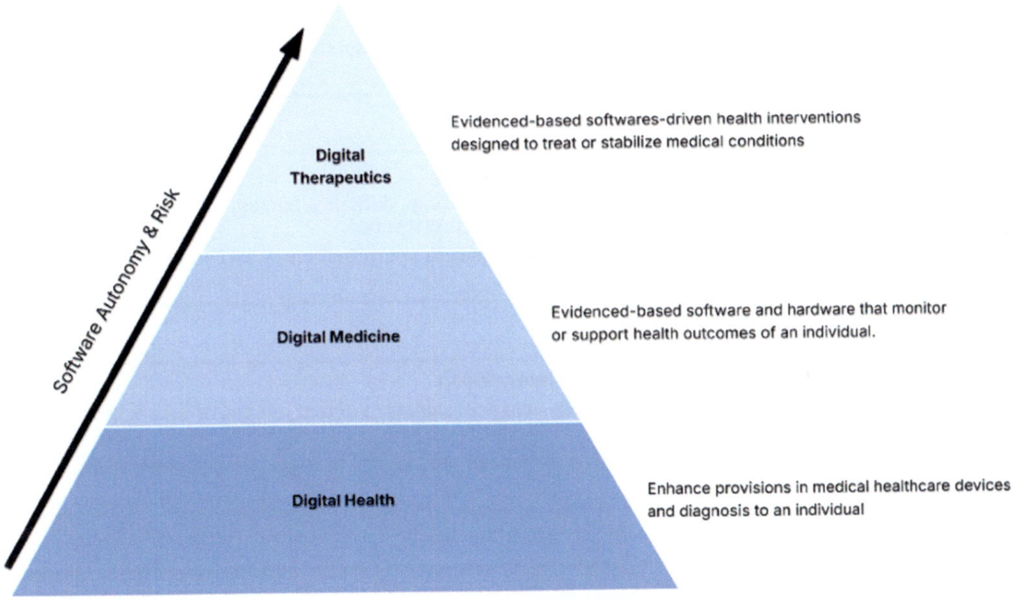

Figure 7.3 Digital health, digital medicine, and DTx—The spectrum of digital interventions in healthcare.

Source: ***Created by the Author.***

This spectrum shows (see Figure 7.3) that greater software autonomy demands stronger clinical validation to protect patients and ensure reliable therapeutic outcomes.

AI-Driven Transformation of DTx

AI is reshaping DTx, making them more adaptive and clinically useful. AI systems can tailor interventions in real time and even anticipate disease progression before symptoms appear. Crucially, these recommendations are embedded within human-in-the-loop (HITL) designs, ensuring that clinicians review and validate outputs rather than relying on automation alone.

Several capabilities underpin this transformation (Figure 7.4). At the foundation lies the ability to handle vast and varied data—from EHRs to speech and movement captured through sensors. AI also enables prediction, detecting early signs of relapse or forecasting disease flares. Personalization is another core capability, where models adapt treatment pathways to the unique needs of each patient. Finally, decision support ensures that insights generated by AI are integrated into clinical workflows, guiding timely and appropriate interventions.

To address privacy concerns, a method called federated learning[a13] is gaining traction. Instead of pooling data in one place, each hospital keeps its records on site and trains the AI model locally. Only the lessons the model learns—like an updated set of rules—are shared with a central system. These updates are then combined to make the model smarter overall, without exposing the underlying patient records. In this way, institutions can collaborate on AI development while keeping sensitive information secure.

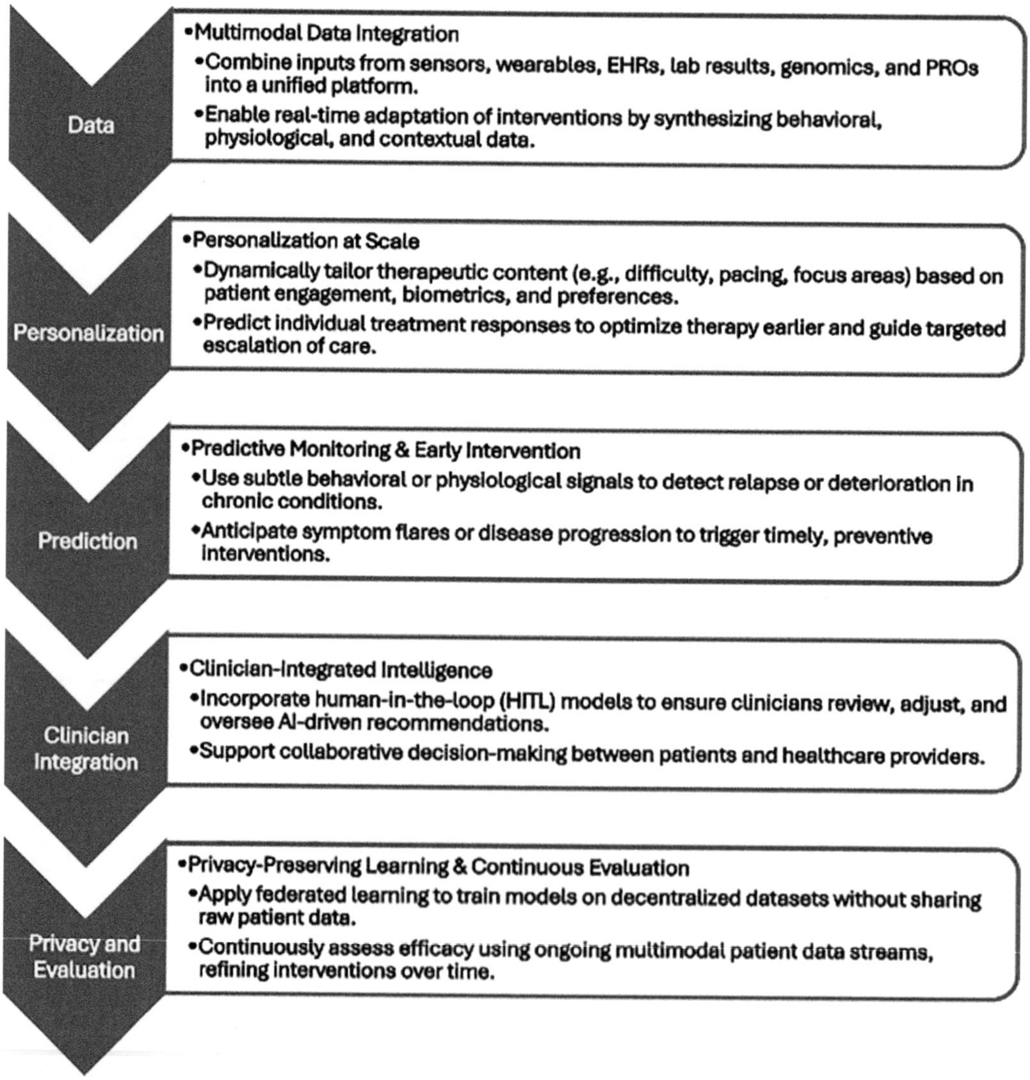

Figure 7.4 Core capabilities of AI in DTx.

Source: Created by the Author.

These capabilities enable personalized, real-time interventions that improve adherence, reduce relapse, and deliver measurable health outcomes.

New Frontier of AI-Driven DTx

Closed-loop DTx represent the next evolution of AI in Healthcare. These systems combine real-time sensing and predictive algorithms to anticipate clinical needs and deliver timely interventions, all while integrating seamlessly with EHRs. Examples of emerging AI-driven digital therapeutics are presented in Table 7.3.

Table 7.3 Therapeutic Areas Leveraging AI-Powered DTx

Therapeutic Area	*AI Capability*	*Examples*	*Intended Use*
Behavioral Health	Conversational AI for cognitive behavioral therapy (CBT)	Woebot[43] Wysa[44]	Support mental health management and self-guided CBT
Diabetes Management	Predictive modeling for behavior change	Omada Health[45] Dario Platform[46]	Prevent and manage type 2 diabetes through lifestyle interventions
Chronic Pain	Computer vision for exercise form correction	Kaia Health[47] RelieVRx[48]	Guide physical therapy and pain management
Hypertension	Personalized AI-driven risk alerts	Hello Heart[49]	Manage blood pressure and improve cardiovascular health
IBS	Adaptive symptom tracking and behavioral coaching	Mahana IBS[50]	Manage irritable bowel syndrome symptoms
Sleep Disorders	AI-based sleep pattern analysis	Sleepio[51] Somryst[52]	Deliver personalized CBT for insomnia

Note: These examples illustrate real conditions where AI-driven software is already improving disease management and patient self-care.

After exploring how AI is driving innovation in DTx, we now examine how similar capabilities are reshaping the management of entire health systems.

Health System Management

AI in healthcare is shifting from isolated applications toward integrated ecosystems that unify data, algorithms, and workflows. This momentum is being driven not only by academic medical centers establishing dedicated AI institutes and training programs,[53–55] but also by significant investments from leading technology and pharmaceutical companies.[56] The shared aim is clear: to embed AI into the infrastructure of healthcare delivery so that decision-making becomes faster, more consistent, and patient-centered (see Table 7.4).[57]

Current efforts tackle some of the system's most pressing challenges: rising costs, workforce shortages, and increasing patient demand.[58] At the organizational level, applications cluster around three domains:

1. Hospital logistics and resource management
AI models forecast demand for supplies and medications, reducing both shortages and overstock.[3] Predictive maintenance systems identify early signs of equipment failure, and scheduling tools optimize the use of operating rooms and staff.[59] In crisis settings, simulation models help stabilize supply chains and direct resources to areas of greatest need.[60]
2. Administrative process automation
LLMs are accelerating billing and claims processing, reducing errors and costly denials.[61] Chatbots and automated document processing relieve staff of routine communication and paperwork. In outpatient imaging, predictive scheduling reduced no-show rates from 19.3% to 15.9% over six months by targeting reminders to patients most at risk of missing appointments.[3]
3. Patient flow and scheduling optimization
AI rescheduling systems dynamically reallocate resources in real time, reducing wait times and maximizing capacity.[62]

AI is also strengthening data security and compliance. Automated monitoring systems detect unusual access patterns and ensure adherence to regulations such as HIPAA and GDPR, reinforcing trust in digital health systems.[63] Overall, AI-driven management tools are helping health systems shift from reactive problem-solving to proactive planning.

Table 7.4 Summary of AI Applications in Health System Management

Area of AI Application	*Example*	*Impact*
Hospital Logistics and Resource Management	Predicting inventory for supplies and medications; AI-optimized HVAC; predictive maintenance/repair; optimized OR scheduling; supply chain planning during crises	Reduced waste and cost; improved uptime; faster response in emergencies
Administrative Process Automation	NLP-based EHR insights; AI claims processing; predicting no-show patients; document parsing; chatbot-based patient engagement; monitoring compliance with privacy rules	Lower administrative burden; improved billing accuracy; increased patient engagement
Patient Flow and Scheduling Optimization	Predicting admissions/ discharges; dynamic rescheduling; predicting wait times; satisfaction-linked communication tools; telehealth scheduling	Reduced wait times; increased patient capacity; improved patient satisfaction

Note: These system-level uses translate directly into shorter wait times, lower costs, and better resource allocation for hospitals and patients.[62]

Precision Medicine and Genomics

AI's analytic power is increasingly being applied at the molecular level, where genomics generate data of staggering complexity.[64] Unlike a supply chain where the variables are finite and relatively predictable, genomic datasets contain billions of data points, each representing a potential clue to health or disease (see Figure 7.5). Making sense of that information is the essence of precision medicine.

Precision medicine seeks to tailor prevention, diagnosis, and treatment for the individual, accounting for factors such as a person's genetic sequence, environment, and lifestyle. AI enables this vision by uncovering genomic patterns that traditional statistical methods often miss and combining these findings with clinical and behavioral data. For instance, AI models can reveal genotype–phenotype associations (how a particular variant influences disease traits), identify biomarkers that indicate risk before symptoms appear, and forecast how an illness is likely to progress.[65,66]

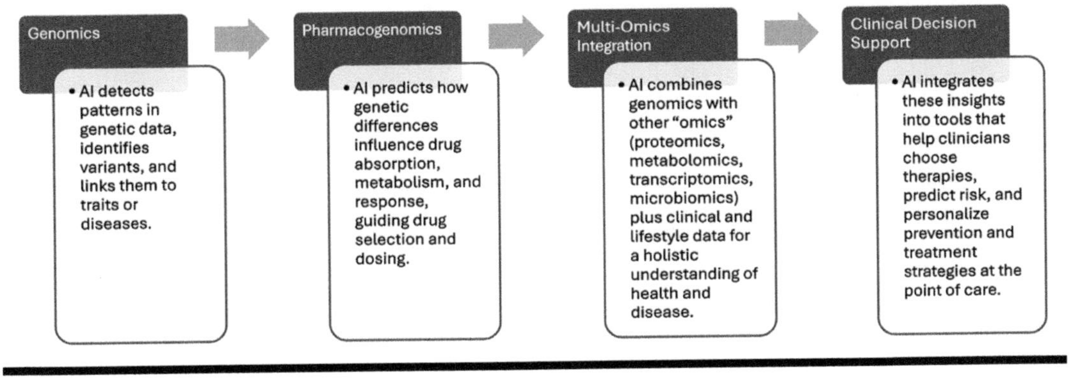

Figure 7.5 How AI powers precision medicine.

Source: Created by the Author.

This progression (see Figure 7.5) shows how AI links genetic and multi-omic data to clinical decision tools, enabling more precise diagnoses and personalized treatments that improve patient outcomes.

Precision medicine now integrates multiple "omics" layers: genomics (genes), transcriptomics (which genes are actively expressed), proteomics (protein structure and function), metabolomics (small-molecule products of metabolism), and environmental or lifestyle factors. AI methods, especially multimodal DL models, can synthesize these layers. This allows for the discovery of complex biomarker signatures that signal disease before symptoms arise, the identification of molecular subtypes of cancer that respond differently to therapy, and the suggestion of novel uses for existing drugs by mapping shared pathways across seemingly unrelated conditions.[67] In other words, AI provides a systems-level view of health that traditional, single-layer analyses cannot deliver.

Pharmacogenomics is a domain where these insights are already being translated into practice. Genetic variation influences how individuals absorb, metabolize, and respond to drugs. AI models are accelerating pharmacogenomics by analyzing variants at scale and recommending drug–dose combinations that minimize harm and maximize benefit.[68] They can flag patients at elevated risk of adverse drug reactions, support adaptive therapy as new genomic data become available, and identify opportunities for drug repurposing by recognizing molecular pathways shared across diseases. These pharmacogenomic recommendations are slowly being built into EHRs, so clinicians encounter them naturally at the point of care.[69]

These same approaches extend precision medicine from individual care to public health. AI can help determine which patients should be prioritized for genetic testing, estimate how frequently particular variants occur in different ancestry groups, and inform screening strategies to catch disease earlier. These insights are crucial for designing representative clinical studies and ensuring that interventions are equitably distributed.[70]

Despite this progress, major challenges persist, including the underrepresentation of diverse populations in genomic datasets and ongoing barriers to data sharing due to privacy concerns.[71] Addressing these barriers will be essential to ensure that the benefits of AI-driven genomics are distributed equitably across all patient groups.

Building on these genomic advances, AI is also playing a growing role in transforming drug discovery and development. Next, we explore how AI is accelerating every stage of the pipeline—from target identification and compound screening to clinical trial design.

Drug Discovery and Development

Drug discovery has long been a marathon: slow, complex, and expensive. On average, bringing a new therapy from concept to clinic costs an estimated $2.6 billion and can take 12–15 years.[72] However, AI is making improvements at every stage.

The first step in discovery is identifying a biological "handle" on disease—a gene, protein, or pathway that can be modulated. AI accelerates this process by mining datasets on a superhuman scale. Knowledge graph models, for instance, map hidden relationships between genes, pathways, and diseases, suggesting new targets. Structural biology is also being transformed: breakthroughs like AlphaFold and RoseTTAFold predict protein 3D structures directly from amino acid sequences, enabling drug designers to model how candidate compounds might interact with these targets with unprecedented accuracy.[72]

Once targets are identified, the search begins for molecules that can bind them. Traditionally, this meant laborious high-throughput assays[a14] testing thousands of compounds. AI compresses this step by running millions of "virtual experiments" in silico.[73] DL models predict binding strength and drug-like properties, rapidly triaging vast libraries of molecules. Generative models such as MegaMolBART and MolFormer go further, designing entirely new compounds optimized for binding affinity, selectivity, and pharmacokinetic features—shortening cycles of design and synthesis from months to days.[74]

Promising "hits"—molecules that show initial activity against a biological target—must then be refined into safe, effective "leads," which are optimized compounds with desirable potency and drug-like properties. Here, AI leverages physiologically based pharmacokinetic (PBPK) models to simulate absorption, distribution, metabolism, and excretion (ADME).[75,76] These simulations help chemists tweak molecular structures to maximize potency while minimizing toxicity long before moving to animal studies.

Before human trials, candidate drugs undergo in vitro and in vivo testing.[77] AI improves efficiency by predicting toxicity, off-target interactions, and drug–drug conflicts earlier in the pipeline.[78] By filtering out unsafe candidates at this stage, AI reduces both cost and ethical burdens, sparing unnecessary animal testing.[79]

Human testing remains the costliest and riskiest bottleneck. AI supports this phase by identifying patients most likely to respond based on genomic and clinical data, stratifying cohorts by biomarkers or disease stage, and optimizing trial protocols. Adaptive designs allow protocols to evolve in real time, while decentralized trials reduce patient burden by shifting components online. Recruitment, often the slowest step, can be accelerated by predicting which hospitals are most likely to yield eligible participants. Innovations like platform trials—exemplified by the RECOVERY trial during COVID-19—demonstrate how AI can coordinate the testing of multiple therapies under a single framework.[3,80–82] Synthetic control arms, which substitute historical or registry data for some control participants, further streamline trials while reducing patient exposure to placebos—an especially important advance for rare diseases.

Approval is not the end of the story. Once drugs reach the market, AI continues to monitor safety by scanning EHRs, insurance claims, adverse-event databases, and even patient forums and social media for early signals of rare side effects. These systems can detect safety concerns in near real time, well before traditional reporting pipelines.

Despite these advances, hurdles remain. Quality of data limits reliability, and using biased data risks embedding health disparities into models. Yet the promise is clear: AI is reshaping drug discovery from a slow relay race into an accelerated, iterative cycle.

Now that we've explored AI's success in drug discovery and development, we turn to Agentic AI, a new frontier of systems that moves beyond prediction to autonomous planning and action.

Agentic AI

Agentic AI refers to systems capable of autonomous planning, reasoning, and action. Unlike predictive models, these systems can execute multistep tasks, monitor outcomes, and adapt based on feedback.[83]

For example, an agentic AI could coordinate a patient's care journey: scheduling follow-up appointments, ordering lab tests, and adjusting reminders based on real-time data. Such capabilities push AI beyond passive analysis toward active orchestration.

The story of AI in drug development shows how algorithms can accelerate even the most complex scientific pipelines. But a new frontier is emerging where AI doesn't just accelerate human work, it orchestrates it.

Most AI systems in widespread use today are extraordinary in their capacity but limited in their posture. They wait on standby, responding only when summoned. They can parse language, analyze patterns, and generate coherent responses, but once their answer is delivered, their work is done.

Agentic AI shifts this stance. These systems are designed to carry actions forward. They integrate reasoning with planning and planning with execution, so that one step flows into the next until a task is complete. To borrow a metaphor: an LLM alone is a brilliant brain without a body—capable of thought but incapable of touch. Agentic AI provides the body. It allows systems to reach outward: to query databases, interact with hospital scheduling platforms, operate within software environments, and even trigger actions in the physical world.[12] In healthcare, that could mean not just recommending how to improve patient scheduling, but actually scanning the clinic's system for open appointments, resolving conflicts, and placing patients into slots automatically. The shift is from language to agency, from insight to action.

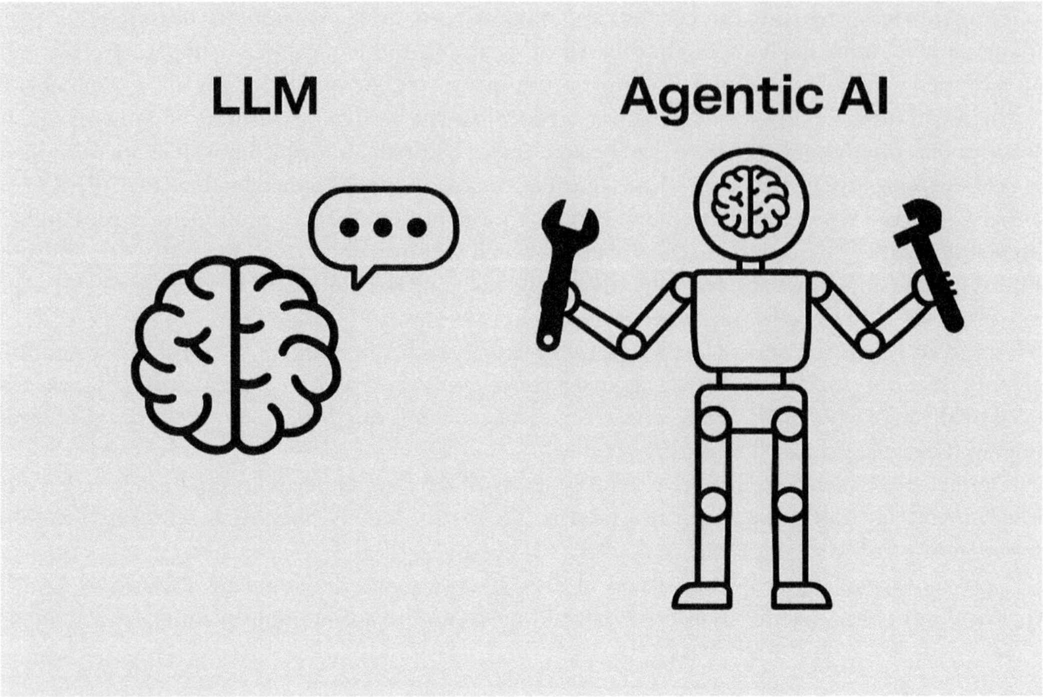

Figure 7.6 Diagram illustrating the difference between LLM and AI agent.
Source: Created by the Author with AI-assisted Illustration Using ChatGPT.

Figure 7.6 illustrates how an LLM provides the "brain" for reasoning while the agent adds the "body" to act, enabling AI to move from insight to real-world clinical action.

What distinguishes agentic AI is autonomy: they can act without continuous prompting. A hospital-based agent, for example, might integrate new lab results into a patient's record the instant they are posted, triggering an alert if the findings shift risk stratification. They also pursue goals. Instead of just scheduling one appointment when asked, an agent could ensure an entire discharge plan is coordinated across specialties, with follow-ups, lab work, and imaging booked in proper sequence.[11]

These agents also possess persistence: they do not start fresh each time, but maintain context across days or weeks, continuously refining recommendations as data accumulate. Crucially, they can act directly in their environment, from entering billing codes into the EHR to dynamically reallocating ICU staff in response to patient surges.[84,85]

The implications for healthcare practice are profound. Consider a multidisciplinary oncology board: an agentic system could gather inputs from radiology, pathology, and genomic profiling, draft a structured case summary, simulate likely outcomes under different regimens, and update its recommendations as new results arrive. Early prototypes hint at this potential. Microsoft's MAI-Dx Orchestrator, for example, deploys a panel of specialized agents—hypothesis testing, stewardship, challenge, checklist, and others—debating cases in sequence before converging on a recommendation. In controlled trials using complex diagnostic cases published in the *New England Journal of Medicine*, this multi-agent system achieved diagnostic accuracies exceeding 85%, far outstripping the 20% baseline of practicing physicians without external resources.[86,87] Systems like MAI-Dx illustrate how agentic AI can move beyond assisting individual clinicians to orchestrating collaborative, debate-driven decision-making at scale.

Research and operations stand to benefit in equal measure. In drug discovery, agent-based systems could cycle through hypothesis generation, molecular modeling, and in silico toxicity screening in iterative loops, while "consulting" specialized AI colleagues trained on proteomics or pharmacokinetics. In health system management, an agent might monitor patient flow in real time, forecast bottlenecks before they appear, and automatically reassign staff or adjust bed allocations to maintain capacity.

Such autonomy, however, raises urgent questions of safety and accountability. When machines can plan and act independently, robust safeguards are non-negotiable. Transparent system design, rigorous validation, and clearly defined human oversight must accompany deployment.[88] But the trajectory is unmistakable: agentic AI is shifting AI from being a passive assistant to an active partner in medicine—one capable of executing multistep tasks, coordinating across systems, and helping clinicians meet the demands of modern care.

Because these autonomous agents can plan and act without continuous prompting, the very capabilities that make them powerful also heighten the need for rigorous human oversight to ensure that every action remains safe, ethical, and clinically appropriate.[88] As this autonomy grows, the need for HITL safeguards becomes even more critical. Next, we examine how HITL approaches ensure that these powerful tools augment rather than replace clinicians, maintaining safety, accountability, and trust in real-world healthcare settings.

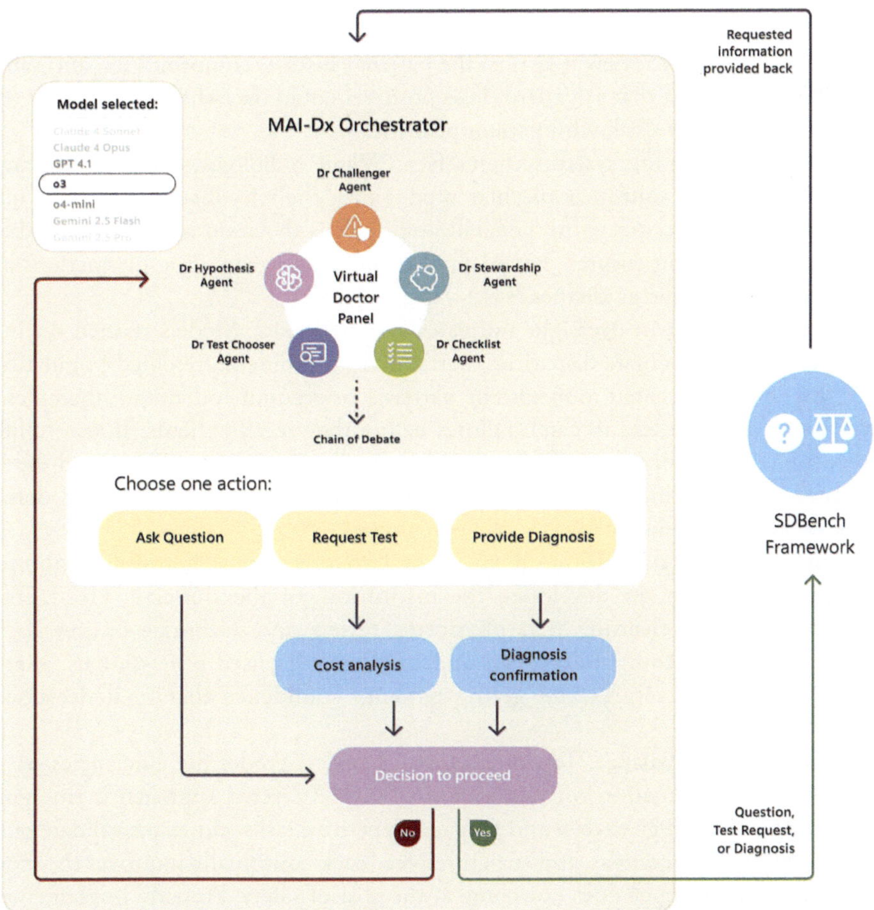

Figure 7.7 MAI-DxO (Microsoft AI Diagnostic Orchestrator): Mimicking healthcare experts.[89]

Figure 7.7 shows the MAI-Dx Orchestrator, a multi-agent AI system for medical diagnostics. It uses a Virtual Doctor Panel to simulate clinical reasoning and interacts with the SDBench framework to evaluate and refine diagnoses.

Human-in-the-Loop

HITL approaches ensure that AI augments clinicians, rather than replacing them, by keeping humans in control of critical decisions. HITL frameworks are essential for safety, accountability, and trust.

For instance, clinical decision support systems should present recommendations that clinicians can accept, modify, or reject. Continuous monitoring and feedback loops allow human experts to correct errors and prevent automation bias.

As AI systems become more powerful in healthcare, keeping humans firmly in the loop is foundational.[90,91] HITL approaches merge ML with the contextual judgment, ethical reasoning, and lived experience of clinicians. The goal is not to sideline professionals but to augment them: AI handles rapid pattern recognition and large-scale data synthesis while humans remain accountable for decisions that shape people's lives.

This principle is directly applicable to diagnostics and treatment planning. An AI model may suggest a cancer therapy matched to a patient's molecular profile. But this output is only a recommendation; a physician must review it against the patient's history, comorbidities, and values before any action is taken. Without that safeguard, false positives could overwhelm emergency teams, and treatment suggestions might clash with patient priorities.

HITL also strengthens the systems themselves. When radiologists correct AI-drawn lesion boundaries or pathologists validate molecular predictions, their feedback loops back into model training, improving both accuracy and generalizability. This dynamic is especially visible in genomics, where expert curation ensures that AI predictions about gene–drug interactions align with established pharmacogenomic guidelines.[92]

Equally important, human oversight mitigates systemic risks. Models trained on incomplete or skewed datasets can perpetuate disparities, particularly for underrepresented populations.[93] Left unchecked, they may hallucinate nonexistent patterns or recommend unsafe therapies. Human review serves as a corrective lens to catch failures before they reach patients. It also fulfills a regulatory imperative: agencies like the U.S. Food and Drug Administration (FDA) and the European Medicines Agency (EMA) increasingly emphasize transparency, explainability, and demonstrable clinician oversight as prerequisites for safe AI deployment.[94,95]

Liability adds another dimension. If an AI system produces a harmful recommendation, responsibility could fall on the developer, the institution, or the clinician. HITL frameworks reduce this ambiguity by ensuring that physicians review and authorize outputs before they guide care. In doing so, accountability stays anchored with licensed professionals, aligning with established malpractice structures and giving patients confidence that final decisions remain human-led.

The challenge, then, is balance. Too much manual review erodes the efficiencies AI promises, while too little invites automation without accountability. A layered approach is emerging as best practice.[96] AI triages the deluge of data and manages repetitive tasks, clinicians validate outputs and integrate them with patient context, and structured feedback continually improves the models. This interplay ensures that efficiency does not come at the cost of safety. Properly implemented, HITL designs illustrate the best of both worlds: machines that extend human reach, and humans who ground machine intelligence in ethical, patient-centered care.

Ethical and Regulatory Considerations

AI's promise in healthcare is immense—but so are the stakes. Alongside opportunities to diagnose earlier, treat more precisely, and manage systems more efficiently come questions that cut to the heart of medicine itself: How do we prevent bias from hardening into digital discrimination? How do we ensure transparency when models are built on billions of parameters that few can fully explain? Where does accountability lie when a machine's recommendation shapes a life-altering decision? And how do we preserve patient trust in a landscape increasingly mediated by algorithms?

These are not abstract concerns. Regulators are already responding: new frameworks are being drafted to govern AI tools before they enter clinical practice.[97,98] Ethical reflection and legal oversight ensure that new technologies are safe, equitable, and worthy of public confidence. As we move forward, these considerations are not peripheral to the story of AI in medicine. They are the conditions that make the story possible, and they set the stage for the deeper examination in the next chapter.

Ensuring that AI in healthcare remains safe, transparent, and accountable depends not only on sound regulations but also on the people who design, deploy, and use these systems. Next, we focus on education—how do we equip the healthcare workforce and future leaders with the skills and knowledge needed to guide these technologies responsibly from concept to clinic?

Education and Workforce Preparation

The arrival of AI in healthcare is both a technological revolution and an educational one. Algorithms may transform operations, but people determine whether those transformations are safe, ethical, and effective. Preparing the next generation of healthcare professionals is as critical as advancing the code itself.

Curricula in medicine, pharmacy, nursing, and allied health are evolving. Beyond anatomy and pharmacology, tomorrow's clinicians must learn the language of data. But technical fluency alone is not enough. Training must also cultivate ethical reasoning, empathy in patient communication, and the capacity for interdisciplinary teamwork.[99]

Hospitals, professional societies, and accrediting bodies are beginning to respond with continuing education that goes beyond "how to use the tool."[100–102] Courses emphasize governance, bias detection, patient safety, and responsible deployment—skills that give professionals confidence not only in using AI, but also in guiding it.

The lesson is clear: the future of AI in healthcare hinges not only on better models, but also on better-prepared people. By equipping practitioners with the knowledge, judgment, and ethical compass to work alongside intelligent systems, we ensure that AI's adoption is thoughtful and inclusive. Education is the bridge between promise and practice, and on that bridge walks the workforce that will decide whether AI in medicine fulfills its potential.

Balancing the Risks and Rewards of AI in Healthcare

The integration of AI has made significant strides in healthcare, revolutionizing various aspects of patient care, medical research, and healthcare management. AI-powered tools have significantly enhanced the accuracy and speed of medical diagnoses. For instance, in radiology, AI algorithms can now detect abnormalities in medical images with remarkable precision, often outperforming human radiologists in certain tasks. Virtual health assistants, powered by AI, are now managing over 85%

of customer interactions in healthcare, reducing the need for human intervention in routine tasks. A report by McKinsey & Company predicts that generative AI could help reduce healthcare costs in the United States by up to $150 billion annually by 2026 through automation of administrative tasks and optimization of clinical workflows.

However, the risks of AI in healthcare are mounting, too. These advanced solutions can lead to breaches in patient trust or privacy, legal issues, new rules to follow, and challenges with new technology.

The potential risks and consequences balance on a fulcrum that consists of AI governance, culture, policies, and standards. Different entities can influence the shape and strength of this fulcrum:

Systemic: Governing bodies such as the FDA or the Centers for Medicare and Medicaid Services (CMS) can implement "top–down" regulations that apply to specific types of algorithms, reducing risk to patients these algorithms are intended to serve. Any healthcare organization developing or deploying these algorithms will be held accountable for complying with these regulations.

Organizational: Each organization will likely have its own framework for how AI should be designed, developed, and delivered within the organization. This "inside–out" approach will build upon the systemic guidelines and reinforce organizational strategies, values, and culture.

Individual: The most important influence on the balance of risk and reward rests with the individuals involved in the AI lifecycle. Those most intimate with the algorithms create a "bottom–up" approach to enforcing standards and strengthening long-term success with AI strategies.

Current Risk Management Approaches and Their Limitations

While the benefits of AI in healthcare are substantial, the technology also presents significant risks that need to be carefully managed. Current risk management strategies often fall short of addressing the unique challenges posed by AI in healthcare.

One significant risk is bias in AI and machine learning algorithms, which often leads to inaccuracies. If a model is biased, it's usually inaccurate, too. The leading cause is poor data quality—garbage in, garbage out. If biased data is fed into the model, a biased model will be produced. Organizations often face a sunk cost effect; they've invested a lot in these models already. To fix this, they might educate physicians or system users to handle inaccuracies or bias in the models.

Consider the example of one of the most common machine learning use cases in healthcare: predicting high-cost or high-needs patients. These models are challenging to build because they need vast historical data to predict future care patterns. However, often, the individuals who suddenly need expensive care don't have the same type and volume of historical data used to train these models. This makes the models biased or inaccurate against these individuals. Despite this, many organizations still want these models in their analytical portfolio. Therefore, tactics to overcome the risk posed by the bias in these models must be purposefully put into the workflow. Options may include an additional step to sort individuals by known vulnerable or marginalized groups and create a stratified risk profile. Additionally, it becomes imperative to train end-users on how to properly leverage stratified risk profiles to allocate resources equally.

Now, let's talk about return on investment (ROI). It's said that 7 out of 10 AI solutions do not deliver the promised value. Some of this is likely due to inflated expectations in the sales process, but often, poor design and implementation play a factor as well. Even if a model is statistically accurate and fair, it will not return the intended value if utilized incorrectly. This misalignment is frequently seen in algorithms that support clinical decision-making.

While clinical, demographic, and utilization factors alone can build a statistically sufficient model, it lacks applicability for nurses who need to make decisions and form care plans from these model outputs. This will become a more pressing issue as providers and payers continue to realize the potential of the social drivers of healthcare, but we still lack the volume of these data to fuel ML/AI models appropriately.

Many organizations face the development and implementation risks previously discussed; others may face the consequences of lack of or deferred adoption. These entities often find themselves paralyzed by the fear of not realizing the anticipated value from AI investments or, even more concerning, the possibility of causing harm to patients or damaging their reputations.

Adopting a cautious approach, these organizations prefer to remain on the sidelines, closely monitoring the successes and failures of their industry peers before determining their own course of action. This wait-and-see strategy frequently leads to costly partnerships with AI consultants, which only serve to prolong the process of AI adoption and implementation further.

The hesitancy exhibited by these companies stems from a valid concern—the potential risks associated with AI implementation are significant and cannot be ignored. However, by delaying the adoption of these transformative technologies, they may inadvertently fall behind their competitors who have embraced AI more proactively. Finding the right balance between prudent risk management and timely adoption of AI solutions is a delicate undertaking that requires careful consideration and strategic planning.

In some cases, organizations may find themselves trapped in a perpetual cycle of exploratory AI pilots and proof-of-concept projects, unable to commit to deploying an operational AI solution at scale. This phenomenon, often referred to as "pilot purgatory," can arise due to various factors, including organizational inertia, risk aversion, lack of strategic alignment, or insufficient resources dedicated to AI initiatives.

Pilot projects serve an essential purpose, allowing organizations to evaluate the feasibility, potential benefits, and challenges associated with AI technologies in a controlled environment. However, when these pilots become an end unto themselves, organizations risk falling behind their competitors who have successfully transitioned from experimentation to full-scale implementation.

While the risks posed by utilizing AI cannot be completely eliminated, there are proactive measures that organizations can implement to minimize their potential impact.

- Conduct a thorough inventory of all ML and AI algorithms currently in use across the organization. This inventory should identify the specific applications, data sources, and individuals responsible for each algorithm's development, deployment, and maintenance. Assigning clear ownership and accountability for each algorithm and its outputs is paramount. This oversight should encompass regular monitoring, validation, and risk assessment processes to identify and address any potential issues or biases promptly. To reinforce the importance of this responsibility, organizations should implement a system of penalties or consequences for algorithms and outcomes that go unaccounted for or unreported. Similarly, individuals who fail to report identified risks or concerns in a timely manner should face appropriate disciplinary actions. This approach underscores the commitment to ethical and responsible AI deployment and encourages a culture of transparency and accountability.
- Aligning Data and AI Maturity: A common misconception is the belief that a robust data strategy must be fully established before embarking on AI initiatives. This notion fails to recognize the dynamic nature of data and the associated workflows. Data and its

surrounding processes are in a constant state of evolution, never reaching a truly finalized state. Consequently, AI leaders should adopt a collaborative mindset and work closely with data leaders to synchronize the maturity levels of both data and AI capabilities within the organization. It is worth noting that data maturity tends to be higher for data generated through core operational processes, such as claims processing or patient record management. These processes are typically well-established and have undergone rigorous refinement over time. As a result, algorithms built upon these data sources are likely to be more robust and reliable, making them an ideal starting point for initial AI model development and deployment.

- Developing an External Evaluation Strategy: In today's rapidly evolving technological landscape, the number of potential external partners is proliferating at an unprecedented rate. While this abundance of options presents exciting opportunities for collaboration and innovation, it also necessitates a significant investment of time and resources in evaluating these prospective partnerships. To navigate this complex landscape effectively, it is crucial for organizations to establish a well-defined process that sets clear, organization-specific standards early in the evaluation process. By doing so, they can streamline the assessment of potential partners, mitigate the risk of wasted efforts, and ensure alignment with their strategic objectives. Consider assessing the performance of external algorithms for subsets of data that are representative of organizational distributions or require shared savings goals when possible.
- Tracking Compliance Nuances: Leveraging robust tools to meticulously monitor and analyze AI policy changes is paramount, as even subtle nuances could significantly impact the inputs, outcomes, or utilization of AI/ML systems. The complexities inherent in this domain stem from a multitude of factors, including but not limited to:
  - Geographical Considerations: Varying state regulations and jurisdictional boundaries can introduce disparities in compliance requirements, necessitating a localized approach to ensure adherence.
  - Model Typology: The compliance implications may differ based on the specific type of model employed, such as Generative AI (GenAI) systems versus traditional ML models, each with its unique characteristics and potential risks.
  - Data Utilization: The nature and provenance of the data leveraged by the AI/ML solution can influence compliance obligations, particularly when dealing with sensitive or regulated information.
  - Patient-Facing Applications: AI/ML solutions intended for direct patient interaction or clinical decision support may be subject to heightened scrutiny and stringent regulatory oversight to safeguard patient safety and privacy.
  - Intended Use: The intended application or use case of the AI/ML model can shape the regulatory landscape, with different requirements potentially applying to systems deployed in diverse domains, such as healthcare, finance, or consumer applications.
- Fostering an Entrepreneurial Culture: The realm of data science and AI engineering is often dominated by a focus on technical prowess and algorithmic mastery. However, the ability to comprehend product-market fit and develop minimum viable products (MVPs) can be a game-changer, setting extraordinary AI teams apart from their average counterparts. The majority of data scientists and AI engineers are not trained to understand the intricate

dynamics of product-market fit, which involves aligning a product or service with the specific needs and demands of a target market. This critical aspect of product development is frequently overlooked in favor of purely technical considerations. Similarly, the concept of MVPs, which involves creating a bare-bones version of a product or service with just enough features to satisfy early customers and gather valuable feedback, is often neglected in the AI domain. The ability to build computationally lightweight and explainable models that address the core needs of end-users is a unique skill set that can significantly enhance the impact and success of AI initiatives.

- Create AI Decision Support: Just as physicians rely on clinical decision support systems to gain deeper insights into their patients' conditions and explore potential treatment options, data scientists can harness the power of AI decision support to better comprehend the nuances of their algorithms and models. These advanced systems act as virtual advisors, providing real-time recommendations and guidance to optimize model performance, identify potential biases, and ensure alignment with organizational goals. By integrating domain-specific knowledge, best practices, and historical data, these systems can provide data scientists with a comprehensive view of their models, enabling them to make informed decisions and mitigate risks effectively. Furthermore, AI decision support systems can facilitate collaboration and knowledge sharing within data science teams by capturing and codifying the collective expertise of experienced data scientists.

Case Study and Exercises

CASE STUDY 1:

Objective: Assess the risks and propose a mitigation strategy for AI deployment in healthcare.

Scenario: A hospital has implemented an AI system to predict patient readmission rates. Early results show that patients from underrepresented communities are disproportionately flagged as high-risk, leading to increased interventions for these groups.

Task:

1. Identify the possible risks associated with the AI system (e.g., bias, resource misallocation).
2. Suggest immediate actions the hospital could take to address these risks.
3. Propose a long-term strategy to prevent similar issues from arising in future AI implementations.

EXERCISE 2 BUILD A RESPONSIBLE AI CHECKLIST

Objective: Create a practical tool for balancing innovation with oversight.

Task: Imagine you are part of a healthcare organization planning to implement a new AI system. Develop a checklist of at least 10 actionable items that ensure risks are identified and addressed throughout the AI lifecycle. Your checklist should include considerations for:

- Data collection and preprocessing
- Algorithm design and testing
- Deployment and monitoring
- Organizational policies and training

- Compare your checklist with others to identify common themes and innovative approaches.

EXERCISE 3 ROLE-PLAYING ACTIVITY

Objective: Explore diverse perspectives on AI risks in healthcare.

Scenario: Your organization is hosting a meeting to decide whether to implement an AI-powered clinical decision support tool. Participants in the meeting include a healthcare administrator, a data scientist, a clinician, and a patient advocate.

Task:

1 Divide participants into groups, assigning each person one of the roles above.
2 Each participant should prepare a short statement outlining their perspective on the potential benefits and risks of the tool, considering their role's priorities and concerns.
3 Conduct a simulated meeting, allowing each participant to present their perspective and then engage in a collaborative discussion to decide whether to implement the tool and how to mitigate its risks.

Chapter Questions

Multiple-Choice Questions

1 **Which of the following is a key reason why healthcare organizations must actively address AI risks in real-time?**
A. To save on operational costs
B. To comply with all regulatory standards

C. To prevent algorithms from causing harm
D. To accelerate innovation without restrictions

Answer: C

2 What is the main limitation of viewing AI governance as merely an 'organizational value'?
A. It discourages innovation
B. It fails to address issues in real-time or prevent future harm
C. It increases the complexity of AI systems
D. It reduces the need for oversight

Answer: B

3 Which of the following best describes the ideal approach to AI risk mitigation in healthcare?
A. Reactive and cost-effective
B. Proactive and aligned with innovation
C. Technology-driven and regulation-focused
D. Decentralized and informal

Answer: B

Short-Answer Questions

1 What are the three forces that effect enterprise AI risk mitigation strategies and why are each important to a well-rounded approach?

Answer: The three forces are:

1 Systemic: Considers external factors like regulations, societal values, and industry standards to align organizational practices with broader expectations.
2 Organizational: Establishes policies, governance structures, and accountability measures to guide AI use responsibly.
3 Individual: Involves training and empowering employees to recognize and address risks effectively.

Each force is crucial to ensure AI risk mitigation is comprehensive, addressing internal operations, personal responsibility, and external influences.

2 Why is it important for risk mitigation strategies in healthcare AI to be approached with creativity and tactical precision?

Answer: Creativity and tactical precision are essential because addressing AI risks requires innovative solutions that keep pace with the rapid development of technology while ensuring patient safety and equity.

3 What does balancing innovation with proactive oversight in AI implementation achieve for healthcare organizations?

Answer: It ensures that AI serves as a tool for good by maximizing its benefits while minimizing unintended consequences and preventing harm to patients.

Assessment Questions

1. Define AI and explain how it differs from traditional computer programming.
2. Identify three subfields of AI relevant to healthcare and give an example of how each is applied.
3. What are two major factors driving the adoption of AI in healthcare today?
4. Choose one historical AI system (e.g., Eliza, MYCIN, INTERNIST-1). What did it attempt to accomplish, and why did it fall short in clinical use?
5. What are DTx, and how do they differ from general digital health tools such as wellness apps?
6. Give one example of how AI can improve hospital operations (e.g., logistics, staffing, or patient flow).
7. In drug development, how might AI-supported synthetic control arms reduce costs and patient burden in clinical trials?
8. Explain the concept of HITL in healthcare AI and why it is important for patient safety.
9. Consider the rise of agentic AI. What new capabilities might autonomous AI systems bring to healthcare teams, and what risks must be managed?
10. How could AI-driven DTx change the way patients and providers interact in managing chronic disease?

Answer Key

1. AI refers to computer systems designed to perform tasks that normally require human intelligence, such as learning, reasoning, understanding language, or recognizing patterns in data. Unlike traditional programming, which follows explicitly written "if–then" rules, AI systems can learn from data and improve over time without being manually reprogrammed for every situation.
2. Three examples of AI subfields: a) ML, which are algorithms that learn patterns from data (e.g., predicting which patients are at risk for heart failure). B) NLP, which are algorithms that can process and generate human language (e.g., summarizing EHRs or creating patient discharge instructions), and c) Computer Vision, which are systems that can interpret images and video (e.g., detecting tumors in radiology scans).
3. Factors driving the adoption of AI in healthcare include a) the explosion of healthcare data from EHRs, genomics, imaging, and wearable devices and b) the ability of AI to process this data quickly and generate insights that improve diagnosis, prevention, and treatment.

4. Eliza (1960s): Simulated a conversation with a therapist, but could not understand the meaning.
   MYCIN (1970s): Recommended antibiotics using "if–then" rules but was limited by manual data entry and rigidity.
   INTERNIST-1 (1970s): One of the first computerized medical consultants, but too complex and impractical for real clinical use.
   Common issue: These systems couldn't adapt or learn from new data and required too much effort to use in practice.
5. DTx are clinically validated, software-based treatments designed to prevent, manage, or treat medical conditions. Unlike general health apps or fitness trackers, DTx must show evidence of effectiveness in clinical trials and often require regulatory approval.
6. AI can predict emergency department arrivals or ICU occupancy, allowing hospitals to allocate staff and beds more efficiently. Similarly, it can automate administrative tasks like billing and scheduling, saving time and reducing costs.
7. Synthetic control arms use historical patient data instead of requiring new patients to be placed in the control group. This reduces the number of participants who must receive placebos, lowers costs, and speeds up trials while still allowing reliable comparisons.
8. HITL means AI supports, but does not replace, human decision-makers. For example, an AI system might flag a possible cancer on an image, but a radiologist reviews and confirms it. This safeguard ensures accuracy, prevents errors, and maintains trust in AI-assisted care.
9. Agentic AI could carry out multistep tasks, such as gathering lab results, drafting summaries, and scheduling follow-ups. This may improve efficiency and coordination. However, risks include errors going unnoticed, overreliance on AI, and unclear accountability if something goes wrong; therefore, oversight and safeguards are essential.
10. AI-driven DTx can adapt to patient behavior in real time. For example, adjusting a diabetes management plan based on glucose readings and activity data. This empowers patients to take a more active role in their own care, while providers receive richer data to guide treatment. The patient–provider relationship may become more collaborative and continuous, rather than limited to office visits.

References

1. Schmidgall S, Opfermann JD, Kim JW, Krieger A. Will your next surgeon be a robot? autonomy and AI in robotic surgery. *Science Robotics*. 2025;10(104). doi:https://doi.org/10.1126/scirobotics.adt0187
2. Gabriel P, Rehani P, Troy T, Wyatt T, Choma M, Singh N. Continuous patient monitoring with AI: real-time analysis of video in hospital care settings. *Frontiers in Imaging*. 2025;4. doi:https://doi.org/10.3389/fimag.2025.1547166
3. Varnosfaderani SM, Forouzanfar M. The role of AI in hospitals and clinics: transforming healthcare in the 21st century. *Bioengineering*. 2024;11(4):1–38. https://www.mdpi.com/2306-5354/11/4/337
4. Weizenbaum J. ELIZA – a computer program for the study of natural language communication between man and machine. *Communications of the ACM*. 1966;9(1):36–45. doi:https://doi.org/10.1145/365153.365168
5. Kaul V, Enslin S, Gross SA. History of artificial intelligence in medicine. *Gastrointestinal Endoscopy*. 2020;92(4):807–812. doi:https://doi.org/10.1016/j.gie.2020.06.040

6. Miller RA, Pople HE, Myers JD. Internist-1, an experimental computer-based diagnostic consultant for general internal medicine. *The New England Journal of Medicine.* 1982;307(8):468–476. doi:https://doi.org/10.1056/NEJM198208193070803
7. Shortliffe EH. Computer programs to support clinical decision making. *JAMA: The Journal of the American Medical Association.* 1987;258(1):61. doi:https://doi.org/10.1001/jama.1987.03400010065029
8. Ferrucci D, Brown E, Chu-Carroll J, et al. Building watson: an qverview of the deepQA project. *AI Magazine.* 2010;31(3):59. doi:https://doi.org/10.1609/aimag.v31i3.2303
9. Malin JL. Envisioning watson as a rapid-learning system for oncology. *Journal of Oncology Practice.* 2013;9(3):155–157. doi:https://doi.org/10.1200/jop.2013.001021
10. Jumper J, Evans R, Pritzel A, et al. Highly accurate protein structure prediction with alphafold. *Nature.* 2021;596(7873):583–589. doi:https://doi.org/10.1038/s41586-021-03819-2
11. Karunanayake N. Next-generation agentic AI for transforming healthcare. *Informatics and Health.* 2025;2(2):73–83. doi:https://doi.org/10.1016/j.infoh.2025.03.001
12. Bandi A, Kongari B, Naguru R, Pasnoor S, Vilipala SV. The rise of agentic AI: a review of definitions, frameworks, *Architectures, Applications, Evaluation Metrics, and Challenges. Future Internet.* 2025;17(9):404–404. doi:https://doi.org/10.3390/fi17090404
13. Turing A. Computing machinery and intelligence. *Mind.* 1950;59(236):433–460. doi:https://doi.org/10.1093/mind/LIX.236.433
14. Nilsson N, Nielson D. Shakey the Robot.; 1984. https://ai.stanford.edu/~nilsson/OnlinePubs-Nils/shakey-the-robot.pdf
15. Silver D, Huang A, Maddison CJ, et al. Mastering the game of Go with deep neural networks and tree search. *Nature.* 2016;529(7587):484–489. doi:https://doi.org/10.1038/nature16961
16. Abràmoff MD, Lavin PT, Birch M, Shah N, Folk JC. Pivotal trial of an autonomous AI-based diagnostic system for detection of diabetic retinopathy in primary care offices. *NPJ Digital Medicine.* 2018;1(1). doi:https://doi.org/10.1038/s41746-018-0040-6
17. Nori H, Daswani M, Kelly C, et al. Sequential diagnosis with language models. *arXiv*.org. Published 2025. https://arxiv.org/abs/2506.22405
18. Bajwa J, Munir U, Nori A, Williams B. Artificial intelligence in healthcare: transforming the practice of medicine. *Future Healthcare Journal.* 2021;8(2):188–194. doi:https://doi.org/10.7861/fhj.2021-0095
19. Hirani R, Noruzi K, Khuram H, et al. Artificial intelligence and healthcare: a journey through history, present innovations, and future possibilities. *Life.* 2024;14(5):557. doi:https://doi.org/10.3390/life14050557
20. Błaziak M, Urban S, Wietrzyk W, et al. An artificial intelligence approach to guiding the management of heart failure patients using predictive models: a systematic review. *Biomedicines.* 2022;10(9):2188. doi:https://doi.org/10.3390/biomedicines10092188
21. Wang SCY, Nickel G, Venkatesh KP, Raza MM, Kvedar JC. AI-based diabetes care: risk prediction models and implementation concerns. *npj Digital Medicine.* 2024;7(1). doi:https://doi.org/10.1038/s41746-024-01034-7
22. Faiyazuddin M, Syed JQR, Anand G, et al. The impact of artificial intelligence on healthcare: a comprehensive review of advancements in diagnostics, treatment, and operational efficiency. *Health Science Reports.* 2025;8(1). doi:https://doi.org/10.1002/hsr2.70312
23. Acumen Research and Consulting. AI in healthcare market is forecasted to reach USD 427.5 Billion by 2032, growing at a CAGR of 44.0% over the forecast period 2023 to 2032. *GlobeNewswire News Room.* Published October 10, 2023. www.globenewswire.com/news-release/2023/10/10/2757664/0/en/AI-in-Healthcare-Market-is-forecasted-to-Reach-USD-427-5-Billion-by-2032-growing-at-a-CAGR-of-44-0-Over-the-Forecast-Period-2023-to-2032.html
24. Khalifa M, Albadawy M. AI in diagnostic imaging: revolutionising accuracy and efficiency. *Computer Methods and Programs in Biomedicine Update.* 2024;5:100146. doi:https://doi.org/10.1016/j.cmpbup.2024.100146

25. Debellotte O, Dookie RL, Rinkoo F, et al. Artificial intelligence and early detection of breast, lung, and colon cancer: a narrative review. *Cureus. Published online February* 18, 2025. doi:https://doi.org/10.7759/cureus.79199
26. Tang AS, Rankin KP, Cerono G, et al. Leveraging electronic health records and knowledge networks for Alzheimer's disease prediction and sex-specific biological insights. *Nature Aging.* Published online February 21, 2024;4(4):523–539. doi:https://doi.org/10.1038/s43587-024-00573-8
27. Młynarska E, Bojdo K, Frankenstein H, et al. Nanotechnology and artificial intelligence in dyslipidemia management—cardiovascular disease: advances, challenges, and future perspectives. *Journal of Clinical Medicine.* 2025;14(3):887. doi:https://doi.org/10.3390/jcm14030887
28. Kai J, Yang L, AbuElela AF, et al. Building simplified cancer subtyping and prediction models with glycan gene signatures. *Cell Reports Methods.* 2025;5(8):101140. doi:https://doi.org/10.1016/j.crmeth.2025.101140
29. Wu S, Roberts K, Datta S, et al. Deep learning in clinical natural language processing: a methodical review. *Journal of the American Medical Informatics Association.* 2019;27(3):457-470. doi:https://doi.org/10.1093/jamia/ocz200
30. Wang D, Zhang S. Large language models in medical and healthcare fields: applications, advances, and challenges. *Artificial Intelligence Review.* 2024;57(11). doi:https://doi.org/10.1007/s10462-024-10921-0
31. Singhal K, Azizi S, Tu T, et al. Large language models encode clinical knowledge. *Nature.* 2023;620(7972):172–180. doi:https://doi.org/10.1038/s41586-023-06291-2
32. Lee P, Bubeck S, Petro J. Benefits, limits, and risks of GPT-4 as an AI chatbot for medicine. Drazen JM, Kohane IS, Leong TY, eds. *New England Journal of Medicine.* 2023;388(13):1233–1239. doi:https://doi.org/10.1056/nejmsr2214184
33. Tavabi N, Singh M, Pruneski J, Kiapour AM. Systematic evaluation of common natural language processing techniques to codify clinical notes. *PloS one.* 2024;19(3):e0298892–e0298892. doi:https://doi.org/10.1371/journal.pone.0298892
34. Peerbolte TF, van Diggelen RJ, van den Haak P, et al. Conversational agents supporting self-management in people with a chronic disease: systematic review. *Journal of Medical Internet Research.* 2025;27:e72309–e72309. doi:https://doi.org/10.2196/72309
35. Sutton R, Pincock D, Baumgart D, Sadowski D, Fedorak R, Kroeker K. An overview of clinical decision support systems: benefits, risks, and strategies for success. *NPJ Digital Medicine.* 2020;3(1):1–10. doi:https://doi.org/10.1038/s41746-020-0221-y
36. Lin Z, Guan S, Zhang W, Zhang H, Li Y, Zhang H. Towards trustworthy LLMs: a review on debiasing and dehallucinating in large language models. *Artificial Intelligence Review.* 2024;57(9). doi:https://doi.org/10.1007/s10462-024-10896-y
37. Thirunavukarasu AJ, Ting DSJ, Elangovan K, Gutierrez L, Tan TF, Ting DSW. Large language models in medicine. *Nature Medicine.* 2023;29(29). doi:https://doi.org/10.1038/s41591-023-02448-8
38. FDA. Policy for device software functions and mobile medical applications. *U.S. Food and Drug Administration.* Published 2019. www.fda.gov/regulatory-information/search-fda-guidance-documents/policy-device-software-functions-and-mobile-medical-applications
39. Coravos A, Goldsack JC, Karlin DR, et al. Digital medicine: a primer on measurement. *Digital Biomarkers.* 2019;3(2):31–71. doi:https://doi.org/10.1159/000500413
40. Digital Therapeutics Alliance. Understanding DTx. Digital Therapeutics Alliance. Published 2024. https://dtxalliance.org/understanding-dtx/
41. Benjamens S, Dhunnoo P, Meskó B. The state of artificial intelligence-based FDA-approved medical devices and algorithms: an online database. *NPJ Digital Medicine.* 2020;3(1):1–8. doi:https://doi.org/10.1038/s41746-020-00324-0
42. Wang C, Lee C, Shin H. Digital therapeutics from bench to bedside. *NPJ Digital Medicine.* 2023;6(1):1–10. doi:https://doi.org/10.1038/s41746-023-00777-z

43. Fitzpatrick KK, Darcy A, Vierhile M. Delivering cognitive behavior therapy to young adults with symptoms of depression and anxiety using a fully automated conversational agent (woebot): a randomized controlled trial. *JMIR Mental Health*. 2017;4(2). doi:https://doi.org/10.2196/mental.7785
44. Inkster B, Sarda S, Subramanian V. An empathy-driven, conversational artificial intelligence agent (Wysa) for digital mental well-being: real-world data evaluation mixed-methods study. *JMIR mHealth and uHealth*. 2018;6(11):e12106. doi:https://doi.org/10.2196/12106
45. Wilson MG, Castro Sweet CM, Edge MD, et al. Evaluation of a digital behavioral counseling program for reducing risk factors for chronic disease in a workforce. *Journal of Occupational and Environmental Medicine*. 2017;59(8):e150–e155. doi:https://doi.org/10.1097/jom.0000000000001091
46. Gershoni T, Ritholz MD, Horwitz DL, Manejwala O, Donaldson-Pitter T, Fundoiano-Hershcovitz Y. Glycemic management by a digital therapeutic platform across racial/ethnic groups: a retrospective cohort study. *Applied Sciences*. 2022;13(1):431. doi:https://doi.org/10.3390/app13010431
47. Priebe JA, Haas KK, Moreno Sanchez LF, et al. Digital treatment of back pain versus standard of care: the cluster-randomized controlled trial, rise-uP. *Journal of Pain Research*. 2020;13:1823–1838. doi:https://doi.org/10.2147/JPR.S260761
48. Maddox T, Garcia H, Ffrench K, et al. In-home virtual reality program for chronic low back pain: durability of a randomized, placebo-controlled clinical trial to 18 months post-treatment. *Regional Anesthesia and Pain Medicine*. 2022;49(5):rapm-104093. doi:https://doi.org/10.1136/rapm-2022-104093
49. Paz E, Pargaonkar VS, Roach BJ, et al. Comprehensive cardiovascular risk factor control with a mobile health cardiovascular risk self-management program. *Journal of the American Heart Association Cardiovascular and cerebrovascular disease*. 2024;13(10). doi:https://doi.org/10.1161/jaha.123.033328
50. Crist C. Digital therapeutics could help patients with IBS. *Medscape. Published February* 27, 2023. www.medscape.com/viewarticle/988848
51. Nevado-Holgado A, Espie C, Liakata M, et al. Personalised recommendations of sleep behaviour with neural networks using sleep diaries captured in Sleepio. *arXiv.org*. Published July 29, 2022. https://arxiv.org/abs/2208.00033
52. Thorndike FP, Morin CM, Ojile J, et al. Effect of a prescription digital therapeutic for chronic insomnia on post-treatment insomnia severity, depression, and anxiety symptoms: results from the real-world DREAM study. *Frontiers in Psychiatry*. 2024;15. doi:https://doi.org/10.3389/fpsyt.2024.1450615
53. Miller School of Medicine. Miller school of medicine launches office of AI in medical education – inventUM. *InventUM*. Published August 5, 2025. Accessed October 25, 2025. https://news.med.miami.edu/miller-school-of-medicine-launches-office-of-ai-in-medical-education/
54. Feinberg School of Medicine. *Home*. Northwestern.edu. Published 2025. www.feinberg.northwestern.edu/sites/artificial-intelligence/index.html
55. Mount Sinai. Mount sinai opens the Hamilton and Amabel James center for artificial intelligence and human health to transform health care by spearheading the AI revolution. *Mount Sinai Health System*. Published November 25, 2024. www.mountsinai.org/about/newsroom/2024/mount-sinai-opens-the-hamilton-and-amabel-james-center-for-artificial-intelligence-and-human-health-to-transform-health-care-by-spearheading-the-ai-revolution
56. IntuitionLabs. Top 20 medtech companies leveraging AI in 2025. *IntuitionLabs*. Published April 18, 2025. https://intuitionlabs.ai/articles/top-20-medtech-companies-using-ai-2025
57. Deakers C. The healthcare AI adoption index. Bessemer venture partners. Published April 14, 2025. www.bvp.com/atlas/the-healthcare-ai-adoption-index
58. Topol EJ. High-performance medicine: the convergence of human and artificial intelligence. *Nature Medicine*. 2019;25(1):44–56. www.nature.com/articles/s41591-018-0300-7
59. Scaife AD. Improve predictive maintenance through the application of artificial intelligence: A systematic review. *Results in Engineering*. 2023;21:101645. doi:https://doi.org/10.1016/j.rineng.2023.101645

60. Gan Z, Fu Z, Dong P, Ju Y, Shen Y. Computational modeling and analysis of medical resource shortages in hospital alliance: a simulation-driven approach. *PLoS ONE*. 2025;20(8):e0330871–e0330871. doi:https://doi.org/10.1371/journal.pone.0330871
61. Islayem R, Gebreab S, AlKhader W, et al. Using large language models for enhanced fraud analysis and detection in blockchain based health insurance claims. *Scientific Reports*. 2025;15(1). doi:https://doi.org/10.1038/s41598-025-15676-4
62. Knight DRT, Aakre CA, Anstine CV, et al. Artificial intelligence for patient scheduling in the real-world health care setting: a metanarrative review. *Health Policy and Technology*. 2023;12(4):100824. doi:https://doi.org/10.1016/j.hlpt.2023.100824
63. Pantanowitz L, Hanna M, Pantanowitz J, et al. Regulatory aspects of AI-ML. *Modern Pathology*. 2024;37(12):100609. doi:https://doi.org/10.1016/j.modpat.2024.100609
64. Maqsood K, Hagras H, Zabet NR. An overview of artificial intelligence in the field of genomics. *Discover Artificial Intelligence*. 2024;4(1). doi:https://doi.org/10.1007/s44163-024-00103-w
65. Mak CCY, Klinkhammer H, Choufani S, et al. Artificial intelligence-driven genotype–epigenotype–phenotype approaches to resolve challenges in syndrome diagnostics. *EBioMedicine*. 2025;115:105677. doi:https://doi.org/10.1016/j.ebiom.2025.105677
66. Prelaj A, Miskovic V, Zanitti M, et al. Artificial intelligence for predictive biomarker discovery in immuno-oncology: a systematic review. *Annals of Oncology*. 2024;35(1):41–55. doi:https://doi.org/10.1016/j.annonc.2023.10.125
67. Wan Z, Sun X, Li Y, et al. Applications of artificial intelligence in drug repurposing. *Advanced Science*. 2025;12(16):2411325. doi:https://doi.org/10.1002/advs.202411325
68. Zack M, Stupichev DN, Moore AJ, et al. AI and multi-omics in pharmacogenomics: a new era of precision medicine. *Mayo Clinic Proceedings Digital Health*. 2025;3(3):100246–100246. doi:https://doi.org/10.1016/j.mcpdig.2025.100246
69. Kidwai-Khan F, Rentsch CT, Pulk R, Alcorn C, Brandt CA, Justice AC. Pharmacogenomics driven decision support prototype with machine learning: a framework for improving patient care. *Frontiers in Big Data*. 2022;5. doi:https://doi.org/10.3389/fdata.2022.1059088
70. Khoury MJ, Bowen S, Dotson D, Kolor K. *Public Health Genomics Priorities Through a Health Equity Lens | Blogs | CDC*. Cdc.gov. Published May 18, 2021. https://blogs.cdc.gov/genomics/2021/05/18/public-health-genomics-priorities/
71. Bentley AR, Callier S, Rotimi CN. Diversity and inclusion in genomic research: why the uneven progress? *Journal of Community Genetics*. 2017;8(4):255–266. doi:https://doi.org/10.1007/s12687-017-0316-6
72. Zhang K, Yang X, Wang Y, et al. Artificial intelligence in drug development. *Nature Medicine*. 2025;31(31):1–15. doi:https://doi.org/10.1038/s41591-024-03434-4
73. Sadybekov AV, Katritch V. Computational approaches streamlining drug discovery. *Nature*. 2023;616(7958):673–685. doi:https://doi.org/10.1038/s41586-023-05905-z
74. Gangwal A, Ansari A, Ahmad I, et al. Generative artificial intelligence in drug discovery: basic framework, recent advances, challenges, and opportunities. *Frontiers in Pharmacology*. 2024;15. doi:https://doi.org/10.3389/fphar.2024.1331062
75. Wu K, Li X, Zhou Z, et al. Predicting pharmacodynamic effects through early drug discovery with artificial intelligence-physiologically based pharmacokinetic (AI-PBPK) modelling. *Frontiers in Pharmacology*. 2024;15. doi:https://doi.org/10.3389/fphar.2024.1330855
76. Habiballah S, Reisfeld B. Adapting physiologically-based pharmacokinetic models for machine learning applications. *Scientific Reports*. 2023;13(1). doi:https://doi.org/10.1038/s41598-023-42165-3
77. Singh N, Vayer P, Tanwar S, Poyet JL, Tsaioun K, Villoutreix BO. Drug discovery and development: introduction to the general public and patient groups. *Frontiers in drug discovery*. 2023;3. doi:https://doi.org/10.3389/fddsv.2023.1201419
78. Lee H, Kim J, Kim JW, Lee Y. Recent advances in AI-based toxicity prediction for drug discovery. *Frontiers in chemistry*. 2025;13:1632046. doi:https://doi.org/10.3389/fchem.2025.1632046

79. Price PS, Hubbell BJ, Hagiwara S, et al. A framework that considers the impacts of time, cost, and uncertainty in the determination of the cost effectiveness of toxicity-testing methodologies. *Risk Analysis.* 2022;42(5):1078–1095. doi:https://doi.org/10.1111/risa.13810
80. The RECOVERY Collaborative Group. Dexamethasone in hospitalized patients with covid-19 — preliminary report. *New England Journal of Medicine.* 2020;384(8):693–704. doi:https://doi.org/10.1056/nejmoa2021436
81. Makutam V, Achanti SY, Doostan M. Integration of artificial intelligence in adaptive travel designs: enhancing efficiency and patient-centric outcomes. *International Journal of Advanced Research.* Published August 17, 2024. Accessed October 25, 2025. www.journalijar.com/article/49739/integration-of-artificial-intelligence-in-adaptive-trial-designs:-enhancing-efficiency-and-patient-centric-outcomes/
82. Rosenthal JT, Beecy A, Sabuncu MR. Rethinking clinical trials for medical AI with dynamic deployments of adaptive systems. *NPJ Digital Medicine.* 2025;8(1). doi:https://doi.org/10.1038/s41746-025-01674-3
83. Nisa U, Shirazi M, Saip MA, Pozi MSM. Agentic AI: the age of reasoning—a review. *Journal of Automation and Intelligence. Published online August* 28, 2025. doi:https://doi.org/10.1016/j.jai.2025.08.003
84. Hinostroza Fuentes VG, Karim HA, Tan MJT, AlDahoul N. AI with agency: a vision for adaptive, efficient, and ethical healthcare. *Frontiers in Digital Health.* 2025;7. doi:https://doi.org/10.3389/fdgth.2025.1600216
85. Barra FL, Rodella G, Costa A, et al. From prompt to platform: an agentic AI workflow for healthcare simulation scenario design. *Advances in Simulation.* 2025;10(1). doi:https://doi.org/10.1186/s41077-025-00357-z
86. Milmo D. Microsoft says AI system better than doctors at diagnosing complex health conditions. *The Guardian.* Published June 30, 2025. www.theguardian.com/technology/2025/jun/30/microsoft-ai-system-better-doctors-diagnosing-health-conditions-research
87. Park A. Microsoft's AI is better than doctors at diagnosing disease. *TIME.* Published July 2, 2025. https://time.com/7299314/microsoft-ai-better-than-doctors-diagnosis
88. Saenz AD, Harned Z, Banerjee O, Abràmoff MD, Rajpurkar P. Autonomous AI systems in the face of liability, regulations and costs. *NPJ Digital Medicine.* 2023;6(1):1–3. doi:https://doi.org/10.1038/s41746-023-00929-1
89. King D, Nori H. The path to medical superintelligence | Microsoft AI. Microsoft AI. Published August 26, 2025. https://microsoft.ai/news/the-path-to-medical-superintelligence/
90. Sezgin E. Artificial intelligence in healthcare: complementing, not replacing, doctors and healthcare providers. *Digital Health.* 2023;9(PMC10328041). doi:https://doi.org/10.1177/20552076231186520
91. Bakken S. AI in health: keeping the human in the loop. *Journal of the American Medical Informatics Association.* 2023;30(7):1225–1226. doi:https://doi.org/10.1093/jamia/ocad091
92. Taherdoost H, Ghofrani A. AI's role in revolutionizing personalized medicine by reshaping pharmacogenomics and drug therapy. *Intelligent Pharmacy.* 2024;2(5). doi:https://doi.org/10.1016/j.ipha.2024.08.005
93. Hasanzadeh F, Josephson CB, Waters G, Adedinsewo D, Azizi Z, White JA. Bias recognition and mitigation strategies in artificial intelligence healthcare applications. *NPJ Digital Medicine.* 2025;8(1). doi:https://doi.org/10.1038/s41746-025-01503-7
94. FDA. Transparency for machine learning-enabled medical devices: guiding principles. Published online June 13, 2024. www.fda.gov/medical-devices/software-medical-device-samd/transparency-machine-learning-enabled-medical-devices-guiding-principles
95. European Medicines Agency. Committee for Medicinal Products for Human Use (CHMP) Committee for Medicinal Products for Veterinary Use (CVMP) Reflection Paper on the Use of Artificial Intelligence (AI) in the Medicinal Product Lifecycle Draft Agreed by Committee for Medicinal Products for Human Use (CHMP) Methodology Working Party Reflection Paper on

the Use of AI in the Medicinal Product Lifecycle. EMA; 2024. www.ema.europa.eu/en/documents/scientific-guideline/reflection-paper-use-artificial-intelligence-ai-medicinal-product-lifecycle_en.pdf
96. Kim Y, Jeong H, Park C, et al. Tiered agentic oversight: a hierarchical multi-agent system for AI safety in healthcare. *arXiv.org*. Published 2025. https://arxiv.org/abs/2506.12482
97. Palaniappan K, Yan E, Vogel S. Global regulatory frameworks for the Use of artificial intelligence (AI) in the healthcare services sector. *Healthcare*. 2024;12(5):562–562. doi:https://doi.org/10.3390/healthcare12050562
98. Schmidt J, Schutte NM, Buttigieg S, et al. Mapping the regulatory landscape for artificial intelligence in health within the European Union. *NPJ Digital Medicine*. 2024;7(1). doi:https://doi.org/10.1038/s41746-024-01221-6
99. Okamoto S, Kataoka M, Itano M, Sawai T. AI-based medical ethics education: examining the potential of large language models as a tool for virtue cultivation. *BMC Medical Education*. 2025;25(1). doi:https://doi.org/10.1186/s12909-025-06801-y
100. AMA EdHub. *Artificial and Augmented Intelligence in Health Care*. edhub.ama-assn.org. Accessed October 25, 2025. https://edhub.ama-assn.org/course/318
101. Institute for Healthcare Improvement. Making AI work for you. *Ihi.org*. Accessed October 25, 2025. www.ihi.org/learn/courses/making-ai-work-for-you
102. Crim A, Skidmore RM, Bowser AD, et al. The alliance for continuing education in the health professions' position on artificial intelligence in CPD. *Journal of CME*. 2025;14(1). doi:https://doi.org/10.1080/28338073.2025.2545647

Appendix 7A

Glossary

1. Neural Networks—NNs are computational models inspired by the brain's structure. They process data through layers of interconnected "neurons" that adjust their weights during training, allowing the system to learn patterns for tasks like image recognition, language processing, or prediction.
2. Supervised Learning—This is a type of ML where an algorithm is trained on labeled data. The model learns the mapping between inputs and outputs, such as using medical records and known diagnoses to predict future cases.
3. Unsupervised Learning—This learning uses data without labels. The goal is to find hidden patterns or groupings, such as clustering patients with similar symptoms even when no diagnosis is given beforehand.
4. Reinforcement Learning—It is a training method where an agent learns by trial and error, receiving rewards or penalties based on its actions. This is used in areas like drug dosing simulations or robotics.
5. Multimodal AI systems—Multimodal AI systems combine different types of input data, such as text, images, and genomic sequences, into one model. This integration allows for richer insights—for example, linking genetic profiles with imaging and clinical notes.
6. CAGR—This is a way to measure the consistent annual growth rate of an investment, market, or technology over time. It smooths out fluctuations to give an average year-on-year percentage increase.
7. Information Extraction (NLP)—Information extraction is the process of automatically pulling out structured facts from unstructured text. For example, scanning clinical notes to identify mentions of symptoms or treatments.

8. Document Classification (NLP)—Document classification involves sorting text into predefined categories. In healthcare, this might mean labeling reports as radiology, pathology, or discharge summaries.
9. Negation Detection (NLP)—Negation detection identifies when a medical condition or symptom is explicitly denied in text, such as distinguishing "no evidence of stroke" from "stroke present."
10. Temporal Reasoning (NLP)—Temporal reasoning interprets time-related information in text. For instance, it helps models recognize that "symptoms began three months ago" is important for diagnosing disease progression.
11. Tokens—These are the smallest units of text that an AI model processes, often words, parts of words, or symbols. They are the building blocks for language models.
12. Dimensions and weights—Dimensions refer to the size of the data representations in a model, while weights are the adjustable parameters that determine how inputs are transformed into outputs during training.
13. Federated Learning—A method where multiple institutions train a shared model without exchanging raw data. Instead, updates are sent and combined, protecting privacy while benefiting from broader datasets.
14. High-Throughput Sequencing—Also called next-generation sequencing, HTS is a fast and large-scale DNA or RNA reading method. It enables rapid analysis of genomes or transcriptomes, critical for personalized medicine and drug discovery.

Appendix 7B

Extended Notes

1. "If–then" expert systems in clinical decision-making—Early AI in medicine often relied on rule-based "if–then" logic. For example, an expert system might encode medical knowledge such as: *if* the patient has chest pain and shortness of breath, *then* check for possible cardiac disease. These systems were transparent and interpretable but limited, as they could not easily adapt to new evidence or uncertainty. They served as early decision-support tools in clinical practice but were eventually replaced by more flexible statistical and ML models.
2. Generative and Foundational models in drug discovery—Generative models create new data samples, such as designing novel drug molecules that follow desired chemical rules. Foundation models, like AlphaFold or LLMs, are trained on massive and diverse datasets, making them highly adaptable to many downstream tasks. In drug discovery, these approaches enable automated molecule generation, prediction of protein structures, and simulation of drug–target interactions. Together, they are transforming early-stage R&D by accelerating hypothesis generation and reducing costs compared to traditional lab-based trial-and-error.
3. Model Tuning (NLP)—Model tuning is the process of adapting a general AI model to perform well on a specific task or dataset. In NLP, this often means fine-tuning a pretrained language model on specialized text—such as medical notes—so it can classify conditions, extract information, or assist in diagnostics. Tuning improves accuracy, reduces errors, and ensures that models capture domain-specific terminology and context. It is particularly valuable in healthcare, where precision and reliability are critical.

4. Application Programming Interface (API)—An API is a standardized way for different software systems to communicate with each other. In practice, it acts like a bridge, allowing an AI tool to integrate into clinical workflows. For example, an NLP model can process EHRs through an API and return structured insights to a hospital's system. APIs are becoming essential in healthcare because they enable secure, modular, and scalable use of AI—letting hospitals and researchers connect advanced models with existing infrastructure without rebuilding systems from scratch.

Chapter 8

Machine Learning in Healthcare

Anthony Blash, PharmD, BCompSc, CPHIMS

Machine Learning Fundamentals

Machine learning (ML) is a transformative force in healthcare, enabling systems to learn autonomously from large datasets. ML algorithms, often grouped under artificial intelligence (AI), build problem-solving models that interpret information, generate predictions, and uncover patterns at speeds exceeding human cognition while reducing bias.[1]

A program is a set of instructions for a task, and a software system comprises interconnected programs and databases, such as electronic health records (EHRs). An algorithm is a generalized set of rules for solving a class of problems, while an AI/ML model is a computable representation created from training data to produce solutions from new inputs.[1]

By revealing subtle relationships in complex healthcare data, ML improves diagnostic accuracy, prognosis, and personalized treatments, while supporting trust, collaboration, and responsible adoption.[1]

Types of ML: Supervised, Unsupervised, and Reinforcement Learning

Machine learning (ML) paradigms are broadly categorized into three main types—supervised learning, unsupervised learning, and reinforcement learning—each suited for different problem sets and applications within healthcare.

Supervised Learning trains ML algorithms using labeled datasets, where each input is paired with a known desired output.[2] The algorithm learns to map inputs to outputs, enabling classification or prediction. In healthcare, supervised learning is widely applied to diagnostic and prognostic tasks using historical data with known outcomes.[3] Common supervised learning algorithms include several well-established methods.

Support vector machines (SVMs) are widely used for classification in clinical epidemiology, for example predicting patient risk stratification for chronic diseases such as cardiovascular conditions

 DOI: 10.4324/9781003593867-11

by analyzing clinical and demographic data.[3] K-Nearest neighbor (KNN) algorithms have been effectively applied to identify patients at risk for heart disease by grouping cases based on similarities in clinical, demographic, and laboratory variables, an intuitive approach supported by multiple healthcare diagnostic reviews.[4] Logistic regression remains a fundamental supervised learning method for binary outcome prediction, such as forecasting hospital readmission within 30 days after discharge; its interpretability and robustness make it a mainstay in clinical risk stratification models.[3] Neural networks (NNs), particularly deep NNs, are central to medical image analysis, exemplified by models that detect diabetic retinopathy from retinal fundus photographs with accuracy comparable to expert ophthalmologists, demonstrating their ability to capture complex nonlinear patterns in healthcare data.[4] Decision trees (DTs) are used for clinical prognostic classification, including triage systems that predict critical illness and support decision-making in emergency departments through sequential evaluation of clinical features, providing transparent decision pathways that help prioritize care.[5] Finally, AdaBoost, an ensemble boosting method, improves predictive accuracy by combining multiple weak classifiers and has been applied in critical care settings to predict sepsis in ICU patients, enhancing early detection and intervention through robust aggregation of simple classifiers.[4]

Together, these algorithms illustrate the breadth of supervised learning techniques in healthcare, each offering distinct advantages depending on the data type and clinical context.

Supervised learning has demonstrated a wide range of clinical applications. For instance, triage systems employing ML models outperform conventional approaches in predicting outcomes for children in emergency departments, enabling earlier identification of critically ill patients. In COVID-19 prognosis, ensemble models have been applied to predict patient mortality risk with high accuracy. Another example is HIV rapid test classification,[1] where convolutional NNs (CNNs) analyze photos of diagnostic test strips to standardize interpretation and reduce errors.[3]

Unsupervised learning, by contrast, analyzes unlabeled datasets to uncover hidden structures or associations without prior knowledge of the output. Algorithms such as K-means clustering, hierarchical clustering, and principal component analysis (PCA) are commonly used to group data, generate novel insights, and reduce dimensionality.[4] Healthcare applications include disease phenotyping,[3] genomic analysis to discover new genotypes, and histopathology slide classification using systems such as Owkin's CHOWDER, which can extract interpretable features and predict survival without human input.[2]

Reinforcement learning (RL) extends ML by training "agents" to learn optimal strategies through repeated interaction with an environment.[6] Agents receive rewards for beneficial actions and penalties for poor ones, gradually refining policies to maximize cumulative rewards. Key concepts include the agent, environment, state, actions, and the rewards or penalties that guide learning, often framed within Markov Decision Processes (MDPs).[6] In healthcare, RL has been applied to resource optimization, such as reducing emergency department waiting times,[3] and to personalized treatment strategies, where models adapt therapies to patient-specific responses.[6] During COVID-19, RL was noted for managing uncertainty, optimizing complex decisions under rapidly changing conditions.[7] The adoption of ensemble and hybrid approaches marks a maturation in ML for healthcare, moving beyond single algorithms to improve accuracy and robustness. Studies show that integrating multiple ML models, such as ensembles predicting COVID-19 mortality, achieved high AUC values.[3] Hybrid and ensemble methods consistently demonstrate high predictive accuracy across diseases,[7] with algorithms like AdaBoost illustrating how weak classifiers can be combined for stronger performance.[4] This trend reflects a shift toward multilayered architectures capable of capturing complex data, providing more reliable and robust clinical tools. However, the "black-box" nature of deep learning and unsupervised models remains a barrier to interpretability, trust, and practical use.[8,9] Clinicians require clear rationales for predictions to ensure safety, accountability, and informed decision-making. Without transparency, adoption is undermined, highlighting the urgent need for continued work in explainable AI (XAI) to make decision-making processes more understandable. RL is poised to revolutionize dynamic, real-time decision-making and resource optimization. Its ability to continuously learn and adapt is especially valuable for evolving scenarios, from sequential treatment strategies to patient flow management.[6] During the COVID 19 pandemic, RL demonstrated its relevance for decision-making under uncertainty,[3] underscoring its role as an evolution from static prediction to adaptive, continuous strategies essential in critical care, chronic disease management, and resource allocation.

The ML Stepwise Process of Development in Healthcare

The development and deployment of ML models in healthcare is a multistage process, integrating best practices from ML, software engineering, and data engineering. This structured approach ensures robust, reliable, and clinically impactful ML solutions.[10]

Identifying the Clinical Scenario

The initial step is to identify clinical scenarios where ML can provide substantial value. This involves assessing the problem's significance, the gap between current and desired performance, and the likelihood that ML can improve outcomes. Prioritization often focuses on risk stratification leading to differential actions and clinical problems causing substantial morbidity or mortality. Successful identification requires a "clinical champion" and a multidisciplinary clinical steering group to ensure alignment with real-world needs and team receptiveness.[10]

Establishing the Data Infrastructure and Utilization

Healthcare ML programs require robust clinical deployment environments with accessible real-world data for developing and testing ML models at scale. EHR data are complex, often unstructured, and evolve over time. Innovative solutions like the SickKids Enterprise-wide Data in Azure Repository (SEDAR) provide validated EHR data in standardized schemas, organizing data into relational tables for comprehensive feature extraction and temporal alignment. Careful cohort and label definition is crucial to prevent data leakage or bias, with safeguards like examining global explanations and conducting ablation experiments. Ablation experiments are systematic tests where parts or features of a model are removed or modified to understand their contribution to overall performance, helping to identify essential components and prevent unintended bias. Data infrastructure should also support fairness evaluation by providing demographic and socioeconomic data.[10]

Data Preprocessing

Healthcare datasets frequently present challenges due to large dimensionality, distortions, missing values, and imbalanced data, which can lower algorithm effectiveness. Preprocessing is crucial for data quality and model performance.[11]

ML in healthcare must contend with several persistent data challenges. Missing values are common, often arising from incomplete documentation, and can lead to suboptimal predictions if not carefully addressed. Outliers represent suspicious or erroneous data points that distort analyses and compromise model reliability. Imbalanced datasets, where one class is overrepresented compared to others, can bias models toward majority categories, frequently resulting in misclassification of the minority group.

A range of techniques has been developed to mitigate these issues. Missing values in healthcare datasets can be effectively handled through approaches such as KNN imputation, which imputes missing values by averaging similar patient data and remains widely applied in clinical research.[12] Recent advancements to KNN address earlier limitations by incorporating dependency and uncertainty handling, improving accuracy, and reducing bias.[13] Regression models such as random forest imputation have also demonstrated strong performance in cohort studies, effectively estimating missing clinical variables while maintaining predictive validity.[13]

Imbalanced data can be managed through resampling strategies, including random resampling, the Synthetic Minority Over-sampling Technique (SMOTE) and its variants, and Adaptive Synthetic Sampling (ADASYN). These methods generate synthetic examples for minority classes to improve classification balance and model performance in healthcare datasets.[14] Together, these methods form a critical toolkit for ensuring the robustness and fairness of ML models in healthcare.[11] Effective preprocessing significantly improves data completeness and accuracy, enhancing model performance.

Model Training and Evaluation

After preprocessing, the model is trained and rigorously evaluated.[5]

For supervised learning, the dataset is typically divided into a training dataset and a test dataset. The training set teaches the algorithm to build its model, while the test set, new to the algorithm, evaluates performance and ensures unbiased predictions, preventing overfitting.[5]

Evaluating ML models in medical applications requires specific metrics beyond simple accuracy, given the critical nature of clinical decisions.[12] These metrics are summarized in Table 8.1, which outlines their definitions, calculations, and relevance in healthcare.

Table 8.1 Key Evaluation Metrics for ML Models in Healthcare[15]

Metric	*Definition*	*Calculation*	*Relevance in Healthcare*
True Positive (TP)	Correctly classified positive samples (e.g., a patient with disease correctly predicted as having it).	N/A	Essential for identifying actual cases, especially critical conditions.
True Negative (TN)	Correctly classified negative samples (e.g., healthy patient correctly predicted as healthy).	N/A	Important for ruling out conditions and avoiding unnecessary interventions.
False Positive (FP)	Incorrectly classified positive samples (e.g., a healthy patient incorrectly predicted as having disease).	N/A	Leads to unnecessary tests, anxiety, and resource waste.
False Negative (FN)	Incorrectly classified negative samples (e.g., a patient with disease incorrectly predicted as healthy).	N/A	Can lead to missed diagnoses, delayed treatment, and adverse outcomes; often the most critical error in healthcare.

(Continued)

Table 8.1 ***(Continued)***

Metric	*Definition*	*Calculation*	*Relevance in Healthcare*
Accuracy (ACC)	Ratio of correctly classified samples to total samples.	(TP+TN)/(TP+FP+TN+FN)	Commonly used, but can be misleading with imbalanced class proportions (e.g., rare diseases).
Recall (REC)/ Sensitivity/True Positive Rate (TPR)	Rate of correctly classified positive samples out of all actual positive samples.	TP/(TP+FN)	Crucial in medical studies; desirable to miss as few positive instances as possible.
Specificity (SPEC)	Rate of correctly classified negative samples out of all actual negative samples.	TN/(TN+FP)	Important for correctly identifying healthy individuals and avoiding false alarms.
Precision (PREC)/ Positive Predictive Value (PPV)	Proportion of retrieved positive samples that are truly relevant.	TP/(TP+FP)	Indicates reliability of positive predictions; high precision means fewer FPs.
F1-Score	Harmonic mean of precision and recall.	2 ×(Precision × Recall)/ (Precision+ Recall)	Provides a balanced measure, especially useful with uneven class distribution.
AUC-ROC (Area Under the Receiver Operating Characteristic Curve)	Measures classifier's ability to distinguish between classes across all possible classification thresholds.	N/A	Represents trade-off between sensitivity and specificity. Higher AUC indicates better overall performance.

The choice of evaluation metrics depends on the clinical context and the consequences of different errors.

Create Machine Learning Operations

Machine Learning Operations (MLOps) bring together practices from ML, software engineering, and data engineering to ensure reliable deployment and management of ML systems in healthcare. Its focus on automation, modularity, versioning, reproducibility, and monitoring supports safe and scalable clinical use. A typical pipeline begins with experimentation, where reproducible steps such as feature extraction, training, and evaluation are automated on static datasets. In classification tasks, thresholds must balance the risks of false positives and missed outcomes, with clinical teams selecting cutoffs based on performance and feasibility.

Deployment follows approval, with configurations, code, and artifacts versioned and tested through continuous integration and continuous delivery (CI/CD) pipelines before release. Before full clinical integration, models undergo a silent trial, generating predictions without delivering them to users, to confirm stability. Continuous monitoring is then essential, as changes in patient populations or practices can erode performance. Tracking meaningful metrics and input data ensures models adapt, remain reliable, and continue to support patient safety.[10]

Integrate into Clinical Workflows

The final stage of the ML lifecycle is thoughtful integration into clinical workflows to ensure adoption and impact. Implementation requires clinical informaticians to align tools with practice, as models are intended to support—not replace—expert judgment. Education, auditing, and ongoing support are critical for fostering trust and sustaining behavioral change.

Equally important is designing workflows and care pathways. Defining who receives alerts and how interventions are triggered ensures predictions lead to action. Leveraging existing clinical decision support (CDS) frameworks enables delivery of outputs through EHR alerts, dashboards, or emails. Structured care pathway documents then standardize responses to positive predictions, promoting consistency, reducing variability, and embedding ML into evidence-based clinical practice.[10]

Ethical Considerations in Healthcare AI

The integration of ML into healthcare introduces a complex array of ethical challenges integral to every stage of ML development and deployment. Key ethical areas include bias, fairness, interpretability, and data privacy.[1]

Algorithmic bias is a pressing ethical concern, potentially perpetuating existing health disparities.[16]

Bias in ML can emerge from several sources. Data bias arises when training datasets are unrepresentative, contain historical inequities, or lack diversity.[17] A clear example is the performance disparity in pulse oximeters, both traditional and newer AI-assisted models, which tend to overestimate oxygen saturation in patients of color due to calibration and validation primarily on lighter populations. This overestimation increases the risk of occult hypoxemia in patients of color, who have been found to experience it nearly three times more often than patients with fair skin.[18] Such bias has significant clinical implications, highlighting the need for diverse data, inclusive algorithm design, and equitable evaluation standards to ensure safety and trust in biomedical AI.[19] Feature selection bias occurs when chosen attributes unintentionally embed skewed assumptions, reinforcing inequities.[20] Algorithmic bias can also develop even with representative data, as model design or optimization may amplify disparities.[17] Addressing these forms of bias is essential to promote fairness, safety, and trust in clinical applications.

Fairness in clinical ML means ensuring models perform consistently for different patient types, without outputs influenced by gender, age, or ethnicity. Any discrepancies across subgroups must be ethically considered. Model fairness (group fairness) focuses on maintaining similar predictive performance across groups, assessed with metrics such as equalized odds or predictive equality. Equalized odds require that a model achieve similar true positive rates and false positive rates across protected groups, ensuring that no population systematically benefits from or is disadvantaged by the model's predictions. Outcome fairness emphasizes monitoring health outcomes, documenting gaps between training data and the actual patient population, and addressing inferior results in underrepresented groups.[21] Both dimensions are essential to prevent inequities in clinical ML applications.

Bias mitigation is central to developing equitable ML applications in healthcare. Building diverse training datasets is crucial to improving model accuracy and reliability, while community engagement ensures underrepresented groups are involved throughout the AI lifecycle. Conducting equity-focused audits during model development helps detect and address disparities early.[17] Debiasing techniques may be applied at multiple stages: in preprocessing, by adjusting sample weights; in-process, by incorporating independence of protected attributes; and in post-processing, by recalibrating scores. Exploring the Rashomon set of nearly optimal models further helps avoid trade-offs between fairness and performance.[21]

Interpretability is equally important for building trust. The "black-box" nature of deep learning models often raises concerns, as clinicians need to understand how predictions are generated to justify treatment decisions or deviations from standard practice.[7] Strategies to improve interpretability include developing explainable artificial intelligence (XAI) tools, which provide insight into model reasoning and increase confidence in use.[8] Transparency in communicating both the benefits and limitations of artificial intelligence (AI), along with acknowledgment of data deficits, strengthens reliability.[17] In some cases, simple models such as logistic regression, decision trees (DTs), or scoring systems may be preferred, as they explicitly display predictor contributions and facilitate communication.[22] Additionally, releasing AI governance scorecards promotes accountability by making development practices publicly available.[17]

Data privacy remains a foundational concern, protecting sensitive patient information from unauthorized access, misuse, or disclosure.[23] This issue is particularly significant for underserved populations who may hesitate to share health information with AI companies. In North America, the Health Insurance Portability and Accountability Act (HIPAA) sets standards for safeguarding electronic protected health information through its Privacy, Security, and Breach Notification Rules. In Europe, the General Data Protection Regulation (GDPR)[17] provides comprehensive protections, treating health data as a "special category" requiring explicit consent and Data Protection Impact Assessments (DPIAs).[24]

Strategies to uphold privacy include establishing strong data governance policies for access,[17] sharing, retention, and disposal; employing encryption and pseudonymization to protect data in transit and at rest; and conducting regular risk assessments to identify vulnerabilities. Ongoing staff training ensures compliance, while third-party risk management holds vendors accountable to privacy standards. Maintaining audit trails and logs enables monitoring of data use, and breach planning ensures organizations are prepared to respond effectively to incidents.[24]

ML Applications in Clinical Settings

ML is rapidly transforming various facets of clinical practice, moving healthcare from a reactive, generalized approach to one that is proactive, personalized, and highly efficient.

Disease Diagnosis and Prognosis Prediction

ML has demonstrated potential to improve disease diagnosis through the identification of complex patterns in clinical data and enhanced diagnostic prediction performance. ML models improve diagnostic accuracy by analyzing EHRs, medical images, genetic data, and lifestyle information. For example, in diabetes management, ML algorithms integrate blood glucose records, genetic information, and BMI to predict diabetes risk, facilitating early intervention.[25] In rare disease diagnosis, AI detects subtle patterns in large-scale medical data, analyzing genetic data, medical imaging, and EHRs to reduce diagnosis time. Examples include genetic syndrome identification and rare cancer detection.[26] For cancer detection, ML strategies like CNNs show high success in medical imaging analysis, leading to greater precision for conditions like lung cancer and diabetic retinopathy.[7]

ML is extensively used to predict patient outcomes and disease progression. For cancer survivability, ML techniques applied to EHRs identify variables affecting patient survivability in breast and prostate cancer, allowing individualized care plans. Algorithms like SVM and KNN have shown high AUC values in predicting survivability.[27] In critically ill patients, ML algorithms predict 30-day quality-adjusted survival in ICUs for cancer patients, providing valuable information for palliative and end-of-life care decisions.[28] ML algorithms also predict dire outcomes in patients with community-acquired pneumonia and 30-day mortality risk in cardiovascular diseases.[29]

Personalized Treatment Optimization

ML is revolutionizing personalized medicine by tailoring therapeutic interventions to individual patient profiles, moving away from a "one-size-fits-all" approach.[30] ML algorithms, including deep NNs and ensemble methods, are increasingly applied to a wide range of healthcare data sources. Genomic sequences derived from DNA analysis, such as gene expression profiles and mutation data, support treatment plans tailored to individual genetic profiles, advancing precision medicine.[29] EHRs provide comprehensive digital documentation of patient histories, integrating diagnoses, medications, laboratory results, and procedures into a unified dataset.[11] Real-time biometrics collected from wearable devices and medical sensors, such as heart rate, glucose levels, and sleep patterns, offer continuous monitoring and enable dynamic adjustments to treatment plans.[31] Finally, imaging and diagnostic data, including X-rays, MRIs, CT scans, and pathology slides, remain central to disease diagnosis and treatment monitoring, with computer vision techniques increasingly employed to detect subtle features and improve clinical accuracy.[32] Together, these multimodal data sources form the foundation for robust ML-driven healthcare solutions.[30]

By analyzing these data, ML algorithms predict individual responses to treatments, crucial for selecting effective therapies and determining optimal dosages to minimize adverse effects.[30] This data-driven approach facilitates early diagnosis and enables dynamic treatment adjustments, reducing traditional trial-and-error. For example, in hypertension management, ML models optimize antihypertensive dosage and medication type.[25]

Drug Discovery and Development

ML is transforming the traditionally lengthy and costly process of drug discovery and development, enhancing both data analysis and predictive modeling.[33] A central application lies in target identification and validation, where ML uncovers novel targets and strengthens evidence for target–disease associations. Algorithms predict druggable genes and molecular targets, including those for anti-aging therapies, while AI tools analyze spectroscopic data to detect bioactive molecules in natural products.[34] Biomarker identification is another critical domain, with ML-based predictive models improving success rates in clinical trials by matching drugs to responsive patients. Similarly, in computational pathology, deep learning analyzes digital pathology images to discover novel biomarkers with greater precision and reproducibility, reducing development time.[34] The integration of AI techniques, ranging from generative models for data synthesis to advanced strategies such as de novo design and drug repurposing, promises to accelerate discovery pipelines and improve outcomes in translational medicine.[33]

Medical Imaging Analysis

ML, particularly deep learning architectures, has transformed medical imaging analysis, enhancing diagnostic accuracy and efficiency across a range of clinical applications. CNNs have become the standard for image-based tasks, as their multilayered structure excels at feature recognition and hierarchical pattern detection.[11,32] Early layers capture simple features such as edges, while deeper layers extract increasingly complex patterns relevant to clinical diagnosis. CNNs support diverse applications, including image classification, such as distinguishing among skin diseases;[11] segmentation, exemplified by automated lung and lobe segmentation from chest CT scans;[35] anomaly detection, such as identifying aneurysms in diabetic retinopathy;[11] quantitative analysis, measuring nodule type and size in lung cancer screening;[35] and direct cancer prediction, where deep learning models can predict actionable lung cancer from CT scans.[35]

Beyond CNNs, recurrent NNs (RNNs) process temporal data by reusing outputs from previous steps as inputs for subsequent predictions. Their ability to capture sequential dependencies makes them useful in healthcare tasks such as predicting post-stroke pneumonia from EHR time series data.[11]

More recently, Transformer architectures, initially developed for natural language processing (NLP), have been adapted for healthcare, including medical imaging.[36,37] Vision Transformers (ViTs) extend this framework to computer vision by dividing images into patches and applying self-attention mechanisms to identify relationships among them. These models demonstrate particular advantages under noisy conditions and are now applied to classification, segmentation, and reconstruction tasks in imaging workflows.[36,37]

Comparisons between CNNs and large language models (LLMs) highlight complementary strengths. CNNs consistently achieve higher performance in precision, recall, accuracy, and F1-score for direct image classification tasks across modalities such as chest X-rays, brain MRI, and chest CT scans. In contrast, LLMs excel at processing unstructured data, such as radiology reports or clinical narratives, contextualizing patient information, and enabling automated report generation and decision support. While LLMs generally underperform CNNs in direct image classification—often exhibiting mismatches between high confidence scores and actual accuracy—they provide valuable complementary insights.[38] The synergy between CNNs' spatial recognition capabilities and LLMs' contextual processing represents a powerful direction for multimodal AI frameworks, integrating strengths from both paradigms to advance medical imaging and clinical decision-making.

EHR Data Analysis and CDS

EHRs are foundational in modern healthcare, containing vast and heterogeneous datasets of both structured and unstructured information. ML is well-suited to process and analyze these complex data sources, providing critical support for clinical decision-making.[11] Large healthcare systems increasingly build data warehouses that integrate EHR data with complementary sources such as claims, imaging, omics, and patient-generated data, creating a rich foundation for ML applications. Omics refers to high-dimensional biological data derived from molecular profiling techniques such as genomics, proteomics, metabolomics, and transcriptomics that characterize the molecular mechanisms underlying health and disease. When integrated with clinical, imaging, and behavioral data, these molecular datasets enable more precise diagnosis, prognosis, and treatment selection. Within this framework, ML assists clinicians in several key areas.

Risk stratification models identify high-risk patients, optimize resource allocation, and guide perioperative decisions, recalculating risk dynamically rather than relying on static statistical models. Patient outcome optimization is another area of impact, with deep RL models capable of learning optimal dosing strategies for sepsis management and guiding ventilator-weaning policies. ML also contributes to early-warning systems, detecting subtle physiological changes and predicting acute decompensation hours before traditional vital signs, enabling timely intervention. Empirical studies further suggest that AI-powered, knowledge-based CDS systems improve diagnostic accuracy, prognosis, and personalization in medical imaging and related use cases.[39]

Genomics and Precision Medicine

The integration of AI and ML into genomics is fundamentally reshaping precision medicine, offering unprecedented opportunities to personalize diagnostics and therapies.[39, 40] Advances in next-generation sequencing (NGS) technologies generate massive volumes of genomic data, presenting both challenges and opportunities for analysis. ML algorithms, including deep learning, SVMs, and random forests, can parse these complex datasets to identify meaningful insights. Key applications include the identification of genetic markers, where ML uncovers subtle variations that inform molecular mechanisms of disease; prediction of disease risk, where models estimate individual susceptibility to conditions based on genetic profiles; and the development of individualized treatment strategies, which use genomic insights to tailor therapies to the unique genetic makeup of each patient. Beyond genomics, the ability of AI to integrate multiomics data, the combined analysis of multiple layers of biological information such as genomics, transcriptomics, proteomics, and metabolomics, further enhances diagnostic precision and supports informed therapeutic decisions.[35] These tools enable a shift toward more patient-centered care, reducing clinical errors, improving predictive scoring, and managing high-risk emergencies.

Wearable Devices and Remote Patient Monitoring

ML integrated with wearable devices has transformed healthcare from a reactive model to one that is proactive and personalized. Continuous monitoring of health metrics supports preventive care, early intervention, and individualized treatment strategies. Wearable technologies collect data such as respiration rate, electrocardiograms, skin temperature, blood glucose levels, and general activity, including step counts and sleep quality. Some devices, like smart canes, extend beyond monitoring to enhance mobility and safety.[31] Advanced AI algorithms process these continuous data streams, identifying patterns, detecting anomalies, forecasting potential health risks, and tailoring personalized health advice delivered directly to patients or through clinician dashboards. The benefits of this integration are wide-ranging: preventive care insights encourage proactive management; continuous monitoring reduces clinic visits and improves chronic disease management; personalized medicine enables tailored treatment; enhanced communication improves patient–provider relationships; and proactive health management supports earlier interventions before severe symptoms emerge. This continuous, data-sharing ecosystem fosters stronger collaboration between patients and clinicians, building trust and engagement in the care process.[31]

Public Health and Epidemiology

ML also plays an expanding role in public health, particularly in surveillance and outbreak management. AI-powered early-warning systems rapidly process large and diverse datasets to identify signals of infectious disease outbreaks.[41] Data sources for such systems range from digital and publicly available information—including news reports, social media, search queries, and health forums—to health system and personal health data, such as case reports, hospital records, and surveillance registries. Increasingly, environmental and contextual data, including climate trends, travel and mobility patterns, pathogen genomic data, and wastewater surveillance, add further predictive power. Integrating these diverse sources creates a more comprehensive and timely understanding of emerging threats. The benefits are clear: earlier outbreak detection, more efficient processing of large datasets, improved predictive accuracy, optimized resource allocation, and enhanced adaptability in resource-constrained settings.[42] Within hospitals, ML also supports epidemiology by assisting in emergency department triage, predicting septic shock, detecting community-acquired pneumonia, and stratifying COVID-19 disposition risk.[41]

Clinical Trial Design and Optimization

ML is poised to transform clinical trials by addressing inefficiencies and reducing high failure rates.[43] In trial design, predictive analytics and simulation models create robust study frameworks, adjusting for patient variability and refining inclusion and exclusion criteria. AI-driven optimization further adapts parameters such as sample size and dosing regimens based on real-time data. Patient recruitment and selection are streamlined through ML models integrated with EHRs, enabling rapid identification of eligible participants. NLP enhances this process by extracting eligibility indicators from unstructured clinical notes, improving diversity and reducing recruitment timelines. ML also supports dropout prediction and retention strategies, identifying risks of nonadherence or adverse events and enabling proactive interventions.[43] In site selection and feasibility assessment, ML analyzes past performance and integrates demographic and geospatial data to identify high-performing, strategically placed trial sites. Finally, real-time monitoring and anomaly detection allow continuous oversight, with wearable technologies feeding trial data directly into monitoring systems, flagging irregularities before they escalate.[44] Collectively, these applications streamline complex tasks, enhance safety, and improve overall trial efficiency and outcomes.

Emerging Trends and Future Directions

Looking ahead, several trends are shaping the field. Multimodal AI integrates diverse data types—structured EHRs, clinical notes, images, genomics, and biometrics—capturing richer patterns for prediction.[8] For example, CNN-based multimodal disease risk prediction systems combine structured and unstructured data for more comprehensive risk assessment. Synergies between LLMs and imaging architectures support automated report generation, decision support, and reduced clinician workload. XAI continues to expand, with methods designed to clarify how predictions are derived and why factors are selected, improving reliability and trust.[22] Federated learning offers solutions to fragmented data by enabling models to train on decentralized datasets without moving sensitive information, supporting privacy under HIPAA and GDPR.[35] Continuous learning is also critical, as adaptive models that update with new data can address concept drift and maintain relevance. Finally, emphasis is shifting toward workflow integration and human–AI collaboration, ensuring systems complement rather than replace clinical expertise.[45] By embedding AI into existing workflows, providing actionable insights, and fostering user trust, ML can evolve into a collaborative partner in patient care.

Exercises and Activities

ACTIVITY 1: ML PIPELINE SIMULATION

Objective: To understand the end-to-end ML pipeline in healthcare and practice identifying potential pitfalls.

Instructions:

1. Divide students into teams. Provide each team with a short dataset (synthetic patient EHR data with missing values, imbalanced classes, and some outliers).
2. Teams must walk through the ML pipeline stages outlined in the chapter:
   - Define a clinical scenario (e.g., predicting hospital readmission).
   - Preprocess data (decide how to handle missing values, outliers, and class imbalance).
   - Choose and justify a model (SVM, DT, NN, etc.).
   - Select performance metrics appropriate for the clinical scenario (e.g., sensitivity vs. specificity).
   - Identify ethical risks (bias, interpretability, privacy).
3. Each team presents a short "deployment plan," highlighting both technical and ethical safeguards.

ACTIVITY 2: CASE STUDY DEBATE—EXPLAINABILITY VS. ACCURACY

Objective: To analyze trade-offs between accuracy and interpretability in clinical AI adoption.

1. Divide students into stakeholder groups. Present the following scenario:
   A hospital is considering deploying a deep NN for cancer survivability prediction (AUC = 0.92) versus a logistic regression model (AUC = 0.85) that clinicians can easily interpret.
2. Divide students into four stakeholder groups. Each group prepares and debates from its perspective:
   - Clinical team: Argue for interpretability to ensure accountability.
   - Data science team: Argue for maximizing predictive accuracy to improve outcomes.
   - Regulatory experts: Evaluate compliance with ethical standards and data privacy.
   - Patient advocates: Emphasize trust, fairness, and patient autonomy.
3. Each team contributes to a short consensus statement, highlighting both technical and ethical safeguards for model adoption.

ACTIVITY 3: ETHICAL RISK MAPPING EXERCISE

Objective: To critically evaluate real-world risks of ML in healthcare.

Instructions:

1. Provide groups with three case studies (e.g., pulse oximeter bias, COVID-19 mortality prediction models, AI in wearable heart monitoring).
2. Students create an Ethical Risk Map identifying:
   - Type of bias (data, feature selection, algorithmic).
   - Impacted population groups.
   - Clinical consequences (e.g., missed diagnoses, inequitable treatment).
   - Mitigation strategies (e.g., diverse training data, fairness audits, explainability protocols).
3. Groups present their maps, followed by a class-wide discussion on trade-offs between fairness, accuracy, and feasibility.

Assessment Questions

1. In the ML pipeline, why is data preprocessing particularly important for healthcare datasets compared to other domains?
2. Compare the ethical trade-offs between using deep NNs and logistic regression in predicting patient mortality.
3. How could RL be applied to optimize ICU resource allocation, and what ethical concerns might arise?
4. Explain how SMOTE can address imbalanced healthcare data. What risks might it introduce?
5. Evaluate how federated learning supports privacy-preserving collaboration across hospitals. What are its limitations in ensuring fairness?
6. A hospital deploys an AI diagnostic tool trained on patients from high-income countries. What justice implications might this raise for deployment in low-income settings?
7. Propose a strategy for auditing an ML model in oncology for gender bias in treatment recommendations.
8. Why is sensitivity often prioritized over specificity in life-threatening conditions? Give an example from the chapter.
9. Draft a patient-facing disclosure for a wearable device that uses AI to predict heart arrhythmias, addressing transparency and consent.
10. Defend or challenge: "Explainability should be prioritized over predictive accuracy in all clinical AI applications."

Answers to Assessment Questions

1. Why is data preprocessing important in healthcare?
   Healthcare data are noisy, incomplete, and imbalanced. Missing values (e.g., incomplete EHR entries) or outliers (erroneous lab results) can lead to unsafe predictions. Preprocessing ensures reliability and patient safety.
2. Trade-offs between deep NNs and logistic regression:
   - DNN: Higher accuracy, captures nonlinear patterns, but opaque ("black box").
   - Logistic regression: Lower accuracy, but interpretable and trusted by clinicians. Ethical trade-off = saving more lives vs. ensuring accountability.
3. RL in ICU resource allocation:
   RL could optimize ventilator use or nurse assignments in real time. Risks: unfair allocation, reinforcing existing inequities, and a lack of transparency in decision-making.
4. SMOTE for imbalanced data:
   SMOTE generates synthetic samples for minority classes (e.g., rare disease patients), improving model sensitivity. Risks: overfitting, synthetic samples not capturing true biological variability.
5. Federated learning and privacy:
   It allows hospitals to train models without sharing raw data, preserving HIPAA/GDPR compliance. Limitations: heterogeneity of local datasets, fairness risks if one hospital's data dominate, and difficulty auditing.
6. Justice implications of high-income datasets:
   Models may underperform on underrepresented populations, worsening inequities. For example, an oncology model trained in the U.S./Europe may misclassify disease progression in African or South Asian populations.
7. Auditing an oncology model for gender bias:
   - Compare prediction accuracy, false negative/false positive rates across male and female patients.
   - Perform subgroup analysis.
   - If discrepancies exist, retrain using balanced datasets or apply fairness constraints.
8. Why prioritize sensitivity in life-threatening conditions?
   Missing a positive case (false negative) can be fatal (e.g., sepsis, cancer, or COVID-19). Example: pneumonia or sepsis detection where underdiagnosis risks death.
9. Patient-facing disclosure (wearable arrhythmia predictor):
   "This device uses artificial intelligence to analyze your heart rhythms and alert you to potential irregularities. The predictions are supportive, not a substitute for medical advice. Your data remain private, stored securely, and you may withdraw consent at any time."
10. Defend or challenge: Explainability>Accuracy:
    - Defend: Trust, accountability, and legal compliance require explainability; clinicians must justify decisions.
    - Challenge: In acute care, saving more lives through higher accuracy may outweigh explainability concerns, provided safeguards exist.
    - Strong answer: a balanced approach (hybrid+XAI) is most ethical.

References

1. Aliferis C. Artificial intelligence (AI) and machine learning (ML) for healthcare and health sciences: the need for best practices enabling trust in AI and ML. In: *Artificial Intelligence and Machine Learning in Health Care and Medical Sciences: Best Practices and Pitfalls*. Bethesda, MD: National Center for Biotechnology Information; 2024. Accessed August 22, 2025. www.ncbi.nlm.nih.gov/books/NBK610550/
2. Owkin, Inc. Unsupervised vs supervised learning: A to Z of AI for healthcare. *Owkin website*. Published 2019. Accessed August 22, 2025. www.owkin.com/a-z-of-ai-for-healthcare/unsupervised-vs-supervised-learning
3. Ono S, Goto T. Introduction to supervised machine learning in clinical epidemiology. *Ann Clin Epidemiol.* 2022;4:e22. Accessed August 22, 2025. https://pmc.ncbi.nlm.nih.gov/articles/PMC10760492/
4. Ahsan MM, Luna SA, Siddique Z. Machine-learning-based disease diagnosis: a comprehensive review. *Healthcare (Basel)*. 2022;10(3):541. Accessed August 22, 2025. https://pmc.ncbi.nlm.nih.gov/articles/PMC8950225/
5. Habehh H, Gohel S. Machine learning in healthcare. *Curr Genomics*. 2021;22(4):291–300. doi:10.2174/1389202922666210705124359
6. Jayaraman P, Desman J, Sabounchi M, Nadkarni GN, Sakhuja A. A primer on reinforcement learning in medicine for clinicians. *NPJ Digit Med.* 2024;7:337. doi:10.1038/s41746-024-01316-0.Accessed August 22, 2025. https://pmc.ncbi.nlm.nih.gov/articles/PMC11599275/
7. Wu Q, Han J, Yan Y, Kuo YH, Shen ZM. Reinforcement learning for healthcare operations management: methodological framework, recent developments, and future research directions. *Health Care Manag Sci.* 2024;27(3):373–390. doi:10.1007/s10729-024-09638-2
8. Machine Learning in Healthcare: Transformative Applications, Challenges, and Future Directions. Frontiers in health informatics. Published online 2024. doi:https://doi.org/10.52783/fhi.63
9. Sy L, Rajappa S. Transforming healthcare with big data: a predictive approach to illness detection. *Int J Innov Res Sci Eng Technol.* 2019;8(11):7969–7976. Accessed August 22, 2025. www.ijirset.com/upload/2019/november/90_Transforming.pdf
10. Yan AP, Guo LL, Inoue J, et al. A roadmap to implementing machine learning in healthcare: from concept to practice. *Front Digit Health.* 2025;7:1462751. doi:10.3389/fdgth.2025.1462751. Accessed August 22, 2025.https://pmc.ncbi.nlm.nih.gov/articles/PMC11788154/.
11. Kale K, Dev D. Data pre-processing technique for enhancing healthcare data quality using artificial intelligence. *Int J Sci Res Sci Technol.* 2024;11(3):299–309. doi:10.32628/ijsrst52411130
12. Stevens JR, Suyundikov A, Slattery ML. Accounting for missing data in clinical research. *JAMA.* 2016;315(5):517. doi:https://doi.org/10.1001/jama.2015.16461
13. Li J, Guo S, Ma R, et al. Comparison of the effects of imputation methods for missing data in predictive modelling of cohort study datasets. *BMC Medical Research Methodology*. 2024;24(1). doi:https://doi.org/10.1186/s12874-024-02173-x
14. Sowjanya AM, Mrudula O. Effective treatment of imbalanced datasets in health care using modified SMOTE coupled with stacked deep learning algorithms. *Applied Nanoscience. Published online February* 3, 2022. doi:https://doi.org/10.1007/s13204-021-02063-4
15. Hicks SA, Strümke I, Thambawita V, et al. On evaluation metrics for medical applications of artificial intelligence. *Sci Rep*. 2022;12(1):5979. doi:10.1038/s41598-022-09954-8
16. Rajagopal A, Shant A, Ryu AJ, et al. Machine learning operations in health care: a scoping review. *Mayo Clin Proc Digit Health*. 2024;2(3):421–437. doi:10.1016/j.mcpdig.2024.06.009
17. Gianfrancesco MA, Tamang S, Yazdany J, Schmajuk G. Potential biases in machine learning algorithms using electronic health record data. *JAMA Intern Med.* 2018;178(11):1544–1547. doi:10.1001/jamainternmed.2018.3763
18. Sjoding MW, Dickson RP, Iwashyna TJ, Gay SE, Valley TS. Racial bias in pulse oximetry measurement. *N Engl J Med.* 2020;383(25):2477–2478. doi:10.1056/NEJMc2029240.

19. Vargas RL, Horowitz NH, Katznelson R, et al. Ensuring that biomedical AI benefits diverse populations. *NPJ Digit Med.* 2021;4(1):105. doi:10.1038/s41746-021-00447-8.
20. Bahangulu JK, Berko LO. Algorithmic bias, data ethics, and governance: ensuring fairness, transparency, and compliance in AI-powered business analytics applications. *ResearchGate*. Published 2025. Accessed August 22, 2025. www.researchgate.net/publication/389397603
21. Hoche M, Mineeva O, Rätsch G, Vayena E, Blasimme A. What makes clinical machine learning fair? A practical ethics framework. *PLOS Digit Health.* 2025;4(3):e0000728. doi:10.1371/journal.pdig.0000728
22. Ning Y, Liu M, Liu N. Advancing ethical AI in healthcare through interpretability. *Patterns (N Y).* 2025;6(8):100914. Accessed August 22, 2025. https://pmc.ncbi.nlm.nih.gov/articles/PMC12191714/
23. Conduah AK, Ofoe S, Siaw-Marfo D. Data privacy in healthcare: global challenges and solutions. *Digit Health.* 2025;11:205520762512345. Accessed August 22, 2025. https://pmc.ncbi.nlm.nih.gov/articles/PMC12138216/
24. UVJ Technologies. HIPAA, GDPR, and beyond: navigating data privacy in healthcare. UVJ Tech. Published 2025. Accessed August 22, 2025. https://uvjtech.com/article/hipaa-gdpr-and-beyond-navigating-data-privacy-in-healthcare/
25. Pan M, et al. Application of artificial intelligence in the health management of chronic disease: bibliometric analysis. *Front Med.* 2025;12:1248. Accessed August 22, 2025. https://pmc.ncbi.nlm.nih.gov/articles/PMC11747633/
26. Gowda M, Mathew J. AI applications in rare disease diagnosis. *ResearchGate*. Published 2025. Accessed August 22, 2025. www.researchgate.net/publication/39223257
27. Safa N, Anouar B, Hamza C. Review paper machine learning applications in rare diseases. Accessed August 22, 2025. www.jobiost.com/article_199030_4b09f9b78781544a113dd0ec2e7bbf70.pdf
28. Dos Santos HG, et al. Machine learning to predict 30-day quality-adjusted survival in critically ill patients with cancer. *J Crit Care.* 2019;54:73–80. doi:10.1016/j.jcrc.2019.08.012
29. Bardhi O, Garcia Zapirain B. Machine learning techniques applied to electronic healthcare records to predict cancer patient survivability. *Computers, Materials & Continua.* 2021;68(2):1595–1613. doi:https://doi.org/10.32604/cmc.2021.015326
30. Sophia E. Machine learning for personalized medicine and treatment optimization. ResearchGate. Published 2025. Accessed August 22, 2025. www.researchgate.net/publication/390726386
31. TDK. How AI and wearable devices are transforming healthcare. TDK website. Published 2024. Accessed August 22, 2025. www.tdk.com/en/tech-mag/past-present-future-tech/ai-and-wearable-technology-in-healthcare
32. Salehi AW, Khan S, Gupta G, et al. A study of CNN and transfer learning in medical imaging: advantages, challenges, future scope. *Sustainability.* 2023;15(7):5930. doi:10.3390/su15075930
33. Gangwal A, Lavecchia A. Artificial intelligence in natural product drug discovery: current applications and future perspectives. *J Med Chem.* 2025;68(13):4991–5008. doi:10.1021/acs.jmedchem.4c01257
34. Vamathevan J, et al. Applications of machine learning in drug discovery and development. *Nat Rev Drug Discov.* 2019;18(6):463–477. doi:10.1038/s41573-019-0024-5
35. Zhou SK, Greenspan H, Davatzikos C, et al. A review of deep learning in medical imaging: imaging traits, technology trends, case studies with progress highlights, and future promises. *Proc IEEE.* 2021;109(5):820–838. doi:10.1109/JPROC.2021.3054390
36. Pinto-Coelho L. How artificial intelligence is shaping medical imaging technology: a survey of innovations and applications. *Bioengineering (Basel).* 2023;10(12):1457. doi:10.3390/bioengineering10121457
37. Nerella S, Bandyopadhyay S, Zhang J, et al. Transformers and large language models in healthcare: a review. *Artif Intell Med.* 2024;154:102900. doi:10.1016/j.artmed.2024.102900
38. Tian D, Jiang S, Zhang L, Lu X, Xu Y. The role of large language models in medical image processing: a narrative review. *Quantitative imaging in medicine and surgery (Online).* 2024;14(1):1108–1121. doi:https://doi.org/10.21037/qims-23-892

39. Khosravi M, Zare Z, Mojtabaeian SM, Izadi R. Artificial intelligence and decision-making in healthcare: a thematic analysis of a systematic review of reviews. *Health Serv Res Manag Epidemiol.* 2024;11:23333928241234863. doi:10.1177/23333928241234863
40. Suura SR. Artificial intelligence and machine learning in genomic medicine: redefining the future of precision diagnostics. *South East Eur J Public Health.* Published online March 7, 2024:955–973. doi:10.70135/seejph.vi.4602
41. Hamilton AJ, Strauss AT, Martinez DA, et al. Machine learning and artificial intelligence: applications in healthcare epidemiology. *Antimicrob Steward Healthc Epidemiol.* 2021;1(1):e24. doi:10.1017/ash.2021.192
42. Villanueva-Miranda I, Xiao G, Xie Y. Artificial intelligence in early warning systems for infectious disease surveillance: a systematic review. *Frontiers in Public Health.* 2025;13. doi:https://doi.org/10.3389/fpubh.2025.1609615
43. Machine Learning and AI in Clinical Trials: Use Cases. Coherent solutions. Published November 4, 2024. www.coherentsolutions.com/insights/role-of-ml-and-ai-in-clinical-trials-design-use-cases-benefits
44. Jordan A. Integrating machine learning for clinical trial optimization. *ResearchGate.* Published May 1, 2025. Accessed August 22, 2025. www.researchgate.net/publication/391347759
45. Ahmad MA, Patel A, Eckert C, Kumar V, Teredesai A. Fairness in machine learning for healthcare. In: *Proceedings of the 26th ACM SIGKDD International Conference on Knowledge Discovery & Data Mining*; July 6, 2020; Virtual. New York, NY: ACM; 2020. doi:10.1145/3394486.3406461

Chapter 9

Types of Data Analytics

Descriptive, Prescriptive, and Predictive Application of Predictive Analytics in Acute and Specialized Care

Rudolph Bedeley, PhD

Why the Healthcare Industry Needs Analytics

Healthcare organizations (HCOs) in the United States are currently under constant pressure to improve their performance by reducing the cost of care while providing better service at the same time.[19] Despite the increasing demand and high expectations, HCOs still have a very promising future due to their increasingly growing data and the widespread analytics systems and technologies.[20]

Concerns about the quality of care and economic sustainability in healthcare have existed for years all over the world.[7] Government agencies and businesses that are involved in providing health coverage for workers and citizens have long called for cost control.[7] In the United States, a published report from the Business Roundtable, which represents CEOs of major companies, has concluded that the US healthcare system has become a liability that hinders companies', as well as HCOs', competitiveness in a global economy.[2] As an additional twist, the report found that higher US spending fails to deliver a healthier workforce, thus creating the largest "value gap" between cost and benefits among healthcare systems.

While analytics have permeated all aspects of business to date, healthcare analytics represent an area of extremely high and untapped potential.[19,12] The McKinsey Global Institute (MGI) estimates

DOI: 10.4324/9781003593867-12

that big data analysis (i.e., analysis of large datasets) could save the US healthcare system 300 billion dollars annually, with two-thirds of that saving in the form of decreasing expenditures by 8%.[10]

The healthcare sector has drawn the attention of many healthcare-providing organizations to seek better ways to reengineer their current methods of operation. As a result, emphasis on the adoption and use of data analytics tools and techniques has since been increasingly enforced by many HCOs as one of the most efficient ways to streamline healthcare processes and operations in order to achieve better quality of care delivery and overall performance.[1,5] However, while there have been several studies on the adoption and impact of analytics on organizational performance, only a few studies in the healthcare sector have investigated analytics impacts on the chain of activities that lead to the creation of value in HCOs.[17,18]

A systematic review of the current literature reveals that several studies have proposed models, typologies, and domains to study the impact of analytics on organizations.[5,21] Other studies have focused on the supply chain analytics capabilities of organization from a resource-based view[3] and dynamic capabilities perspectives.[8,4] While these studies have generally shown that a relationship exists between analytics adoption and organizational performance (operations, finance, etc.), there is a scarcity of studies that have yet systematically investigated or shown how analytics is being utilized in HCOs to improve quality of care and financial performance.

Thus, the healthcare industry currently lags behind significantly in taking full advantage of current and emerging state-of-the-art analytics tools and methods.[9,16] Many HCOs are struggling today with the implementation of analytics techniques and technologies even though they invest in numerous analytics systems and applications with the hope of achieving major transformation in their daily care processes and performance.[13,17] Moreover, evidence from a survey also shows that 60% of HCOs surveyed fail to develop a clear, integrated enterprise strategy and vision for analytics deployment across a broad range of functions.[6] One of the reasons for the low interest in analytics implementation in HCOs is basically a result of a lack of understanding of the economic potential and implications of analytics adoption.[11,13] This chapter explores how analytics can be leveraged to reshape the healthcare industry.

Analytics

Analytics is defined as the process of making sense of data by cleaning, reformatting, and visualizing data. Analytics is carried out with the intention of discovering trends, patterns, and findings in data that describe real-life phenomena. You have probably carried out extensive data analysis in applications like Excel, Python, R, or with visualization applications like Tableau and Microsoft Power BI. Analytics can also be referred to as data products that describe datasets and how they behave. These data products are generated from data analytics and visualization processes, and the people who are generally functioning within a data analytics role would be titled something like analytics specialist or data analyst. Data analytics is "the study of data to discover potential trends, analyze the effects of certain decisions or events, or to evaluate the performance of a given tool or scenario, with the goal of improving outcomes through greater knowledge."[15]

Data Analytics Specialist: Typical Traits

Data analytics professionals are the liaison between the more complex data roles and the business requirements. Analytics professionals work as an interface between the advanced and technical data scientists and engineers. Data analysts use applications to analyze data so they are not using code to do complex data analysis or make complex predictions. They have a solid background in mathematics and understand the inner workings of the business very well. They enjoy using data insights to improve business and are not into spending hours and days doing deep analysis, sitting by themselves coding, and trying to get into advanced math and statistical modeling aspects of making predictions.

In terms of typical tasks, data analytics specialists are constantly engaged in performing various tasks. Among some of the tasks executed are: generating predictive, prescriptive, and descriptive data insights; uncovering correlations and causations in business data to support business decision-making so they operate in a decision support function; and deploying analytics technologies and software applications to generate their findings and then return those to the business decision-makers to help them lead their organizations and become more data driven. However, they achieve this by using applications, not doing custom coding to uncover those *correlations* (a statistical measure that describes the strength and direction of a relationship between two variables) and *causations* (the relationship between a cause and its effect, where one event [the cause] makes another event [the effect] happen.

Types of Analytics

There are four main categories of analytics in healthcare and these are (i) *descriptive analytics*, (ii) *diagnostic analytics*, (iii) *predictive analytics*, and (iv) *prescriptive analytics*. Definitions and explanations of each of these analytics types are provided in the following sections.

a. **Descriptive analytics**
   Descriptive analytics is the kind of analytics performed by summarizing historical data to identify trends and patterns, and it helps in answering the question, "*what happened?*". Descriptive analytics often apply basic statistical techniques to provide descriptive analysis of what is evident from the data, and it involves gathering, organizing, tabulating, visualizing, and summarizing data. Among some of the statistics or information obtained from descriptive analytics are the mean or average, median, standard deviation, mode, range, skewness, kurtosis, etc. A typical example of application of this kind of analytics skills is the analysis of hospital readmission rates or average length of stay across departments.
b. **Diagnostic analytics**
   Diagnostic analytics explores and usually attempts to address "*Why did it happen?*" kind of question. It often involves root cause analysis to understand anomalies or undesirable outcomes. A typical example of the application of this kind of analytics is identifying why the rate of infection increases in a given population.
c. **Prescriptive analytics**
   Prescriptive analytics is the type of analytics where the optimum output can be prescribed based on results from descriptive and predictive analytics. It is usually used to suggest actions to achieve desired outcomes. It often applies optimization and simulation models to recommend treatment plans, resource allocation, and or staffing strategies.
d. **Predictive analytics**
   Predictive analytics is the kind of analytics that utilizes historical data, statistical models, and machine learning techniques to foretell or forecast events that are likely to occur in the future. An example of such type of analytics is using historical data and statistical models to

predict patient hospital readmission rate or emergency department demand. In the following section, we introduce a Python coding platform called "Google Colab," which is one of the most popular and extensively used environments for carrying out various types of data analytics and statistical computing in most industries and academic institutions.

Analytics Programming Platform – Python and Google Colab

Invented in the Netherlands in the early 1990s by Guido van Rossum, Python is an open-source scripting language that is used extensively in academia and industry for programming, statistical and numerical analysis, data mining, machine learning, etc. It is different from other programming language software such as Java and C++ because, unlike others, Python's script does not require any compilation and it is evaluated by the interpreter, line by line. There are several different ways and platforms available to run Python code or programs. One way to do this is by using the iPython console, which operates on open-source platforms such as Google Colab. An example code executed in such a platform or programming environment is illustrated below.

```
In [167]: 3+3
Out [167]: 6
```

This option is very convenient and interactive, and as such, a lot of data scientists prefer using such a platform to carry out their work. This chapter was written with example Python programs or codes executed in Google Colab.

Google Colab

The main programming platform used in this chapter is Google Colab, which is a free, open-source Python programming environment that runs entirely in the cloud. Most importantly, Google Colab does not require any download, installation, or initial setup, and the notebooks that you create can be simultaneously edited remotely by your team members – just as the way you would work collaboratively with your team members in Google Docs. Colab supports many popular data mining and machine learning libraries that can be easily loaded in your notebook.

Colab Environment Tutorial

In this section, you will learn how to create and execute your first Colab notebook. The following is a step-by-step walkthrough to guide you through the process. Note that Colab implicitly uses Google Drive for storing your notebooks and therefore you must first ensure that you are logged into your Google Drive or Gmail account before proceeding further.

Step 1 – Open the following URL in your browser: https://colab.research.google.com

Your browser would display the following screen (see Figure 9.1) if and only if you are logged into your Google Drive or Gmail account.

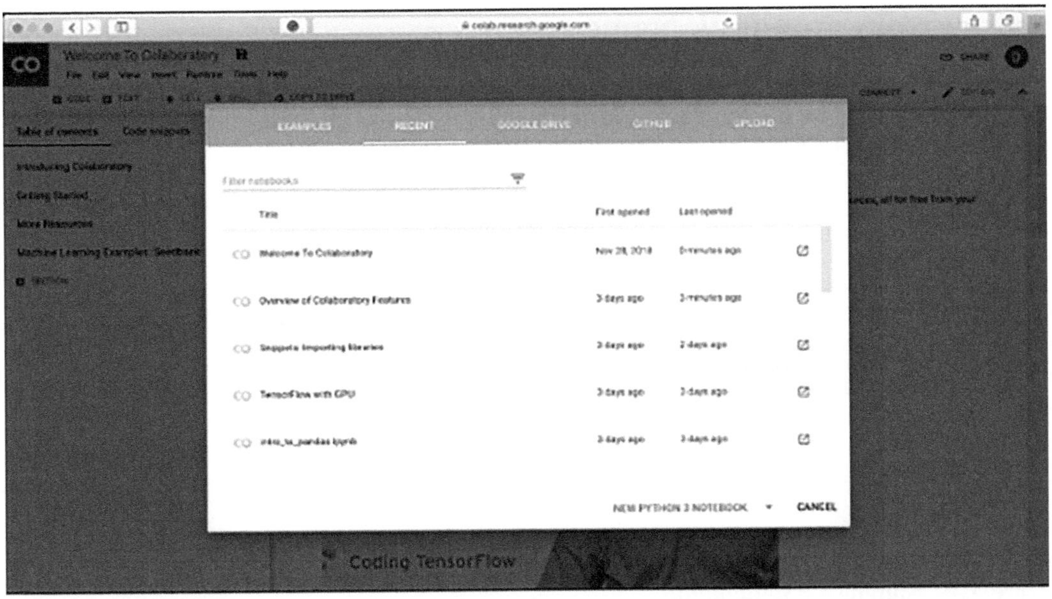

Figure 9.1 Opening Google Colab coding platform.

Step 2 – Click on the NEW PYTHON 3 NOTEBOOK link at the bottom of the screen. A new notebook would open up as shown in Figure 9.2.

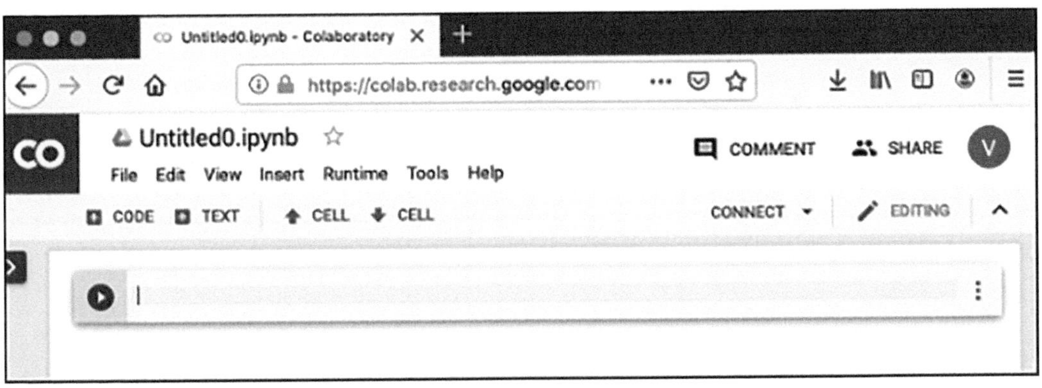

Figure 9.2 An opened new notebook in a Google Colab platform.

If you are familiar with the Jupyter Notebook environment, you will notice that the Google Colab notebook interface is quite similar to that of the Jupyter interface. The Colab interface opens in a Google browser with a code window in which you would enter your Python code or program.

Setting Your Notebook Name

By default, the notebook uses the naming convention "UntitledXX.ipynb." The .ipynb file extension is an acronym for "iPython Notebook." To rename the notebook, click on this name and type in the desired name in the edit box, as shown in Figure 9.3.

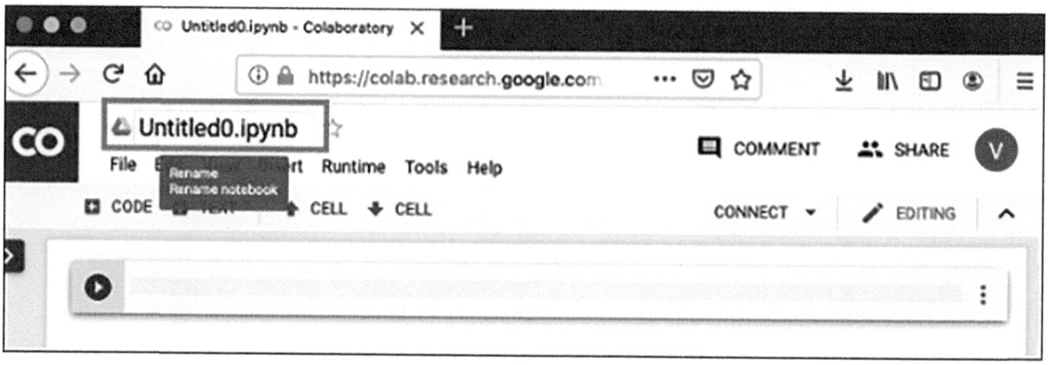

Figure 9.3 Naming a notebook file.

We will name this notebook as "MyFirstColabNotebook" so type in this name in the edit box and hit enter. The notebook will acquire the name that you have given it now.

Entering Your Code

You will now enter a simple Python code in the code window and execute it. Enter the following two Python statements in the code window (see Figure 9.4).

```
import math
print(math.pi)
```

Figure 9.4 Example Python code execution in Google Colab.

Executing Your Code

To execute the code, click on the white arrow with the dark circle around it on the left side of the code window and wait for your code to run. After a little while, you will see the output underneath the code window, as shown in Figure 9.5.

```
import math
print(math.pi)

3.141592653589793
```

Figure 9.5 Displayed output from running a Google Colab code cell.

You can clear the output anytime by clicking the icon on the left side of the output display.

Adding New Code Cells

To add more code to your notebook, just hover the mouse at the bottom center of the Code cell. When the **CODE** and **TEXT** buttons appear, click on the CODE to add a new cell. This is shown in the screenshot below. A new code cell will be added below as shown in Figure 9.6, the current cell.

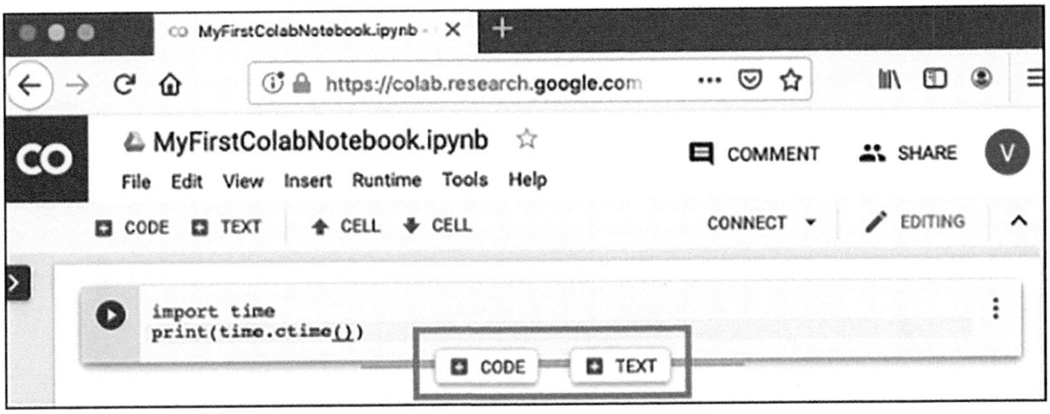

Figure 9.6 Adding a new code block in a notebook.

The most commonly used analytics technique, used for making predictions, is Linear Regression. In the following section, we elaborate and demonstrate the application of the Linear Regression technique for making predictions.

Application of Analytics using Linear Regression Modeling

One of the most popular and widely used techniques in predictive analytics is regression analysis. It captures the relationship between two or more variables, helps in predicting an outcome of a target variable based on several input variables, and it helps in making assessments and robust predictions by determining which of the relationships matter the most and which we can ignore.

Simple linear regression fits a straight line to the data. In regression, one variable is considered an independent (predictor) variable (x) and the other the dependent (outcome) variable (Y). The output of a regression is a function that predicts the dependent variable based on values of the independent variable. The mathematical representation of a linear regression model is shown below:

$$Y = \alpha + \beta X$$

Where:

Y=the dependent (outcome) variable.
X=the independent variable.

α = the intercept (i.e., y-intercept) or the point at which the regression line intersects with the y-axis.
β = the slope, coefficient, or the magnitude of impact of the independent variable (X).

Figure 9.7 is a graphical representation of the same mathematical linear regression equation.

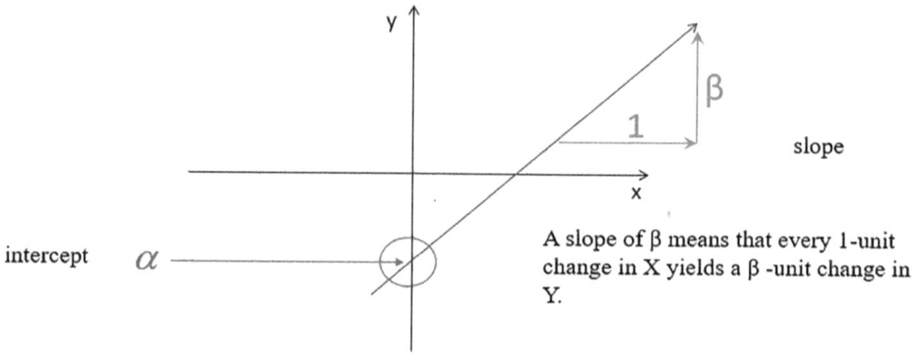

Figure 9.7 Linear regression graphical representation.

Regression models are known to perform well for making predictions. Sometimes, they fail to establish a cause-and-effect relationship between the variables because of the nonexperimental nature of most applications. A regression model may appear to search for causality when, in actual fact, it detects correlation. Causality can only be established through randomized experiments and/or advanced statistical models.

Linear Regression Model Formulation

To formulate a linear regression model, we use a mathematical model that captures the relationship between the response variable y and the k predictor variables, $x_1, x_2, \ldots, x_k$. The model must also account for the randomness that is part of real life. The model formulation begins with a deterministic component that approximates the relationship and then adds a random error term to it that makes the relationship a stochastic one. The formulation process concludes with the use of economic theory, intuition, and statistical measures to determine which predictor might best explain the response variable.

Data Types for Regression Modeling

A regression model treats all predictor variables as numerical. A numerical variable assumes meaningful numeric values. A categorical variable reflects categories. A dummy variable is used to describe two categories of a categorical variable. The letter, *d*, is often used to denote a dummy variable, with

d=1 for one of the categories, and d=0 for the other(s). The category with d=0 is called the reference or benchmark category. All comparisons are made relative to this category.

Simple Linear Regression Model

A simple linear regression model uses only one predictor variable. It is mathematically formulated as: $y = \beta_0 + \beta_1 x_1 + \varepsilon$.

β_0 is the unknown intercept, β_1 is an unknown slope, $\beta_0 + \beta_1 x_1$ is the deterministic component, and ε is the stochastic component or the random error term. The expected value of y for a given value of x_1 lies on a straight line: $E(y) = \beta_0 + \beta_1 x_1$.

Multiple Linear Regression Model

A model with more than one predictor is called a multiple linear regression model. It is mathematically formulated as: $y = \beta_0 + \beta_1 x_1 + \beta_2 x_2 + \ldots + \beta_k x_k + \varepsilon$. Replace x with d for a dummy variable. The population parameters $\beta_0, \beta_1, \beta_2, \ldots, \beta_k$, are unknown and must be estimated using sample data. Sample data: n observations of $y, x_1, x_2, \ldots, x_k$. Use sample data to obtain $b_0, b_1, b_2 \ldots, b_k$, which are estimates of $\beta_0, \beta_1, \beta_2, \ldots, \beta_k$.

$b_0, b_1, b_2 \ldots, b_k$ form the sample regression equation $\hat{y} = b_0 + b_1 x_1 + b_2 x_2 + \ldots + b_k x_k$.

$\hat{y}$(read as y-hat) is the predicted value of the response variable given specified values of the predictor variables. The difference between the observed and the predicted values is the residual: $e = y - \hat{y}$. The coefficients or the slopes are estimated using Ordinary Least Square (OLS) algorithm, which chooses the sample regression equation by minimizing the error sum of squares, $SSE = \Sigma(y - \hat{y})^2 = \Sigma e^2$.

Interpretation of Regression Estimates

Being able to interpret the estimated regression coefficients is very important to data scientists. For example, b_0 is the estimate of β_0, which means the predicted value of $\hat{y}$ when each predictor variable assumes a value of 0. b_j is the estimate of β_j, which is interpreted as the change in the predicted value of the response given a unit increase in x_j, holding all other predictor variables constant. It is also referred to as the partial influence of x_j on $\hat{y}$.

Executing a Regression Code in Python

Let's fabricate some data that shows a roughly linear relationship between internet data usage and amount purchased (see Figures 9.8, 9.9 and 9.11).

```
# import the needed libraries
import numpy as np
from pylab import *

%matplotlib inline
```

```
# Using random number generator to create the fabricated data

internetData = np.random.normal(4.0, 2.0, 500)
amountPurchased = 500 - (internetData + np.random.normal(0, 0.2, 500)) * 2
```

```
# Making a scatterplot of your dataset

scatter(internetData, amountPurchased)
xlabel("Internet Data")
ylabel("Amount Purchased")
```

Figure 9.8 Code used to generate fabricated data and create a scatter plot (Internet data vs amount purchased).

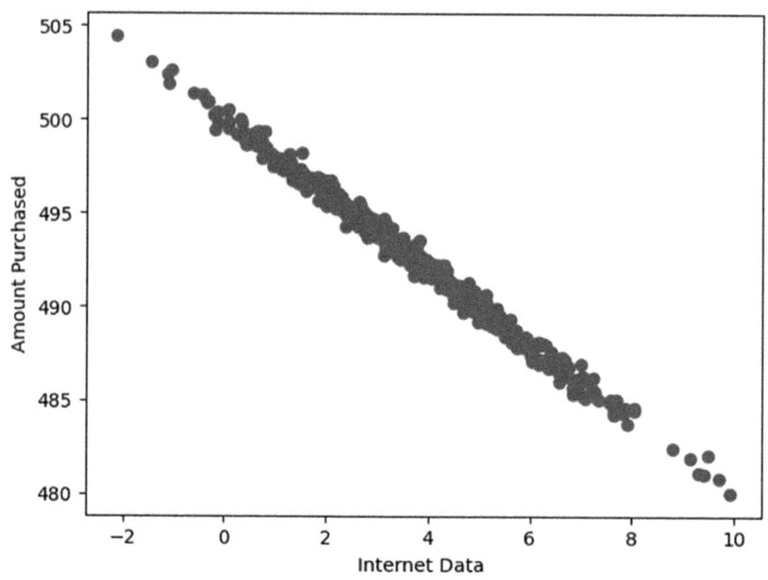

Figure 9.9 A scatter plot of Internet data and amount purchased.

Since we only have two features, we can keep it simple and just use scipy.state.linregress (see Figures 9.10 and 9.11).

```
from scipy import stats

slope, intercept, r_value, p_value, std_err = stats.linregress(internetData, amountPurchased)
```

```
# Determining the goodness-of-fit or r-square

r_value ** 2
```

```
0.990812583050744
```

```
# Let's use the slope and intercept we got from the regression to plot predicted values vs. observed values;

import matplotlib.pyplot as plt

def predict(x):
    return slope * x + intercept

fitLine = predict(internetData)

plt.scatter(internetData, amountPurchased)
plt.plot(internetData, fitLine, c='r')
plt.show()
```

Figure 9.10 Code used to compute linear regression parameters and r^2, and plot predicted vs observed values.

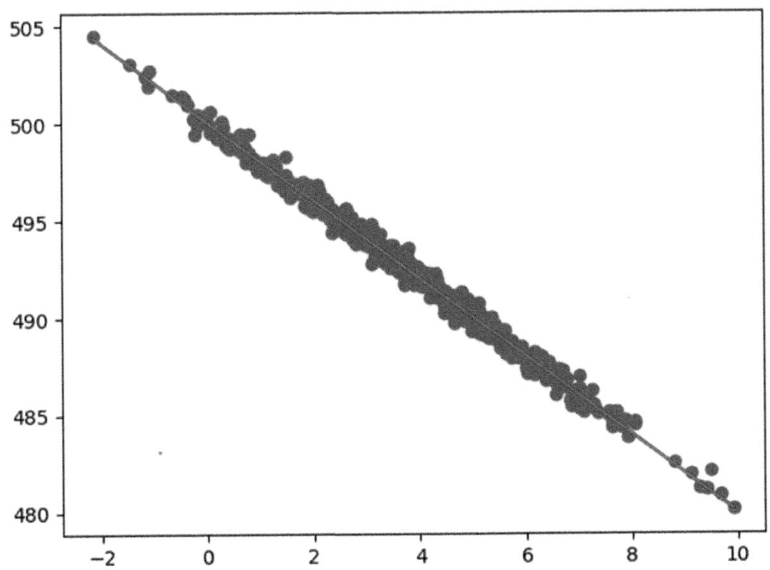

Figure 9.11 A regression plot of Internet data and amount purchased.

Bivariate Linear Regression with Python

Bivariate regression analysis investigates multiple predictor variables' influence on an outcome variable. The example below walks you step-by-step through the process of conducting a bivariate regression and it is designed to help you build upon linear regression concepts while also introducing the Python methodologies to analyze and model relationships between two variables. We will be accessing an archive of machine learning datasets from the UCI Machine Learning Repository.

Practical Example with Python

In this example, we will use the Gapminder dataset to explore the relationship between Life Expectancy variable and GDP per capita variable for countries of the world. The Google Colab tutorial code and the results are shown in Figures 9.12 – 9.22 below .

```
# Importing needed Python library
import pandas as pd
```

```
# Loading the data and previewing it.

data_url = 'http://bit.ly/2cLzoxH'

gm = pd.read_csv(data_url)
gm.head()
```

	country	year	pop	continent	lifeExp	gdpPercap
0	Afghanistan	1952	8425333.0	Asia	28.801	779.445314
1	Afghanistan	1957	9240934.0	Asia	30.332	820.853030
2	Afghanistan	1962	10267083.0	Asia	31.997	853.100710
3	Afghanistan	1967	11537966.0	Asia	34.020	836.197138
4	Afghanistan	1972	13079460.0	Asia	36.088	739.981106

Figure 9.12 A tutorial on using Python in Google colaboratory for data analysis, focusing on data loading and linear regression.

```
# Filter the data so that only the year 2007 is maintained in the data frame.

gm_07=gm[gm['year']==2007]
print(gm_07.shape) # recall, this tells us the dimensions
gm_07.head()
```

```
(142, 6)
```

	country	year	pop	continent	lifeExp	gdpPercap
11	Afghanistan	2007	31889923.0	Asia	43.828	974.580338
23	Albania	2007	3600523.0	Europe	76.423	5937.029526
35	Algeria	2007	33333216.0	Africa	72.301	6223.367465
47	Angola	2007	12420476.0	Africa	42.731	4797.231267
59	Argentina	2007	40301927.0	Americas	75.320	12779.379640

Figure 9.13 Filtering the dataset to year 2007 and previewing the filtered dataframe.

```
# Data Preprocessing
# Always take some time to understand the data set
# Determine the dimensions of the data frame

gm_07.shape
```

```
(142, 6)
```

```
# Check all of the data types in the data frame

gm_07.dtypes
```

```
country       object
year           int64
pop          float64
continent     object
lifeExp      float64
gdpPercap    float64
dtype: object
```

Figure 9.14 Data preprocessing checks: Dataset dimensions and variable data types.

```
# Exploratory Data Analysis
# Next, we take a look at the distributions of some of the variables by creating histograms

import numpy as np
import matplotlib.pyplot as plt
%matplotlib inline

# make sure the independent variable is the log of gdpPercap
x=gm_07['gdpPercap']
# specify the dependent variable as life expectancy
y=gm_07['lifeExp']

gdp_hist=plt.hist(x)
plt.xlabel('GDP')
plt.ylabel('Frequency')
plt.title('Distribution of GDP in Countries of the World, 2007')
plt.show()

gdp_hist=plt.hist(np.log(x))
plt.xlabel('log(GDP)')
plt.ylabel('Frequency')
plt.title('Distribution of log(GDP) in Countries of the World, 2007')
plt.show()

gdp_hist=plt.hist(y)
plt.xlabel('Life Expectancy')
plt.ylabel('Frequency')
plt.title('Distribution of Life Expectancy in Countries of the World, 2007')
plt.show()
```

Figure 9.15 Code used to generate histograms for GDP, Log(GDP), and life expectancy.

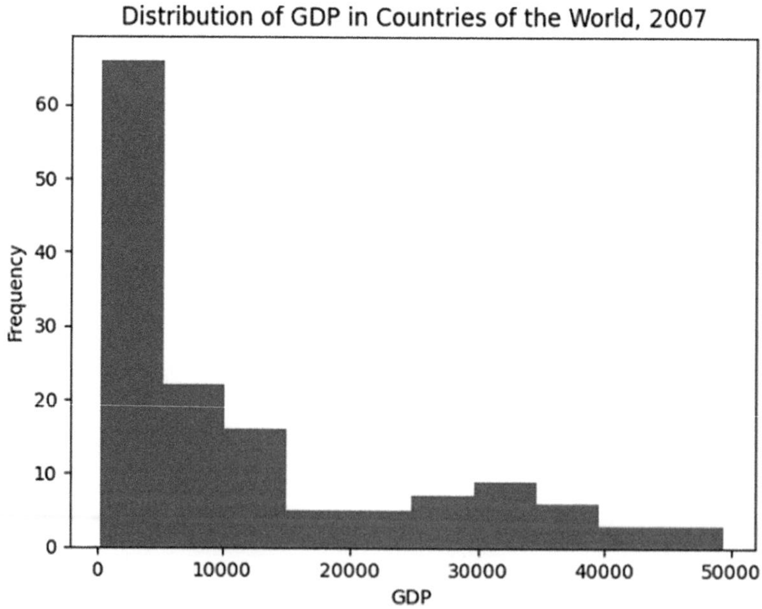

Figure 9.16 A frequency distribution plot of GDP.

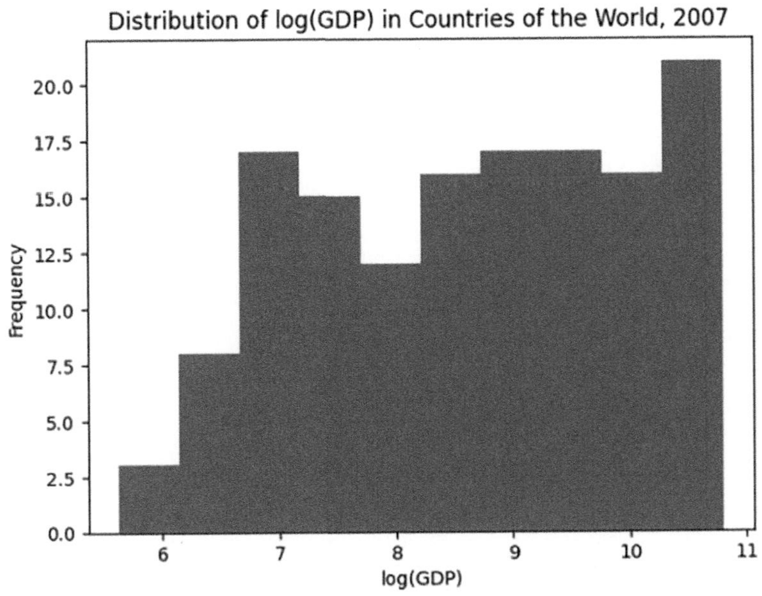

Figure 9.17 A frequency distribution plot of Log(GDP).

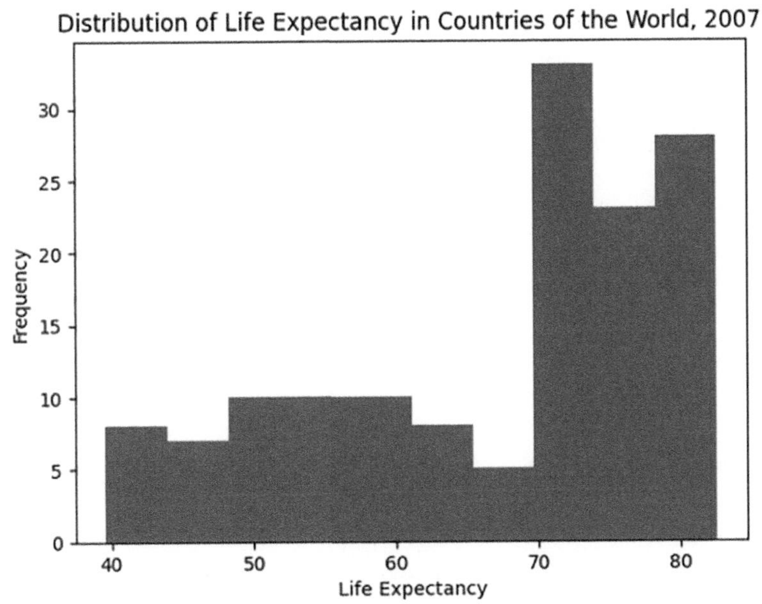

Figure 9.18 A frequency distribution plot of life expectancy.

```
import matplotlib.pyplot as plt
%matplotlib inline


# make sure the independent variable is the log of gdpPercap
x=gm_07['gdpPercap']
# specify the dependent variable as life expectancy
y=gm_07['lifeExp']

plt.scatter(x,y)

plt.title('life Expectancy vs. GDP')
plt.xlabel('GDP')
plt.ylabel('Life Expectancy')
plt.show()
```

Figure 9.19 Code used to produce a scatter plot of life expectancy vs GDP.

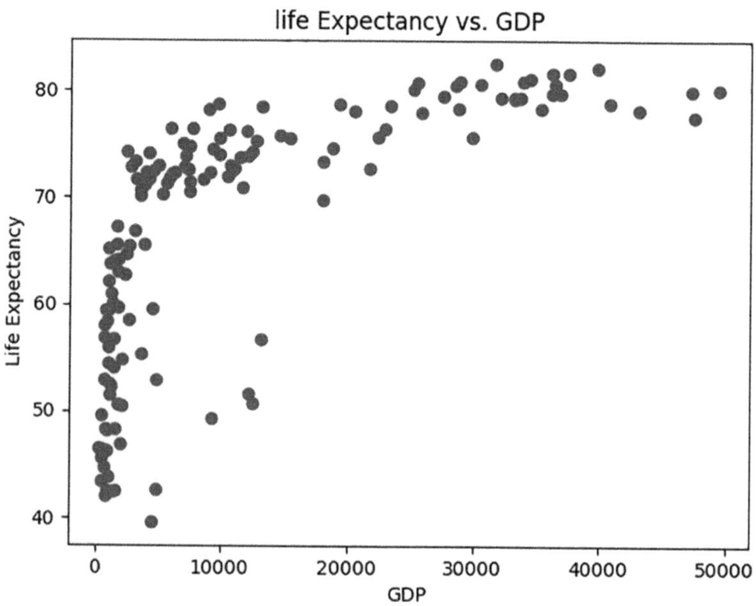

Figure 9.20 A scatter plot of life expectancy vs GDP.

```
import matplotlib.pyplot as plt
%matplotlib inline

# make sure the independent variable is the log of gdpPercap
x=np.log(gm_07['gdpPercap'])
# specify the dependent variable as life expectancy
y=gm_07['lifeExp']

plt.scatter(x,y)

plt.title('life Expectancy vs. GDP')
plt.xlabel('GDP (transformed)')
plt.ylabel('Life Expectancy')
plt.show()
```

Figure 9.21 Code used to produce a scatter plot of life expectancy vs Log(GDP).

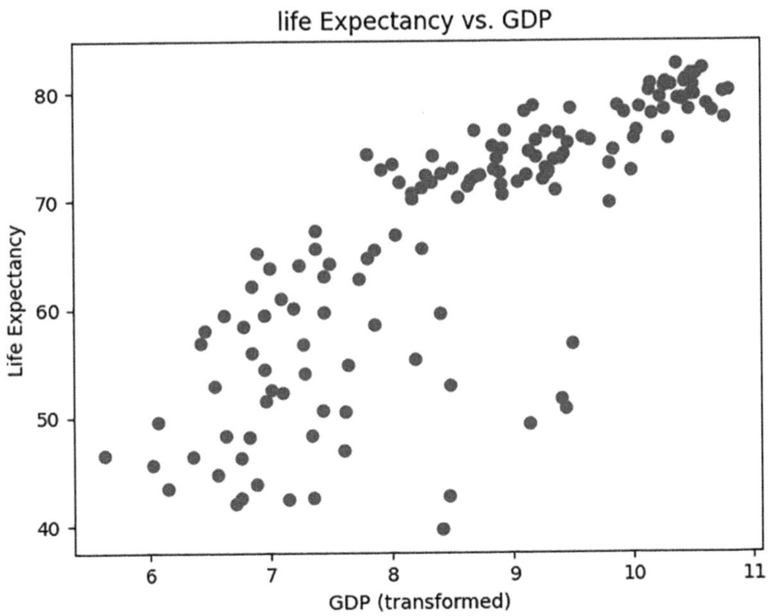

Figure 9.22 A scatter plot of life expectancy vs GDP (transformed).

Measuring Strength – Correlation Analysis

We run correlation analysis by calculating the values that indicate how strong the linear association between the variables is. We calculated the correlation among the variables in the dataset as shown in Figure 9.23.

```
# Calculting the correlation among three of the variables

gm_07_q=gm_07[['pop','lifeExp','gdpPercap']]

corr=gm_07_q.corr()
corr
```

	pop	lifeExp	gdpPercap
pop	1.000000	0.047553	-0.055676
lifeExp	0.047553	1.000000	0.678662
gdpPercap	-0.055676	0.678662	1.000000

Figure 9.23 Correlation matrix output for population, life expectancy, and GDP per capita.

It can be inferred from the above correlation results that the correlation between gdpPercap and lifeExp is r=0.68. This indicates a relatively strong association between the two variables. Correlation ranges between 1 and –1, with a correlation value close to 0 meaning the strength of the relationship is weak, a correlation value close to 0.5 or –0.5, means the strength of the relationship is moderate, and a correlation close to 1 or –1 means a strong relationship.

Next, we use a tool in seaborn to make a visual of the correlations, where the color corresponds to the value of the correlation (see Figure 9.24). There are a lot of customizations that can be added to this kind of plot. Figure 9.25 is a heat map.

```
# Seaborn version of correlation analysis

import seaborn as sns

# Generate a mask for the upper triangle
mask = np.triu(np.ones_like(corr, dtype=bool))

sns.heatmap(corr, mask=mask, cmap='coolwarm', annot=True)
```

Figure 9.24 Code used to generate a seaborn correlation heat map.

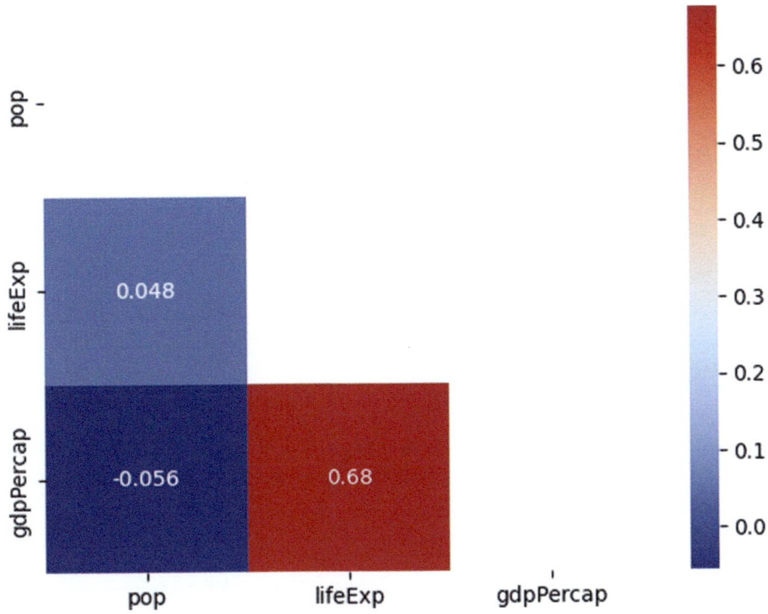

Figure 9.25 A heat map of population, life expectancy, and GDP per capita.

The Regression Analysis

We perform a basic linear regression analysis using the statsmodels library and a bit of the NumPy library. The regression method uses least squares to optimize a model to approximate the relationship between the variables. When specifying the linear regression model using the statsmodels formula module, we use the expression "LifeExp ~ log_GDP." In other words, we model the Life Expectancy variable as a function of log(GDP). The GDP variable is transformed using the logarithmic function (i.e., log_GDP). Figures 9.26 and 9.27 are the Python code and resultant output of the regression analysis.

```
# Transforming the 'gdpPercap' variable using log function
log_GDP=np.log(gm_07['gdpPercap'])
```

```
# import statsmodels.api as sm <-- tool appears to be depricated
# delete the pandas.utils....
import statsmodels.formula.api as smf

# use smf.ols function to generate the linear model (ordinary least squares regression)
results=smf.ols('lifeExp ~ log_GDP', data=gm_07).fit()
print(results)

# inspect the results with the summary() method

print(results.summary())
```

Figure 9.26 Code used to fit an OLS Regression Model predicting life expectancy from Log(GDP).

```
                            OLS Regression Results
==============================================================================
Dep. Variable:                lifeExp   R-squared:                       0.654
Model:                            OLS   Adj. R-squared:                  0.652
Method:                 Least Squares   F-statistic:                     265.2
Date:                Thu, 16 May 2024   Prob (F-statistic):           4.12e-34
Time:                        05:03:58   Log-Likelihood:                -479.26
No. Observations:                 142   AIC:                             962.5
Df Residuals:                     140   BIC:                             968.4
Df Model:                           1
Covariance Type:            nonrobust
==============================================================================
                 coef    std err          t      P>|t|      [0.025      0.975]
------------------------------------------------------------------------------
Intercept      4.9496      3.858      1.283      0.202      -2.677      12.576
log_GDP        7.2028      0.442     16.283      0.000       6.328       8.077
==============================================================================
Omnibus:                       40.647   Durbin-Watson:                   2.154
Prob(Omnibus):                  0.000   Jarque-Bera (JB):               72.274
Skew:                          -1.341   Prob(JB):                     2.02e-16
Kurtosis:                       5.240   Cond. No.                         57.0
==============================================================================
```

Figure 9.27 Regression analysis results.

Interpreting Regression Output

Slope (The second value in the "coef" column): For each unit increase in the log(GDP) variable, the model predicts a 7.2 year increase in the Country's life expectancy. R-squared: 65% of the variation in Life Expectancy is explained by the linear regression predicting Life Expectancy from log(GDP). P-value: The p-value is approximately 0, meaning the observed relationship is unlikely to occur by chance. It is more plausible to conclude that the observed relationship is a product of a meaningful phenomenon rather than a random occurrence.

The regression output helps us quantify the relationship between the variables and evaluate the model as far as its usefulness in predicting Life Expectancy from GDP. The p-value suggests that the linear relationship is statistically significant (unlikely to happen by chance alone). The R-squared value tells us that the linear model predicting Life Expectancy from GDP explains 65% of the variation in Life Expectancy. In general, a low p-value, high R-squared provide strong validation that the model is appropriate and meaningful for these data.

Fitting a Model to a Scatterplot

A tool from NumPy library called polynomial was used to fit the linear model to the scatterplot (see Figures 9.28 and 9.29).

```
import matplotlib.pyplot as plt
%matplotlib inline
from numpy.polynomial.polynomial import polyfit
import numpy as np

# make sure the independent variable is the log of gdpPercap
x=np.log(gm_07['gdpPercap'])
# specify the dependent variable as life expectancy
y=gm_07['lifeExp']

# Fit with polyfit
b, m = polyfit(x, y, 1)

plt.scatter(x,y)
plt.plot(x, b + m * x, '-')
plt.title('life Expectancy vs. log(GDP)')
plt.xlabel('log(GDP)')
plt.ylabel('Life Expectancy')
plt.show()
```

Figure 9.28 Code used to fit and overlay a trendline on life expectancy vs Log(GDP).

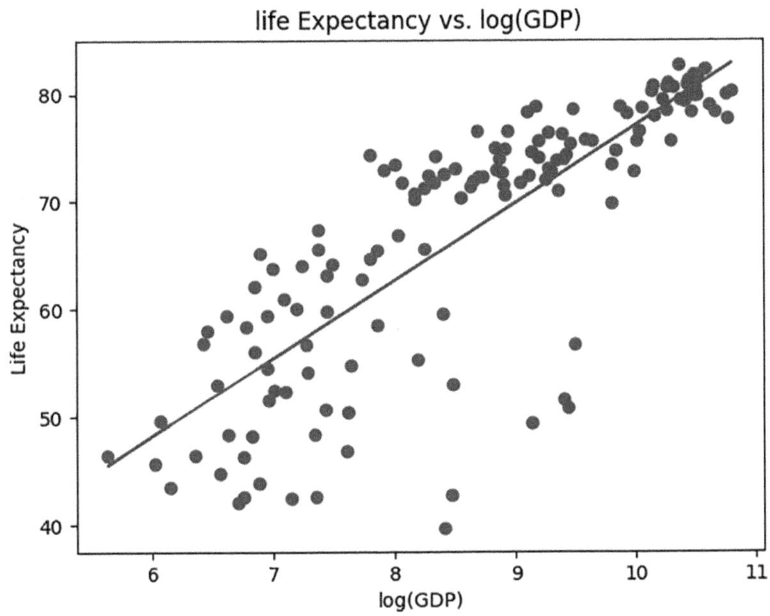

Figure 9.29 A scatter plot with a trendline showing life expectancy vs Log(GDP).

Predictive Analytics Application in Predicting the Relationship between Sleep and Health Quality

Sleep is arguably one of the most important human bodily functions. According to the National Heart, Lung, and Blood Institute,[14] "sleep plays a vital role in good health and well-being throughout your life."[14] Further, "during sleep, your body is working to support healthy brain function and maintain your physical health."[14] Specifically, getting enough sleep can play an important role in your weight, emotional well-being, blood pressure, diabetes, mental and physical performance, and more."[14] While there is no doubt that sleep is imperative for a healthy lifestyle, proper sleep is often hard to come by. Quality sleep can be affected by many things such as busy schedules, kids, anxiety, and technology. With that, it is important to identify variables that can enhance sleep quality.

This project aimed to predict how various factors might influence sleep quality and overall health. Specifically, these factors include heart rate variability, body temperature, movement during sleep, sleep duration hours, sleep quality score, caffeine intake, stress level, bedtime consistency, and light exposure. The purpose of this project is to identify the relationships between these specific factors and sleep quality. Another goal is to determine which factors have the greatest influence on sleep quality and overall health. By identifying which factors significantly influence sleep patterns, the results can be used to increase sleep quality.

Data: Sources and Preprocessing

The dataset, "Sleep and Health Metrics," was obtained from Kaggle.com, a data science community for downloading free publicly available datasets. To access this data, you need to create an account and log in to your account on the Kaggle website (www.kaggle.com/) as shown in Figure 9.30. The dataset was uploaded onto by Kaggle website by Laksika Tharmalingam. Once you sign in, click on the link to the dataset with #48 to take you to the dataset homepage. While on the dataset homepage, you will find a download button on the top right. Click on it to open a window, and then click on the "Download dataset as a zip" option to download the dataset into your download folder. In your downloads folder, find the zip file containing the dataset, unzip it, and then open it to preview the dataset.

Figure 9.30 Kaggle data source.

This dataset included a detailed overview of how various factors might influence sleep quality and overall health. The dataset presented 1000 different cases, as shown in Figure 9.31. Each individual was measured on a variety of factors such as heart rate, body temperature, movement during sleep, sleep duration in hours, sleep quality score, caffeine intake in milligrams, stress level, bedtime consistency, and light exposure. Once downloaded, the dataset was very clean and organized. But, in order to make sure that the data was as clean as it could be, it was checked for duplicate and redundant data and blank cells. There were no duplicate individuals found. And, the cells were trimmed in order to take away excess white spaces. A YouTube video by Mynda Treacy was watched to clean the data (Treacy). The table on the next page displayed the final datasheet that was imported into Google Colab, which will be used for linear regression analysis. The sleep quality score was used as the outcome variable. The other variables of heart rate, body temperature, movement during sleep, sleep duration in hours, caffeine intake in milligrams, stress level, bedtime consistency, and light exposure were the predictor variables. Because the outcome variable was numerical, a linear regression model was used.

wearable_tech_sleep_quality_1

Heart_Rate_Variability	Body_Temperature	Movement_During_Sleep	Sleep_Duration_Hours	Sleep_Quality_Score	Caffeine_Intake_mg	Stress_Level	Bedtime_Consistency	Light_Exposure_hours
79.93428306	37.19967772	1.324821725	4.638288663	1	107.6240318	2.771837284	0.657037016	7.933949473
67.23471398	36.96231684	1.855481329	6.209422484	1	104.6585892	3.738138333	0.144463808	6.992699479
82.95377076	36.52981518	1.207580079	6.8795917	10	0	3.115879633	0.64294913	7.655250085
100.4605971	36.17653161	1.69203847	10.33153149	1	116.9909808	3.904008363	0.453255188	9.429463455
65.31693251	36.84911166	0.106385333	8.334829687	1	223.2829082	4.571699379	0.641491542	10.55571331
65.31726086	36.69674269	2.213293707	5.496777646	7.122152667	22.57678809	6.674308973	0.655386338	9.140974662
101.5842563	36.94759661	2.001205475	8.229054434	1	254.8482651	4.357681923	0.821583012	8.203446417
85.34869458	36.8175859	1.182911369	5.179044017	1	198.7774821	1.828748586	0.77069073	10.99602354
60.61051228	37.02477636	2.659245668	9.124036581	2.409237055	76.5766678	7.280135693	0.769314333	7.374327054
80.85120087	36.23238239	2.937570138	6.793313022	1	135.8470363	3.325819733	0.788734064	10.06183868
60.73164614	37.15869703	0.392440136	7.359545717	1	309.8321808	4.882559146	0.558275797	7.423874403
60.68540493	36.5987998	1.237275221	9.488694971	1	223.3547814	5.893073014	0.506437017	8.862045916
74.83924543	37.53763044	1.23085765	5.569254647	1	150.8783655	5.399220837	0.674563417	7.77287487
31.73439511	36.15540609	1.060096899	5.404322722	1	126.2316683	7.188359095	0.64641619	7.888295635

Figure 9.31 Preview of the "Sleep and Health Metrics" dataset (sample rows and variables).

Model

A linear regression model has been used to predict the value of a variable based on the value of another variable. A linear regression model was used to predict the sleep quality score variable by factoring in heart rate variability, body temperature, movement during sleep, sleep duration, caffeine intake, stress level, bedtime consistency, and light exposure. This technique was used because the outcome variable, the sleep quality score, was numerical. The predictors were heart rate variability, body temperature, movement during sleep, sleep duration, caffeine intake, stress level, bedtime consistency, and light exposure. The following code, shown in Figure 9.32, was input into Google Colab to partition the data into the outcome variable and predictors.

```
[9] predictors = ['Heart_Rate_Variability','Body_Temperature', 'Movement_During_Sleep
    outcome = 'Sleep_Quality_Score'
```

Figure 9.32 Code used to predictors and outcome variable for the Sleep Quality Regression Model.

After the variables were partitioned into outcome and predictor variables, the next step was to train the dataset. Training the dataset allowed the best regression line to be fit to the data. In other words, training the dataset prevented overfitting or underfitting the data. This was essential to ensure accurate and reliable results. The following code, shown in Figure 9.33, was used to fit a regression model to the dataset by training the dataset through the use of dummy variables and defining x and y (outcome and predictor variables). A value of 40% was used in the validation test partition.

```
predictors = ['Heart_Rate_Variability','Body_Temperature', 'Movement_During_Sleep', 'Sleep_D
outcome = 'Sleep_Quality_Score'
x = pd.get_dummies(sleep[predictors], drop_first = True)
y = sleep[outcome]
train_x, valid_x, train_y, valid_y = train_test_split(x,y,test_size=0.4, random_state=1)
sleep_Im = LinearRegression()  # Define the model
sleep_Im.fit(train_x,train_y)   # Train the model
```

Figure 9.33 Code used to partition data and train a Linear Regression Model (train/validation split).

Results and Discussion

After the predictors and outcome variables were defined, along with training the dataset, the regression results were output. In order to determine which outcome variable should be used for this dataset, multiple variables were used as the outcome variable. And, a subsequent regression summary was output. However, the only outcome variable that gave the best and most accurate R-square and was the closest to 1 was the outcome variable of sleep quality score. The following screenshot shows (see Figure 9.34) the regression summary from the outcome variable of sleep quality score.

```
print(results.summary())

                            OLS Regression Results
==============================================================================
Dep. Variable:     Sleep_Quality_Score   R-squared:                       0.533
Model:                             OLS   Adj. R-squared:                  0.529
Method:                  Least Squares   F-statistic:                     141.2
Date:                 Tue, 15 Apr 2025   Prob (F-statistic):          6.08e-158
Time:                         18:26:22   Log-Likelihood:                -2129.8
No. Observations:                 1000   AIC:                             4278.
Df Residuals:                      991   BIC:                             4322.
Df Model:                            8
Covariance Type:             nonrobust
===========================================================================================
                              coef    std err          t      P>|t|      [0.025      0.975]
-------------------------------------------------------------------------------------------
Intercept                   6.0055      4.806      1.249      0.212      -3.426      15.438
Heart_Rate_Variability      0.0036      0.003      1.100      0.272      -0.003       0.010
Body_Temperature           -0.0107      0.130     -0.082      0.935      -0.266       0.245
Movement_During_Sleep      -0.2030      0.066     -3.081      0.002      -0.332      -0.074
Sleep_Duration_Hours        0.1324      0.042      3.145      0.002       0.050       0.215
Caffeine_Intake_mg         -0.0229      0.001    -33.129      0.000      -0.024      -0.022
Stress_Level               -0.0418      0.032     -1.311      0.190      -0.104       0.021
Bedtime_Consistency        -0.5801      0.319     -1.820      0.069      -1.205       0.045
Light_Exposure_hours        0.0033      0.032      0.104      0.918      -0.059       0.066
==============================================================================
Omnibus:                      110.208   Durbin-Watson:                   2.046
Prob(Omnibus):                  0.000   Jarque-Bera (JB):               86.264
Skew:                           0.625   Prob(JB):                     1.85e-19
Kurtosis:                       2.287   Cond. No.                     1.40e+04
==============================================================================

Notes:
[1] Standard Errors assume that the covariance matrix of the errors is correctly specified.
[2] The condition number is large, 1.4e+04. This might indicate that there are
strong multicollinearity or other numerical problems.
```

Figure 9.34 OLS regression results output for Sleep Quality Score (multiple predictors).

As can be seen, the R-squared value was 0.533. This value is closer to 1 than 0. So, this model was highly explained by the independent variables/predictors. Additionally, analyzing the p-value of the regression results determined which independent variables are most significant. A p-value was significant if it was more than 0.05. Therefore, the independent variables that were significant were heart rate variability, body temperature, stress level, bedtime consistency, and light exposure. The predictors that were not significant are movement during sleep, sleep duration, and caffeine intake.

Another model that was created was the determinants of coefficients for the predictor variables; a screenshot of the model is included below (see Figure 9.35). According to Jim Frost, "a positive coefficient indicates that as the value of the independent variable increases, the mean of the dependent variable tends to increase. A negative coefficient suggests that as the independent variable increases, the dependent variable tends to decrease" (Frost). As it relates to this model, heart rate variability, body temperature, and sleep duration changed the dependent variable (sleep quality score) the most.

```
[ ] print(pd.DataFrame({'Predictor':x.columns, 'Coefficient':sleep_Im.coef_}))

                 Predictor  Coefficient
0  Heart_Rate_Variability     0.002288
1        Body_Temperature     0.120507
2   Movement_During_Sleep    -0.211954
3    Sleep_Duration_Hours     0.122652
4      Caffeine_Intake_mg    -0.022249
5            Stress_Level    -0.007145
6      Bedtime_Consistency   -0.545123
7     Light_Exposure_hours   -0.005495
```

Figure 9.35 Predictor Coefficients output for the Sleep Quality Score Model.

A third model that was created compares the model's predictions to the actual values and also shows residual errors. In other words, these results identified how far off the model was for each prediction. The following screenshot was the output of this model (see Figure 9.36). According to Newcastle University, the residual value is the difference between the predicted value and the actual value. If there is a negative residual value, the predicted value is too high. If there is a positive residual value, the predicted value is too low.

```
       Actual  Predicted  Residual
507  9.731204   5.652768  4.078436
818  7.668166   5.144456  2.523710
452  1.000000  -1.205195  2.205195
368  1.584278   3.995589 -2.411311
242  1.000000   0.153287  0.846713
929  1.000000   1.702156 -0.702156
262  1.000000   1.297641 -0.297641
810  1.000000  -0.235310  1.235310
318  1.000000   3.176204 -2.176204
49   1.000000   3.228041 -2.228041
446  9.029235   5.309848  3.719387
142  1.000000   0.060352  0.939648
968  1.000000   2.516021 -1.516021
345  1.000000  -1.146116  2.146116
971  1.000000   2.001686 -1.001686
133  1.000000   1.643722 -0.643722
104  1.000000   1.729024 -0.729024
6    1.000000   0.196562  0.803438
600  1.000000   3.210945 -2.210945
496  1.000000   3.093798 -2.093798
```

Figure 9.36 Actual vs predicted values with residual errors (Sleep Quality Model).

Because the actual, predicted, and residual values have been determined, the next step was to gather the metrics for the overall performance of the model. In order to measure this, a model was run to find the mean error (ME), the Root Mean Squared Error (RMSE), the Mean Absolute Error (MAE), the Mean Percentage Error (MPE), and the Mean Absolute Percentage Error (MAPE). A screenshot of the output was included below (see Figure 9.37).

```
[ ] print(regressionSummary(train_y, sleep_Im.predict(train_x)))

Regression statistics

                      Mean Error (ME) : 0.0000
       Root Mean Squared Error (RMSE) : 2.0122
            Mean Absolute Error (MAE) : 1.6697
          Mean Percentage Error (MPE) : -39.1084
Mean Absolute Percentage Error (MAPE) : 113.4669
None
```

```
[ ] print(regressionSummary(valid_y, sleep_Im.predict(valid_x)))

Regression statistics

                      Mean Error (ME) : 0.1752
       Root Mean Squared Error (RMSE) : 2.0824
            Mean Absolute Error (MAE) : 1.7081
          Mean Percentage Error (MPE) : -30.3546
Mean Absolute Percentage Error (MAPE) : 110.4292
None
```

Figure 9.37 Regression performance metrics for training and validation sets (ME, RMSE, MAE, MPE, MAPE).

According to Shittu Olumide from Arize.com, a value of 0 for RMSE "indicates that the expected and actual values match precisely. Low RMSE values show that the model makes more accurate predictions and fits the data well. Higher levels, on the other hand, imply more significant mistakes and fewer accurate forecasts" (Olumide). Therefore, after analyzing the model above, the RMSE showed that the model makes mostly accurate predictions.

Lastly, the final linear regression model equation is the following: Y=0+0.002288 (Heart_Rate_Variability)+0.120507 (Body_Temperature)+–0.211954 (Movement_During_Sleep)+0.122652 (Sleep_duration_hours)+–0.022249 (Caffeine_Intake_mg)+–0.007145 (stress_level)+–0.0545123 (Bedtime_Consistency)+–0.005495 (Light_Exposure_hours).

The purpose of this model was to be able to predict a healthy sleep quality score based on a variety of factors such as heart rate, body temperature, movement during sleep, sleep duration in hours, caffeine intake in milligrams, stress level, bedtime consistency, and light exposure. Based on our linear regression model, the variables that were most significant in predicting the sleep quality score were heart rate variability, body temperature, stress level, bedtime consistency, and light exposure. Additionally, the two most significant variables that were found were body temperature and light exposure. The predictors that were not significant are movement during sleep, sleep duration, and caffeine intake. It was found through the predictor and coefficient model that heart rate variability, body temperature, and sleep duration change the dependent variable (sleep quality score) the most.

This data and model could be used to help others who are interested in improving their sleep. It was suggested that individuals first regulate their bedroom temperature in order to regulate their body temperature. A dark bedroom was also suggested. Other variables that individuals should pay attention to are regulating heart rate, stress levels, and bedtime consistency. Factors that were not as significant but could still impact sleep in a small way included movement during sleep, sleep duration, and caffeine intake. According to Mayo Clinic, some practical ways to improve sleep quality are to create a restful environment such as dark rooms and calming activities before bed such as a bath or relaxing. Further, practicing stress management can also help lower stress levels (Six Steps to Better Sleep). Overall, the model was able to identify which factors are most important for sleep which in turn impacted one's overall sleep score.

Concluding Remarks

This chapter has discussed and demonstrated data analytics capabilities and how the healthcare industry can leverage these capabilities to their advantage. Analytics has become an indispensable pillar of modern healthcare, transforming how providers deliver care, manage resources, and make strategic decisions. By leveraging advanced data techniques – including predictive modeling, prescriptive modeling, and real-time dashboarding – HCOs can identify trends earlier, personalize treatment plans, streamline operations, and improve population health outcomes. These insights help reduce clinical variation, minimize costs, and enhance patient safety and satisfaction.

As the industry continues to generate vast and complex datasets – from electronic health records to wearables, imaging, genomics, and administrative systems – analytics offers a powerful pathway to convert this information into actionable intelligence. However, the full realization of analytics' potential requires continued investment in data quality, interoperability, privacy protections, and workforce development.

Ultimately, the integration of robust analytics within healthcare not only strengthens evidence-based decision-making but also supports a more proactive, equitable, and patient-centered healthcare system. As capabilities continue to advance, analytics will remain central to shaping the future of care delivery and improving outcomes for individuals and communities alike.

References

1. Agarwal, R., Gao, G., DesRoches, C., & Jha, A.K., (2010). Research Commentary—The Digital Transformation of Healthcare: Current Status and the Road Ahead. *Information Systems Research, 21* (4), 796–809.
2. Alonso-Zaldivar, R. (2009). U.S. Healthcare Lags in Bang for the Buck. *San Francisco Chronicle*, March 12, p. 1.
3. Barney, J. (1991). Firm Resources and Sustained Competitive Advantage. *Journal of Management, 17*(1), 99–120.

4. Chae, B., & Olson, D. L. (2013). Business analytics for supply chain: A dynamic-capabilities framework. *International Journal of Information Technology & Decision Making 12*(1), 9–26.
5. Chen, H., Chiang, R. H. L., & Storey, V. C. (2012). Business Intelligence and Analytics: From Big Data to Big Impact. *MIS Quarterly*, 36(4), 1165–1188.
6. Deloitte Center for health Solutions (2015). Health System Analytics: The Missing Key to Unlock Value-based Care. *Deloitte Development LLC.*
7. Dinev, T., Albano, V., Xu, H., D'Atri, A., & Hart, P. (2016). Individuals' Attitude Towards Electronic Healthcare Records: A Privacy Calculus Perspective. *Advances in Healthcare Informatics and Analytics*, 19–50.
8. Eisenhardt, K. M., & Martin, J. A. (2000) Dynamic Capabilities: What are They, *Strategic Management Journal, 21*(1), 1105–1121.
9. Ferranti, J.M, Langman, M.K., Tanaka, D., McCall, J. & Ahmad, A. (2010) Bridging the Gap: Leveraging Business Intelligence Tools in Support of Patient Safety and Financial Effectiveness, *Journal of American Medical Information Association, 17*(2):136–43. doi: 10.1136/jamia.2009.002220.
10. Gartner. (2012). Gartner Says Worldwide Business Intelligence, Analytics and Performance Management Software Market Surpassed the $12 Billion Mark in 2011, (available at www.gartner.com/newsroom/id/1971516; retrieved May 1, 2016).
11. Groves, P., Kayyali B., Knott D., & Van Kuiken, S. (2013). The Big Data Revolution in Healthcare. *Center for US Health System Reform Business Technology Office,* January 2013, Copyright © McKinsey & Company.
12. Holsapple, C., Lee-Post, A., & Pakath, R. (2014). A Unified Foundation for Business Analytics. *Decision Support Systems, 64,* 130–141.
13. Murdoch, T.B. & Detsky, A.S. (2013) The Inevitable Application of Big Data to Health Care, *Journal of American Medical Association, 3*(13), 1351–1352
14. National Heart, *Lung and Blood Institute.* How Sleep Works, 2022
15. Reiner, B.I. (2013). Creating Accountability in Image Quality Analysis. *Part 4: Quality Analytics Journal of Digital Imaging,* 26, 825–829.
16. Shah, N.D, & Pathak J. (2014) Why Health Care May Finally Be Ready for Big Data. *Harvard Business Review,* December 2014. https://hbr.org/2014/12/why-health-care-may-finally-be-ready-for-big-data
17. Sharma, R., Mithas, S., & Kankanhalli, A. (2014). Transforming Decision-Making Processes: A Research Agenda for Understanding the Impact of Business Analytics on Organizations. *European Journal of Information System, 23*(4), 433–441.
18. Wang, Y., Kung, L-A., & Byrd, T.A. (2016). Big Data Analytics: Understanding its Capabilities and Potential Benefits for Healthcare Organizations, *Technological Forecasting & Social Change,* 12(6), 3–13. http://dx.doi.org/10.1016/j.techfore.2015.12.019
19. Ward, M.J., Marsolo, K.A, & Froehle, C.M. (2014). Applications of Business Analytics in Healthcare, *Journal of Business Horizon,* 57, 571–582
20. Wixom, B. H., Yen, B., & Relich, M. (2013). Maximizing Value from Business Analytics, *MIS Quarterly Executive,* 12(2), 111–123.
21. Yang, J.-J., Li, J., Mulder, J, Wang, Y., Chen, S., Wu, H., Wang, Q., & Pan, H. (2015). Emerging Information Technologies for Enhanced Healthcare, *Journal of Computers in Industry,* 69, 3–11.

Chapter 10

AI-Assisted Clinical Decision Support Systems

Anthony Blash, PharmD, BCompSc, CPHIMS

Overview of AI in Clinical Decision Support

Artificial intelligence (AI) has emerged as a transformative force in healthcare, particularly in the realm of clinical decision support systems (CDSS). AI-assisted CDSS leverage advanced computational techniques such as machine learning (ML), natural language processing (NLP), and deep learning to analyze large and complex datasets, providing healthcare professionals with actionable insights to improve patient care.[1] These systems are not designed to replace clinicians but to augment their decision-making, offering evidence-based recommendations that can enhance diagnostic accuracy, optimize treatment plans, and predict patient outcomes.

The integration of AI into CDSS represents a significant evolution from traditional rule-based systems. Early CDSS relied heavily on static, predefined algorithms and structured knowledge bases, which often struggled to adapt to the complexity and variability of clinical practice. These early systems could not keep pace with the exponential growth of biomedical knowledge and the increasing diversity of clinical data. By contrast, modern AI-driven CDSS can learn from real-world data, continuously refining their performance and adapting to emerging evidence. This adaptability is particularly valuable in contemporary healthcare, where the volume of information generated from electronic health records (EHRs), medical imaging, genomic sequencing, and wearable devices is increasing at unprecedented rates.[5, 10, 11]

The Evolution of CDSS

The concept of CDSS dates back to the 1970s, when pioneering systems such as MYCIN were created to assist clinicians in diagnosing infections and recommending antibiotics.[11] These early systems were primarily rule-based, depending on a set of "if-then" rules derived from clinical guidelines and expert knowledge. While groundbreaking, they were limited by their inability to process complex, unstructured data or adapt to new information without manual updates.

DOI: 10.4324/9781003593867-13

The advent of ML and big data analytics in the 21st century revolutionized CDSS. Modern AI-assisted CDSS can process structured and unstructured data, including clinical notes, laboratory test results, imaging data, and genomic sequences, to generate insights that were previously inaccessible.[2] For instance, deep learning algorithms have been applied to radiology and pathology, demonstrating diagnostic performance comparable to, and sometimes exceeding, that of human experts.[7] Recent advances have also integrated multimodal data sources, combining EHRs, imaging, and genomic profiles to produce more holistic and personalized decision support.[5]

AI-Assisted CDSS

AI has fundamentally reshaped the design and operation of CDSS, ushering in a new era of data-driven, adaptive healthcare. At the heart of this transformation are several interrelated technologies, such as ML, NLP, deep learning, and predictive analytics, that collectively enable modern CDSS to analyze complex datasets, generate actionable insights, and support clinicians in real time.

ML forms the foundation of most AI-assisted CDSS innovations. Algorithms such as random forests, gradient boosting, and neural networks can uncover intricate patterns within large volumes of patient data and construct predictive models of clinical outcomes. These systems have already demonstrated significant impact in predicting conditions such as sepsis, cardiac arrest, and acute kidney injury in hospitalized patients, allowing for earlier and more targeted interventions.[3]

NLP represents another cornerstone of AI-driven CDSS. This technology enables the interpretation of unstructured text, including physician notes, discharge summaries, and diagnostic reports, which often contain essential details not captured in structured EHR fields. The integration of large language models (LLMs) has propelled NLP forward, empowering systems to extract risk factors in real time, summarize patient histories, and even draft preliminary clinical documentation.[4]

Deep learning, a specialized subset of ML, leverages multilayered neural networks to process highly complex data modalities such as medical imaging, waveforms, and genomic sequences. Convolutional neural networks (CNNs) have achieved remarkable accuracy in detecting diseases like diabetic retinopathy, breast cancer, and pneumonia. More recently, transformer-based architectures have expanded these capabilities to include multimodal data inputs, combining text, imaging, and numerical data, thereby creating more holistic and context-aware decision support systems.[5]

Complementing these methods, predictive analytics allows CDSS to anticipate clinical events by analyzing historical and real-time data. These systems can forecast hospital readmissions, disease progression, or treatment responses, enabling proactive interventions that improve outcomes and reduce complications. By 2023, AI-driven predictive models had been widely adopted within population health initiatives, helping healthcare organizations identify at-risk cohorts and implement preventive strategies at scale.[6]

Benefits of AI-Assisted CDSS

The integration of AI into CDSS offers profound benefits across diagnostic accuracy, personalization, efficiency, and preventive care.

One of the most significant advantages lies in improved diagnostic accuracy. AI algorithms can process vast datasets to detect subtle patterns that may be missed by human observers. Research published in 2023 demonstrated that AI-enhanced radiology systems were capable of identifying early-stage cancers with greater sensitivity than traditional diagnostic workflows, reducing error rates and improving patient prognosis.[7]

Equally transformative is the capacity for personalized treatment. AI-assisted CDSS can integrate genomic, phenotypic, and lifestyle data to generate individualized therapeutic recommendations. Such personalization not only optimizes treatment efficacy but also minimizes adverse effects—a particularly vital capability in oncology and rare disease management, where tailored therapies are essential to success.

AI also contributes to enhanced clinical efficiency. By automating labor-intensive administrative processes such as data extraction, coding, and documentation, AI systems reduce clinician workload and mitigate burnout. This operational streamlining allows providers to redirect valuable time toward direct patient care and complex decision-making.[8]

Finally, AI-enabled proactive care represents a major step toward preventive medicine. Predictive analytics tools can identify patients at high risk for acute exacerbations of chronic conditions such as heart failure or chronic obstructive pulmonary disease (COPD). Early detection enables timely outpatient interventions, which not only improve patient outcomes but also reduce costly hospitalizations and overall healthcare expenditures.[9]

Recent Developments and Challenges

Since 2023, several notable developments have shaped the field. First, explainable AI (XAI) has become increasingly important for building clinician trust. CDSS platforms now integrate interpretable models that not only provide recommendations but also explain their reasoning in human-understandable terms. Second, federated learning has gained traction as a means of training robust AI models without transferring sensitive patient data, thus addressing privacy and regulatory challenges. Third, integration with wearable and remote monitoring devices has expanded the reach of CDSS beyond hospitals into patients' homes, enabling continuous monitoring and real-time interventions.[10]

Nevertheless, challenges persist. Algorithmic bias remains a critical concern, as models trained on unrepresentative datasets risk perpetuating healthcare disparities. Regulatory oversight, interoperability standards, and medico-legal responsibilities also continue to evolve as AI becomes more deeply embedded into clinical workflows. Importantly, balancing automation with human oversight remains essential to ensure safe and ethical use of AI in CDSS.[11]

Applications and Case Studies

AI is rapidly transforming the landscape of CDSS, enabling more accurate diagnostics, enhanced predictive capabilities, and personalized treatment approaches.[1] As healthcare continues to generate vast amounts of complex data, AI-driven CDSS are emerging as essential tools for improving patient outcomes, optimizing workflows, and supporting evidence-based decision-making. This section explores four major applications, including diagnostic support, predictive analytics, personalized medicine, and clinical workflow optimization, which are illustrated with real-world examples that demonstrate how these technologies are reshaping modern healthcare.

Diagnostic Support

Among the most transformative uses of AI in CDSS is its ability to enhance diagnostic accuracy. ML algorithms have achieved remarkable performance in interpreting medical images, including X-rays, MRIs, and CT scans. A landmark study published in 2022 reported that an AI model trained on a large dataset of chest X-rays detected pneumonia with a sensitivity of 94% and a specificity of 92%, outperforming many radiologists.[7] This advancement is particularly valuable in resource-limited environments where access to specialist expertise is scarce.

By 2023, AI applications in diagnostic support expanded beyond radiology to dermatology, ophthalmology, and pathology. AI-based models were shown to match or exceed human specialists in recognizing complex disease patterns such as melanoma, diabetic retinopathy, and cervical dysplasia.[7]

One notable example comes from a hospital in the United Kingdom, which implemented an AI-assisted CDSS to support radiologists in interpreting mammograms. The system analyzed more than 10,000 mammograms and identified early signs of breast cancer in 15% of cases initially missed by human readers.[5] Early detection enabled timely intervention and improved survival outcomes. Similar AI systems are now being deployed across Europe and North America, where they have demonstrated reductions in both false positives and false negatives. As a result, AI in radiology has become one of the most mature and widely adopted CDSS applications.[5]

Predictive Analytics

Another major domain of AI-assisted CDSS involves predictive analytics, which uses data-driven algorithms to forecast future clinical events. By analyzing structured and unstructured data from EHRs, laboratory results, medication histories, and clinical notes, predictive models can identify patients at elevated risk for adverse outcomes. These tools support early intervention, enabling clinicians to act before deterioration occurs.

In 2023, predictive analytics systems were increasingly deployed at the population level, allowing health systems to stratify patients by risk and direct preventive measures toward those most likely to benefit.[6] A study published that year demonstrated how an AI model predicted the risk of heart failure among patients with diabetes with over 90% accuracy.[3] By analyzing blood pressure, cholesterol levels, and medication histories, the model helped clinicians identify high-risk individuals and implement early interventions, such as lifestyle modification and pharmacologic optimization, reducing heart failure incidence by 25%.[3] Similar successes have been reported in hypertension, chronic kidney disease, and COPD, further validating the potential of predictive analytics to reduce long-term morbidity and healthcare costs.[9]

Personalized Medicine

AI-assisted CDSS also plays a pivotal role in the evolution of personalized medicine. These systems integrate genomic, proteomic, phenotypic, and lifestyle data to tailor therapeutic strategies for each patient. By identifying genetic mutations and molecular markers, AI can predict drug response and optimize treatment plans, particularly in oncology and rare diseases where individual variability significantly influences outcomes.[8]

A 2022 implementation at a major U.S. cancer center exemplified this approach. The center deployed an AI-assisted CDSS to guide treatment selection for lung cancer patients based on tumor genomic profiles. The system recommended targeted therapies aligned with specific genetic alterations, resulting in a 20% improvement in treatment response and a 15% reduction in adverse effects.[5] By 2023, similar oncology platforms had evolved to include liquid biopsy data, enabling clinicians to monitor tumor evolution in real time and adjust therapy dynamically. This adaptive capability is revolutionizing cancer care, shifting treatment paradigms from reactive to proactive and individualized precision medicine.[5]

Clinical Workflow Optimization

Beyond diagnostics and treatment planning, AI-assisted CDSS is transforming clinical operations through workflow optimization. These systems reduce administrative burden, streamline data management, and enhance overall efficiency. Intelligent automation tools can extract and summarize key patient information, prioritize cases based on severity, and even assist with documentation and coding while maintaining compliance with clinical and regulatory standards.[4]

A 2023 study highlighted the potential of AI-driven documentation systems to reduce charting time by 30%, allowing providers to redirect attention toward patient care.[8] The AI system automatically extracted relevant details from clinical narratives and populated corresponding EHR fields. Hospitals implementing this approach reported not only improved operational efficiency but also higher clinician satisfaction and reduced burnout. These results underscore that AI-assisted CDSS can enhance both clinical effectiveness and workforce well-being by aligning technological capability with human-centered design principles.

Impact on Clinical Practice

The integration of AI-assisted CDSS into clinical practice has the potential to revolutionize healthcare delivery. By providing clinicians with real-time, evidence-based recommendations, these systems enhance diagnostic accuracy, optimize treatment plans, and improve patient outcomes.[1] In recent years, the adoption of AI-driven tools has accelerated across diverse specialties, from emergency medicine to oncology, where they have been shown to reduce errors, improve efficiency, and strengthen clinical decision-making through continuous learning from real-world data.

Enhanced Diagnostic Accuracy

Diagnostic errors remain one of the most significant sources of patient harm worldwide. AI-assisted CDSS has demonstrated considerable promise in addressing this challenge. For example, a 2023 multicenter study found that implementing AI-assisted CDSS in emergency departments reduced diagnostic errors by nearly 30%.[3] These improvements were particularly notable in cases involving complex or ambiguous presentations such as sepsis, pulmonary embolism, and acute myocardial infarction. By analyzing patient data in real time, including vital signs, laboratory results, and imaging studies, the system generated prioritized differential diagnoses and highlighted high-risk conditions that required urgent attention. Clinicians reported that the tool functioned as a valuable "second set of eyes," improving confidence in decision-making while also accelerating the initiation of life-saving treatments. Challenges remained, however, including alert fatigue and the need to integrate seamlessly with existing workflows, underscoring the importance of thoughtful system design and clinician engagement.

Beyond emergency settings, diagnostic support tools powered by AI have proven effective in radiology and pathology, fields where the interpretation of complex imaging and tissue data is critical. AI-assisted mammography review systems in 2023 were shown to detect subtle early-stage cancers that had been missed by human radiologists in approximately 12% of cases.[7] Similarly, AI-assisted pathology platforms achieved superior detection rates of rare malignancies compared with standard manual review, thereby reducing delays in diagnosis and enabling earlier initiation of treatment. These systems not only improved diagnostic accuracy but also enhanced efficiency by automating routine tasks, allowing clinicians to focus on the most complex cases. Nevertheless, issues such as algorithm transparency, variability in image quality across institutions, and the risk of overreliance on automated outputs highlighted the ongoing need for balanced implementation strategies that prioritize both technological innovation and human oversight.

Optimized Treatment Plans

AI-assisted CDSS is also transforming the way treatment plans are developed and implemented. These systems combine patient medical history, laboratory results, imaging studies, and genomic information to generate personalized treatment recommendations. In 2023, a large oncology trial demonstrated that AI-assisted CDSS improved adherence to evidence-based chemotherapy protocols by 20%, while simultaneously reducing treatment-related adverse events.[5] Patients treated with AI-guided plans had higher response rates, improved quality of life, and fewer unplanned hospitalizations. Clinicians noted that the system's ability to synthesize vast amounts of clinical and molecular data in real time facilitated more precise dosing strategies and better sequencing of therapies, ultimately leading to more consistent outcomes across diverse patient populations.

Furthermore, AI has expanded the scope of pharmacogenomics by integrating genomic sequencing into CDSS. This enables the tailoring of medication regimens based on a patient's genetic profile, reducing adverse drug reactions and enhancing therapeutic efficacy.[8] For example, AI-assisted prescribing systems in cardiology have been used to adjust anticoagulation therapy more precisely, significantly lowering the risk of bleeding while maintaining protection against stroke. This integration of genomic data into treatment planning highlights the shift toward truly individualized medicine, where interventions are optimized not only for disease characteristics but also for patient-specific biology. While challenges such as cost, access to sequencing technologies, and the need for clinician education remain, these innovations demonstrate how AI-assisted CDSS can advance precision medicine and reshape the standards of care across multiple specialties.

Improved Workflow Efficiency

The integration of AI-assisted CDSS into clinical workflows has the potential to significantly improve efficiency by reducing the time and effort required for routine tasks. A 2023 study of hospitalist physicians reported that AI-supported documentation and order-entry systems decreased charting time by 28% without compromising accuracy.[4] The time savings allowed physicians to increase direct patient contact and reduce after-hours charting, thereby improving clinician satisfaction and reducing burnout. Hospitals adopting these systems also observed measurable improvements in throughput, with faster discharge processing and fewer delays in initiating evidence-based care plans. Nevertheless, successful implementation required thoughtful workflow redesign, clinician training, and ongoing monitoring to ensure that automation complemented rather than disrupted clinical practice.

In addition, AI-based triage systems have been adopted in large emergency departments, where they automatically prioritize patients based on presenting symptoms, vital signs, and comorbidities. These systems reduced average wait times by 15 minutes and improved time-to-treatment for high-acuity cases such as stroke and trauma.[6] Workflow improvements extend beyond the hospital setting; primary care clinics employing AI-assisted virtual scribes have reported lower administrative burden and higher patient satisfaction, as providers were able to maintain better eye contact and more conversational visits. Collectively, these examples illustrate how AI-CDSS can streamline processes, enhance patient-centered care, and support workforce well-being. However, they also underscore the importance of interoperability, data governance, and addressing clinician concerns about overreliance on automated decision-making to ensure these benefits are fully realized.

Population Health Management

AI-assisted CDSS is also playing a key role in population health management. By analyzing aggregated patient data, these systems enable healthcare organizations to identify health disparities, predict disease outbreaks, and implement targeted interventions.[9] In 2023, predictive CDSS platforms were deployed at the regional level in the United States to forecast influenza outbreaks up to two weeks in advance, allowing for the timely distribution of vaccines and staffing adjustments in hospitals. This example highlighted how AI not only improves patient-level outcomes but also strengthens the resilience of healthcare systems by informing resource allocation, guiding public health policy, and reducing the strain on emergency services during seasonal surges. Importantly, the ability to incorporate social determinants of health data, such as housing, transportation, and socioeconomic status, further enhanced the precision and equity of these interventions.

Similarly, chronic disease management has benefited from AI-assisted CDSS at the population level. A 2023 review found that AI-driven platforms analyzing EHR and wearable device data reduced hospital admissions for diabetes complications by 22% and improved blood pressure control rates in hypertensive patients.[2] These systems support a shift from reactive to proactive healthcare by enabling population-level prevention strategies, particularly in underserved communities. The applications underscore the potential of AI to close care gaps, personalize outreach campaigns, and optimize chronic disease management programs across large patient cohorts. However, the success of these initiatives depends on addressing challenges such as interoperability between health systems, ensuring data privacy, and providing equitable access to digital tools, so that the benefits of AI-driven population health management are distributed fairly across all populations.

Challenges and Ethical Considerations

Despite the potential benefits, the integration of AI-assisted CDSS into clinical practice presents several challenges. One major issue is algorithmic bias, which occurs when models are trained on datasets that do not adequately represent the diversity of real-world patient populations. A 2023 investigation revealed that some sepsis prediction models performed less effectively in minority populations, underscoring the importance of inclusive training datasets and continuous validation.[10]

Another critical challenge lies in transparency and explainability. Clinicians often hesitate to rely on AI tools that function as "black boxes" without providing a clear rationale for their recommendations. Recent developments in XAI have sought to address this limitation by incorporating interpretable models that present supporting evidence alongside predictions.[11] However, widespread adoption will require regulatory frameworks that mandate both technical performance standards and ethical safeguards to ensure accountability, patient safety, and trust in AI-driven decision-making.

Finally, legal liability considerations must be addressed as AI becomes a copilot in decision-making. Questions of liability whether resting on clinicians, healthcare organizations, or AI vendors, remain unresolved. Professional societies have begun issuing guidance, but consistent standards across regions and specialties are still lacking.[12] Addressing these ethical and regulatory issues will be essential to ensuring that AI-assisted CDSS are used safely, fairly, and effectively.

Future Directions and Innovations

AI-CDSS are entering a period of accelerated maturation, evolving from isolated pilot programs into enterprise-level platforms that span service lines, care settings, and data modalities. The next phase of innovation will be defined by advances in model architectures, particularly foundation and multimodal models, together with privacy-preserving learning, explainability, interoperability, and safety engineering designed for day-to-day clinical reliability.[1] These developments promise to enhance care quality, patient safety, equity, and operational performance, aligning AI-driven systems with the rigor of regulated clinical practice.[1]

Foundation models, including LLMs and vision-language architectures, are moving rapidly from research settings into regulated clinical workflows. Within CDSS, domain-adapted LLMs are being fine-tuned to summarize longitudinal charts, propose differential diagnoses, draft patient-specific orders, and surface guideline citations directly at the point of care.[5] Retrieval-augmented generation (RAG) and institutional guardrails, covering policy, vocabulary, and formulary constraints, are improving factual grounding and reducing hallucination risk, allowing recommendations to remain consistent with evidence and local protocols.[4] Compared with earlier narrow models, foundation models can adapt swiftly as clinical guidelines evolve and support multiservice deployments where a single core model underpins pharmacy verification, inpatient triage, and outpatient care-gap closure.[4,5]

Emerging multimodal and longitudinal modeling further extends the reach of AI-CDSS by combining text, numerical data, images, and genomic or social determinants inputs into unified patient representations.[5] These systems integrate vitals, laboratory values, notes, imaging, and SDOH data to produce continuously updating state assessments that inform "next best action" recommendations.[5,3] New architectures capable of handling long temporal contexts, spanning months or years of EHR history, allow clinicians to ask context-rich questions such as, "What happened the last time this patient presented like this?" or "Which therapy sequence historically worked best for similar cohorts?"[5,3] For pharmacists, these models enable safer therapeutic drug monitoring by synthesizing renal function trends, serum drug levels, and interaction networks in real time.[2,3]

Digital-twin technology represents another frontier for AI-enabled clinical optimization. These virtual replicas mirror patients, departments, or entire health systems, allowing teams to simulate therapy sequences, staffing models, or bed-management strategies before implementation. By combining mechanistic knowledge, such as pharmacokinetics, with observational learning, digital twins generate counterfactual scenarios that forecast outcomes under different choices.[3] Pharmacy services can apply digital twins to infusion-center management to predict drug waste or scheduling bottlenecks, while surgical units can test peri-operative pathways under simulated surge conditions.[3] The same methodology supports scenario planning for formulary adjustments, antimicrobial stewardship, and discharge readiness thresholds, strengthening operational resilience across the care continuum.[2,3]

Scaling these innovations safely requires privacy-preserving learning frameworks. Federated learning enables institutions to collaboratively train shared models on decentralized data without transferring patient-level records, thereby reducing reidentification risk while preserving the data diversity crucial for model generalizability.[11] However, this approach faces threats such as poisoning attacks where malicious actors insert corrupted data into training sets to degrade model performance or induce biased outputs[18] and membership inference attacks which exploit subtle differences in model behavior to reveal whether an individual's data contributed to training,[14] *risking patient privacy. T*o mitigate these, current federated learning practices incorporate federated averaging with secure aggregation, while next-generation pipelines augment defenses with differential privacy noise and robust aggregation techniques.[2,11] Additionally, synthetic data generation and split learning configurations are being tested to support collaboration when raw data cannot be moved, promoting fairness and consistent model calibration across sites.[11]

As deployment broadens, explainability and transparency have become indispensable. Modern explainable-AI methods move beyond retrospective feature attribution toward decision-centric transparency that highlights which guideline passages, clinical trials, or patient cohorts support a given recommendation.[10] Salient contrasts such as "why A over B," confidence intervals, and counterfactual explanations, for example, "to recommend B, creatinine would need to be ≤1.3 mg/dL," allow clinicians to reason through uncertainty.[8] Workflow-aware user interfaces that display concise justifications near order buttons reduce cognitive load and alert fatigue, fostering clinician trust and appropriate overrides.[10,17]

Safety engineering now parallels medication-safety disciplines. Health systems are implementing full model-lifecycle management: versioned datasets, prospective validation on shifted populations, drift detection, and rollback mechanisms when thresholds are exceeded.[1,7] Independent, device-style evaluations that measure clinical impact, usability, and equity outcomes are emerging as regulatory expectations.[1] Many organizations are adopting formal safety cases, structured arguments supported by evidence, and incident-response playbooks, to demonstrate that an AI-CDSS is safe for a defined clinical use.[7]

Reliable, real-time performance also depends on robust interoperability. FHIR-native data pipelines and event-driven architectures allow AI models to process vital signs, orders, and laboratory results as they are generated, returning actionable recommendations integrated within workflows such as medication reconciliation or order entry.[7] Tight linkage to eMAR, CPOE, and inventory systems ensures that dosing adjustments or therapeutic substitutions can be accepted with a single confirmation.[5,7] As TEFCA expands cross-network data liquidity, CDSS will be able to incorporate external encounters and diagnostics, closing information gaps that previously limited safe decision-making.[7]

Edge-based AI, or the deployment of AI models and algorithms directly on local devices such as mobile phones, wearables, and clinical instruments, is extending decision support beyond hospital walls.[15] By enabling real-time data processing and analysis on-site, it supports continuous cardiometabolic and respiratory monitoring even without constant connectivity, allowing earlier detection of decompensation and prompting timely outreach.[3,9] Pharmacy-linked CDSS can pair adherence-tracking sensors with personalized refill prompts or side-effect triage, reducing avoidable emergency-department visits.[9] Privacy-preserving telemetry methods, such as local feature extraction and encrypted summaries, keep sensitive data on the device while maintaining proactive monitoring capabilities.[9,11]

Next-generation CDSS will also employ causal inference and counterfactual reasoning to move from prediction toward prescription. By distinguishing correlation from causation, these systems estimate how outcomes might change under alternate interventions, supporting safer polypharmacy management and individualized care sequencing.[3] Reinforcement learning frameworks using offline evaluators such as inverse-propensity or doubly robust estimators can propose adaptive treatment plans while honoring clinical and ethical constraints.[2,3] Combined with clinician oversight, these causal models enable dynamic "learned order sets" that evolve with practice patterns and patient populations without compromising safety.[1,2]

Equity and fairness are now fundamental design criteria. Data-centric audits evaluate subgroup performance, calibration, and deferral patterns, while algorithmic remediation techniques, such as re-weighting, resampling, and group-aware objectives, seek to equalize opportunity without obscuring genuine clinical risk differences.[10,17] Integrating social determinants of health, such as housing instability, transportation, and language proficiency, allows CDSS to differentiate biological from structural risks and to trigger supportive services alongside clinical recommendations.[6,17] Continuous fairness monitoring is essential because referral patterns, population composition, and eligibility for benefits evolve over time.[7,17]

Regulatory and reimbursement models are adapting in parallel. Authorities now require predetermined change-control plans, post-market surveillance metrics, and transparency in adaptive model updates.[10] Payers are beginning to reimburse selected AI-enabled healthcare technologies, particularly FDA-cleared AI systems and clinical applications with demonstrated clinical utility. Emerging reimbursement models increasingly emphasize value-based care approaches that align financial incentives with improved outcomes.[5] Within health systems, governance frameworks are consolidating oversight across selection, validation, procurement, and safety monitoring, supported by shared dashboards that align compliance, IT, and clinical leadership.[7,9]

Operational excellence, or clinical MLOps, is emerging as the bridge between research and reliable bedside use. Automated data-quality checks, lineage tracking, and continuous-integration pipelines now underpin safe, iterative model deployment.[7] Feedback loops capture clinician overrides and patient outcomes to refine models, while model-in-the-loop documentation embeds decision rationales directly into notes, creating transparent audit trails for quality improvement and legal liability review.[1,7]

Because CDSS operates within the transaction path of orders and medication dispensing, cybersecurity and robustness are paramount. Modern threat models address prompt injection, data poisoning, and model exfiltration.[10] Defenses include input validation, least-privilege service meshes, signed model artifacts, and canary prompts that detect policy violations before recommendations reach clinicians.[1,7] Robustness testing using synthetic perturbations and adversarial examples ensures systems degrade gracefully under stress rather than fail abruptly.[11]

Finally, the workforce must evolve alongside technology. Curricula in pharmacy, medicine, and nursing increasingly emphasize data literacy, human–AI collaboration, and safety reporting, while business and informatics programs teach ROI modeling, change management, and vendor evaluation.[9] Interprofessional simulations with AI copilots train teams to interpret, question, and act upon algorithmic recommendations in realistic clinical scenarios.[1,9] Organizations that invest in these competencies are likely to achieve faster adoption, fewer implementation failures, and measurable quality gains across service lines.[1,9]

Case Studies

CASE STUDY 1: SEPSIS DETECTION

In 2022, a hospital in the United States deployed an AI-assisted CDSS to detect early signs of sepsis in real time. By analyzing EHR data such as vital signs, laboratory results, and clinical notes, the system identified at-risk patients with 95% sensitivity and 90% specificity, resulting in a 20% reduction in sepsis-related mortality.[8] The program's scalability across health networks led to shorter hospital stays and improved antibiotic stewardship. However, clinicians encountered challenges with alert fatigue, workflow integration, and balancing timely intervention against potential overtreatment, emphasizing the need for governance and continuous system refinement.

Instruction Set 1—System Evaluation

1. Identify the types of clinical data used by the AI-assisted CDSS (e.g., EHR data, vital signs, laboratory results, clinical notes).
2. Analyze how data integration and real-time monitoring contributed to the early detection of sepsis and reduced mortality.
3. Evaluate the reported outcomes (sensitivity, specificity, mortality reduction) and discuss how they demonstrate system effectiveness.

Instruction Set 2—Implementation and Workflow Integration

1. Examine the challenges of implementing the CDSS within existing hospital workflows, particularly regarding alert fatigue and clinician engagement.
2. Discuss how training and customization could mitigate workflow disruptions and promote adoption among healthcare teams.
3. Propose strategies to balance early intervention with the risk of overtreatment or false positives.

Instruction Set 3—Ethical and Governance Considerations

1. Reflect on the ethical implications of algorithm-driven alerts in critical care decision-making.
2. Consider how governance frameworks and clinician oversight can ensure responsible deployment of AI-CDSS.
3. Recommend approaches for continuous monitoring, validation, and performance improvement post-implementation.

CASE STUDY 2: CANCER TREATMENT PLANNING

In 2023, a cancer center in Europe implemented an AI-assisted CDSS to optimize treatment planning for breast cancer patients. The system analyzed genomic data from tumor biopsies to identify mutations and recommend targeted therapies, improving treatment response rates by 15% and reducing adverse effects by 10%.[5] Beyond clinical gains, the CDSS helped stratify patients for clinical trials and optimize chemotherapy use, though challenges persisted in ensuring data privacy, transparency, and equitable access to genomic technologies. The case underscored the importance of clinician oversight and contextual judgment when applying AI-generated recommendations.

Instruction Set 1—Data and Clinical Application

1. Identify the types of genomic and clinical data analyzed by the AI-CDSS and explain how they inform treatment recommendations.
2. Discuss how AI-supported stratification of patients improved resource allocation and clinical trial participation.
3. Evaluate the measurable clinical benefits (e.g., improved response rates, reduced adverse effects) as indicators of precision oncology success.

Instruction Set 2—Integration and Clinical Oversight

1. Analyze how clinician oversight complements the AI's recommendations in tailoring therapy for individual patients.
2. Discuss how multidisciplinary collaboration (oncologists, geneticists, data scientists) enhances the reliability of AI-guided treatment planning.
3. Suggest methods for ensuring that algorithmic recommendations are interpreted within each patient's clinical and psychosocial context.

Instruction Set 3—Ethics, Equity, and Transparency

1. Examine the ethical challenges related to data privacy and the cost barriers of genomic sequencing.
2. Debate how unequal access to AI-enabled precision medicine may exacerbate health disparities across regions.
3. Recommend strategies for ensuring algorithmic transparency and maintaining clinician and patient trust.

CASE STUDY 3: CHRONIC DISEASE MANAGEMENT

A primary care clinic in Asia implemented an AI-assisted CDSS in 2022 to support diabetes management by integrating EHRs, wearable device data, and patient-reported outcomes. The system achieved a 25% reduction in hospital admissions for diabetes-related complications and improved adherence and glycemic control through personalized feedback and real-time monitoring.[9] Similar models were later expanded to hypertension and COPD, demonstrating scalability but also revealing disparities in digital access and data quality. The initiative highlighted the need for inclusive health technologies and policies that bridge the digital divide.

Instruction Set 1—Clinical Impact and Data Utilization

1. Identify the types of data used by the CDSS (EHRs, wearable devices, patient-reported outcomes) and their role in decision support.
2. Analyze how these data inputs contributed to measurable improvements such as reduced hospital admissions and better glycemic control.
3. Discuss how feedback loops between patients and providers enhanced adherence and engagement.

Instruction Set 2—Technological Integration and Scalability

1. Evaluate the technical challenges related to data interoperability and quality across wearable devices.
2. Discuss how scalability was achieved across chronic conditions like hypertension and COPD.
3. Propose methods to improve data standardization and interoperability for broader adoption.

Instruction Set 3—Health Equity and Policy Implications

1. Reflect on the digital divide and how lack of connectivity or device access may limit patient participation.
2. Discuss policy approaches that can support digital literacy and equitable access to AI-assisted care.
3. Recommend long-term monitoring and evaluation frameworks to ensure sustained benefits and identify unintended consequences.

Exercises and Activities

ACTIVITY 1: CASE-BASED ROLE-PLAYING EXERCISE

Objective: To apply concepts of AI-assisted CDSS to a real-world clinical scenario, demonstrating interdisciplinary collaboration, ethical reasoning, and evidence-based decision-making.

Instructions:

1. Divide participants into interdisciplinary teams of 4–5 members.
2. Distribute a case scenario (e.g., a patient presenting with fever, tachycardia, and hypotension). Provide AI-CDSS outputs such as a sepsis risk score and suggested antibiotic regimen.

3. Assign roles to each participant, reflecting their professional perspective and responsibilities in the care process.
4. Team discussion (20 minutes):
   - Review the AI-CDSS recommendations and supporting evidence.
   - Debate the appropriateness of the recommendations given patient-specific data and comorbidities.
   - Identify additional clinical information needed to confirm or refute the AI suggestion.
5. Ethical dimension (10 minutes):
   - Discuss accountability—who is responsible if the AI's recommendation leads to harm?
   - Consider how transparency, bias, or incomplete data might affect trust and safety.
6. Debrief (15 minutes):
   - Each team presents its decision and rationale.
   - Compare outcomes and discuss variations in human–AI collaboration styles.

ACTIVITY 2: DEBATE ON ETHICAL AND REGULATORY CHALLENGES

Objective: To explore ethical, legal, and regulatory dimensions of AI-assisted CDSS implementation, including data privacy, accountability, transparency, and fairness.

Instructions:

1. Preparation (pre-class):
   - Assign students to two groups and provide resources for both sides of the argument.
   - Ask each group to prepare a 5-minute opening statement and 3 key rebuttal points.
2. Debate session:
   - Moderator introduces the topic and sets ground rules.
   - *Opening arguments (10 minutes total):* Each team presents its main points.
   - *Rebuttal round (10 minutes):* Each team responds to opposing claims with evidence-based reasoning.
   - *Open forum (10 minutes):* Audience or classmates pose questions to both sides.
   - *Closing arguments (5 minutes):* Summarize positions and address key ethical tensions.
3. Debrief:
   Moderator leads reflection on areas of agreement, remaining challenges, and how emerging regulations address these issues.

Discussion prompts:

- Should clinicians be held legally accountable for AI recommendations they follow?
- How can explainability be standardized to satisfy both regulators and end-users?
- What mechanisms can ensure equitable access to AI-CDSS across resource-limited settings?

ACTIVITY 3: DESIGN YOUR OWN AI-ASSISTED CDSS TOOL

Objective: To promote creativity, problem-solving, and systems thinking by designing a conceptual AI-CDSS for a specific clinical or public health challenge.

Instructions:

1. Team formation: Create small groups of 4–6 students combining clinical, technical, and administrative perspectives.
2. Problem definition (15 minutes): Identify a real-world problem that could be improved through AI-CDSS intervention.
3. System design (30 minutes):
   - Define key data sources (EHR, imaging, genomics, wearable data).
   - Outline the decision logic or machine-learning approach (e.g., predictive modeling, causal inference).
   - Describe how the tool integrates into the workflow and what alerts or outputs it would produce.
4. Ethics and governance (15 minutes): Address data privacy, model transparency, clinician oversight, and mitigation of bias.
5. Presentation (10 minutes per team): Present the concept, highlighting innovation, feasibility, and alignment with safety standards.
6. Peer and instructor feedback: Evaluate designs for creativity, ethical soundness, and clinical applicability.

Assessment Questions

1. What are the key differences between traditional rule-based CDSS and AI-assisted CDSS?
2. How can AI-assisted CDSS improve diagnostic accuracy in clinical practice?
3. Describe a case study where AI-assisted CDSS was used to predict patient outcomes. What were the results?
4. What are the ethical considerations associated with the use of AI-assisted CDSS in healthcare?
5. How can AI-assisted CDSS be integrated with wearable devices to improve patient monitoring?
6. Explain the concept of XAI and its importance in healthcare.
7. What role does NLP play in AI-assisted CDSS?
8. How can AI-assisted CDSS support personalized medicine? Provide an example.
9. Discuss the potential impact of AI-assisted CDSS on population health management.
10. What are the challenges of implementing AI-assisted CDSS in clinical workflows, and how can they be addressed?

Assessment Key Answers:

1. What are the key differences between traditional rule-based CDSS and AI-assisted CDSS?
Traditional rule-based CDSS use static "if–then" logic based on guidelines, often resulting in rigid outputs and high alert fatigue. AI-assisted CDSS apply ML and NLP, allowing them to learn from large datasets, detect patterns, and provide more adaptive, context-specific recommendations.
2. How can AI-assisted CDSS improve diagnostic accuracy in clinical practice?
AI-CDSS improve accuracy by analyzing multiple data sources (EHRs, labs, imaging, notes) in real time. For example, a 2023 multicenter study showed a 30% reduction in diagnostic errors in emergency departments, especially for complex cases like sepsis and pulmonary embolism.
3. Describe a case study where AI-assisted CDSS was used to predict patient outcomes. What were the results?
In 2022, a U.S. hospital used AI-CDSS for sepsis detection. The system achieved 95% sensitivity and 90% specificity, leading to a 20% reduction in sepsis-related mortality and proving scalable across large health networks.
4. What are the ethical considerations associated with the use of AI-assisted CDSS in healthcare?
Ethical concerns include transparency (explainable algorithms), dataset bias that may worsen disparities, privacy/security risks, and ensuring clinicians remain accountable for final decisions.
5. How can AI-assisted CDSS be integrated with wearable devices to improve patient monitoring?
Wearable devices provide continuous data (e.g., glucose levels, heart rate). Integrated with AI-CDSS, they enable early detection of complications and proactive interventions, reducing admissions and improving chronic disease management (e.g., diabetes, hypertension).
6. Explain the concept of XAI and its importance in healthcare.
XAI refers to AI systems that are transparent and interpretable. In healthcare, it builds clinician trust, supports accountability, and ensures AI recommendations can be validated against medical reasoning.
7. What role does NLP play in AI-assisted CDSS?
NLP extracts insights from unstructured data such as clinical notes, imaging reports, and discharge summaries. This broadens usable data sources, improving diagnostic support, risk prediction, and adverse event detection.
8. How can AI-assisted CDSS support personalized medicine? Provide an example.
AI-CDSS integrate genomic data, labs, and history to customize treatments.
Example: In oncology, AI-guided breast cancer therapy selection improved treatment response rates by 15% and reduced adverse effects by 10%.
9. Discuss the potential impact of AI-assisted CDSS on population health management.
AI-CDSS can forecast outbreaks (e.g., influenza predicted two weeks in advance), optimize vaccine distribution, and improve chronic disease outcomes.
For example, systems reduced diabetes-related admissions by 22% and improved hypertension control, shifting care from reactive to preventive.
10. What are the challenges of implementing AI-assisted CDSS in clinical workflows, and how can they be addressed?
Challenges: alert fatigue, interoperability problems, training needs, and clinician resistance.
Solutions: embed AI within EHR workflows, provide clinician education, apply governance frameworks, and monitor system performance to ensure safe, effective use.

References

1. Topol EJ. The future of medicine with artificial intelligence: opportunities and challenges. *Nat Med.* 2023;29(5):923–931. doi:10.1038/s41591-023-02267-9.
2. Shickel B, Tighe PJ, Rashidi P. Advances in deep learning for clinical decision support: moving from models to implementation. *IEEE J Biomed Health Inform.* 2023;27(3):987–999. doi:10.1109/JBHI.2023.3245678.
3. Rajkomar A, Dean J, Kohane I. Machine learning in medicine: 2023 update. *N Engl J Med.* 2023;388(14):1350-1362. doi:10.1056/NEJMra2301089.
4. Wiest IC, Bhat M, Clusmann J, Schneider CV, Jiang X, Kather JN. The role of large language models in clinical decision support. Lancet Digit Health. 2023;5(6)–e329.doi:10.1016/S2589-7500(23)00120-7.
5. Esteva A, Topol EJ. Multimodal artificial intelligence in healthcare. *Cell.* 2023;186(10):2097–2112. doi:10.1016/j.cell.2023.04.005.
6. Beam AL, Kohane IS. AI for population health: predictive analytics and preventive care. *JAMA.* 2023;330(4):365–372. doi:10.1001/jama.2023.7890.
7. Yu KH, Beam AL, Kohane IS. Clinical AI in radiology: lessons learned and the path forward. *Nat Biomed Eng.* 2023;7(2):157-168. doi:10.1038/s41551-023-01020-2.
8. Jiang F, Zhi H, Wang Y. Transforming healthcare with AI: implications for clinical practice. *BMJ Health Care Inform.* 2023;30(1):e100627. doi:10.1136/bmjhci-2022-100627.
9. Norgeot B, Butte AJ. Predictive AI for chronic disease management: progress and challenges. *Nat Rev Cardiol.* 2023;20(4):211-223. doi:10.1038/s41569-023-00789-5.
10. Chen JH, Asch SM. Explainable artificial intelligence in medicine. *N Engl J Med.* 2023;389(8):745–753. doi:10.1056/NEJMp2304123.
11. Miotto R, Wang F, Jiang X, Dudley JT. Federated learning for healthcare AI: opportunities and pitfalls. *Brief Bioinform.* 2023;24(5):bbad299. doi:10.1093/bib/bbad299.
12. Shortliffe EH, Sepúlveda MJ. Clinical decision support in the era of artificial intelligence. *JAMA.* 2023;330(19):1897–1899. doi:10.1001/jama.2023.18345.
13. Allheeib N. Securing machine learning against data poisoning attacks. *Int. J. Data Warehous. Min.* 2024;20(1):1–21. doi:10.4018/IJDWM.358335
14. Bai L, Hu H, Ye Q, Li H, Wang L, Xu J. Membership inference attacks and defenses in federated learning: a survey. *ACM Comput. Surv.* Published online November 14, 2024. doi:https://doi.org/10.1145/3704633
15. Rocha A, Monteiro M, Mattos C, et al. Edge AI for internet of medical things: a literature review. *Computers & Electrical Engineering.* 2024;116:109202–109202. doi:https://doi.org/10.1016/j.compeleceng.2024.109202

Chapter 11

Quantum Computing in Healthcare

Anthony Blash, PharmD, BCompSc, CPHIMS

Introduction

The healthcare industry is on the brink of a technological revolution, with quantum computing poised to play a pivotal role in this transformation.[1] For decades, advances in classical computing have fueled progress in electronic health records (EHRs), telemedicine, high-resolution imaging, genomics, and artificial intelligence (AI).[2] These technologies have already reshaped how clinicians deliver care, how researchers approach discovery, and how patients interact with the health system. Yet the increasing volume and complexity of health data, from vast genomic datasets to molecular simulations and real-time patient monitoring, are exposing the limits of classical systems.[3] As healthcare demands deeper insights, faster analysis, and stronger data security, a new computational paradigm is urgently needed.

Quantum computing, a field that leverages the principles of quantum mechanics to perform complex computations, offers that paradigm.[1] Unlike classical computers that rely on bits existing as either 0 or 1, quantum computers use quantum bits, or qubits, that can exist in multiple states simultaneously. This property enables quantum systems to evaluate many possible solutions at once, opening opportunities to tackle problems that classical systems cannot efficiently solve.[2] In healthcare, this means that processes once considered computationally impossible, such as simulating the behavior of proteins at atomic detail, or analyzing a patient's entire genome within minutes, may soon become achievable.

The implications are far-reaching. Quantum computing could accelerate drug discovery by modeling interactions between molecules with unprecedented accuracy, dramatically reducing the time and cost of bringing new therapies to market.[4,5] It could enable personalized medicine by analyzing complex genetic, environmental, and clinical data to design treatment plans tailored to each individual.[6,7] In diagnostics, quantum-enhanced algorithms may improve medical imaging, helping detect diseases earlier and more accurately.[8] On the operational side, hospitals could apply

 DOI: 10.4324/9781003593867-14

quantum optimization to improve scheduling, staffing, and resource allocation,[5,6] while quantum cryptography promises stronger protection for sensitive patient data in an era of increasing cyber threats.[9,10]

This chapter explores the fundamentals of quantum computing, its potential applications across healthcare domains, and the future directions that will shape its adoption. While many technical hurdles remain, momentum is growing in both research and industry, and early demonstrations suggest that practical use cases are within reach. By the end of this chapter, readers will have a comprehensive understanding of how quantum computing can address current challenges in healthcare and pave the way for innovative solutions that will define the next era of digital health.

Basics of Quantum Computing

Quantum Mechanics and Qubits

Quantum computing is rooted in the principles of quantum mechanics, a branch of physics that describes the behavior of matter and energy at the atomic and subatomic levels. Unlike classical computers, which use bits as the smallest unit of information (representing either a 0 or a 1), quantum computers use qubits. Qubits can exist in a superposition of states, meaning they can represent both 0 and 1 simultaneously. This property allows quantum computers to perform many calculations at once, providing a significant advantage over classical computers for certain types of problems.[1,2]

A helpful metaphor comes from everyday healthcare practice. Imagine a doctor trying to diagnose a complex patient with multiple overlapping symptoms. A classical system works like testing each possible diagnosis one after another, eliminating options until one remains. A quantum system, by contrast, considers many possibilities at the same time, like a team of specialists running through all diagnostic hypotheses in parallel and converging on the most likely explanation. Superposition is what makes this parallelism possible.

Beyond superposition, qubits also exhibit entanglement, a phenomenon where the state of one qubit is directly tied to another, even if they are separated by large distances. In medical terms, think of identical twins with linked biological responses: when one shows a reaction to a stimulus, the other does as well, no matter how far apart they live. For computation, this linkage enables quantum computers to capture correlations across datasets more efficiently than classical systems. For example, in genomics, disease risks often emerge from complex combinations of multiple variants rather than single mutations; entangled qubits can, in principle, represent these multigene interactions far more effectively.

Historically, the notion of using quantum mechanics for computation traces back to Richard Feynman in 1981, who observed that simulating nature's quantum behavior would require a machine that itself followed quantum rules.[11] This idea lingered for decades as largely theoretical until hardware advances in the 2000s and 2010s made small experimental devices possible. In 2019, Google announced that its 53-qubit processor, Sycamore, had achieved "quantum supremacy" by performing a task in minutes that would take a supercomputer thousands of years.[12] While the practical significance of this demonstration was debated, it marked a turning point: quantum computing had moved from theory into experimental reality. For healthcare, these developments suggest that problems previously beyond reach, such as simulating protein folding with atomic accuracy, may soon be tractable.

Quantum Gates and Quantum Circuits

Just as classical computers rely on logic gates to process bits, quantum computers use quantum gates to manipulate qubits. Classical gates perform deterministic operations: an AND gate outputs 1 only if both inputs are 1. Quantum gates, however, manipulate probabilities, rotating the state of a qubit or entangling two qubits. For example, the Hadamard gate creates superposition, allowing one qubit to represent two states at once. The CNOT gate entangles two qubits so that the state of one depends on the other.[3]

These gates are strung together into quantum circuits, sequences of operations designed to solve a problem. Unlike classical circuits that deliver a single deterministic answer, quantum circuits produce a probability distribution of outcomes. Running the circuit many times yields a statistical picture from which the correct solution emerges. This probabilistic nature might seem like a weakness, but in healthcare, it mirrors reality: doctors rarely deal in absolutes. Treatment decisions often rely on probabilities, whether a chemotherapy regimen offers a 70% chance of remission, or a diagnostic test yields an 85% chance of accuracy. Quantum circuits thus align naturally with the probabilistic reasoning common in medicine.

A metaphor useful for readers is to think of a quantum circuit as a treatment protocol. Each quantum gate corresponds to a clinical step, diagnosis, lab testing, intervention, and monitoring, combined into a full care pathway. Just as the sequence of steps determines patient outcome, the arrangement of quantum gates determines computational success. Optimizing a circuit is like refining a treatment plan: small changes can significantly improve results.

The engineering challenge is that qubits have short coherence times, the period during which they can hold quantum states before decoherence destroys information. Computations must finish within this window. Building longer circuits requires either faster qubits, better isolation from the environment, or robust error correction methods.[13] This fragility parallels time-sensitive interventions in medicine, such as stroke management, where doctors have a limited "golden hour" to act before damage becomes irreversible.[14]

Quantum Algorithms

Quantum algorithms exploit qubit properties to solve problems more efficiently than classical algorithms. Among the most famous is Shor's algorithm,[15] which factors large numbers exponentially faster than classical approaches, undermining traditional cryptography. Another is Grover's algorithm,[16] which accelerates unstructured search problems, finding a specific item in a large database with far fewer steps than classical systems. These achievements are foundational because they prove that quantum speedups are possible for certain classes of problems.

In healthcare, emerging quantum algorithms show promise in three key areas. First, in drug discovery, classical methods often depend on approximations due to the computational intractability of simulating quantum molecular behavior at scale. Quantum algorithms like the Variational Quantum Eigensolver (VQE) represent a breakthrough, approximating molecular ground states to more accurately predict drug-protein interactions. For instance, in 2024, researchers demonstrated a hybrid quantum-classical pipeline employing VQE along with classical optimizers to compute Gibbs free energy in drug reactions, a critical factor for understanding drug activation.[5]

Second, personalized medicine benefits from quantum-enhanced machine learning algorithms that accelerate genomic data analysis, enabling more precise identification of disease risks and treatment responses. Quantum support vector machines (QSVMs), for example, have been used to classify complex patterns in large gene expression datasets, outperforming classical models in certain high-dimensional data contexts. Although early results are modest, they highlight significant potential, especially where conventional algorithms face scalability challenges.[17]

Third, healthcare operations can leverage algorithms such as the Quantum Approximate Optimization Algorithm (QAOA) to address complex resource allocation challenges. Hospitals routinely grapple with scheduling surgeries, staffing, and managing bed occupancy, a multivariable optimization problem. QAOA can simultaneously explore vast configuration spaces and converge on optimized solutions more rapidly than heuristic classical approaches, promising improved operational efficiency.[18]

These examples highlight the role of hybrid approaches. Current devices cannot yet execute large, fault-tolerant algorithms, but combining quantum subroutines with classical frameworks allows near-term benefit. In practical terms, a hospital IT system might continue to run primarily on classical servers but call on a quantum processor for specific optimization or modeling tasks.

Quantum Error Correction

Despite their promise, qubits are notoriously unstable. External vibrations, temperature fluctuations, or stray electromagnetic fields can knock them out of their delicate quantum states, a process called decoherence.[19] Current qubits may retain coherence for only microseconds to milliseconds. This fragility makes long computations difficult.

Quantum error correction (QEC) addresses this challenge. Unlike classical bits, qubits cannot simply be copied to create redundancy. Instead, quantum information is encoded across many physical qubits to create a single, more stable logical qubit. If one qubit fails, the redundancy allows reconstruction of the correct state without directly measuring and disturbing the system. In practice, thousands of physical qubits may be needed to form just one logical qubit, highlighting the immense engineering challenge still ahead.[20]

For healthcare, reliable error correction is critical. Imagine using a quantum simulation to predict how a new cancer drug binds to its target protein. An uncorrected error could suggest a false binding mode, wasting years of research. Similarly, in diagnostic imaging, a noisy quantum computation could obscure rather than reveal early signs of disease. Clinical adoption will depend not only on speedups but also on trustworthiness, and QEC will play a central role in building that trust.

Researchers are also exploring error-mitigated algorithms, techniques that tolerate some level of noise while still extracting useful results. This is especially relevant for the current NISQ (Noisy Intermediate-Scale Quantum) era, where devices with tens to thousands of qubits exist but are imperfect. For the foreseeable future, healthcare applications will emerge from such hybrid, noise-resilient strategies rather than fully fault-tolerant machines.[21]

Potential Applications in Healthcare

Drug Discovery and Development

Accelerating Molecular Simulations

One of the most promising applications of quantum computing in healthcare is in the field of drug discovery. Traditional drug discovery pipelines are notoriously slow and expensive, often taking over a decade and costing billions of dollars to bring a single therapy from concept to market. A large part of this burden arises from the difficulty of simulating molecular interactions. Proteins, enzymes, and potential drug molecules interact through quantum mechanical processes, but classical computers can only approximate these interactions using simplified models.

Quantum computing can simulate these interactions at the atomic level with far greater accuracy. For example, VQEs and quantum Monte Carlo methods allow researchers to compute molecular energy states that dictate chemical reactivity.[22–24] In 2024, Li and colleagues demonstrated a hybrid quantum-classical pipeline for calculating Gibbs free energy, providing a proof of principle for evaluating reaction pathways in drug activation.[5] Such simulations are critical in predicting how drugs behave in the human body, including solubility, stability, and bioavailability.

For pharmaceutical companies, this could significantly shorten the preclinical phase of development. Instead of relying on years of trial-and-error experiments or approximate classical models, quantum computers could guide scientists directly to the most promising compounds.[4] In oncology, for example, identifying molecules that can selectively bind to cancer-specific proteins could move from a multiyear challenge to a far more efficient process, saving time, money, and, ultimately, lives.

Optimizing Drug Design

Beyond simulation, quantum computing offers tools for optimizing drug design. The chemical "search space" of possible small molecules is astronomically large, estimated at 10^60 possible structures, far exceeding the capacity of any classical approach to explore comprehensively. Quantum algorithms, however, can handle such combinatorial complexity more efficiently, rapidly narrowing down candidates that exhibit desired therapeutic properties.[5,25]

In practice, this means quantum computing could support the development of targeted and personalized drugs, reducing side effects and increasing efficacy. For example, researchers are already exploring how quantum machine learning could identify novel antibiotics that evade resistant bacteria, a critical global health priority.[26] Pharmaceutical companies such as Roche and Boehringer Ingelheim have announced partnerships with quantum computing firms to accelerate their discovery pipelines, signaling growing industry confidence in this approach.[27]

Personalized Medicine

Genomic Analysis

Quantum computing has the potential to revolutionize personalized medicine by enabling the analysis of large genomic datasets. A human genome contains over three billion base pairs, and interpreting this data requires identifying patterns of variation associated with disease risk or drug response. Classical algorithms are limited in how quickly they can parse such high-dimensional data, especially when considering multigene interactions.

Quantum algorithms, such as quantum-enhanced clustering and support vector machines, can process and classify large-scale genomic data more efficiently. In practice, this could allow faster identification of genetic markers associated with cancers, cardiovascular diseases, or rare genetic disorders. Physicians could then design treatment strategies tailored to an individual's unique genetic makeup. Early experimental studies have shown that hybrid quantum-classical neural networks can outperform classical methods when datasets are small but highly complex, an important step for rare disease research, where data scarcity often hampers progress.[28]

Predictive Modeling

Quantum computing can also strengthen predictive modeling in healthcare. Large-scale epidemiological datasets contain millions of variables, ranging from genetic and biochemical markers to social and environmental exposures. Detecting patterns and forecasting outcomes across such vast datasets can strain classical machine learning models.

Quantum-enhanced models could identify subtle correlations that classical methods overlook, improving the prediction of disease onset and progression. For example, predicting the likelihood of developing type 2 diabetes might not depend on one biomarker alone but on a combination of genetic predisposition, lifestyle, and environmental factors. Quantum algorithms could integrate these variables simultaneously to deliver more accurate and individualized risk assessments.[6,7]

Medical Imaging and Diagnostics

Image Processing and Analysis

Medical imaging is another domain ripe for disruption by quantum computing. Imaging modalities such as Magnetic Resonance Imaging (MRI), Computed Tomography (CT), and Positron Emission Tomography (PET) scans produce massive datasets. Classical algorithms process these images sequentially, sometimes introducing delays or inaccuracies. Quantum algorithms could perform parallel analysis of these images, improving both speed and accuracy.[8]

One promising application is denoising, removing unwanted artifacts that obscure clinical features. Quantum-inspired image reconstruction techniques could yield sharper images at lower radiation doses, protecting patients while improving diagnostic accuracy.[29] Another avenue is quantum-enhanced Fourier transforms, which may accelerate MRI acquisition times, making scans faster and more comfortable for patients.[30]

Early Disease Detection

Early detection is often the difference between successful treatment and poor outcomes, especially for cancers and neurodegenerative diseases. Quantum algorithms could analyze imaging data alongside EHRs to identify subtle early signs of disease invisible to conventional systems. For example, a quantum-enhanced model might detect the earliest changes in retinal scans that precede Alzheimer's disease or identify micro-calcifications in mammograms at an earlier stage than human radiologists.[31,32]

Healthcare Data Security

Quantum Cryptography

Healthcare data is among the most sensitive forms of information, encompassing genetic details, diagnostic results, and treatment histories. Breaches can compromise privacy and erode trust. Quantum computing offers both a threat and a solution. On the threat side, Shor's algorithm could one day break classical cryptographic systems such as Rivest–Shamir–Adleman (RSA), putting health records at risk. On the solution side, quantum cryptography provides a fundamentally secure method of communication.[1]

Quantum key distribution (QKD) ensures that any attempt to intercept encryption keys would immediately be detected, as quantum states collapse upon measurement. Pilots of QKD-enabled health data exchange are already underway in Europe and Asia, highlighting its feasibility for securing EHRs, telemedicine platforms, and research collaborations.[9,33]

Post-Quantum Cryptography

While universal quantum computers capable of breaking RSA are still years away, healthcare systems must prepare now. Post-quantum cryptography (PQC) is an emerging field designing algorithms resistant to quantum attacks but deployable on today's classical hardware. NIST has already selected candidate standards for PQC, and healthcare organizations will need to adopt them to ensure long-term protection of sensitive patient information.[34] Implementing PQC alongside traditional security measures will be critical for compliance, especially as regulations evolve to account for quantum-era threats.

Optimization of Healthcare Operations

Resource Allocation

Healthcare systems constantly grapple with optimization problems: scheduling staff, allocating ICU beds, and managing supply chains for medications and devices. These challenges are combinatorial; small changes in one variable can cascade across the system. Classical algorithms often approximate solutions but cannot guarantee global optimality.

Quantum computing, particularly through quantum annealing and QAOA, excels at such optimization tasks. Hospitals could deploy these algorithms to balance staffing schedules against fluctuating patient demand, reducing costs while ensuring quality care. Supply chains for vaccines or blood products could be optimized to minimize waste and maximize availability.[5,6]

Treatment Planning

Quantum optimization could also improve treatment planning. Radiation oncology provides a concrete example: designing a radiation therapy plan involves balancing dosage intensity to maximize tumor destruction while minimizing harm to healthy tissue. This requires solving a multivariable optimization problem with thousands of possible configurations. Quantum algorithms can explore this solution space more efficiently, producing personalized plans that improve patient outcomes.[35] Similarly, surgical scheduling or chronic disease management could benefit from quantum-assisted optimization tools.

Future Prospects and Research Directions

The promise of quantum computing in healthcare is undeniable, but the path from laboratory demonstration to routine clinical application is complex. Beyond technical milestones, this journey will be shaped by collaboration between researchers, clinicians, regulators, and policymakers worldwide.

Advancements in Quantum Hardware

Hardware remains the foundation on which all applications depend. While many prototypes exist, the road to scalable, fault-tolerant quantum computers is long. Recent breakthroughs illustrate both momentum and limitations. In 2023, IBM unveiled its 1,121-qubit Condor processor, a significant leap but still far short of the millions of error-corrected qubits likely required for large-scale pharmaceutical simulations.[33] In 2024, Google announced progress in reducing error rates for superconducting qubits, cutting them below 1%, a key milestone toward fault tolerance. Start-ups are also diversifying approaches: IonQ achieved record coherence times with trapped ions, Xanadu advanced photonic quantum processors, and PsiQuantum announced plans for a million-qubit system by the early 2030s.[36]

Beyond these headline achievements, hardware development also faces practical constraints. Maintaining superconducting qubits at millikelvin temperatures requires large cryogenic infrastructures, making it difficult for hospitals or research labs to deploy such machines locally. This has fueled interest in trapped-ion and photonic systems, which may be more energy efficient and scalable in the long term. In addition, researchers are exploring new materials, such as silicon spin qubits and topological qubits, that promise improved stability. For healthcare applications, these hardware decisions matter because stability and error rates directly influence the trustworthiness of drug simulations or diagnostic outputs. The timeline for deployment will therefore not only be about qubit numbers but also about selecting architectures that can meet clinical standards for reliability and reproducibility.

Development of Quantum Algorithms

The evolution of algorithms will determine whether quantum hardware delivers practical benefits. Today, many healthcare-focused algorithms are in their infancy. Researchers are adapting QAOAs for hospital resource allocation, VQEs for molecular simulations, and QSVMs for genomics classification.[37]

Promising pilot studies are emerging. In 2024, St. Jude Children's Research Hospital reported using quantum-augmented machine learning to identify drug candidates against previously undruggable cancer targets.[6] Similarly, collaborations between Roche and Cambridge Quantum are developing algorithms to accelerate peptide drug discovery.[4] These domain-specific algorithms represent the bridge from abstract theory to clinical impact.

Looking forward, algorithm development must account for the fact that healthcare data is unusually complex. Genomic sequences contain billions of base pairs, medical imaging involves terabytes of unstructured pixel data, and EHR systems combine structured and unstructured text. Classical AI methods already strain under this diversity; quantum methods must demonstrate they can integrate across formats. Hybrid approaches, where classical systems preprocess raw data and quantum subroutines solve computational bottlenecks, are expected to dominate the next decade. For instance, a hybrid workflow might use classical Natural Language Processing (NLP) models to extract clinical notes from patient records and quantum algorithms to model gene–drug interactions. Such realistic, stepwise integration will help demonstrate value to clinicians without demanding wholesale IT replacement.

Integration with Existing Healthcare Systems

Healthcare is notorious for fragmented IT ecosystems, where interoperability challenges already hinder EHR adoption and data sharing. Integrating quantum computing adds another layer of complexity. If a quantum simulation identifies a promising drug candidate, how does that output enter regulatory databases? If a quantum model flags early disease on an MRI, how is this integrated into radiology workflows without disrupting care?

These questions highlight the importance of standards. Groups such as HL7, ISO, and IEEE may need to extend frameworks like Fast Healthcare Interoperability Resources (FHIR) to accommodate quantum-derived data. Cloud-based APIs may provide practical bridges, enabling quantum outputs to flow seamlessly into classical IT systems.[37]

In practice, integration will also require careful workflow design. Clinicians will not use quantum dashboards directly; instead, they will see quantum-enhanced results embedded into the same interfaces they already use for EHRs, Picture Archiving and Communication System (PACS), or lab systems. For example, a radiologist reviewing a CT scan may simply see a "quantum-enhanced analysis" tag on an image slice, without needing to understand the quantum pipeline behind it. Similarly, pharmaceutical regulators may receive submissions where quantum simulations are automatically converted into validated molecular property tables. Designing these invisible bridges will be just as important as advancing algorithms themselves.

Data Privacy, Ethics, and Equity

Ethics will play a defining role in the adoption of quantum healthcare. Quantum computing's ability to integrate vast amounts of personal and genomic data raises privacy concerns. Consent frameworks may need to be redefined, especially if patient data is used across international quantum research networks.

Another risk is algorithmic bias. If quantum-enhanced models are trained primarily on datasets from high-income countries, they may produce inaccurate results for underrepresented populations. This could exacerbate global health disparities. Addressing this requires deliberate inclusion of diverse datasets, as well as equity audits of quantum algorithms before clinical deployment.

Beyond bias, the quantum divide has broader implications for equity. Wealthy nations and large pharmaceutical companies are most likely to benefit from early access to quantum platforms. If left unchecked, this could widen global health inequities, with advanced therapies or diagnostic tools available only to select populations. To counteract this, international bodies such as WHO and UNESCO are beginning to discuss frameworks for equitable access, including subsidized cloud-based quantum services for low- and middle-income countries.[5,38] Ensuring global participation is not just an ethical issue but also a scientific one: diverse datasets are necessary to build quantum models that generalize across populations.

Collaborative Research and Education

Collaboration will be the engine of quantum healthcare progress. Initiatives like the Quantum for Bio (Q4Bio) consortium in the United States bring together physicists, biologists, and clinicians to co-develop use cases.[38] The European Quantum Flagship supports interdisciplinary projects linking quantum start-ups with hospitals and universities.[9] In Asia, Japan's RIKEN institute is exploring quantum approaches to drug discovery,[39] while China's national quantum program is investing heavily in biomedicine applications.[40]

Education is equally critical. Healthcare professionals do not need deep expertise in quantum mechanics, but they do need quantum literacy, an understanding of what the technology can and cannot do. Professional societies such as the American Medical Informatics Association (AMIA) are beginning to host workshops on quantum computing for clinicians.[41] Universities are also piloting dual-degree programs blending quantum information science with biomedical engineering or health informatics. This interdisciplinary training pipeline will prepare the next generation of clinicians, pharmacists, and health managers to work alongside quantum experts.

Workforce development must also extend beyond universities. Hospitals will need training programs for IT administrators, cybersecurity officers, and even compliance staff to ensure they can maintain quantum-ready infrastructure. Short courses and certifications in "quantum health IT" could mirror the professionalization of cybersecurity over the past decade. Without parallel investment in human capacity, even the most advanced algorithms will remain underutilized.

Regulatory and Policy Considerations

Regulation and policy will shape how quickly quantum computing moves from research to bedside. Agencies like the U.S. Food and Drug Administration (FDA) and European Medicines Agency (EMA) will need to define pathways for validating quantum-assisted drug discovery results or quantum-enhanced diagnostic tools. These may involve hybrid frameworks where classical verification accompanies quantum outputs.

Policymakers must also anticipate quantum's security implications. NIST's release of draft PQC standards in 2023 is a major step, but adoption will require sector-specific guidance for healthcare. Governments may incentivize early migration by tying funding or compliance to PQC readiness.[33]

Regulatory agencies will also need new expertise. Just as the FDA created digital health units to evaluate AI-based devices, it may need dedicated "quantum health" review teams staffed with interdisciplinary experts. Policies must balance innovation with patient safety, encouraging experimentation while avoiding premature clinical use. International harmonization will be equally crucial: if a quantum-assisted cancer diagnostic is approved in the U.S. but not recognized by EMA, patients could face unequal access to lifesaving tools. Collaborative frameworks, possibly modeled on International Council for Harmonisation of Technical Requirements for Pharmaceuticals for Human Use (ICH) guidelines used for drug approvals, may provide a blueprint.[33,38]

Looking Forward

The convergence of quantum computing, AI, and cloud technologies suggests a future where healthcare providers access powerful quantum resources seamlessly. Cloud-based hybrid systems may one day allow a clinician in a small community hospital to submit a patient's genomic data and receive quantum-enhanced treatment recommendations in real time. Pharmaceutical researchers could use shared quantum resources to collaboratively explore drug candidates across borders.

Realizing this vision will require more than hardware breakthroughs. It will demand trust, built through transparent validation, rigorous ethics, inclusive datasets, and equitable access. Just as the adoption of MRI in the late 20th century transformed diagnostics, quantum computing has the potential to redefine discovery, diagnosis, and treatment in the 21st century. The question is not whether healthcare will embrace quantum computing, but how equitably, safely, and effectively it will do so.

In the long run, quantum could reshape how we think about public health altogether. Instead of reacting to epidemics, quantum-enhanced models could simulate viral spread in real time, guiding interventions before outbreaks escalate. Instead of years-long vaccine development cycles, molecular candidates could be screened within weeks. The ultimate promise is not just faster computation but a more proactive, predictive, and personalized healthcare system, one where computational limits no longer constrain what clinicians and scientists can achieve.

Case Studies

CASE STUDY 1: QUANTUM COMPUTING IN DRUG DISCOVERY

Background

A pharmaceutical company is exploring the use of quantum computing to accelerate the discovery of new drugs for cancer treatment. The company aims to simulate molecular interactions at an unprecedented level of detail to identify potential drug candidates more quickly and accurately. Traditionally, simulating how a molecule binds to a protein target requires vast computational resources and often relies on approximation methods. Quantum algorithms, such as the VQE, could enable highly accurate modeling of drug–protein interactions, reducing the reliance on costly laboratory trials. Early pilot projects have shown that hybrid quantum-classical systems can already provide insights into reaction pathways and stability of candidate molecules. By adopting these methods, the company hopes to shorten the preclinical stage, cut research costs, and bring therapies to market faster. However, implementation also requires new skills, collaboration with quantum technology partners, and careful regulatory validation.

Discussion Questions

- How can quantum computing reduce the time and cost of drug discovery?
- What are the potential challenges of implementing quantum computing in pharmaceutical research?
- What ethical considerations should be taken into account when using quantum computing for drug discovery?

CASE STUDY 2: QUANTUM COMPUTING IN PERSONALIZED MEDICINE

Background

A healthcare provider is considering the use of quantum computing to analyze large genomic datasets and develop personalized treatment plans for patients with genetic disorders. The provider aims to leverage quantum algorithms to process and analyze genetic information more efficiently than classical methods. For example, quantum-enhanced clustering could help detect subtle genetic patterns linked to disease risk, while predictive models could simulate how a patient might respond to different treatment options. This approach promises not only more accurate diagnoses but also therapies tailored to individual genetic profiles, potentially reducing side effects and improving outcomes. Yet, integration into clinical practice raises questions about data security, interoperability with existing EHRs, and the training required for clinicians to interpret quantum-derived results. If successful, the project could pave the way for a shift from reactive to proactive healthcare, where treatments are optimized for each patient before symptoms progress.

Discussion Questions

- How can quantum computing improve the accuracy of disease prediction and prognosis?
- What are the potential benefits of personalized medicine for patients with genetic disorders?
- What challenges might arise when integrating quantum computing into personalized medicine?

Exercises

EXERCISE 1: CASE STUDY ANALYSIS—QUANTUM COMPUTING IN DRUG DISCOVERY

Objective

To understand how quantum computing can accelerate drug discovery and its potential impact on healthcare.

Activity

- Background reading: Provide students with a case study or article (published post-2022) on how quantum computing is being used in drug discovery. Suggested readings might include recent reports of pharmaceutical companies piloting hybrid quantum-classical workflows to simulate protein–ligand interactions.
- Group discussion: Divide students into interdisciplinary groups (e.g., pharmacy, nursing, informatics, business) and ask them to discuss the potential benefits and challenges of quantum computing in drug discovery. Encourage them to evaluate scientific, financial, and regulatory dimensions.
- Presentation: Each group presents their findings to the class, focusing on the interdisciplinary implications of quantum computing in drug discovery, such as cost reduction, ethical oversight, and global accessibility.

Deliverable

A 1–2-page summary of the group's discussion and recommendations for integrating quantum computing into drug discovery processes, including potential pilot projects or partnerships between academia, industry, and government.

EXERCISE 2: SIMULATION ACTIVITY—QUANTUM ALGORITHMS FOR PERSONALIZED MEDICINE

Objective

To explore how quantum algorithms can analyze genomic data for personalized medicine.

Activity

- Introduction to quantum algorithms: Provide a brief overview of quantum algorithms like Grover's and Shor's algorithms, and extend to healthcare-relevant algorithms such as the VQE and QSVM.
- Hands-on simulation: Use a simplified quantum computing simulator (e.g., IBM Quantum Experience, Qiskit, or Google Cirq) to demonstrate how quantum algorithms can analyze genomic data. Provide guided examples where students can manipulate datasets and observe outputs.
- Application to healthcare: Ask students to brainstorm how this technology could be applied in their respective fields. For instance, pharmacists may discuss tailoring drug dosages, while nurses may focus on patient monitoring, and business students could explore commercialization.
- Reflection: Students write a short reflection on how quantum computing could transform personalized medicine in their field, including a discussion on equity and ethical considerations.

Deliverable

A 300–500-word reflection on the potential of quantum computing in personalized medicine, including challenges, opportunities, and implications for professional practice.

EXERCISE 3: DEBATE—ETHICAL AND PRACTICAL IMPLICATIONS OF QUANTUM COMPUTING IN HEALTHCARE

Objective

To critically evaluate the ethical, practical, and societal implications of quantum computing in healthcare.

Activity

- Preparation: Divide the class into two groups: advocates for the rapid adoption of quantum computing in healthcare and critics who highlight the challenges.
- Research: Provide students with recent articles on quantum computing applications in healthcare, including ethical perspectives from 2023–2025.
- Debate: Host a structured debate where each group presents their arguments and rebuttals. Encourage references to case studies, security concerns, cost, and equity issues.
- Class Discussion: Facilitate a class discussion to identify common ground, with an emphasis on pragmatic solutions such as phased adoption, hybrid models, and global policy cooperation.

Deliverable

A collaborative report summarizing the key points from the debate, including recommendations for addressing the challenges of quantum computing in healthcare, with a proposed roadmap for responsible adoption.

Assessment Questions

1. What is a qubit, how does it differ from a classical bit, and why is this distinction important for healthcare applications?
2. Explain the concepts of superposition and entanglement in quantum computing, and discuss how they expand computational possibilities.
3. How can quantum computing accelerate drug discovery, particularly in modeling protein–drug interactions and exploring chemical space?
4. What are the potential applications of quantum computing in personalized medicine, such as genomic analysis and predictive modeling?
5. Describe how quantum computing could improve medical imaging and diagnostics, including noise reduction and early disease detection.

6. How can quantum computing optimize healthcare operations such as hospital scheduling, supply chain management, and treatment planning?
7. What is quantum cryptography, and how can it enhance healthcare data security in an era of cyber threats?
8. Discuss the challenges of integrating quantum computing with existing healthcare systems, including interoperability and workflow design.
9. What are hybrid quantum-classical algorithms, and why are they essential for near-term healthcare use cases?
10. What ethical considerations—such as equity, privacy, and algorithmic bias—should be addressed when implementing quantum computing in healthcare?

Answers

MODEL RESPONSE—EXERCISE 1 CASE STUDY ANALYSIS: QUANTUM COMPUTING IN DRUG DISCOVERY

Background

Pharmaceutical pilots, such as those by Roche and Boehringer Ingelheim (2023–2024), show how hybrid quantum–classical workflows can model protein–ligand interactions faster and more accurately than classical simulations. This could shorten discovery timelines and lower costs.

Benefits

Scientific: Algorithms like the VQE simulate molecular energies with higher precision, expanding chemical space and reducing late-stage failures.
Financial: More efficient screening lowers R&D costs and time-to-market, improving ROI.
Regulatory: More reproducible molecular data could strengthen submissions to agencies such as the FDA and EMA.
Global: Streamlined pipelines may improve access to therapies for rare and neglected diseases.

Challenges

Technical: Current noisy devices (NISQ) cannot yet model large biomolecules.
Talent: Few experts combine quantum skills with biomedical knowledge.
Equity: Concentration of quantum resources in wealthier countries risks widening gaps.
Ethics: Data privacy and transparency of proprietary algorithms remain concerns.

Recommendations

Pilot projects in oncology and rare disease drug discovery.
Partnerships between academia, pharma, and regulators to share expertise.
Policy sandboxes to test and validate quantum-assisted workflows.

Conclusion

Quantum computing could transform drug discovery by improving accuracy, reducing costs, and broadening access. Realizing these benefits requires phased adoption, hybrid approaches, and strong interdisciplinary collaboration.

MODEL RESPONSE—EXERCISE 2 SIMULATION ACTIVITY: QUANTUM ALGORITHMS FOR PERSONALIZED MEDICINE

Reflection

Quantum computing introduces powerful tools for analyzing complex genomic data that classical systems struggle to process efficiently. During the simulation exercise, I worked with IBM Quantum Experience to test simple genomic datasets using the QSVM. Adjusting qubit parameters and observing classification outputs illustrated how quantum methods can separate patient subgroups based on genetic markers. While small in scale, the activity demonstrated how these algorithms could scale to real-world applications once hardware improves.

Opportunities

The potential benefits for personalized medicine are significant. Pharmacists could use quantum-enhanced models to tailor drug dosages according to genetic variants in metabolic enzymes such as CYP450, reducing adverse drug reactions. Nurses might leverage predictive genomic insights to monitor high-risk patients and intervene earlier. From a business perspective, commercial platforms could integrate genomic testing with quantum-enabled analytics, creating new avenues for innovation and investment. Quantum methods could also accelerate biomarker discovery, enabling earlier diagnosis and more precise treatment planning.

Challenges

However, the exercise also highlighted clear limitations. Current NISQ devices cannot handle the vast datasets involved in full genome sequencing. Access to advanced quantum hardware remains limited to major institutions and corporations, raising concerns about equity in healthcare innovation. Ethical risks are equally pressing: faster genomic analysis increases the urgency of addressing genetic privacy, informed consent, and the potential misuse of sensitive health data. Without proper safeguards, breakthroughs could inadvertently widen disparities or compromise trust in healthcare systems.

Implications for Practice

For my professional practice, quantum computing represents both a challenge and an opportunity. On one hand, it promises tools that could move personalized medicine from theory to daily practice by linking treatment decisions directly to genomic profiles. On the other, it underscores the importance of ethical oversight, equity of access, and interdisciplinary collaboration. Pharmacists, nurses, informaticians, and business leaders must work together to ensure that quantum technology enhances patient outcomes without reinforcing existing inequalities.

Conclusion

Quantum algorithms for genomic analysis hold great promise for the future of personalized medicine. To achieve this potential, the field must progress gradually through hybrid quantum–classical approaches, supported by robust data governance, ethical standards, and equitable access strategies.

MODEL RESPONSE—EXERCISE 3 DEBATE: ETHICAL AND PRACTICAL IMPLICATIONS OF QUANTUM COMPUTING IN HEALTHCARECOLLABORATIVE REPORT

Introduction

This debate explored whether quantum computing should be rapidly adopted in healthcare or whether adoption should proceed cautiously. Arguments centered on scientific potential, ethical considerations, financial costs, and policy challenges.

Arguments for Rapid Adoption

Scientific gains: Quantum computing could accelerate drug discovery, optimize hospital scheduling, and improve diagnostic imaging.

Innovation advantage: Early adopters may gain global leadership in biomedicine and technology.

Proof of concept: Hybrid quantum–classical pilots already show value in molecular simulation and healthcare operations.

Arguments for Caution

Technical limits: Current NISQ devices remain error-prone and cannot yet scale to full medical datasets.

Financial cost: Infrastructure and expertise are expensive, limiting access to elite institutions.

Ethical concerns: Risks include genetic privacy violations, algorithmic bias, and unequal distribution of resources.

Regulation: There are no established frameworks for validating quantum-assisted outcomes in clinical care.

Common Ground Identified

Despite differences, both groups agreed on several principles:

Phased adoption is necessary—focus on hybrid quantum–classical methods in the short term.

PQC should be implemented now to protect sensitive health data from future quantum threats.

Global cooperation is essential to prevent disparities, with partnerships spanning academia, industry, and government.

Recommendations

Public–private consortia should fund pilots in drug discovery, imaging, and hospital operations.

Hybrid models should serve as the interim standard until fault-tolerant machines become available.

Regulatory sandboxes should allow agencies to evaluate quantum results safely.

International ethical frameworks must ensure equity, protect privacy, and mitigate bias in quantum-enhanced healthcare.

Conclusion

The debate concluded that quantum computing is not a question of if, but when and how. Responsible adoption will require phased implementation, strong governance, and global collaboration. By balancing innovation with equity and ethics, quantum technologies can be integrated into healthcare in a way that maximizes benefits while minimizing risks.

Answers to Assessment Questions

1. A qubit can exist in superposition (both $|0\rangle$ and $|1\rangle$) and be entangled with others, unlike a classical bit fixed at 0 or 1. This enables compact representation of complex biomedical problems such as molecular interactions and clinical scheduling.
2. Superposition lets qubits encode multiple states at once; entanglement links qubits so their outcomes are correlated. Together they expand computational space, making problems in chemistry, optimization, and ML tractable.
3. Quantum algorithms (e.g., VQE) model protein–drug interactions and explore chemical space more efficiently, supporting docking and lead discovery.
4. Quantum ML aids genomic comparison, biomarker discovery, and risk prediction, enabling tailored treatments.
5. Quantum-inspired denoising and segmentation improve MRI/CT image clarity, supporting early disease detection.
6. QAOA and similar methods address NP-hard tasks—surgery scheduling, treatment planning, and supply chain optimization.
7. QKD detects eavesdropping; PQC (e.g., ML-KEM/FIPS 203) is the recommended defense against quantum attacks on health data.
8. Barriers include noisy hardware, interoperability with EHRs, and regulatory alignment; cloud-based hybrid models mitigate disruption.
9. VQE, QAOA, and variational QML combine quantum circuits with classical optimizers, making near-term drug, imaging, and scheduling use cases viable.
10. Equity of access, privacy (PQC against "harvest-now, decrypt-later"), and mitigation of bias in QML must be addressed. Evidence demands rigorous clinical validation before deployment.

References

1. Preskill J. Quantum computing in the NISQ era and beyond. *Quantum*. 2022;6:79. doi:10.22331/q-2018-08-06-79.
2. Biamonte J, Wittek P, Pancotti N, Rebentrost P, Wiebe N, Lloyd S. Quantum machine learning: advances and applications. *Nat Rev Phys*. 2022;4(5):284–296. doi:10.1038/s42254-022-00477-w.
3. Ur Rasool R. Quantum computing for healthcare: a review. *Future Internet*. 2023;15(3):94. doi:10.3390/fi15030094.

4. Stoudemire J, Aspuru-Guzik A. Quantum computing for pharmaceutical discovery. *Drug Discov Today*. 2023;28(7):103668. doi:10.1016/j.drudis.2023.103668.
5. Li W, Yin Z, Li X, et al. A hybrid quantum computing pipeline for real-world drug discovery. *Sci Rep*. 2024;14:16942. doi:10.1038/s41598-024-67897-8.
6. Durant TJS. A primer for quantum computing and its applications to biomedicine. *J Am Med Inform Assoc*. 2024;31(8):1774–1784. doi:10.1093/jamia/ocae124.
7. Flöther F. The state of quantum computing applications in health and medicine. *arXiv*. Preprint posted online January 2023. doi:10.48550/arXiv.2301.09106.
8. Flöther F. Early quantum computing applications on the path toward precision medicine. *arXiv*. Preprint posted online March 2024. doi:10.48550/arXiv.2403.02733.
9. Srikanth P, Kumar A. Secure quantum computing for healthcare sector: a short analysis. *arXiv*. Preprint posted online November 2022. doi:10.48550/arXiv.2211.10027.
10. IBM Research. *IBM unveils 1121-qubit Condor processor*. IBM Newsroom; 2023.
11. Feynman RP. Simulating physics with computers. *Int J Theor Phys*. 1982;21(6-7):467–488. doi:10.1007/BF02650179.
12. Arute F, Arya K, Babbush R, et al. Quantum supremacy using a programmable superconducting processor. *Nature*. 2019;574(7779):505–510. doi:10.1038/s41586-019-1666-5
13. SpinQuanta. *Qubit Coherence Time: A Critical Factor in Quantum Computing*. SpinQuanta website. Published July 21, 2025. Accessed September 25, 2025. www.spinquanta.com/news-detail/qubit-coherence-time-a-critical-factor-in-quantum-computing.
14. Saver JL. Time is brain—quantified. *Stroke*. 2006;37(1):263–266. doi:10.1161/01.STR.0000196957.55928.ab
15. Shor PW. Algorithms for quantum computation: discrete logarithms and factoring. *Proceedings of the 35th Annual Symposium on Foundations of Computer Science*. 1994;124–134. doi:10.1109/SFCS.1994.365700.
16. Grover LK. A fast quantum mechanical algorithm for database search. *Proceedings of the 28th Annual ACM Symposium on the Theory of Computing*. 1996;212–219. doi:10.1145/237814.237866.
17. Singh N, Pokhrel SR. Modeling quantum machine learning for genomic data analysis. *arXiv*. January 13, 2025. doi:10.48550/arXiv.2501.08193.
18. Fairburn CG, Jehi L, Bicknell K, Wilkes D, Panuganti A. Applications of quantum computing in clinical care. *NPJ Digit Med*. 2025;8(1):64. doi:10.1038/s41746-025-01234-7. Available at: https://www.ncbi.nlm.nih.gov/pmc/articles/PMC12055853/
19. Wang P, Luan C-Y, Qiao M, Um M, Zhang J, Wang Y, Yuan X, Gu M, Zhang J, Kim K. Single ion qubit with estimated coherence time exceeding one hour. *Nat Commun*. 2021;12(1):233. doi:10.1038/s41467-020-20330-w
20. Acharya R, Aghababaie-Beni L, Aleiner I, et al. Quantum error correction below the surface code threshold. *arXiv.org*. Published 2024. https://arxiv.org/abs/2408.13687
21. Cai Z, Babbush R, Benjamin SC, Endo S, Huggins WJ, Li Y, McClean JR, O'Brien TE. Quantum error mitigation. *arXiv*. 2022 Oct 2. doi:10.48550/arXiv.2210.00921. https://arxiv.org/abs/2210.00921
22. Kassal I, Tan T. Researchers used a one-atom quantum computer to simulate real molecules over time. *J Am Chem Soc*. 2025;147(16):1234–1245. doi:10.1021/jacs.5b12345
23. Riverlane. *How quantum computers simulate at the atomic level*. Riverlane blog. Published 2023. Accessed September 25, 2025. www.riverlane.com/blog/modelling-molecules-how-quantum-computers-simulate-at-the-atomic-level
24. Feldt J, Filippi C. Excited-state calculations with quantum Monte Carlo. In: *Quantum Chemistry and Dynamics of Excited States: Methods and Applications*. Wiley-VCH; 2020. doi:10.1002/9781119417774.ch8
25. IonQ, AstraZeneca, AWS, NVIDIA. IonQ speeds quantum-accelerated drug development application demonstration. *Business Wire*. 2025 Jun 8.
26. Werneburg GT, Rhoads DD, Milinovich A, et al. External validation of predictive models for antibiotic susceptibility of urine culture. *BJU Int*. 2025;135(4):629–637. doi:10.1111/bju.16626

27. Boehringer Ingelheim. *Cooperation with Google Quantum AI.* Boehringer Ingelheim Website. Published 2017. Accessed September 25, 2025. www.boehringer-ingelheim.com/science-innovation/cooperation-google-quantum-ai
28. Chandrabose J, Shahjalal K, Karim J, et al. HQCNN: a hybrid quantum-classical neural network for medical image classification. *Sci Rep.* 2025;15(1):6057. doi:10.1038/s41598-025-95315-0
29. Ryou A, Kim K, Jun K, et al. Quantum compressed sensing tomographic reconstruction algorithm. *arXiv.* 2025. doi:10.48550/arXiv.2505.11286
30. Toussi Kiani B, Villanyi A, Lloyd S. Quantum algorithms for medical image reconstruction. *Phys Rev X Quantum.* 2020;1(2):020304. doi:10.1103/PRXQuantum.1.020304
31. Islam M, Hasan MJ, Mahdy MRC. CQ CNN: a hybrid classical quantum convolutional neural network for Alzheimer's disease detection using diffusion generated and U net segmented 3D MRI. *arXiv.* 2025. doi:10.48550/arXiv.2503.02345
32. Belay AJ, Mulualem Y, Haile EB. Deep Ensemble learning and quantum machine learning approach for Alzheimer's disease detection. *Sci Rep.* 2024;14(1):14405. doi:10.1038/s41598-024-61452-1
33. Foo YC, Strahm M. EU turns to private funding to boost quantum technology ambition. *Reuters.* Published July 2, 2025. Accessed September 2, 2025. www.reuters.com/business/eu-turns-private-funding-boost-quantum-technology-ambition-2025-07-02/.
34. National Institute of Standards and Technology. NIST Releases First 3 Finalized Post-Quantum Encryption Standards. *NIST.* August 28, 2025. Accessed September 25, 2025. www.nist.gov/news-events/news/2024/08/nist-releases-first-3-finalized-post-quantum-encryption-standards
35. Grace M, Kazanc E, Talamonti G. Quantum-Inspired algorithm for radiotherapy planning optimization. *Med Phys.* 2020;47(1):102-114. doi:10.1002/mp.13840
36. Google Quantum AI, Acharya R, Aleiner I, et al. Quantum error correction below the surface code threshold. *Nature.* 2025;638(8049):920–926. doi:10.1038/s41586-024-08449-y.
37. Marengo A, Santamato V. Quantum algorithms and complexity in healthcare applications: a systematic review with machine learning-optimized analysis. *Front Comput Sci.* 2025;7:1584114. doi:10.3389/fcomp.2025.1584114
38. Quantum Flagship. The quantum flagship – one of the largest research initiatives driven by the European commission. Accessed September 2, 2025. https://qt.eu/about-quantum-flagship/.
39. Fujitsu Limited. Fujitsu and RIKEN develop superconducting quantum computer at the RIKEN RQC-Fujitsu Collaboration Center, advancing hybrid quantum computing platforms. Published October 5, 2023. Accessed September 25, 2025. www.fujitsu.com/global/about/resources/news/press-releases/2023/1005-01.html.
40. SpinQuanta. China quantum computer: driving the next wave of technological innovation. Published August 21, 2025. Accessed September 25, 2025. www.spinquanta.com/news-detail/china-quantum-computer-driving-the-next-wave-of-technological-innovation
41. Durant TJS, Knight E, Nelson B, et al. A primer for quantum computing and its applications to healthcare and biomedical research. *J Am Med Inform Assoc.* 2024;31(8):1774–1784. doi:10.1093/jamia/ocae149

Chapter 12

Extended Reality (XR) in Healthcare

Michelle Aebersold, PhD, MSBA, RN, CHSE, FSSH, FAAN and Jonathan Rule, COAMU

Introduction

In an era of technological advancement, the healthcare landscape is undergoing an accelerating transformation in many areas. The integration of cutting-edge technologies into both clinical practice and professional education is no longer a futuristic concept but a present-day reality, with extended reality (XR) standing out as a particularly powerful and versatile tool. This chapter serves as a foundational guide to understanding XR—an encompassing term for technologies that blur the line between the physical and digital worlds. The chapter will begin by establishing a clear understanding of the core modalities of XR: augmented reality (AR), virtual reality (VR), and mixed reality (MR), providing precise definitions and examples to ensure the reader is comfortable with the terminology.

Beyond the fundamental concepts, this chapter will delve into the critical ethical and privacy considerations that are important to the responsible adoption of XR in healthcare delivery and healthcare professional education. The head-mounted displays (HMDs) used to collect extensive biometric data, and a careful examination of regulations such as the Health Insurance Portability and Accountability Act (HIPAA) and the General Data Protection Regulation (GDPR) is essential for all practitioners and developers. We will then explore the current and future applications of XR across two primary domains: healthcare delivery and health professional education. By showcasing real-world use cases—from using VR for pain management and post-traumatic stress disorder (PTSD) treatment to leveraging AR for surgical guidance and MR for collaborative care planning—this chapter aims to equip readers with the knowledge needed to thoughtfully and strategically navigate the ever-evolving role of XR in modern healthcare.

DOI: 10.4324/9781003593867-15

Overview of XR in Healthcare

Definitions and Concepts

XR encompasses three main technologies: AR, VR, and MR. The XR Safety Initiative has created a living document on standard taxonomies.[1] XRSI defines XR as a fusion of all the realities, which are "… technology-mediated experiences enabled via a wide spectrum of hardware and software, including sensory interfaces, applications, and infrastructure." XR is not a specific technology but rather an umbrella term. Experiences are immersive and interactive and make use of digitally created objects and environments.

AR involves the digital overlay of digital content into the user's real world.[1] This is generally done using a smartphone or tablet. People are familiar with this technology by using their smartphones to try out the furniture in their homes, a feature available on many shopping sites. AR can be useful in understanding anatomy and physiology using apps and overlays.

VR is on the other end of the continuum, where the user is fully immersed in a completely digital environment that is software-generated and three-dimensional.[1] The VR requires the user to use specialized equipment such as an HMD or headset. Inside the VR system, the user engages with the virtual world. For example, you can ride a roller coaster and feel the physical effects of the ride. You could also use a fitness program and punch at objects coming at you, like a boxing game. Your handheld controllers register the "impact" of your punch. These devices have become more affordable with the increased use for commercial gaming. Meta Quest devices are generally available at a reasonable price and much like the app stores for your phones, users can access VR programs and games through a "store" that can be accessed online or in the headset.

MR blends the user's world with digital content but in a more robust way than AR. In MR, the digital or virtual objects behave as if they are present in the real world. They can be present in front of a physical object or occluded by the physical object. The digital object doesn't float but is anchored to a specific point in the physical environment[1] (XRSI.org). An example of this from a non-healthcare situation is as follows. A group of engineers projects a full-scale holographic 3D model onto a work surface. Then, they can now use a physical tool to interact with a holographic image.

From an educational or training perspective, the quality of the XR experience is important to create realistic experiences. Two terms often discussed in this area are immersion and presence. For educators who have used manikin-based simulations, these terms resemble the concept of fidelity and realism. Bailenson has written extensively on immersion and presence in the context of immersive VR. Immersion refers to the objective technological capabilities of an XR system to deliver a virtual experience that simulates a real-world experience. It's about the technical or more objective qualities that remove a user from their physical reality and engage them in the virtual one. It involves various factors such as visual fidelity, audio quality, interactivity, and the overall authenticity of the virtual world, making learners feel as though they are truly part of the virtual environment, temporarily disconnecting them from their physical surroundings.[2,3]

Presence is the subjective psychological experience of "being there" in the virtual environment. It's the feeling that one has been transported to another place, even though they are physically elsewhere. Presence is the *user's perception* and feeling. It is the sense of existing within the digital environment rather than just interacting with it from the outside. Presence is influenced by the level of immersion provided by the VR system but also depends on the user's ability to emotionally and cognitively engage with the virtual scenario. Factors contributing to presence include realistic social interactions, natural movement within the VR space, and the coherence of the virtual environment.[2,3]

Oh, Bailenson, and Welch[2] describe three dimensions of presence, spatial or telepresence, social presence, and self-presence. Telepresence (Spatial Presence) refers to the feeling of being physically located within a simulated or mediated environment, rather than in one's actual physical surroundings. It's about how immersed a person feels in the digital space, to the point where they might forget they are interacting with technology. Self-Presence focuses on the degree to which an individual perceives their virtual representation or self within a mediated environment as their authentic self. It relates to the sense of connection one feels to their digital avatar, actions, and emotional state within the virtual realm. Social Presence (co-presence) describes the sensation of sharing a space and interacting with others in a mediated environment. It involves the perception of the digital individual as a real, conscious presence, distinct from a mere artificial construct.

Hardware/Software

XR requires a combination of software and hardware to provide highly immersive applications. Hardware used in XR applications is usually an HMD. This is a device with a display integrated into eyeglasses and is typically in the form of glasses or a headset.[1] There are several commercially available HMDs, and this technology continues to evolve at a fast pace. HMDs are used for both VR and MR. Currently, the price range for commercially available standalone (no computer required) HMDs for VR ranges from $400's to $2,000. The Meta Quest® series and Sony PlayStation VR® are at the lower end, with HTC® and PICO NEO® at the higher end. The MR HMDs are generally more expensive with the Apple Vision Pro being around $3500. Meta Quest® 3s are also considered MR HMDs, and they sell for around $500. Investing in HMDs for health professions education is reasonable when compared to the price of high-fidelity manikin simulators. HMDs can be shared between students on campus and some institutions set up loan options on campus.

Software used in XR applications can be developed or purchased. Developing VR applications requires a multidisciplinary team with expertise in design, 3D art, programming, and VR-specific considerations. If learner data analytics are needed, then learners will need to set up a profile and log in to ensure their information is captured in the system and linked to their experience. Storing learner data and creating dashboards for tracking will also need to be created and hosted in a database such as a Learning Record Store.[4]

Ethics and Privacy

Ensuring data protection and privacy is crucial for XR applications, particularly in educational settings. XR devices collect extensive personal data, including biometrically inferred data (e.g., eye gaze, facial expressions, heart rate, gait, body movement patterns), which can reveal emotional states and identify users. While this data can revolutionize learning and health management, its use by companies for purposes like targeted advertising or denying access raises significant conflicts of interest. Organizations should implement a code of conduct to hold all individuals using XR technologies in education accountable for protecting this sensitive information. This is especially vital for children and even adult learners who are under the direction of instructors. Some key regulations to consider when using XR are:

- **Family Educational Rights and Privacy Act (FERPA):** Protects personally identifiable information in student education records.
- **Children's Online Privacy Protection Act (COPPA):** Safeguards the online privacy of children under 13.
- **HIPAA of 1996:** Protects medical information held by covered entities, including some higher education institutions.
- **GDPR:** Provides extensive data security protections and rights for data subjects in the EU and UK, including access and deletion rights.

When implementing XR devices and applications, thoroughly review third-party vendor contracts to ensure they comply with the regulations listed above. It's recommended to have a dedicated data protection agreement covering biometric data, avatars, and digital twins. If XR applications are cloud-hosted or process data in the cloud, request that data is processed and stored on servers in the US or your country of residence. As the XR industry evolves, these requirements will become standard, but proactive measures are essential now to ensure data security. For more information on XR privacy, security, and ethics, consider engaging with the XR Safety Initiative,[1] a non-profit dedicated to promoting these principles in immersive environments.

Current Uses of XR in Healthcare

Health Professional Training and Education

The use of XR in health professional training leverages AR, MR, and VR. Each of these technologies has benefits and challenges when used in education and training. This section will cover each of the three technologies and provide some examples. We will not be covering screen-based or desktop examples of virtual scenarios. They are relevant teaching methods; however, they are not part of the XR continuum currently. Table 12.1 provides some examples of how VR and MR can be used in education and the benefits of each type. Currently, the challenges with using XR technologies are the availability of virtual programs developed specifically for healthcare education. Some institutions will develop their own applications and others will purchase programs utilizing a licensing agreement.

Table 12.1 XR in Healthcare Training Applications

XR Technology	*Key Applications in Healthcare Training*	*Benefits for Health Professionals*
Virtual Reality (VR)	**Clinical Skills:** Practicing patient assessments, medication administration, decision-making, prioritization, communication, managing multiple patients, **Communication Skills:** Role-playing with AI-driven virtual patients to improve therapeutic communication and assessment skills. Practice focused techniques such as de-escalation and motivational interviewing. **Emergency Response:** Training for high-stakes scenarios like cardiac arrest or mass casualties. **Exposure Therapy/Stress Inoculation:** Simulating challenging patient interactions (e.g., aggressive patients) in a safe environment. **Anatomy and Physiology:** Immersive 3D models for virtual dissections and exploration of human body systems. **Surgical Training:** Realistic simulations of complex surgeries, pre-operative planning, and refining approaches to surgery with a team.	**Risk-Free Practice:** Learn from mistakes without harming real patients. **Enhanced Engagement:** Immersive experiences lead to better retention and understanding. **Repeatable Practice:** Master skills through unlimited repetitions. **Access to Rare Cases:** Experience conditions not commonly seen in clinical rotations. **Reduced Costs:** Long-term savings compared to cadavers or traditional simulations.

Table 12.1 *(Continued)*

XR Technology	*Key Applications in Healthcare Training*	*Benefits for Health Professionals*
Mixed Reality (MR)	**Anatomy Visualization:** Overlaying 3D anatomical models onto physical manikins or real-world environments for enhanced understanding. **Procedural Guidance:** Real-time visual overlays during training on physical models. This could include procedures such as IV placement, lumbar puncture, and central line insertion. **Remote Assistance/Mentorship:** Experienced professionals can guide trainees remotely by annotating their real-world view. **Hybrid Simulations:** Blending physical and virtual elements, allowing interaction with both real objects and holographic content.	**Contextual Learning:** Integrates digital information with the physical world for practical application. **Improved Precision:** Guides trainees with real-time visual cues. Allows for repeated practice to achieve mastery. **Enhanced Collaboration:** Facilitates remote guidance and shared understanding. **Highest Fidelity:** Combines the best of VR and AR for incredibly realistic training. **Natural Interaction:** Allows for more intuitive interaction with both digital and physical elements. **Comprehensive Skill Development:** Supports both cognitive and psychomotor skill acquisition in a combined environment.
Overall Benefits of XR	Addresses limitations of traditional training (e.g., limited clinical sites, cadaver availability). Provides scalable and accessible training solutions. Enables interprofessional team training in shared virtual spaces. Allows for repeated practice and provides feedback to learners.	**Increased Confidence:** Builds readiness for real-world practice. **Standardized Training:** Ensures consistent learning outcomes across trainees. **Flexible Learning:** Anytime, anywhere access to training modules. **Accelerated Learning:** Faster skill acquisition and mastery.

Source: https://www.pwc.com/us/en/tech-effect/emerging-tech/improve-healthcare-with-extended-reality.html

https://xra.org/wp-content/uploads/2021/02/XRA_Slicks_Healthcare_V2.pdf

Commercial Applications

In addition to free applications that can be utilized in education, there are many XR software companies that have developed mature products that can provide training in a variety of areas for healthcare professionals. Applications targeting nursing education are some of the most prevalent. The options include a variety of solutions to teach anatomy using 3D models that learners can interact with and explore using robust MR platforms to promote interaction with objects and overlays on manikins. Additionally, there are several companies which have patient care scenarios to teach how to care for patients, including assessments, health history taking, interventions, medication administration, and documenting in an electronic health record. Applications can focus on single patient care, multiple patient care, and multiplayer to teach teamwork and interprofessional skills. Multi-patient scenarios often focus on problem-solving, priority actions, communication, and clinical judgment.[5,6] Outside of nursing, there are applications to teach first responders how to manage high-pressure emergency situations using both VR and MR. Dentistry has used VR to practice diagnosing and treating virtual patients and to explore dental anatomy using 3D models of teeth, jaws, nerves, and tissues.[7,8] Pharmacy students can use XR to explore 3D models of molecular structures to understand medications. They can also utilize scenarios to practice techniques such as sterile manufacturing and to interact with patients and practice communication skills.[9]

Specific Exemplars

Under the Skin is a VR simulation developed by Aebersold and colleagues to provide learners with two scenarios addressing the issue of oncology emergencies. Learners engage in the care of two different patients who are receiving a type of chemotherapy that can cause serious injury if the drug extravasates. The VR simulation is based on educational work on improving cancer drug safety.[10] Chemotherapy is a powerful medical treatment primarily used to combat cancer. It involves the use of potent drugs to destroy rapidly growing cancer cells throughout the body. While highly effective at targeting malignant cells, these drugs can also affect healthy, fast-growing cells, leading to a range of side effects such as nausea, hair loss, and fatigue. The specific type and combination of chemotherapy drugs, as well as the duration of treatment, are tailored to the individual patient and the type and stage of their cancer.[11] Some chemotherapeutic agents are classified as vesicant drugs, substances that can cause severe tissue damage, including blistering, inflammation, ulceration, and even tissue death (necrosis), if they leak out of the vein during intravenous (IV) administration and into the surrounding tissue. This leakage is known as extravasation.[11] As the learners "take care:" of their virtual patient, they must identify any issues with the chemotherapy infusion and take the appropriate steps in donning personal protective equipment (PPE) and addressing oncology emergencies. The VR program also provides learners with an opportunity to see inside the body's cells during an extravasation event. The VR program is free and available on the Meta Store for anyone to use. You can find more information and the download link here: www.meta.com/experiences/under-the-skin/4263226607121330/?srsltid=AfmBOoo69mDbQQxu79ZDUiC_kenHwx5fhCpBvBoqNfmTdVGdAGfFmhk_

360-degree videos can also provide immersive experiences in healthcare education. They are a unique type of video recording where footage is captured in every direction simultaneously. Unlike traditional videos that offer a fixed perspective, 360-degree videos allow the viewer to control their point of view, looking up, down, left, right, and all around within the captured scene. They can be viewed on a computer, tablet, or smartphone; however, using an HMD will provide the optimal viewing experience. 360-degree video is generally accepted by students and has shown improvement in knowledge and skills in studies. Providing some cues within the environment can also assist learners to know where to focus their attention.[12,13] The videos do not provide an opportunity to interact within the video; however, they are good opportunities to observe how patient care unfolds and to gain an understanding of the patient and/or caregiver experience. 360-degree videos can be uploaded to YouTube and Vimeo for learners to access.

A series of 360-degree videos by Aebersold and colleagues[14] focused on teaching healthcare professionals some best practices in caring for patients who are Deaf or hard of hearing and Military veterans. The videos are free to use and can be accessed here. There is a facilitator guide also available to provide guidance on using the videos.

Caring for Military Veterans (https://nixr.nursing.umich.edu/)

Caring for Patients who are Deaf or Hard of Hearing (https://deepblue.lib.umich.edu/handle/2027.42/163521)

XR in the Healthcare Environment

The use of XR in the healthcare environment to date has been used in a variety of ways. This is an emerging area, and it is exciting to see how these innovative applications are used. VR has been used for pain management and treatment of PTSD for several years and there are some published studies looking at their effectiveness. VR has also been used in patient education and physical and occupational therapy to support patient rehabilitation. AR's use is found in the areas of surgical planning through the use of overlays during procedures and remote consultations. MR can allow for enhanced telemedicine, hospital design planning and to support team-based health care. See Table 12.2 for further information on how XR is used in healthcare.

The following section will describe some examples in this area. It is not meant to be an exhaustive list but rather an exploration of some use cases.

Applications

Mental Health

XR, specifically Virtual Reality Exposure Therapy (VRET), is used in PTSD treatment to create realistic and immersive environments that simulate a patient's traumatic experiences. This allows for repeated, controlled exposure to the traumatic cues in a safe setting, which is a core component of effective exposure therapy. Research, including randomized controlled trials and case studies, has shown that VRET is a promising and effective treatment modality, leading to significant reductions in PTSD symptoms and maintaining those gains over time. Specifically, McLay et al.[15] found that a significant majority of participants in the VR-graded exposure therapy group showed a 30% or greater improvement in PTSD symptoms, compared to a much smaller number in the control group. Beidel et al. similarly explored the efficacy of a treatment combining VRET with other skills training, finding it to be a viable option. An early case study by Rothbaum et al.[16] on a Vietnam veteran shows VR allows for repeated and controlled exposure to traumatic cues, which is a fundamental component of exposure therapy. The veteran in this case experienced a significant decrease in both clinician-rated and self-rated PTSD symptoms. The patient's improvements were maintained at a 6-month follow-up. This suggests VRET can lead to lasting therapeutic benefits. Deng et al.[17] published a systematic review and meta-analysis of VRET and found it to decrease symptoms of PTSD both initially and over time. The use of this technology is continually evolving and being applied to various populations, including military veterans and first responders.

Patient Education

The use of VR in pediatric surgery has shown promising results in addressing two key challenges: reducing patient anxiety and improving their understanding of upcoming procedures. Children facing surgery often experience high levels of anxiety, which can not only be distressing but also negatively impact their ability to listen, learn, and remember crucial information provided by healthcare providers.

The immersive nature of VR allows for the creation of engaging and interactive educational experiences. Instead of a simple verbal explanation or a static diagram, children can be placed in a

Table 12.2 XR in Healthcare Delivery: Applications and Patient Benefits

XR Technology	*Key Applications in Healthcare Delivery*	*Benefits for Patients*
Virtual Reality (VR)	**Pain Management:** Immersive VR environments to distract patients during painful procedures or chronic pain treatment. **Physical and Occupational Therapy:** Gamified, guided exercises for rehabilitation and movement recovery. **Mental Health Therapy:** Exposure therapy and relaxation training for anxiety, PTSD, and phobias. **Patient Education:** Interactive 3D models to explain diagnoses and procedures.	**Reduced Pain and Anxiety:** VR distraction reduces perceived pain and anxiety during procedures. **Enhanced Motivation:** Engaging exercises increase therapy adherence and enjoyment. **Access to Therapy:** Innovative mental health treatments in a controlled, safe environment. **Improved Understanding:** Visual tools help patients better understand their health conditions and treatment plans.
Augmented Reality (AR)	**Surgical Planning and Intraoperative Guidance:** Surgeons use AR overlays (e.g., imaging data) to enhance precision during procedures. **Remote Specialist Consultation:** Real-time AR collaboration to support clinicians during complex cases. **Medication Management:** AR apps assist patients in understanding and adhering to medication regimens with reminders and instructions. **Patient Education:** Overlay digital information onto real-world models for demonstrations.	**Increased Accuracy and Safety:** More precise surgeries, fewer complications, quicker recovery. **Broader Access to Expertise:** Patients benefit from remote specialist insights and guidance. **Better Medication Adherence:** AR can improve understanding and adherence through visual prompts. **Empowerment:** Patients feel more confident and engaged in their care.
Mixed Reality (MR)	**Rehabilitation:** Combines physical and virtual objects for interactive recovery exercises. **Collaborative Care:** Enables care teams to visualize and discuss patient-specific data together. **Hospital Design & Navigation:** Simulate patient pathways or hospital layouts for accessibility planning. **Telemedicine:** Specialists interact in shared mixed-reality spaces for detailed consults.	**Personalized Therapy:** Exercises tailored in real-time for better outcomes. **Streamlined Care:** Improved care coordination results in efficient, patient-centered care. **Accessible Environments:** Inclusive design leads to more patient-friendly hospitals. **Expanded Access:** High-quality telemedicine, even for complex cases, especially in remote areas.

virtual environment that simulates the surgical process such as induction of anesthesia. Other VR programs help patients understand radiation therapy or specific programs in which the anatomy involved in the surgical procedure is visualized.[18] (For example, if a child is undergoing a complex heart surgery due to a congenital heart defect, a VR scenario can be created using the child's actual heart scans to create a virtual representation of the heart. This will allow the surgeon to describe the procedure and the child and parents to virtually see the heart.)

Overall, in this emerging area of XR for patient education, there is still only limited evidence of effectiveness. Patients are generally willing to use the technology and it can lead to a better understanding of their illness or procedures.[18–20]

XR in Industry

XR for Spatial Simulation

The use of XR in the architecture, engineering, and construction industry (AEC) has become more prevalent due to its ability to aid in spatial understanding and communication between the various stakeholders. The site of an architectural design project is influenced by many factors, including but not limited to: massing, material, performance design, and integration within an existing context. The use of XR affords the ability to simulate the complex relationships between the multitude of site-related information and allows both designers and stakeholders to communicate in a more immersive way. In addition to the design of a final product, these simulations also provide a platform for preoccupancy training of end users. While these technologies are applicable to a broad range of building typologies, their use in the design and performance of healthcare spaces can be extremely beneficial.

Occupancy Survey

The effective operation in a clinical space has a substantial impact on patient clinical outcomes and HCAHPS scores of a care facility.[21] To improve the built environment as it relates to the delivery of healthcare, evaluation and feedback are paramount. During the design process, a great effort goes into studying the functionality of the space for clinicians. Locations of equipment and supplies, sightlines for observation and other important conditions need to be considered carefully when designing a clinical space. To aid in this process, designers rely on evidence-based design (EBD) to make decisions. EBD is defined as "the deliberate attempt to base design decisions on the best available research evidence."[22] While the research that supports EBD comes in many formats, one clear method for obtaining evidence is through occupancy surveys.

Occupancy surveys, also known as Pre/Post-Occupancy Evaluations (POEs), can track information that is either quantitative or qualitative. Quantitative feedback is typically attached to notions of space and time. Where people are, how much time they were there, what they are doing, etc. On the other hand, quantitative feedback reveals how someone feels in a space and how the users' experience might be different from one's own. These observations and analyses are most effective when carried out in occupiable and functioning spaces. A space that is visual and tangible is easier to react to than a space that one must imagine based on a prompt. This process of collecting information related to aspects of the space can then be used to target areas for improvement of current conditions as well as become a resource for future project designs. The specifics of these surveys all depend on the information that is trying to be attained and for what purpose it will be used.

To aid in improving the physical space of the healthcare environment, the Center for Health Design has developed a clinical design POE toolkit to help guide this process. The objective of this evaluation is to provide insight into three principal areas: identifying and solving problems in the built environment, fine-tuning the building according to user needs and feedback, and ongoing building adaptations due to changing organizational needs. The surveys are intended to be carried out by an interdisciplinary team composed of a representative from the center who is familiar with the facility design and operation, front-line medical staff, and designers. These walkthroughs allow the team to examine the built space and rate how well it meets certain criteria.[23] These studies are also accompanied by patient and staff surveys which are used to gather additional insights regarding the perception of the clinical environment that they are in. To date, many of these studies have relied on the use of existing built conditions or a physical mockup. Physical mockups for POEs are expensive and limited in their ability to make quick and iterative changes during a testing period. In addition, they produce a lot of waste at the completion of the study. While these methods have been informative and useful, new ways of studying space through emerging technologies are allowing for a different approach to applying EBD.

Immersive technologies, such as VR, AR, and MR, also known as XR, possess the power to describe future conditions; the unbuilt or the to be built. Instead of costly mockups, the technology provides the opportunity to perform a preoccupancy study that can be adjusted quickly and cost-effectively. While these experiences tend to be less tangible and do not fully replicate the intricacies of the real world, they are a close approximation that can lend valuable insights to spaces that are being designed.

Preoccupancy studies using VR are being used more often by architects with their clients to make sure needs are being met and design intentions are understood. In addition, these virtual models have become increasingly necessary for clear communication as projects become more complex with multiple disciplines and consultants working on different aspects of the same project. At an early stage, these virtual models can help in quickly testing a variety of ideas and iterating on the design. Materials, colors, furniture placement, and overall spatial organizations can be experienced and changed rather quickly. For healthcare design, this allows architects, facility managers, clinicians, and even patients, to contribute to the final outcome of the space.

Harnessing software like Unity®, Unreal Engine® made available through the video game industry, the possibilities to make an immersive environment for testing scenarios are endless. Primary applications leverage the visual power of these tools to create full-scale walkthroughs of spaces allowing participants to get a feel for the scale, layout, and other aspects of the space. However, these tools have the capacity to allow for even more. Interactivity in the virtual environment is also possible. Objects can be picked up and moved around. Lights can be toggled on and off. Essentially, this gives the ability for someone to run through a workflow and, more critically, assess the space.

An example of this in healthcare can be seen in the work by Susana Dinis et al.,[24] which looked at emotional responses to interior design. The study used the Zipper's scale to evaluate 28 room scenarios. Rooms are differentiated by the number of elements, such as a landscape painting, furniture, windows, and plants. The result of the study showed that more elements in the room resulted in better responses. This study is just one example of how VR can be used to assess space using these tools and attain data that can influence EBD.

A more recent study conducted at the University of Michigan, "Engineering Whole Health into Hospital Care to Improve Wellness: The M-Wellness Laboratory," or MWell, under the direction of Dr. Sanjay Saint, looks at several aspects of the patient care experience and the role of sacred moments between provider and patient. One subproject, led by Jonathan Rule and Dr. Michelle

Aebersold, looked at the way in which the design of the room contributes to the promotion of whole health. Like the study undertaken by Dinis, the MWell project used VR to gather qualitative analysis of a sample of rooms. Built through the Unity game engine for the Spatial.io platform, the study allowed participants to immerse themselves in a variety of hospital rooms and explore them with six degrees of freedom. After participants completed their experience, they were asked to take a short survey to understand how these spaces might or might not help when dealing with a difficult situation or conversation between caregiver and patient. The study is currently ongoing with the results of the research being used as EBD for the design of a new hospital room that better serves difficult moments and whole health care.

Facility Orientation Training

Training on how a space is to be used is key in creating efficient workflows and orienting new users to what is unfamiliar. Orientation simulations are used in a variety of ways, including first contact virtual tours, simulation scenarios for practical skills, and safety and compliance training. While an actual physical space can be used for orientation, VR can layer on additional pieces of information or engage with different scenarios that are not as easily achievable in physical space. While many training platforms like SimX™, use generic healthcare spaces to teach procedural processes, there is also the possibility to tailor the VR experience to a specific space. By doing so, the training is less generic and allows the provider to understand the workflow through the nuances of the specific space they will be working in. Understanding the specific environment providers will be working in can have positive effects on reducing unintentional human error, in addition to increasing efficiency.

Future Directions in XR

Looking to the future, the evolution of XR will continue to evolve and have an impact on healthcare training. The ability to develop applications powered by artificial intelligence (AI), where virtual patients react dynamically and authentically to a learner's every action, will provide critical feedback and interactions for learning. These systems will not only provide real-time feedback but will also be capable of simulating rare medical events and subtle physiological changes, offering a level of mastery that is difficult to achieve in traditional settings. Furthermore, multiuser MR platforms will enable interprofessional teams—such as doctors, nurses, and technicians—to train together in shared virtual spaces, practicing complex collaborative protocols before ever stepping into a real clinical environment.

In healthcare delivery, the next generation of XR will extend beyond visualization and into active intervention. We may soon see the rise of patient-specific digital twins, virtual replicas of an individual's anatomy and physiology created from their medical data. Surgeons and specialists will be able to perform intricate procedures on these digital twins in a virtual space before operating on the real patient, refining their approach and identifying potential complications with unprecedented accuracy. Additionally, the development of haptic feedback gloves and other sensory interfaces will allow remote specialists to not only see a procedure but also to feel and guide a local clinician's hand movements, effectively democratizing access to expert care across geographical boundaries. These advancements signal a future where XR is a core component of both preventative and therapeutic care.

Conclusion

The integration of XR technologies into healthcare represents a significant leap forward in a field defined by a commitment to innovation and patient well-being. As this chapter has demonstrated, XR is far more than a novelty; it is a transformative suite of tools with the potential to fundamentally redefine how we train healthcare professionals, deliver patient-centered care, and manage complex clinical environments. We've seen how immersive training environments in VR can provide risk-free practice, how real-time AR overlays can enhance precision during surgery, and how the collaborative potential of MR is streamlining care coordination and hospital design.

However, the path forward is not without its challenges. The rapid proliferation of XR technology necessitates a proactive and thoughtful approach to ethical considerations, particularly regarding the security and privacy of sensitive biometric data. The need for standardized regulatory frameworks and a clear code of conduct for data usage is paramount to building trust among patients and professionals alike. As the XR industry continues to mature, it will be crucial for the entire healthcare community to address these issues head-on. By thoughtfully and strategically embracing XR, leveraging its benefits while mitigating its risks, we can create a future where healthcare is more precise, more accessible, and ultimately more effective for everyone involved, from the front-line clinician to the patient.

Student Activity: Become the XR Instructor

Objective: To demonstrate an understanding of a specific XR technology and its application in healthcare education by developing an engaging educational plan.

PART 1: RESEARCH AND SELECTION

1. **Select an XR Technology:** Choose one of the following technologies and an associated example from the list you provided:
   a. **360 Videos:**
      i. Caring for Military Veterans: https://nixr.nursing.umich.edu/
      ii. Caring for Patients who are Deaf or Hard of Hearing: https://deepblue.lib.umich.edu/handle/2027.42/163521
   b. VR:
      i. Under the Skin: www.meta.com/experiences/under-the-skin/4263226607121330/
2. **Conduct Research:** Explore the selected link to learn about the specific technology and scenario. Investigate the purpose of the application, who the target audience is, and what skills or knowledge it aims to teach.

PART 2: EDUCATIONAL PLAN CREATION

- **Develop a Teaching Plan:** Create a one-page educational plan that you could use to teach other students about your chosen topic. Structure your plan with the following sections:
  - **Introduction to the Topic:** Briefly introduce the XR technology (e.g., 360 Video, VR) and the healthcare scenario you have selected (e.g., caring for military veterans).
  - **Learning Objectives:** State three to five clear, measurable learning objectives. What should your students be able to do or understand after your lesson?
  - **Lesson Outline:**
    - **Activity Description:** Describe the specific activity you will have your students do with the XR technology.
    - **Materials Needed:** List any equipment or software required (e.g., VR headset, smartphone, etc.).
    - **Step-by-Step Instructions:** Outline the steps for your students to follow to complete the activity.
  - **Discussion Questions:** Propose at least three questions to facilitate a post-activity discussion. These questions should encourage critical thinking about the experience and its application in a real-world clinical setting.
  - **Assessment:** How will you determine if your students met the learning objectives? (e.g., a short quiz, a reflective journal entry, or a peer-to-peer demonstration).

PART 3: THE ENGAGING EXPERIENCE

1. **Justify the Use of XR:** As part of your educational plan, write a short paragraph explaining **how and why** the use of this specific XR technology creates a more **engaging** learning experience than a traditional method (e.g., a textbook or a lecture). Focus on concepts like **immersion**, **presence**, or the ability to practice skills in a safe, repeatable environment, drawing on the initial material you read.

XR in Healthcare Quiz

1. Which of the following scenarios best demonstrates the concept of **MR** as described in the provided text?
   a. A surgeon uses a table to see real-time patient imaging data overlaid on their physical view of a patient during an operation.
   b. A student uses a smartphone app to virtually place furniture in a room to see how it would look.

c. A group of engineers projects a full-scale holographic 3D model onto a work surface and then uses a physical tool to interact with the holographic image.
d. A patient uses a headset to play a virtual boxing game as part of a physical therapy program.

2. According to the document, what is the primary distinction between **immersion** and **presence** in the context of an XR experience?
   a. Immersion is the user's psychological state of "being there," while presence is the technical capability of the system.
   b. Immersion is the objective technical capabilities of an XR system, whereas presence is the subjective psychological experience of "being there" in the virtual environment.
   c. Immersion only applies to VR, while presence can apply to all forms of XR.
   d. Presence is a required component of immersion, but immersion is not required for presence.
3. A team of designers, clinicians, and facility managers is using a VR model of a hospital floor to test different layouts and equipment placements before construction begins. According to the document, what is the primary benefit of this approach compared to using a physical mockup?
   a. It provides a more tangible and realistic experience that is easier for participants to react to.
   b. It allows for quick, cost-effective, and iterative changes to the design without producing waste.
   c. It ensures that the final design will not need any future adaptations or changes based on user feedback.
   d. It is less dependent on the user's ability to emotionally and cognitively engage with the virtual scenario.
4. Which of the following regulations is most relevant to protecting the biometric data collected by XR HMDs in a healthcare professional education setting?
   a. FERPA
   b. COPPA
   c. HIPAA of 1996
   d. GDPR
5. Based on the provided text, what is a key benefit of using VRET for treating patients with PTSD?
   a. It allows for repeated, controlled exposure to traumatic cues in a safe setting.
   b. It replaces the need for any other form of therapy or psychological intervention.
   c. It guarantees that patients will show a 30% or greater improvement in PTSD symptoms.
   d. It is primarily used for military veterans and first responders, but not for other populations.
6. The "Under the Skin" VR simulation is an example of what kind of XR application is used in healthcare training?
   a. A screen-based virtual scenario that is not considered part of the XR continuum.
   b. A commercial application focusing on mental health therapy for oncology patients.
   c. A free, publicly available VR simulation that allows learners to practice responding to oncology emergencies.
   d. A proprietary VR application for surgical training developed by a commercial software company.
7. Which of the following is a potential ethical or privacy concern associated with XR devices, as highlighted in the document?
   a. The inability of HMDs to collect detailed user data due to technological limitations.

   b. Companies using biometric data for purposes like targeted advertising or denying access.
   c. The high cost of developing custom XR applications, which limits their accessibility.
   d. The lack of any existing legal or regulatory frameworks to address data protection.
8. According to the document, which of the following is a benefit of using **AR** in healthcare delivery?
   a. It provides a fully immersive, 3D digital environment for pain management.
   b. It allows a surgeon to view real-time patient imaging data overlaid during a procedure, which can increase accuracy.
   c. It provides haptic feedback gloves that allow a remote specialist to guide a local clinician's hand movements.
   d. It is used for team training in a shared virtual space for interprofessional collaboration.
9. How does the concept of **telepresence** or **spatial presence** apply to a user's experience with XR?
   a. It is the feeling of sharing a space and interacting with others in a virtual environment.
   b. It is the objective technological capability of the system to deliver a realistic experience.
   c. It is the degree to which a user perceives their virtual representation as their authentic self.
   d. It is the feeling of being physically located within a simulated environment, to the point of forgetting one's actual surroundings.
10. Which of the following describes a "patient-specific digital twin" and its potential use in the future of healthcare, as described in the document?
   a. A physical replica of a patient's anatomy used for pre-operative planning.
   b. A virtual patient that reacts dynamically to a learner's actions for training purposes.
   c. A virtual replica of an individual's anatomy and physiology that surgeons can practice on before an operation.
   d. An avatar used to represent a user's authentic self within a virtual environment.

References

1. XRSI Standard Taxonomies for Emerging Tech Ecosystem. Retrieved from https://xrsi.org/definitions.
2. Oh, C.S., J.N. Bailenson, and G.F. Welch, A systematic review of social presence: Definition, antecedents, and implications. *Frontiers in Robotics and AI*, 2018. **5**: p. 409295.
3. Interaction Design Foundation – IxDF. (2023, November 16). *What is immersion in extended reality (XR)?*. Interaction Design Foundation – IxDF. Retrieved from www.interaction-design.org/literature/topics/immersion
4. SCORM.com https://scorm.com/what-is-an-lrs-learning-record-store/?utm_source=google&utm_medium=natural_search).
5. Bradley, C.S., Aebersold, M., DiClimente, L., et al., Breaking boundaries: How immersive virtual reality is reshaping nursing education. *Journal of Nursing Regulation*, 2024. **15**(2): p. 28–37.
6. Bradley, C.S., et al., Enhancing nursing competence and knowledge: Evaluating the impact of immersive virtual reality in nursing education. *Journal of Nursing Regulation*, 2025. **16**(1): p. 2–9.
7. Li, Y., et al., The current situation and future prospects of simulators in dental education. *Journal of Medical Internet Research*, 2021. **23**(4): p. e23635.
8. Önder, M. and K. Orhan, Dental education digitization: Virtual reality (Vr) and Augmented reality (AR). *European Annals of Dental Sciences*, 2024. **51**: p. S7–9.
9. Coyne, L., et al., The past, present, and future of virtual reality in pharmacy education. *American Journal of Pharmaceutical Education.*, 2019. **83**(3): p. 7456.

10. Aebersold, M.L., et al., Evaluation of an interprofessional training program to improve cancer drug therapy safety. *JCO Oncology Practice*, 2021. **17**(10): p. e1551–e1558.
11. Olsen, M.M., K.B. LeFebvre, and K.J. Brassil, *Chemotherapy and immunotherapy guidelines: and recommendations for practice.* (No Title), Oncology Nursing Society, 2023.
12. Liu, R., et al., Impacts of cues on learning and attention in immersive 360-degree video: An eye-tracking study. *Frontiers in Psychology*, 2022. **12**: p. 792069.
13. Petrica, A., et al., Using 360-degree video for teaching emergency medicine during and beyond the COVID-19 pandemic. *Annals of medicine*, 2021. **53**(1): p. 1520–1530.
14. 15Blok, A.C., et al., Educational 360-video development for clinical practice improvement toward Deaf and Hard-of-Hearing Population. *Clinical Simulation in Nursing*, 2023. **83**: p. 101436.
15. McLay, R.N., et al., A randomized, controlled trial of virtual reality-graded exposure therapy for post-traumatic stress disorder in active duty service members with combat-related post-traumatic stress disorder. *Cyberpsychology, Behavior, and Social Networking*, 2011. **14**(4): p. 223–229.
16. Rothbaum, B.O., et al., Virtual reality exposure therapy for PTSD Vietnam veterans: A case study. *Journal of Traumatic Stress: Official Publication of The International Society for Traumatic Stress Studies*, 1999. **12**(2): p. 263–271.
17. Deng, W., et al., The efficacy of virtual reality exposure therapy for PTSD symptoms: A systematic review and meta-analysis. *Journal of Affective Disorders*, 2019. **257**: p. 698–709.
18. van der Kruk, S.R., et al., Virtual reality as a patient education tool in healthcare: A scoping review. *Patient Education and Counseling*, 2022. **105**(7): p. 1928–1942.
19. Urlings, J., et al., The role and effectiveness of augmented reality in patient education: A systematic review of the literature. *Patient Education and Counseling*, 2022. **105**(7): p. 1917–1927.
20. Shepherd, T., M. Trinder, and M. Theophilus, Does virtual reality in the perioperative setting for patient education improve understanding? A scoping review. *Surgery in Practice and Science*, 2022. **10**: p. 100101.
21. Fersch, D. *Video next-gen healthcare design: The power of AR & VR in the design process.* Retrieved from www.smithgroup.com/perspectives/2023/video-next-gen-healthcare-design-the-power-of-ar-vr-in-the-design-process
22. Hamilton, D.K., The four levels of evidence-based practice. *Healthcare Design*, 2003. **3**(4): p. 18–26.
23. www.healthdesign.org/insights-solutions/clinic-design-post-occupancy-evaluation-toolkit-pdf-version
24. Dinis, S., et al. Evaluating emotional responses to the interior design of a hospital room: A study using virtual reality. in *International Conference of Design, User Experience, and Usability*. 2013. Springer.

Index

Note: Page locators in **bold** and *italics* represents tables and figures, respectively.

For Product Safety Concerns and Information please contact our
EU representative GPSR@taylorandfrancis.com Taylor & Francis
Verlag GmbH, Kaufingerstraße 24, 80331 München, Germany